Microsoft Azure Compute
The Definitive Guide

Avinash Valiramani

Microsoft Azure Compute: The Definitive Guide

ISBN-13: 978-0-13-756444-6
ISBN-10: 0-13-756444-9

Library of Congress Control Number: 2022935534

1 2022

TRADEMARKS

WARNING AND DISCLAIMER

SPECIAL SALES

For information about buying this title in bulk quantities, or for special sales opportunities (which may include electronic versions; custom cover designs; and content particular to your business, training goals, marketing focus, or branding interests), please contact our corporate sales department at corpsales@pearsoned.com or (800) 382-3419.

For government sales inquiries, please contact governmentsales@pearsoned.com.

For questions about sales outside the U.S., please contact intlcs@pearson.com.

EDITOR-IN-CHIEF
Brett Bartow

EXECUTIVE EDITOR
Loretta Yates

SPONSORING EDITOR
Charvi Arora

DEVELOPMENT EDITOR
Kate Shoup

MANAGING EDITOR
Sandra Schroeder

SENIOR PROJECT EDITOR
Tracey Croom

TECHNICAL EDITOR
Thomas Palathra

COPY EDITOR
Sarah Kearns

INDEXER
Timothy Wright

PROOFREADER
Donna Mulder

EDITORIAL ASSISTANT
Cindy Teeters

COVER DESIGNER
Twist Creative, Seattle

COMPOSITOR
codeMantra

GRAPHICS
codeMantra

Pearson's Commitment to Diversity, Equity, and Inclusion

Pearson is dedicated to creating bias-free content that reflects the diversity of all learners. We embrace the many dimensions of diversity, including but not limited to race, ethnicity, gender, socioeconomic status, ability, age, sexual orientation, and religious or political beliefs.

Education is a powerful force for equity and change in our world. It has the potential to deliver opportunities that improve lives and enable economic mobility. As we work with authors to create content for every product and service, we acknowledge our responsibility to demonstrate inclusivity and incorporate diverse scholarship so that everyone can achieve their potential through learning. As the world's leading learning company, we have a duty to help drive change and live up to our purpose to help more people create a better life for themselves and to create a better world.

Our ambition is to purposefully contribute to a world where:

- Everyone has an equitable and lifelong opportunity to succeed through learning.

- Our educational products and services are inclusive and represent the rich diversity of learners.

- Our educational content accurately reflects the histories and experiences of the learners we serve.

- Our educational content prompts deeper discussions with learners and motivates them to expand their own learning (and worldview).

While we work hard to present unbiased content, we want to hear from you about any concerns or needs with this Pearson product so that we can investigate and address them.

- Please contact us with concerns about any potential bias at https://www.pearson.com/report-bias.html.

Contents at a Glance

Contents

Chapter 4   Azure Virtual Desktop   193

About the Author

Avinash Valiramani is an IT Infrastructure and Cloud Architect with more than 15 years of expertise in areas of Microsoft Technologies such as Microsoft Azure, Microsoft 365, Office365, Windows Server, Microsoft Exchange, SCCM, Intune, Hyper-V, and others. He is a certified Architect on Azure and Microsoft365 and primarily helps enterprises globally in their Cloud Roadmap Architecture and Onboarding/Migration Strategies & Implementation. Avinash is publishing four books on Microsoft Azure Best Practices series including this current one, collating real-world experiences to deliver a comprehensive and concise experience for new and budding technologists. Avinash also holds certifications in Barracuda, AWS, Citrix, VMware, and many other IT/Security industry certifications to complement his Microsoft expertise. He has authored a course of Azure Virtual Desktop for Oreilly Media and is planning many others in the coming months. You can follow Avinash on Twitter at @avaliramani.

Acknowledgments

I would like to thank Loretta Yates for trusting me with this huge responsibility. These books would not have been possible without your confidence in me and I will be forever grateful for that. I would like to thank Charvi Arora and the entire Microsoft Press/Pearson team for their constant support and guidance on this project. I would especially like to thank Kate Shoup for editing and reviewing this book and for all her guidance and attention to detail throughout these series of books. Kate, it has been a wonderful experience writing these four books with you and I could not have asked for a better collaborator. Thanks to Thomas Palathra for his thoughtful technical edits, Sarah Kearns for the amazing copy editing and Tracey Croom for adding the final touches to bring this to fruition. This book is the fruit of all our labor, and I am extremely happy we worked together on it.

I would also like to thank my family with gratitude, especially my brother Junaid and uncle Chandru on this effort. Your assistance in helping me organize my life and ensuring I could stay on track while wearing multiple hats was invaluable. This has been the biggest reason I managed to get this mammoth series of books out and it would not have been possible without all your support during this process. I would like to thank my mom for all her strength and belief throughout the years even when things were not going well and for believing in me throughout. Love you all.

Introduction to Azure compute services

Welcome to *Azure Compute: The Definitive Guide*. This book was developed to provide in-depth information about the different Azure services that provide computing capabilities and best practices based on real-life experiences with the product in use in different environments. *Azure Compute: The Definitive Guide* is the first in a series of what will eventually include three additional titles: *Azure Monitoring and Management: The Definitive Guide; Azure Networking: The Definitive Guide;* and *Azure Storage: The Definitive Guide.*

This book is largely based on the version of Azure compute services generally available during 2021, taking into account the development work done on these services over the years. At the time of this writing, a few features and functionalities were under preview and could potentially change before they are generally available. Most of these will be covered in subsequent editions of this book.

Overview

Over the years, Microsoft has introduced different services related to Azure compute. It started with Azure virtual machines (VMs) before introducing additional platform-as-a-service solutions like Azure App Service, Azure Container Service, Azure Functions, and Azure Virtual Desktop.

Following is a brief timeline of the announcement of each of these services in public preview:

- **Azure VMs**   June 2012
- **Azure App Service**   March 2015
- **Azure Container Service**   September 2015
- **Azure virtual machine scale sets (VMSS)**   November 2015
- **Azure Functions**   March 2016
- **Azure Virtual Desktop**   March 2019

Each service added new dimensions and capabilities to Azure's compute stack that have provided customers with more varied options to leverage compute services depending on their requirements. Over time, each service has helped increase scalability and reliability while reducing the cost and complexity of managing cloud infrastructure workloads.

As you go through each service in more detail in this book, you will find that every service, if used correctly, has the potential to transform an organization's infrastructure and business applications environment. In subsequent chapters, you will dive into each compute service to better understand how each one works and associated best practices. You will initially focus on factors to consider when selecting and designing each workload. Thereafter, you will focus on deployment considerations and strategies, with step-by-step walkthroughs for a better understanding of deployment methods, followed by some best practices.

Cloud service categories

Let's start by defining the different types of cloud service categories:

- **Infrastructure as a service (IaaS)**   Using VMs with storage and networking is generally referred to as infrastructure as a service (IaaS). This is a traditional approach to using cloud services in line with on-premises workloads. Most on-premises environments use virtualization technologies such as Hyper-V to virtualize Windows and Linux workloads. Migrating to IaaS from such an environment is considered to be a much easier first step than migrating to PaaS or FaaS (defined next). Over time, as an organization's understanding of various other types of cloud services grows, it can migrate to PaaS or FaaS.

- **Platform as a service (PaaS)**   One of the biggest benefits of using a cloud service is the capability to offload the management of back-end infrastructure to the service provider. This model is called platform as a service (PaaS). Examples of back-end infrastructure include different layers of the application, such as the compute layer, storage layer, networking layer, security layer, and monitoring layer. Organizations can use PaaS to free up their IT staff to focus on higher-level tasks and core organizational needs instead of on routine infrastructure monitoring, upgrade, and maintenance activities. Azure App Service and Azure Container Service are examples of Azure PaaS offerings.

- **Function as a service (FaaS)**   Function as a service (FaaS) offerings go one step beyond PaaS to enable organizations to focus only on their application code, leaving the entire back-end infrastructure deployment and management to the cloud service provider. This provides developers with a great way to deploy their code without worrying about the back-end infrastructure deployment, scaling, and management. It also enables the use of microservices architectures for applications. An example of an Azure FaaS offering is Azure Functions.

> **NOTE**   In addition to IaaS, PaaS, and FaaS, there is software as a service (SaaS). This is another type of cloud service category. However, because it is not applicable in the context of Microsoft Azure, this book will not delve into it further.

Not all services fall cleanly within the scope of one of these cloud service categories. For example:

- Azure Virtual Desktop, a virtualized Windows desktop hosting service, combines IaaS and PaaS to provide a cohesive solution.
- Azure VMSS, an automated VM scaling service, combines IaaS and PaaS to provide auto-scaling features.

Each of these cloud service categories has various features and limitations. Limitations might relate to the application, technological know-how, and costs for redevelopment, among others. As a result, most organizations use some combination of different types of services to maximize their cloud investments.

Each service provides a different level of control and ease of management. For example:

- IaaS provides maximum control and flexibility in migration and use.
- FaaS provides maximum automation for workload deployment, management, and use.
- PaaS provides a mix of both at varying levels, depending on the PaaS service used.

Each service also offers varying levels of scalability. For example:

- IaaS requires the use of additional services to achieve true scalability and load balancing—for example, VMSS or Azure Load Balancer.
- PaaS and FaaS services are generally designed with built-in scalability and load-balancing features.

Cost-wise, each service provides varying levels of efficiency. For example:

- FaaS offerings charge for compute based only on the usage hours for compute services, making it extremely cost-effective.
- IaaS products charge for compute services regardless of usage once the compute service (for example, a VM) is online.

- PaaS offerings are a mixed bag depending on how the services are configured. Some PaaS products charge for compute resources regardless of usage, while others, if configured correctly, charge based on usage alone.

Migration factors and strategies

Along with these features and limitations, there are certain migration factors to consider when deciding which category of cloud service might be the best solution in an organization's cloud journey. (See Figure I-1.) Of course, organizations can always start with one category (IaaS) and migrate to a second category (PaaS or FaaS) over time as their understanding of the cloud matures.

Let's examine the flow chart shown in Figure I-1 in more detail:

- **Lift-and-shift migration strategy**   In a lift-and-shift migration, the organization migrates its existing on-premises environment as-is to the cloud, without redeveloping or redesigning the application stack. This is a preferred migration approach for organizations in which:

  - A hardware refresh or procurement is planned.

  - Scaling or security limitations require the organization to migrate to the cloud as quickly as possible, with the least amount of disruption.

  - A lift-and-shift migration strategy generally involves less effort because no code changes are necessary. Application components remain as-is and are migrated in their current state to the cloud. This is generally the preferred approach for organizations that want to mainly use IaaS to host their application and database workloads.

- **Cloud-optimized strategy**   With cloud-optimized migrations, the organization redesigns or recodes its application as necessary to use PaaS and FaaS services. This enables the organization to use microservice architectures, enabling it to truly benefit from the scalability and cost benefits that a cloud service like Azure provides.

Organizations can use a lift-and-shift migration strategy, a cloud-optimized migration strategy, or a combination of the two. For example, an organization might use the flexibility provided by cloud services to start its migration using a lift-and-shift approach to quickly benefit from the scaling and global availability of Azure. Then, over time, the organization could migrate to more cloud-optimized PaaS and FaaS services.

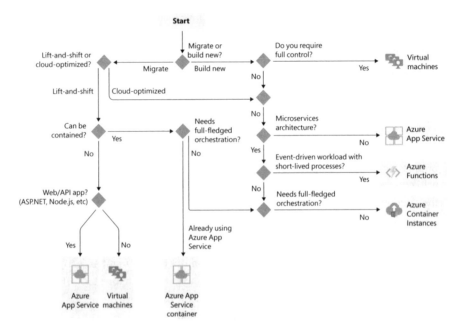

FIGURE I-1 Cloud-migration considerations. Please refer to *https://docs.microsoft. com/en-us/azure/architecture/guide/technology-choices/compute-decision-tree* for more information on Figure I-1.

Who this book is for

Microsoft Azure Compute: The Definitive Guide is for anyone interested in Azure infrastructure solutions: IT and cloud administrators, security professionals, developers, and engineers.

This book is designed to be useful for the entire spectrum of Azure users. Whether you have basic experience on Azure or other on-premises or cloud virtualization technologies, or you are an expert, my hope is that you will still derive value from this book. This book provides introductory, intermediate, and advanced coverage on each compute service.

The book especially targets those who are working in medium to large enterprise organizations and have at least one year of experience in administering, deploying, managing, monitoring, upgrading, migrating, and designing infrastructure services such as virtual machines, as well as related infrastructure such as storage, networking, and backups.

How this book is organized

This book is organized into six chapters:

Chapter 1: Azure virtual machines

Chapter 2: Azure virtual machine scale sets

Chapter 3: Azure App Service

Chapter 4: Azure Virtual Desktop

Chapter 5: Azure Container Instances

Chapter 6: Azure Functions

Each chapter focuses on a specific Azure compute service and includes in-depth coverage of the inner workings of each service, walkthroughs to guide you on how to build and test the service, and real-world best practices to help you maximize your Azure investments.

The approach adopted for the book is a unique mix of didactic, narrative, and experiential instruction. Didactic instruction is used to introduce to you the core aspects of each service. Narrative instruction leverages what you already understand to help you grasp new concepts. Finally, the experiential instruction conveys real-world experiences and challenges of small and large environments and the factors to consider while designing and implementing your own workloads. This includes step-by-step guided walkthroughs on how to configure each Azure compute service and its related features and options to gain all the benefits each service has to offer.

System requirements

To follow along with this book, you'll need an Azure subscription. At the time of this writing, Microsoft provides a 30-day, $200 trial subscription, which you can use to explore most of the services discussed in this book. Some services, however, such as dedicated hosts, are not supported by this trial subscription; these require a paid subscription.

The following list details the minimum system requirements needed to run the content in the book's companion website (*MicrosoftPressStore.com/AzureComputeTDG/detail*):

- Windows 10/11, with the latest updates from Microsoft Update Service
- Azure PowerShell (*https://docs.microsoft.com/en-us/powershell/azure/install-az-ps*)
- Azure CLI (*https://docs.microsoft.com/en-us/cli/azure/install-azure-cli*)
- Display monitor capable of 1024 x 768 resolution
- Microsoft mouse or compatible pointing device

About the companion content

The companion content for this book can be downloaded from the following page:

MicrosoftPressStore.com/AzureComputeTDG/downloads

The companion content includes the following:

- PowerShell code for each walkthrough in the book (where applicable)
- CLI code for each walkthrough in the book (where applicable)

Errata, updates, & book support

We've made every effort to ensure the accuracy of this book and its companion content. You can access updates to this book—in the form of a list of submitted errata and their related corrections—at:

MicrosoftPressStore.com/AzureComputeTDG/errata

If you discover an error that is not already listed, please submit it to us at the same page.

For additional book support and information, please visit

MicrosoftPressStore.com/Support.

Please note that product support for Microsoft software and hardware is not offered through the previous addresses. For help with Microsoft software or hardware, go to *http://support.microsoft.com.*

Stay in touch

Let's keep the conversation going! We're on Twitter: *http://twitter.com/MicrosoftPress.*

## Chapter 1

Azure virtual machines

Overview

Azure virtual machines are the basic building blocks in most Azure architectures and implementations. They are one of the most used services in the Microsoft Azure Cloud. Most organizations migrating from on-premises environments to the Microsoft Azure Cloud leverage Azure virtual machines (along with Azure Storage, Azure Networking, and related services). This chapter introduces the features of Azure virtual machines so you can use these services better.

What is an Azure VM?

A virtual machine (VM) is an image file that acts as an actual computer. Put another way, a VM is a computer hosted inside another computer.

A VM is generally sandboxed from the rest of the host (hypervisor) system and the other VMs (guests) running on that host. This enables you to build an isolated environment to run different workloads while optimizing hardware resources like compute (CPUs, memory), networking interfaces, and storage available on that host. You can separate or connect each VM with other VMs depending on your needs. This has the added benefit of ensuring that the effects of malware (such as viruses) and cyber-attacks can be restricted to specific exposed or interconnected VMs.

> **NOTE** Since their introduction, VMs have largely replaced traditional server-storage designs, which were highly inefficient from a cost, scalability, and reliability perspective.

With Azure VMs, the same virtualization principle is extended to physical servers hosted in different Azure regions across the world. In a traditional virtualization environment, the organization hosting the VMs would also manage the physical host infrastructure, including all related infrastructure workloads like firewalls, routers, switches, and so on. In an Azure-hosted VM, Microsoft is largely responsible for ensuring that the back-end hardware services are up and running for customer consumption as and when needed. This removes the overhead of maintaining, upgrading, and managing the physical infrastructure layer from in-house IT teams.

TIP It is imperative for IT teams to plan and design their Azure VM infrastructure well before deployment to avoid reliability and cost challenges, which could require significant redesign.

Organizations use Azure VMs in a few different ways. Five common examples are as follows:

- **To run test and dev workloads** Organizations that are heavily invested in on-premises infrastructure generally find it easier to deploy test and dev workloads in Azure VMs. This enables their IT teams to become familiar with the cloud while also testing and verifying their on-premises applications to better plan for future migrations to the cloud. Organizations might also initiate new application builds or transformation projects by hosting the initial test and dev workloads in the cloud, so the application code will be built with cloud-native features for maximum benefits.

- **To run applications requiring scalability and flexibility** VMs are often used to accommodate applications that require the ability to scale quickly or in short bursts for temporary or infrequent loads.

- **To provide redundancy for the datacenter** Some organizations use Azure VMs to host their disaster-recovery environment and/or redundant infrastructure.

- **To reduce on-premises hardware footprint** Some organizations move to Azure VMs when refreshing or upgrading hardware to reduce the hardware footprint in the on-premises or co-located datacenters. This also helps reduce related datacenter costs, such as for power, cooling, security, and compliance audits.

- **To reduce on-premises management overhead** Some organizations use Azure VMs to reduce the management overhead of underlying hardware, hypervisors and upgrades, and other interconnected components, such as networking, security solutions, and so on.

Is VM the correct workload type?

One of the critical factors to consider when selecting VMs is whether they are the best service for hosting your workload. There are a number of factors to consider when making this decision, including the following:

- Do you require full control of the back-end infrastructure hosting your application?

- Does your application support only VMs, or is it designed to work better with other Azure compute services to leverage CI/CD and scaling capabilities available in serverless technologies?

- Will your IT team prefer to manage the security and OS updates for their environment?

Answering these questions should help you obtain clarity on whether VMs are the right solution for your workload. Although other factors such as budget allocation, operational needs, and redundancy needs might also influence your decision, you should ask the preceding questions first in identifying or eliminating VMs as the right hosting platform.

Operating system support

Microsoft Azure supports both Windows- and Linux-based VMs. However, make sure to check that your version of Windows or Linux is supported, as these change over time. (See Table 1-1.) Also, although versions older than Windows Server 2008 R2 are supported, clients must bring their own images and have an active support agreement with Microsoft for operating systems that have reached their end-of-life.

TABLE 1-1 OS support for Azure VMs

Distribution	Version
Windows Server	2008 R2, 2012, 2012 R2, 2016, 2019
CentOS	CentOS 6.x, 7.x, 8.x
Debian by Credativ	8.x, 9.x, 10.x
Flatcar Container Linux by Kinvolk	Pro, Stable, Beta
Oracle Linux by Oracle	6.x, 7.x, 8.x
Red Hat Enterprise Linux by Red Hat	6.x, 7.x, 8.x
SUSE Linux Enterprise by SUSE	SLES/SLES for SAP 11.x, 12.x, 15.x
openSUSE by SUSE	openSUSE Leap 15.x
Ubuntu by Canonical	Ubuntu Server and Pro 16.x, 18.x, 20.x

VM series

Microsoft provides various specialized Azure VM series. It's critical that you understand these series, as well as your application requirements, so you can decide which VM series to run your workloads on. As of early 2022, some of these series are as follows:

- **A-series VMs** These are basic, entry-level VMs with CPU performance and memory configurations best suited for workloads used for test and development. A-series VMs might also be good for low-traffic web servers, small to medium databases, servers for proof of concepts, and code repositories. They provide a low-cost option to get started with Azure.

- **Bs-series VMs** These are a great option for workloads that typically require low to moderate baseline CPU utilization, but occasionally require significantly higher CPU utilization for brief periods when demand rises. Web servers handling low traffic volumes are an ideal workload to host on such servers. Bs-series VMs are an economical option to use even for dev and test workloads, where CPU utilization levels are not that high for most of the development cycle. Other use cases include small databases, micro services, servers used for proof of concepts, and low-intensity workloads, such as AD domain controllers, print servers, Windows Update servers, and similar workloads in most environments.

- **D-series VMs** D-series VMs are the most versatile Azure VM series. There are multiple VM subseries available under the D-series: Ds, Dds, and Das-series, each with different VM types. Each VM type uses different processor types and can achieve different levels of CPU performance, providing multiple options based on the application requirements. The CPU and memory combinations available in the D-series address the needs of most production environments. In addition to the use cases mentioned in the preceding bullets, D-series VMs work well for analytics workloads and workloads requiring in-memory caching.

- **DC-series VMs** DC-series VMs use the latest generation of Intel XEON E-2288G processor with SGX technology. They include Software Guard Extensions (SGX), which are a set of instructions that increases the security of the in-memory application code and data to protect it from tampering. This makes them ideal for workloads that require confidential data processing and storage. Some use cases for DC-series VMs include blockchain, intelligence analysis, fraud detection, confidential machine learning, and so on.

- **E-series VMs** E-series VMs are optimized for memory-intensive workloads; they have a higher memory-to-core ratio. Ideal use cases include SQL, Oracle, or SAP HANA databases (which require more in-memory capacity), business intelligence and in-memory analytics workloads, and so on.

- **F-series VMs** F-series VMs are built to support more CPU-intensive workloads; they have a higher core-to-memory ratio. They are ideal for workloads that run compute-intensive applications, such as batch, gaming, and web servers.

- **H-series VMs** Also called high-performance computing VMs, H-series VMs are optimized to support large computing and modeling application requirements, such as financial modeling, weather-pattern analysis, computational chemistry, and similar applications. These VMs have a very high resource capacity and are optimized for intensive computing.

- **N-series VMs** N-series VMs are GPU-enabled VMs that are ideal for graphics-intensive workloads, such as gaming, deep learning, graphics rendering, and so on. There are different VM offerings within this series that are aimed for different computing scenarios. Some of these VM offerings support InfiniBand connections, which provide extremely high networking throughput and performance.

Azure regions

Azure VMs are available in datacenters spread globally across 54 regions, with new regions added on a near-constant basis to address area needs. Each region consists of a set of datacenters located within very low latency perimeters. Regions are connected together with dedicated high-speed networks.

The location of the users who will employ your VMs will be a key factor in deciding which region to choose for your workloads. For example, if most of your users are based on the east coast of the U.S., you will most likely choose to use VMs in that location. This will improve the likelihood that your users will have the best possible experience when accessing these resources. If, on the other hand, your users are split among multiple geographies, you will have to choose by possibly hosting test and dev workloads to determine which region might be best-suited for your needs.

Depending on your application design, you might opt to use VMs across multiple regions to host your workloads, thereby providing an optimal experience to users in different geographic areas. Be sure you have a clear understanding of application functionality and hosting requirements before making your decision about which region(s) to choose.

If the primary users of your application(s) are external-facing customers, where you choose to host certain workloads might depend on where those users are based. For example, the location of external-facing application workloads could reflect where your customers are, while the location of internal-facing workloads, for employees, might depend on where those employees are.

You should review the list of Azure regions available to select the region based on your needs, accounting for the factors that will affect the usage and growth of your workloads. When determining which region should host your workloads, latency is a particularly critical factor. Fortunately, there are online tools to enable you to gauge the average latency between your location (or other locations or ISPs used within your organization) and various Azure datacenters around the world. For example, Figure 1-1 shows the average latency from my workstation to the different datacenters in the U.S. Datacenters in the West US region have the lowest latency, but the West US 2 region has acceptable latency, too. So, in my case, I would specify the West US region as my primary datacenter candidate (meaning I would use the VMs in datacenters in this region by default) and the West US 2 region as my secondary datacenter candidate (meaning I would use VMs in datacenters in this region if there were not adequate VMs in the US West region).

Geography	Region	Physical Location	Average Latency (ms)
US	Central US	Iowa	89 ms
US	East US	Virginia	98 ms
US	East US 2	Virginia	101 ms
US	North Central US	Illinois	90 ms
US	South Central US	Texas	83 ms
US	West Central US	Wyoming	78 ms
US	West US	California	21 ms
US	West US 2	Washington	56 ms

FIGURE 1-1 Latency to different Azure regions.

> **NOTE** What you consider to be acceptable latency will depend on the requirements of your workload(s). So, be sure to identify these in advance, working closely with your application teams.

Compute sizing and pricing

In addition to selecting the appropriate VM series and region, you need to choose the right compute size for your workloads. Your choice will depend on your performance needs as well as your budgetary constraints.

As shown in Figure 1-2, the compute resources with different VM types have various prices. These are based on a number of factors, including the processor, memory, and network resources available on the underlying hardware level. Prices will vary depending on when you run the comparison, so it is imperative to look at VM prices near or on the date of workload creation rather than relying on earlier cost comparisons, especially if those comparisons are weeks or months old.

VM Name ↑F	vCPUs	Memory (GiB)	Region	Currency	Linux Cost	Windows Cost
Standard_B2ms	2	8	West US 2	USD	60.74	66.58
Standard_D2_v3	2	8	West US 2	USD	70.08	137.24
Standard_D2_v4	2	8	West US 2	USD	70.08	137.24
Standard_D2_v5	2	8	West US 2	USD	70.08	137.24
Standard_D2a_v4	2	8	West US 2	USD	70.08	137.24
Standard_D2ads_v5	2	8	West US 2	USD	75.19	142.35
Standard_D2as_v4	2	8	West US 2	USD	70.08	137.24
Standard_D2as_v5	2	8	West US 2	USD	62.78	129.94
Standard_D2d_v4	2	8	West US 2	USD	82.49	149.65

FIGURE 1-2 Monthly VM pricing comparison in the West US 2 region (January 2022).

Naturally, price is important. But when comparing prices for VMs, you must ensure that the VMs you are choosing from meet your technical needs. A VM that does not support your application's technical requirements will generally cause more harm than good in terms of cost savings. On a similar note, if a particular datacenter is the only one capable of meeting your needs with regard to latency, then there's no need to compare VM costs across regions.

> **TIP** Be sure to test different VM series against your workload types to determine which series will work best while also delivering maximum value for your Azure spends.

Azure VM creation walkthrough

The following sections step you through the process of creating an Azure VM using the Azure Portal, Azure PowerShell, and Azure CLI.

USING THE AZURE PORTAL

To create a VM using the Azure Portal, follow these steps:

1. Log in to the Azure Portal and type **virtual machines** in the search bar.

2. Under **Services**, click **Virtual Machines**.

3. On the Virtual Machines page, click **Create** and choose **Virtual Machine** to start the Create a Virtual Machine wizard.

4. In the **Basics** tab of the Create a Virtual Machine wizard, enter the following information (see Figure 1-3):

   - **Subscription**   Select the subscription to create the VM.

   - **Resource Group**   Select an existing resource group or create a new one to host the VM.

   - **Virtual Machine Name**   Enter a name for the VM. It should not be longer than 15 characters to avoid having DNS/NetBIOS issues later on.

   - **Region**   Select the Azure region you want to host the VM.

   - **Availability options**   Leave this at the default value (**No Infrastructure Redundancy Required**) for now. You will explore availability options later in this chapter.

   - **Image**   Select the OS image to use for the VM—in this case, **Windows Server 2019 Datacenter – Gen 1**.

   - **Azure Spot Instance**   Leave this unchecked for now.

   - **Size**   Select a size. Because this is a test VM, choose a smaller size to save on costs.

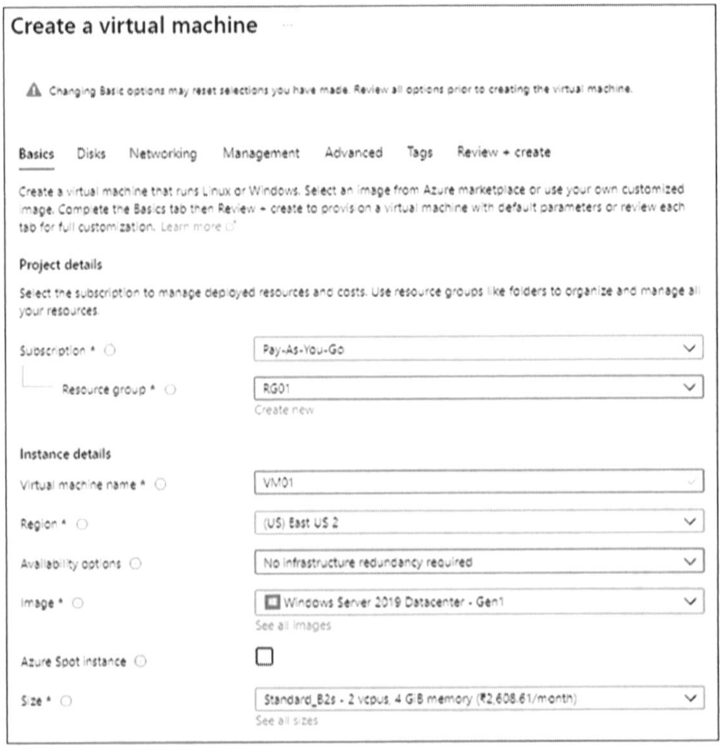

Create a virtual machine ...

⚠ Changing Basic options may reset selections you have made. Review all options prior to creating the virtual machine.

Basics   Disks   Networking   Management   Advanced   Tags   Review + create

Create a virtual machine that runs Linux or Windows. Select an image from Azure marketplace or use your own customized image. Complete the Basics tab then Review + create to provision a virtual machine with default parameters or review each tab for full customization. Learn more ⧉

Project details

Select the subscription to manage deployed resources and costs. Use resource groups like folders to organize and manage all your resources

Subscription * ⓘ	Pay-As-You-Go ⌄
Resource group * ⓘ	RG01 ⌄
	Create new

Instance details

Virtual machine name * ⓘ	VM01 ⌄
Region * ⓘ	(US) East US 2 ⌄
Availability options ⓘ	No infrastructure redundancy required ⌄
Image * ⓘ	☑ Windows Server 2019 Datacenter - Gen1 ⌄
	See all images
Azure Spot instance ⓘ	☐
Size * ⓘ	Standard_B2s - 2 vcpus, 4 GiB memory (₹2,608.61/month) ⌄
	See all sizes

FIGURE 1-3   The Basics tab of the Create a Virtual Machine wizard.

5. Still in the **Basics** tab, under **Administrator Account**, enter the following information. Then click **Next**. (See Figure 1-4.)

   - **Username**   Enter a username for the default local administrator account for the VM.
   - **Password**   Set a strong password based on organizational password requirements.
   - **Confirm Password**   Re-enter the same password.
   - **Public Inbound Ports**   Leave this at the default value of **Allow Selected Ports**.
   - **Select Inbound Ports**   Leave this at the default value of **RDP (3389)**.
   - **Licensing**   Leave this unchecked.

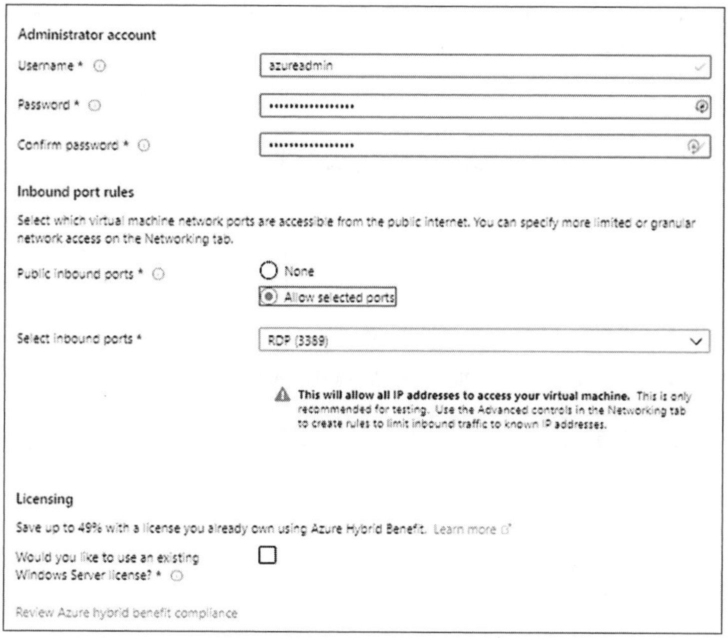

FIGURE 1-4 Setting up the Administrator Account, Networking Rules, and Licensing.

6. In the **Disks** tab, leave all the default settings as is (see Figure 1-5), and click **Next**.

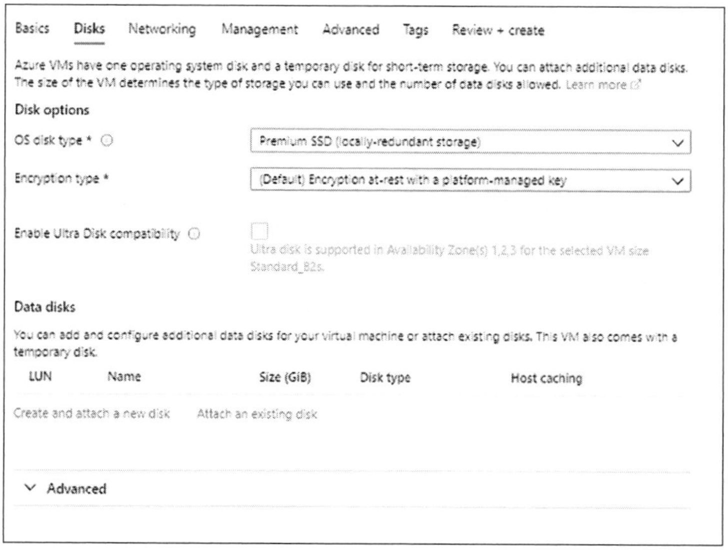

FIGURE 1-5 The Disks tab of the Create a Virtual Machine wizard.

7. In the **Networking** tab, enter the requested information in the following boxes. (See Figure 1-6.) Then click **Next**.

- **Virtual Network**   Select an existing virtual network or let the wizard create a new one.

- **Subnet**   Select an existing subnet or let the wizard create a new one.

- **Public IP**   Select an existing unused public IP or let the wizard create a new one.

- **NIC Network Security Group**   Set this to **Basic** to allow the wizard to create a network security group with the default configuration.

- **Public Inbound Ports**   Leave this at the default setting, **Allow Selected Ports**.

- **Select Inbound Ports**   Leave this at the default setting, **RDP (3389)**, to allow the use of RDP to log in to the VM after you create it.

- **Accelerated Networking**   Depending on the VM size, you might be able to set up accelerated networking. Leave this at the default setting (unchecked).

- **Load Balancing**   Leave this at the default setting (unchecked).

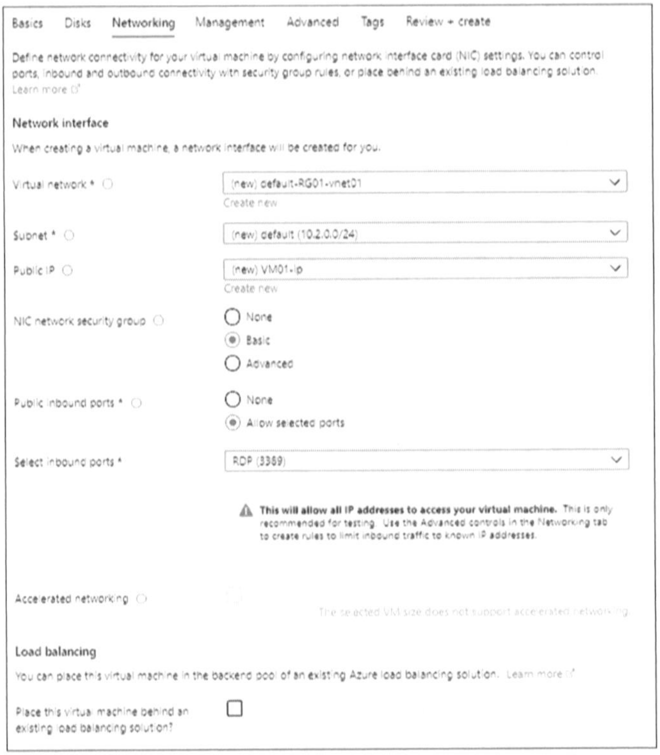

FIGURE 1-6   The Networking tab of the Create a Virtual Machine wizard.

8. In the **Management** tab, leave the default settings as is (see Figure 1-7) and click **Next** to continue.

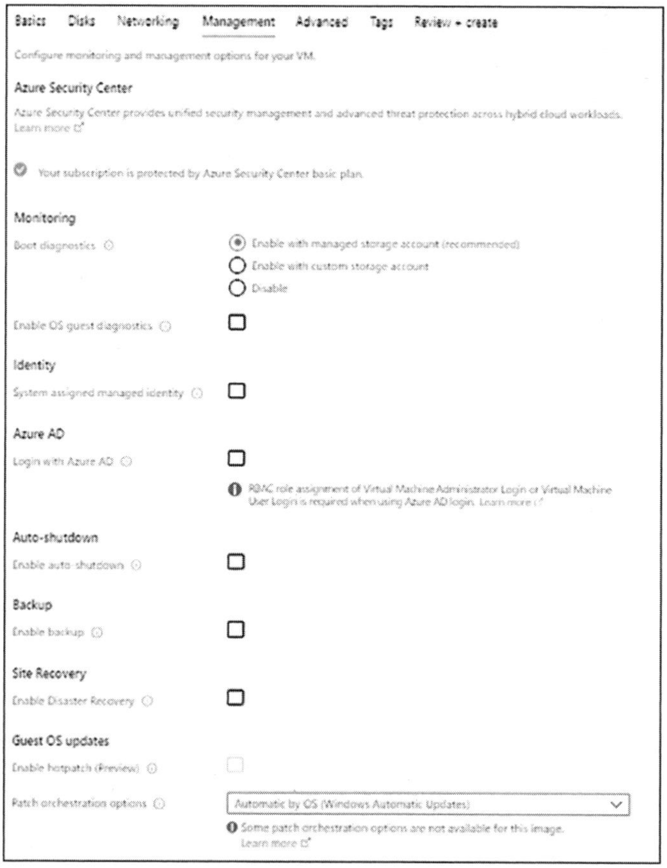

FIGURE 1-7 The Management tab of the Create a Virtual Machine wizard.

9. In the **Advanced** tab, leave the default settings as is (see Figure 1-8) and click **Next** to continue.

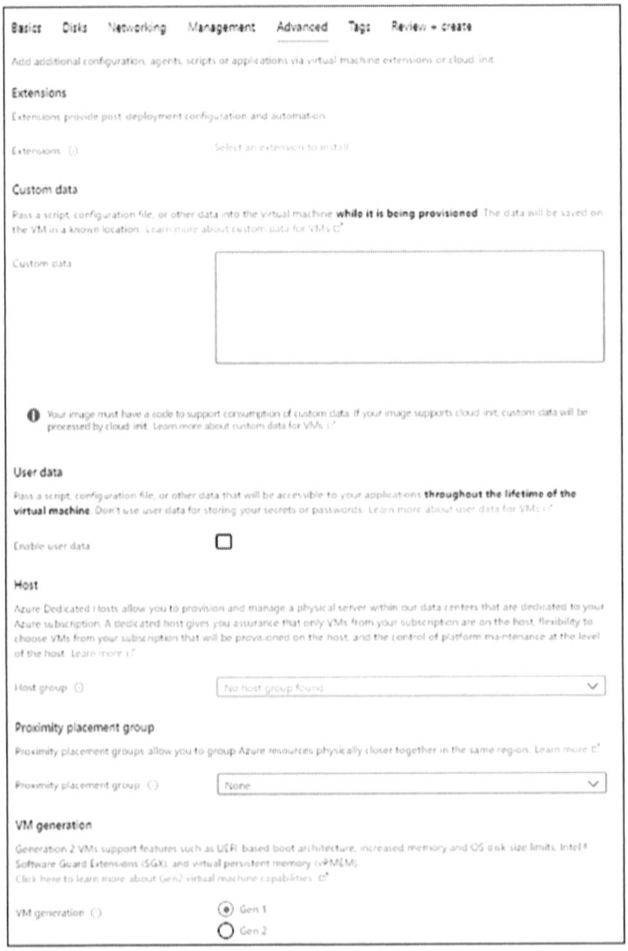

FIGURE 1-8 The Advanced tab of the Create a Virtual Machine wizard.

10. In the **Tags** tab, enter any tags that you would like to apply to the VM or leave the default settings as is (see Figure 1-9) and click **Next** to continue.

FIGURE 1-9 The Tags tab of the Create a Virtual Machine wizard.

11. In the **Review + Create** tab, review your settings and click **Create** to create the VM.

USING AZURE POWERSHELL

You can create VMs using the Azure PowerShell `New-AzVM` command with various switches to specify the VM's parameters. For example, the following code shows how to create the same VM as before using Azure PowerShell:

```
#Define required variables
$rg = "RG01"
$vmname = "VM01"
$location = "EastUS"
$vnet = "vNET01"
$subnet = "Subnet01"
$nsg = "NSG01"
$publicip = "publicIP01"
#Create resource group for VM
New-AzResourceGroup -Name $rg -Location $location
#Create VM
New-AzVm `
    -ResourceGroupName $rg `
    -Name $vmname `
    -Location $location `
    -VirtualNetworkName $vnet `
    -SubnetName $subnet `
    -Image Win2019Datacenter `
    -SecurityGroupName $nsg `
    -PublicIpAddressName $publicip `
    -OpenPorts 3389
```

USING THE AZURE CLI

You can use the Azure CLI to create VMs by using the `az vm create` command with various switches to specify the VM's parameters. For example, the following Bash script shows how to create the same VM as before using the Azure CLI:

```
#Define required variables
rg = "RG01"
location = "EastUS"
vmname = "VM01"
nsg = "NSG-01"
publicip = "publicIP-01"
#Create resource group for VM
az group create --name $rg --location $location
#Create VM and open RDP
az vm create \
    --resource-group $rg \
    --name $vmname \
    --image Win2019Datacenter \
```

```
    --nsg $nsg \
    --public-ip-address $publicip \
    --public-ip-sku Standard \
    --nsg-rule RDP \
    --admin-username azureuser

az vm open-port -g $rg -n $vmname --port 3389 --priority 100
```

High-availability considerations

Different types of VM workloads require different levels of redundancy and high availability. Certain mission-critical applications and database servers might require 100% availability (or close). In other instances, you might require that latency between servers be kept at a minimum. It is therefore important to understand and consider the various high-availability options provided by Microsoft in Azure. These include the following:

- Availability sets
- Availability zones
- Proximity placement groups

> **NOTE** You can choose to deploy different VM workloads with or without one or more of these options based on the individual VM requirements.

Availability sets

An *availability set* is a group of two or more VMs hosted in the same Azure datacenter but on different hardware. This ensures that if the datacenter experiences a physical hardware failure, one or more VMs will remain online. The VMs in an availability set are generally of the same configuration and host the same application or service, so there is redundancy if one VM goes offline. Microsoft offers a 99.95% SLA for availability sets.

> **NOTE** There is no additional cost attached to creating an availability set. You can add a VM to an availability set only when you create the VM. If the VM has already been created, you cannot add it to an availability set.

For configurations in which multiple web servers or application front-ends are located in the same Azure region and are hosting the same workload across multiple servers for redundancy and scalability, adding VMs to an availability set would be highly recommended. Database servers set up with DB replication would also benefit from using availability sets.

> **NOTE** Availability sets do not perform data replication. If you require data replication, you should manage it at the application or database level.

Each availability set is assigned three fault domains and 20 update domains, and each VM in an availability set is assigned to one fault domain and one update domain. If the number of VMs exceeds three, the fourth VM will share the same fault domain as the first VM. (See Figure 1-10.)

- A *fault domain* is a set of VMs that are using the same storage, power source, and networking resources. Any sudden hardware or physical infrastructure failure in an Azure datacenter that pertains to hard disks, power, or networking in a physical rack can result in unplanned downtimes. In such unplanned maintenance events, Azure automatically fails over any VMs hosted on the affected fault domain to another fault domain, assuming those VMs are part of an availability set.

- An *update domain* is a set of VMs that receive Microsoft updates at the same time. As you know, Microsoft patches any security vulnerabilities on a periodic basis. This helps to improve security, reliability, and performance. Generally, when these updates are performed, it does not affect the hosted VMs. However, on occasion, patched VMs require a reboot for the updates to take effect. In a large cloud environment, such a complex operation is planned well in advance to minimize the business impact on affected clients. This is where update domains come in. Update domains enable Azure to reboot VMs in groups rather than all at once. When the VMs in one update domain are finished updating, Azure can move onto the next one.

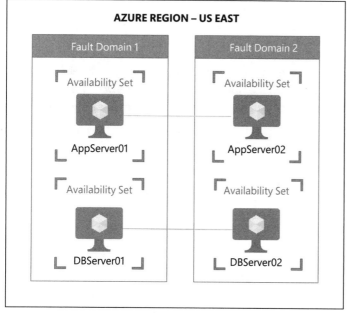

FIGURE 1-10 Fault domains for VMs.

Availability set walkthrough

The following sections step you through the process of creating an availability set using the Azure Portal, Azure PowerShell, and Azure CLI.

USING THE AZURE PORTAL

To create an availability set using the Azure Portal during VM creation, follow these steps:

1. Follow the steps in the "Azure VM creation walkthrough" section to start the Create a Virtual Machine wizard and create a VM.

2. In the **Basics** tab, locate the **Instance Details** section. Then, under the **Availability Set** drop-down list, click the **Create New** link. (See Figure 1-11.)

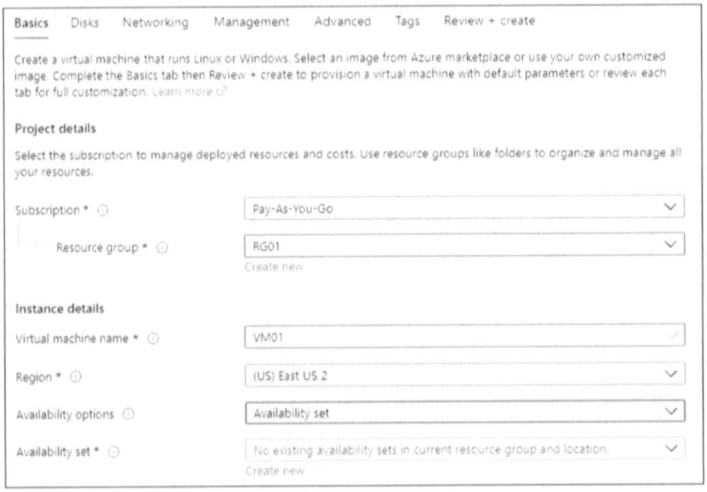

FIGURE 1-11 Creating a new availability set.

3. In the Create Availability Set dialog box, set the following parameters (see Figure 1-12), type a name for the availability set in the **Name** box, use the **Fault Domain** slider to specify how many fault domains to use, and use the **Update Domains** slider to choose how many update domains to use.

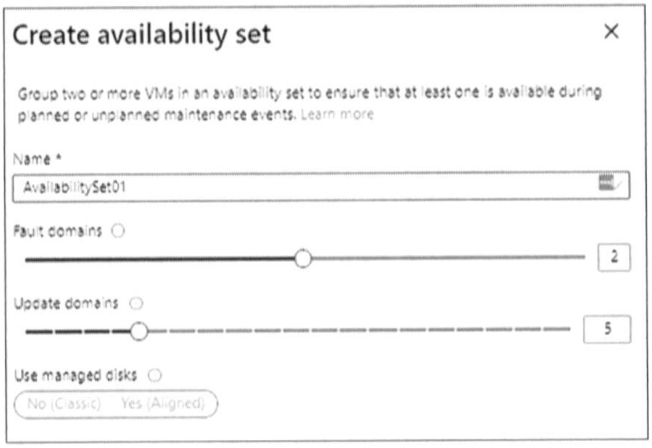

FIGURE 1-12 Setting up the fault and update domains.

4. Click **Create** to return to the Create a Virtual Machine wizard and continue creating the VM as described in the section, "Azure VM creation walkthrough."

USING AZURE POWERSHELL

You can create an availability set using Azure PowerShell by using the New-AzAvailabilitySet command. You can then add VM(s) to the availability set by using the -AvailabilitySetName parameter of the New-AzureVMConfig cmdlet, as shown here:

```
#Define variables
$rg = "RG01"
$location = "EastUS"
$avs = "AVSet-01"
$vm = "vm-01"
$vNet = "vNET-01"
$subnet = "Subnet01"
$nsg = "NSG-01"
$publicip = "PublicIP-01"
#Create an availability set
New-AzAvailabilitySet `
   -Location $location `
   -Name $avs `
   -ResourceGroupName $rg `
   -Sku aligned `
   -PlatformFaultDomainCount 2 `
   -PlatformUpdateDomainCount 5
#Create a VM in the availability set
New-AzVm `
         -ResourceGroupName $rg `
         -Name $vm `
         -Location $location `
         -VirtualNetworkName $vNet `
         -SubnetName $Subnet `
         -SecurityGroupName $nsg `
         -PublicIpAddressName $publicip `
         -AvailabilitySetName $avs
```

USING AZURE CLI

You can create an availability set using the Azure CLI by using the az vm availability-set create command. You can then add VM(s) to the availability set by using the --availability-set parameter of the az vm create cmdlet, as shown here:

```
#Define variables
rg="RG02"
avs="AVSet-01"
```

```
vm="VM-02"
vnet="vNET-01"
subnet="Subnet-01"
avs="AVSet-01"
publicip="publicip-01"
#Create availability set
az vm availability-set create \
    --resource-group $rg \
    --name $avs \
    --platform-fault-domain-count 2 \
    --platform-update-domain-count 5
# Create VM inside the availability set
az vm create \
    --resource-group $rg \
    --name $vm \
    --availability-set $avs \
    --vnet-name $vnet \
    --subnet $subnet \
    --public-ip-sku Standard \
    --public-ip $publicip \
    --image Win2019Datacenter \
    --admin-username azureuser
```

Availability zones

Each Azure region is made up of three availability zones. (See Figure 1-13.) An *availability zone* consists of one or more datacenters equipped with their own power, cooling, and networking. If one datacenter in the availability zone experiences an outage, VMs in another datacenter in the availability zone will still be available. For this reason, availability zones provide a higher level of redundancy than availability sets. Microsoft offers 99.99% SLA for availability zones.

> **NOTE** You can assign an availability zone to a VM only when you create the VM. If you want to apply an availability zone to an existing VM, you must re-create the VM with the original VM disks.

The concepts of fault domains and update domains also apply to availability zones. Azure automatically ensures that VMs are split between fault domains and update domains, even between availability zones.

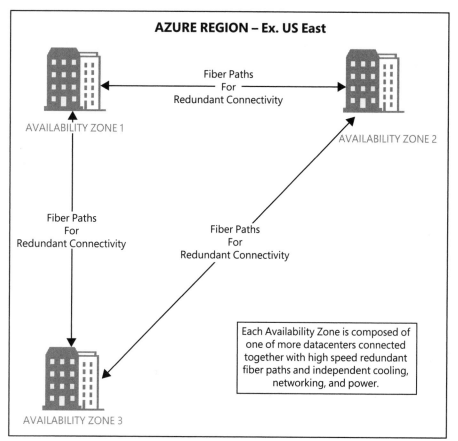

FIGURE 1-13 Availability zones in an Azure region.

NOTE Not all VM SKUs are supported for use with availability zones. Consider this before finalizing a VM SKU for the workload.

Availability zones walkthrough

The following sections step you through the process of assigning a VM to an availability zone using the Azure Portal, Azure PowerShell, and Azure CLI.

USING THE AZURE PORTAL

To assign a VM to an availability zone using the Azure Portal during VM creation, follow these steps:

1. Follow the steps in the "Azure VM creation walkthrough" section to start the Create a Virtual Machine wizard and create a VM.

2. In the **Basics** tab, locate the **Instance Details** section. Then, open the **Availability Options** drop-down list and choose **Availability Zone**. (See Figure 1-14.)

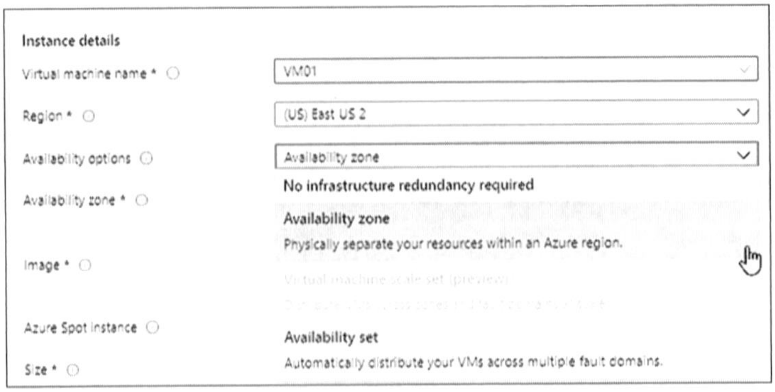

FIGURE 1-14 Setting up an availability zone during VM creation.

3. Open the **Availability Zone** drop-down list and choose the availability zone to which you want to assign the VM. (See Figure 1-15.) Then, continue creating the VM as described in the section, "Azure VM creation walkthrough."

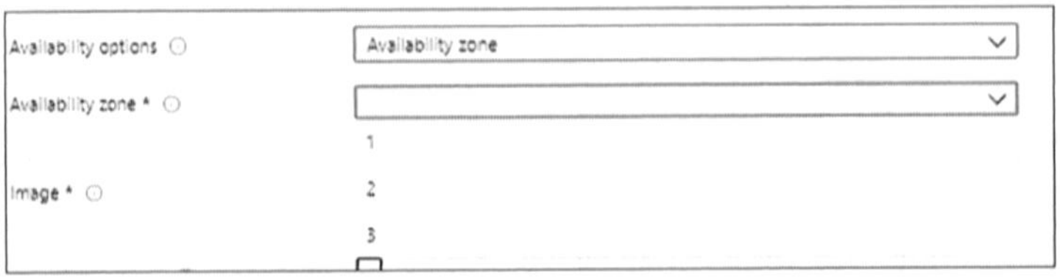

FIGURE 1-15 Selecting the availability zone.

USING AZURE POWERSHELL

You can assign a VM to an availability zone using Azure PowerShell by using the –zone parameter when creating the VM using the New-AzVM command, as shown here:

```
#Define variables
$rg = "RG01"
$location = "EastUS2"
$vm = "vm01"
$vNet = "vNET-01"
$subnet = "Subnet01"
$nsg = "NSG-01"
$publicip = "PublicIP-01"
#Create a VM in the availability zone
New-AzVm `
        -ResourceGroupName $rg `
        -Name $vm `
        -Location $location `
        -VirtualNetworkName $vNet `
        -SubnetName $Subnet `
```

```
        -SecurityGroupName $nsg `
        -PublicIpAddressName $publicip `
                -Zone 2
```

USING THE AZURE CLI

You can assign a VM to an availability zone using the Azure CLI by using the –zone parameter when creating the VM with the az vm create command, as shown here:

```
#Define variables
rg="RG01"
location="EastUS2"
vm="vm01"
# Create VM
az vm create --resource-group $rg --name $vm --location $location
--image Win2019Datacenter --zone 2
```

Proximity placement groups

As your use of VMs grows, those VMs might be placed in different datacenters across an Azure region. This can result in higher than acceptable network latency between VMs. Placing your VMs in proximity placement groups ensures that the VMs are located as close to each other as possible. This enables you to achieve the lowest possible latency and avoid performance issues. This might be important for interconnected workloads, such as applications and databases.

Proximity placement groups walkthrough

The following sections step you through the process of creating a proximity placement group as assigning a VM to it during VM creation using the Azure Portal, Azure PowerShell, and Azure CLI.

USING THE AZURE PORTAL

To create a proximity placement group and assign a VM to it during VM creation using the Azure Portal, follow these steps:

1. In the Azure Portal, type **proximity placement group** in the search bar and click the **Proximity Placement Groups** entry under **Services**. (See Figure 1-16.)

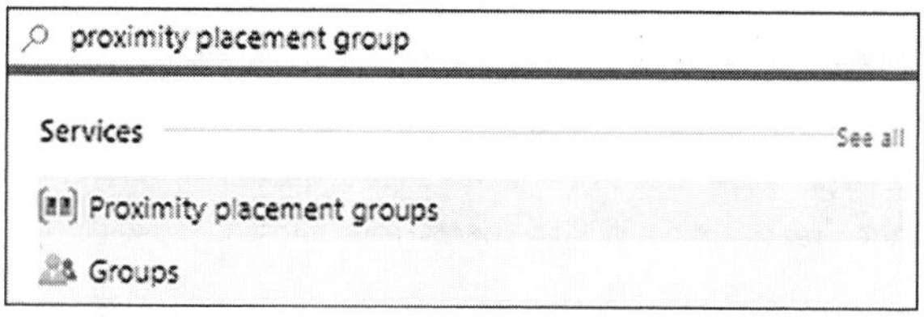

FIGURE 1-16   Search for the proximity placement groups service.

2. Click the **Create Proximity Placement Group** button (see Figure 1-17) to start the Create Proximity Placement Group wizard.

No proximity placement groups to display

A proximity placement group is a logical grouping used to make sure that Azure compute resources are physically located close to each other. Proximity placement groups are useful for workloads where low latency is a requirement.

Create proximity placement group

Learn more ⬚

FIGURE 1-17 Create a proximity placement group.

3. In the **Basics** tab of the Create Proximity Placement Group wizard, enter the following information (see Figure 1-18) and click **Next** to continue:

- **Subscription** Select the subscription to create the proximity placement group.
- **Resource Group** Select an existing resource group or create a new one to host the proximity placement group.
- **Region** Select the Azure region you want to host the proximity placement group. Make sure it is the same region as your VMs that will be a part of this group.
- **Proximity Placement Group Name** Enter a unique name for the proximity placement group.

Create Proximity Placement Group   ...

Basics   Tags   Review + create

Project details

Select the subscription to manage deployed resources and costs. Use resource groups like folders to organize and manage all your resources.

Subscription * ○	Pay-As-You-Go	∨
Resource group * ○	RG01	∨
	Create new	

Instance details

| Region * ○ | East US 2 | ∨ |
| Proximity placement group name * ○ | ProximityPlacementGroup01 | |

FIGURE 1-18 The Basics tab of the Create Proximity Placement Group wizard.

4. In the **Tags** tab, enter any tags that you would like to apply to the proximity placement group or leave the default settings as is (see Figure 1-19) and click **Next** to continue.

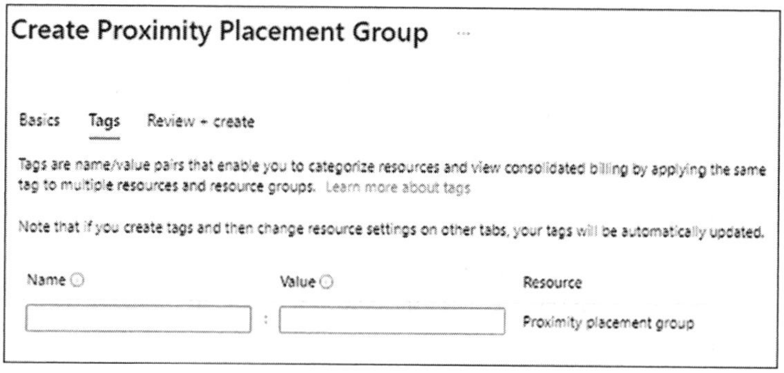

FIGURE 1-19 The Tags tab of the Create Proximity Placement Group wizard.

5. In the **Review + Create** tab (see Figure 1-20), review your settings and click **Create** to create the proximity placement group.

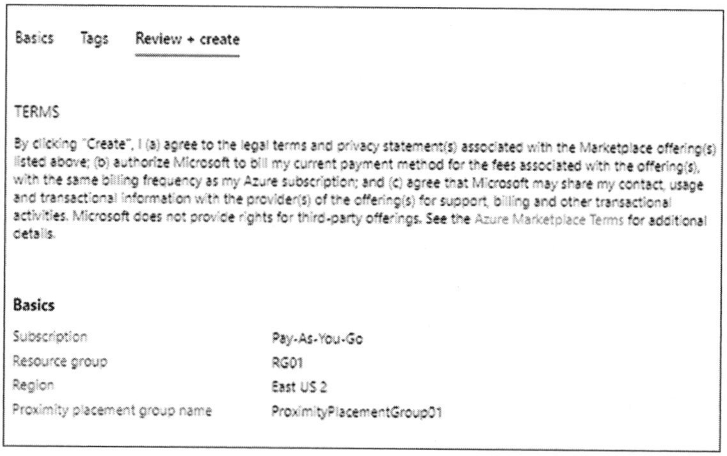

FIGURE 1-20 The Review + Create tab of the Create Proximity Placement Group wizard.

After you create the proximity placement group, you can add VMs to it during the VM-creation process.

6. In the **Advanced** tab of the Create a Virtual Machine wizard, locate the **Proximity Placement Group** section. Then, open the **Proximity Placement Group** drop-down list and choose the placement proximity group you created. (See Figure 1-21.) Then continue creating the VM as described in the section, "Azure VM creation walkthrough."

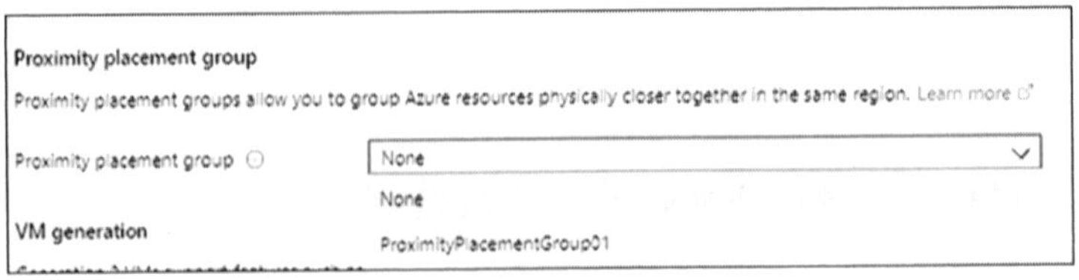

FIGURE 1-21 Selecting the proximity placement group.

USING THE AZURE POWERSHELL

You can create a proximity placement group using Azure PowerShell by using the `New-AzProximityPlacementGroup` command. You then reference it using the `-ProximityPlacementGroup` parameter when creating a new VM with the `New-AzVM` shell command, as shown here:

```
#Define the required variables
$resourceGroup = "RG01"
$location = "East US 2"
$ppgName = "PPG-01"
$vmName = "VM01"
# create the proximity placement group
$ppg = New-AzProximityPlacementGroup `
    -Location $location `
    -Name $ppgName `
    -ResourceGroupName $resourceGroup `
    -ProximityPlacementGroupType Standard
#create a VM in the Proximity Placement Group
New-AzVm `
    -ResourceGroupName $resourceGroup `
    -Name $vmName `
    -Location $location `
    -ProximityPlacementGroup $ppg.Id
```

USING THE AZURE CLI

You can create a proximity placement group using the Azure CLI by using the `az ppg create` command. You then reference it using the `--ppg` parameter when creating a new VM with the `az vm create` Bash command, as shown here:

```
#Define the required variables
resourcegroup = "RG01"
location = "East US 2"
ppgname = "PPG-01"
vmname = "VM01"
#Create a Proximity placement group
```

```
az ppg create -n $ppgname \
    -g $resourcegroup \
    -l $location \
    -t standard
#Create a VM in the Proximity Placement Group
az vm create \
    -n $vmname \
    -g $resourcegroup \
    --image Win2019Datacenter \
    --ppg $ppgname \
    --size Standard_D3_v4 \
    -l $location
```

Storage disks for VMs

VMs can use two types of disks for storage: managed disks and unmanaged disks. Generally speaking, managed disks are recommended because they provide a much higher level of redundancy, resiliency, and reliability than unmanaged disks. However, in certain situations, it might be necessary to use unmanaged disks. This section explores each disk type in detail to enable you to choose the disk type that is right for you.

Managed disks

Managed disks do not require an Azure storage account in the back end to host the disk. This removes all applicable limitations on the storage account. Managed disks can scale independently and have much higher levels of availability and durability.

Some key features of managed disks are as follows:

- **Secure by default**   Managed disks support disk encryption by default using both Azure-managed and customer-managed encryption keys. Encryption can be performed on the OS level, too, providing an additional layer of protection.
- **Built-in high availability**   Designed for 99.999% availability, managed disks are extremely durable and highly available by default. In addition, managed disks always maintain three replicas of data, making them highly tolerant against failures.
- **Zone resilient**   Managed disks offer support for availability zones, making them resilient to zone failures.
- **Scalable**   Managed disks can support up to 50,000 VM disks per region, making them highly scalable—especially when compared to unmanaged disks.
- **Easier to manage**   Managed disks offer support for role-based access controls (RBAC), allowing for granular access control.
- **Higher performance**   Compared to unmanaged disks, managed disks provide predictable and high IOPS for all disk types.
- **Backup support**   Azure Backup can be used to back up and restore managed disks.

Unmanaged disks

Unmanaged disks require you to create an Azure storage account to hold the VM disk files. So, they are subject to all the limitations that apply to the storage account level, such as IOPS throttling, the number of disks supported per storage account, and so on.

Some key characteristics of unmanaged disks are as follows:

- **Performance limitations** IOPS limitations on the Azure storage account level apply to all standard unmanaged disks sharing a storage account. Premium disks provide predictable performance levels.

- **Scalability limitations** It is recommended to have a maximum of 40 disks per standard storage account.

- **Customer-managed encryption** Encryption is performed on the storage-account level and must be enabled manually.

- **Geo-redundancy options** You can set up geo-redundancy for unmanaged disks using either the GRS or RA-GRS options during disk creation.

- **Support for migration to managed disks** Unmanaged disks can be easily migrated to managed disks, which provide higher resiliency and security and offer more features.

> **NOTE** It is highly recommended that you use managed disks for any new deployment. If you have older deployments using unmanaged disks, it is advisable to migrate them to managed disks as soon as possible.

Disk roles

Azure VMs support three main disk roles (see Figure 1-22):

- **OS disk** An OS disk is a default disk that is attached to every VM and contains the operating system running on the VM. In addition to hosting the OS, this disk can be used to host small applications or web services that do not have high IOPS or storage needs.

- **Data disk** A data disk is an additional disk that can be attached to a VM to store applications, databases, or other data required for the VM to perform its functions. Multiple data disks can be attached to a VM (depending on the VM SKU limitations). Each disk is provided a custom drive letter and can be scaled to up to 32 TB in size.

- **Temporary disk** The Azure platform provides a temporary disk on most VMs. The size of the disk depends on the VM SKU. This disk is to be used only for paging or swap files, as the data on this disk is not persistent; a forced VM restart or platform-level maintenance can result in data loss. It is not recommended to store any application, database, or other critical files on this disk.

NOTE Each of these is to be used for a specific purpose and should be set up based on the application requirements.

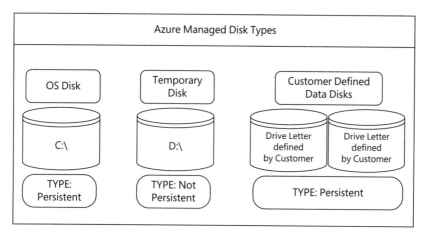

FIGURE 1-22 The different types of disk roles used within a VM.

Disk SKUs

Azure currently provides four disk SKUs. Each of these can be selected in different scenarios based on OS, app, or database requirements:

- **Standard HDD** This SKU provides low-cost reliable HDD disks to Azure VMs. The performance of Standard HDDs is highly variable and unpredictable, making them ideal for low-intensity or low-criticality workloads, such as for dev/test VMs, AD domain controllers, low-traffic web servers, and so on.

- **Standard SSD** This SKU provides cost-effective SSD disks that are optimized for workloads that require lower IOPS at a consistent level. It is a good entry-level SSD disk experience and, considering the cost, is ideal for workloads that do not work well on Standard HDD disks but do not require the high levels of performance provided by Premium and Ultra SSD disks. Standard SSD disks are more reliable and provide lower latency than Standard HDD disks, making them ideal for most web servers and lightly used application servers.

- **Premium SSD** This SKU provides a high-level of IOPS and low latency. It is suitable for workloads requiring high-performing disks. Premium SSD disks are an ideal choice for most mission-critical workloads, including SAP HANA, Microsoft SQL databases, and Enterprise ERP applications.

- **Ultra disk** This SKU provides the highest levels of throughput and IOPS coupled with low levels of latency compared to the other disk types available in Azure. Ultra disks support dynamic disk performance optimization without affecting the workload running on top. This makes them ideal for data-intensive workloads, such as with relational databases, enterprise applications such as SAP HANA, and other transaction-intensive workloads.

> **TIP** For environments using enterprise applications like SAP HANA, using a combination of Ultra disks as data disks (OS disk support is not currently available) and a Premium disk as an OS disk would be ideal. Make the final decision based on inputs from an SAP expert and the application stakeholders, keeping the preceding recommendation in mind.

Networking for VMs

Every VM must be configured with different networking components to ensure connectivity with other resources, as well as user connectivity while ensuring required security is in place. These components include the following:

- Network interfaces
- IP addresses (private and public)
- Network security groups

Network interfaces

Network interfaces connections (NICs) allow VMs to be connected within an Azure virtual network so they can communicate with other resources or accept traffic from users. Every VM requires a minimum of one NIC; some VM SKUs support multiple network NICs. Each NIC connects a VM to a specific subnet.

> **TIP** In environments containing multiple VNETs, it is important to identify the right VNET and appropriate subnet to host a VM based on the connectivity, access, security requirements, and other dependencies the VM might have. Once the VNET and subnet are identified, the NIC can be created. Unlike the subnet configuration, the VNET configuration cannot be changed later, so it is best to plan this out correctly at the outset.

IP addresses

Every VM NIC must be assigned a private IP address, but it can also be assigned a public IP address depending on the VM's access and connectivity requirements and the network design.

The private IP address is used primarily for internal communications within a VNET, which is an interconnected on-premises network. Internet communications are possible using network address translation (NAT) via a web application firewall (WAF) or Azure Firewall, which must be defined for every VM. The public IP address is used when VMs require direct internet connectivity for inbound and outbound communications or when communicating with other Azure services not connected to a VNET. Assigning a public IP address is optional and should be done with caution, as exposing every VM to the public internet is not recommended.

Public IP addresses can be defined on a VM level. However, the recommended approach is to use external load balancers or WAFs to manage internet-based ingress traffic and routes to the VMs' private IPs. This protects VMs from being attacked directly from the internet.

> **NOTE** Both private and public IP addresses support static and dynamic IP allocation. It is recommended to set up VM IPs statically for workloads that are accessed using their IP address or in environments where dynamic DNS updates are not in place to ensure they are assigned the same IP after every reboot.

Network security groups

To protect a VM's inbound and outbound communication, you can set up a network security group (NSG) on the VM NIC or on the subnet where the VM is hosted. An NSG allows you to define rules to restrict or allow network traffic from other Azure resources, IP addresses, or IP ranges. It is recommended that you define NSGs for critical workloads or publicly exposed VMs either on the VM NIC or on the subnet level to only allow the required traffic to and from the VM. This will reduce the VM's attack surface.

> **NOTE** VMs with multiple NICs can be assigned multiple NSGs, different NSGs for each NIC, or NSGs on a specific NIC to control traffic only on required interfaces.

Cost-optimization options

Azure provides various cost-optimization strategies to reduce the cost of your VM workloads.

Reserved instances

Reserved instances (RIs) are VMs that are reserved on the Azure platform for a specific period of time, which can vary from one to three years. When a VM is set up as a reserved instance, the underlying hardware resources for that VM are reserved, ensuring that the VM will have access to them regardless of whether it is placed offline during the reservation period, no matter how long. There is no performance difference between a regular VM and a reserved VM of the same model and size. However, the reservation unlocks value in terms of large cost savings for your organization, as Microsoft provides discounts ranging from 20% to 60% on VM compute costs.

Understanding RI cost savings

Before you commit to using RIs, it is recommended that you run your VM workloads without RIs and gather consumption data. This data will help you understand your actual server usage, which will enable you to make a more informed decision about the VM size to reserve.

Microsoft offers different levels of savings for RIs. These depend on the number and size of the RIs you need to cover your projected workload and the term for which you want to reserve. Because RIs require upfront payment, you should review the pricing guidelines before you buy. Figure 1-23 shows the savings at the time of this writing for a D16a v14 VM hosted in the West US 2 datacenter. As you can see, the cost changes dramatically for the same instance when moving from a one-year RI to a three-year RI.

Region	VM Instance	CPU	RAM	OS	Tier	Reserved Instance	Compute Cost (per month)	Savings
West US 2	D16a v14	16 vCPUs	64GB	Windows	Standard	No Reservation / Pay-as-you-Go (PAYG)	USD 560.64	NA
West US 2	D16a v14	16 vCPUs	64GB	Windows	Standard	1 year reserved	USD 334.00	~40%
West US 2	D16a v14	16 vCPUs	64GB	Windows	Standard	3 years reserved	USD 215.11	~62%
West US 2	D16a v14	16 vCPUs	64GB	Linux (Cent OS)	Standard	No Reservation / Pay-as-you-Go (PAYG)	USD 560.64	NA
West US 2	D16a v14	16 vCPUs	64GB	Linux (Cent OS)	Standard	1 year reserved	USD 334.00	~40%
West US 2	D16a v14	16 vCPUs	64GB	Linux (Cent OS)	Standard	3 years reserved	USD 215.11	~62%

FIGURE 1-23   Savings under RIs (courtesy of https://azure.microsoft.com/en-us/pricing/calculator, as of January 2022).

Therefore, you should consider the instance sizing requirements, based on either monitored use (Azure/on-premises) or specifications from the application developer, and the minimum timeframe for the load and subsequent usage that the application will experience to make a final decision.

> **NOTE**   Azure can provide recommendations regarding reservation size if it has access to sufficient monitoring data. These recommendations are based purely on past usage patterns, though; it does not take into account any growth plans or application build changes your organization may be anticipating.

Adjust the reservation size

f you realize that you have selected the wrong size for an RI, you can easily change it. If your RI is too small, you can exchange it for a larger one. When you do, a prorated refund for your old RI is applied to the purchase of the new one.

If, however, your RI is too large, and you need a smaller one, your only option is to request a cancellation. This will result in a prorated refund of the balance amount of the RI minus an early-termination fee. (This fee is currently set to zero, but it could change; be sure to check it before canceling your RI.) Therefore, you must take this cancellation fee into account when calculating any potential savings you may incur by moving to a smaller RI.

Reservations walkthrough

The following section steps you through the process of creating a reservation using the Azure Portal.

USING THE AZURE PORTAL

To create a reservation using the Azure Portal, follow these steps:

1. In the Azure Portal, type **reservations** in the search bar. Then, under **Services**, click **Reservations**. (See Figure 1-24.)

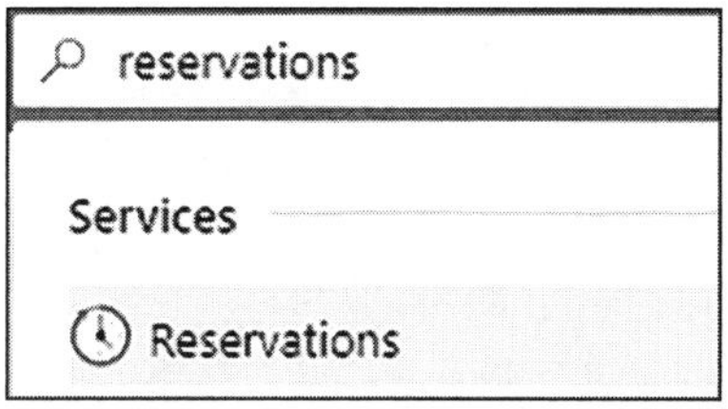

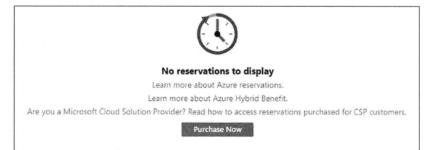

FIGURE 1-24 Search for the reservations service.

2. Click **Purchase Now** to start the Purchase Reservations wizard. (See Figure 1-25.)

No reservations to display

Learn more about Azure reservations.
Learn more about Azure Hybrid Benefit.
Are you a Microsoft Cloud Solution Provider? Read how to access reservations purchased for CSP customers.

Purchase Now

FIGURE 1-25 Start the Purchase Reservations wizard.

3. In the **Products** tab of the Purchase Reservations wizard, click Virtual Machine. (See Figure 1-26.)

4. The Select the Product You Want to Purchase page opens, with recommended reservations based on your usage history. (See Figure 1-27.) Click one of the recommended reservations to select it. Alternatively, click **All Products** and select a different VM SKU. Then click the **Add to Cart** button.

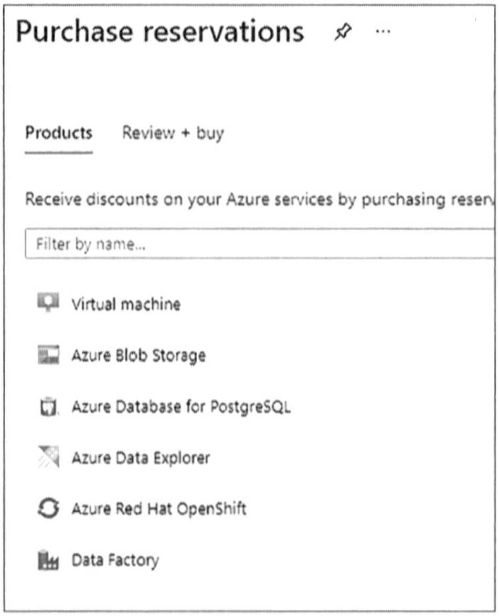

FIGURE 1-26 The Products tab of the Purchase Reservations wizard.

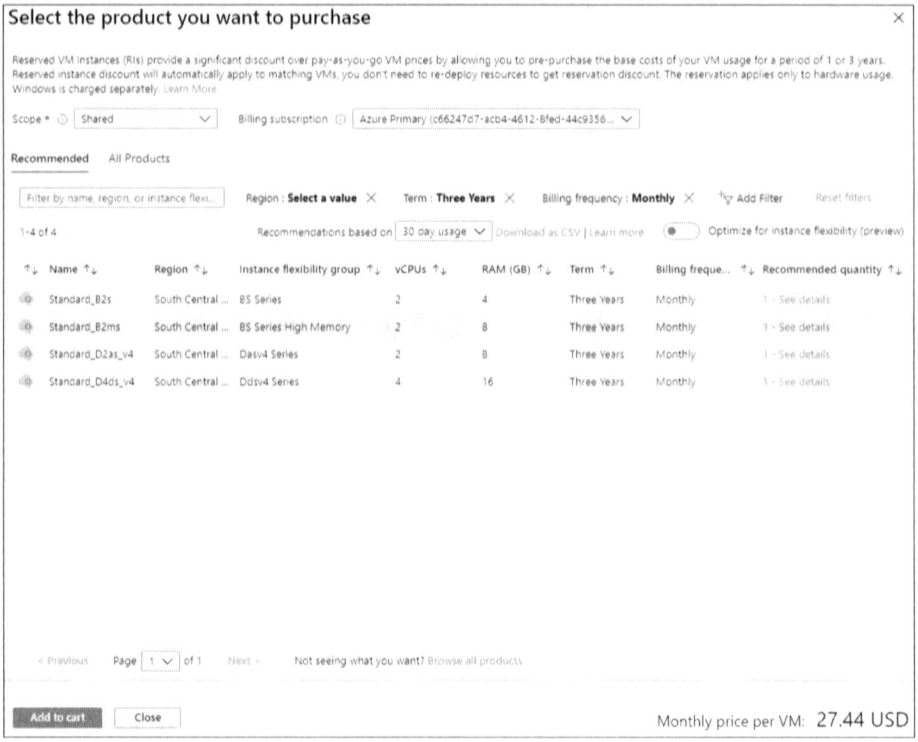

FIGURE 1-27 Select the VM SKU to purchase.

5. In the **Products** tab, enter the following information (see Figure 1-28), and click **Review + Buy**:

- **Reservation Name**   Enter a unique name for the reservation.
- **Billing Frequency**   Choose **Upfront** or **Monthly** to specify how you want to be billed.
- **Quantity**   Enter how many VMs you want to reserve.

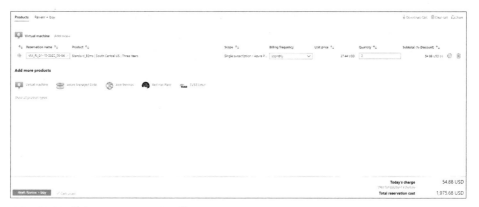

FIGURE 1-28   Set up procurement options.

6. On the **Review + Buy** tab, verify your settings and click the **Buy Now** button. (See Figure 1-29.)

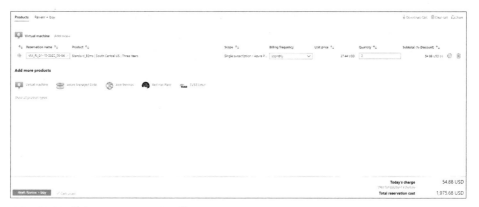

FIGURE 1-29   The Review + Buy tab of the Purchase Reservations wizard.

Azure initiates the procurement of the reservation. This can take a few hours, during which the reservation status will show as Pending. (See Figure 1-30.)

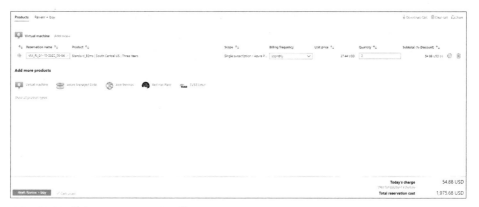

FIGURE 1-30   The reservation is pending.

7. Monitor the status of the reservation to ensure that it is procured. (See Figure 1-31.)

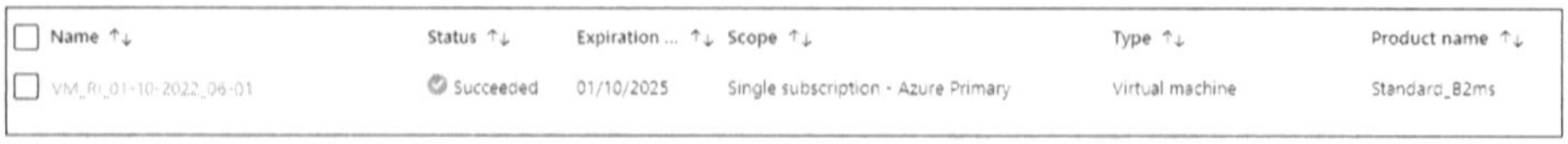

Name ↑↓	Status ↑↓	Expiration ... ↑↓	Scope ↑↓	Type ↑↓	Product name ↑↓
VM_RI_01-10-2022_06-01	✓ Succeeded	01/10/2025	Single subscription · Azure Primary	Virtual machine	Standard_B2ms

FIGURE 1-31   Successful reservation procurement.

8. Select the reservation. You will see the following options (see Figure 1-32):

   - **Refund**   Click this to initiate a refund if you no longer require this reservation.
   - **Exchange**   Click this to exchange this reservation for a higher VM SKU.
   - **Rename**   Click this to rename the reservation.
   - **Change Directory**   Click this to move the reservation to a different Azure subscription.

> **NOTE**   It will take 24 hours to detect the VM(s) in your environment associated with the VM SKU that you have reserved and apply the reservation. The price discount for the VM(s) will be assessed after that takes place.

FIGURE 1-32   Reservation options.

Azure Hybrid Benefit

Another great way to reduce costs is to leverage Azure Hybrid Benefit for Windows, SQL Server, RedHat, and SUSE Linux workloads. Azure Hybrid Benefit is a licensing configuration that can help you significantly reduce the expenses associated with running your workloads in the cloud. It works by allowing you to use your on-premises Software Assurance–empowered Windows Server and SQL Server licenses on Azure. Presently, this advantage applies to RedHat and SUSE Linux workloads too.

By using this benefit, you can reduce your licensing costs while running your workloads in Azure by 20 to 80% (or more), depending on your licensing contracts. To better understand how to leverage this benefit, consult your licensing partner(s), who helped you procure your license.

Azure Hybrid Benefit walkthrough

The following sections step you through the process of setting up Hybrid Use Benefit for a Windows VM workload using the Azure Portal, Azure PowerShell, and the Azure CLI.

USING THE AZURE PORTAL

To set up Azure Hybrid Benefit using the Azure Portal while creating a Windows VM, follow these steps:

1. Follow the steps in the "Azure VM creation walkthrough" section to start the Create a Virtual Machine wizard and create a VM.

2. In the **Basics** tab, locate the **Licensing** section. Then select the **Would You Like to Use an Existing Windows Server License** check box. (See Figure 1-33.)

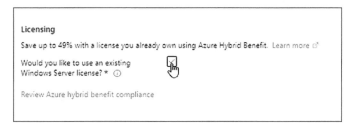

FIGURE 1-33 Setting up OS licensing for a VM.

A second check box appears under the one you just selected.

3. Select the **I Confirm I Have an Eligible Windows Server License...** check box. (See Figure 1-34.) Then click **Next** and continue creating the VM as described in the section, "Azure VM creation walkthrough."

FIGURE 1-34 Confirming license eligibility.

USING AZURE POWERSHELL

You can enable Azure Hybrid Benefit using Azure PowerShell by using the `-LicenseType` parameter and setting its value to "`Windows_Server`" or "`Windows_Client`" (Windows) or "RHEL_BYOS" or "SLES_BYOS" (Linux, depending on your OS distribution), as shown here:

```
#Define variables
$rg = "RG01"
$vm = "VM01"
$location = "East US"
#Create VM
New-AzVm `
    -ResourceGroupName $rg `
    -Name $vm `
    -Location $location `
    -ImageName "Win2019Datacenter" `
    -LicenseType "Windows_Server"
```

AZURE CLI

You can enable Azure Hybrid Benefit using the Azure CLI by adding the `--licensetype` parameter and setting its value to `Windows_Server` or `Windows_Client` (Windows) or "RHEL_BYOS" or "SLES_BYOS" (Linux, depending on your OS distribution), as shown here:

```
#Define variables
rg = "RG01"
vm = "VM01"
location = "East US"
#Create VM
az vm create \
    --resource-group $rg \
    --name $vm \
    --location $location \
    --image win2019datacenter \
    --license-type Windows_Server
```

Spot instances

Azure spot instances offer significant cost savings when performing scale-out operations. Spot instances enable you to run your workloads at a discount when there is unused capacity in the region where your VMs are hosted. Using spot instances is ideal for organizations running different types of workloads, such as the following:

- Test/dev workloads (including continuous delivery and integration workloads)
- Batch-processing jobs, large compute workloads, or graphics rendering applications or jobs
- Analytics and big data workloads

If the Azure platform determines that it needs the capacity back to handle a workload request from a pay-as-you-go client in the same region (who is charged a higher rate), it will terminate, or evict, the spot instance. Azure supports two eviction models:

- **Capacity only**   With this eviction model, the VM instance is evicted only if Azure needs the capacity for a pay-as-you-go instance request in that region.
- **Price or capacity**   With this eviction model, you set a maximum price (per hour) that you are willing to pay to run the spot instance. So, if Azure needs to free up capacity to handle a pay-as-you-go request, it will perform a price comparison. If the maximum price you set is more than the pay-as-you-go price, Azure will continue handling your spot instance. If not, your spot instance will be evicted.

> **NOTE**   Azure informs the spot instance of its impending eviction and allows it 30 seconds to complete as many pending jobs as it can. Any remaining pending jobs are reinitiated when the workload is brought back online if supported by your workload. Keep this in mind when selecting workloads for spot instances.

The eviction process is managed by an eviction policy, which you set up when you create a spot instance. The eviction policy also enables you to specify whether a VM should be deallocated or deleted when a spot instance is de-provisioned:

- When a VM is deallocated, the compute capacity is removed, and any charges associated with this capacity no longer apply. However, the underlying disks remain in place—meaning, those charges do still apply.
- When a VM is deleted, the underlying disks are also deleted. This reduces the costs associated with the workload, which can be significant depending on your disk size, disk top, the number of spot instances you put in place, and so on. However, when you are ready to reinstate the workload, you will need to retrieve the source data from its original location, which can take time.

Deallocating rather than deleting the VM enables you to quickly spin your workload back up when you need it or when capacity becomes available. The option you choose will depend on your application design and requirements.

> **NOTE**   Not all VM types support spot instances. Be sure to check the updated list of supported VM types before deciding which type to use for your workload. You should also check pricing information for spot instances, as this can vary depending on the VM SKU and Azure region.

Azure spot instance walkthrough

The following sections step you through the process of setting up spot instances for VM workloads using the Azure Portal, Azure PowerShell, and the Azure CLI.

USING THE AZURE PORTAL

To set up spot instances using the Azure Portal, follow these steps:

1. Follow the steps in the "Azure VM creation walkthrough" section to start the Create a Virtual Machine wizard and create a VM.

2. In the **Basics** tab, locate the **Instances** section. Then select the **Enable Spot Instance** check box. (See Figure 1-35.)

FIGURE 1-35   Setting up an Azure spot instance.

Two **Eviction Type** options become available:

- **Capacity Only**   You choose this to base the eviction policy on capacity only.
- **Price or Capacity**   You choose this to base the eviction policy on both capacity and maximum price.

3. Select the **Price or Capacity** option button. (See Figure 1-36.)

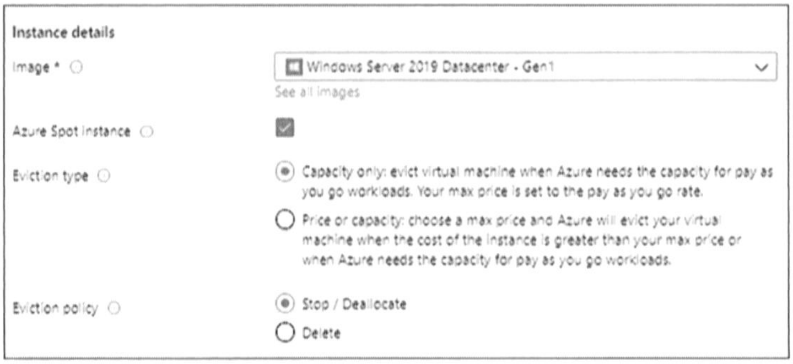

FIGURE 1-36   Setting the eviction type.

4. Open the **Size** drop-down list and choose a size for this spot instance workload. Then enter your maximum price in the **Maximum Price You Want to Pay Per Hour** box, based on your budget available. (See Figure 1-37.)

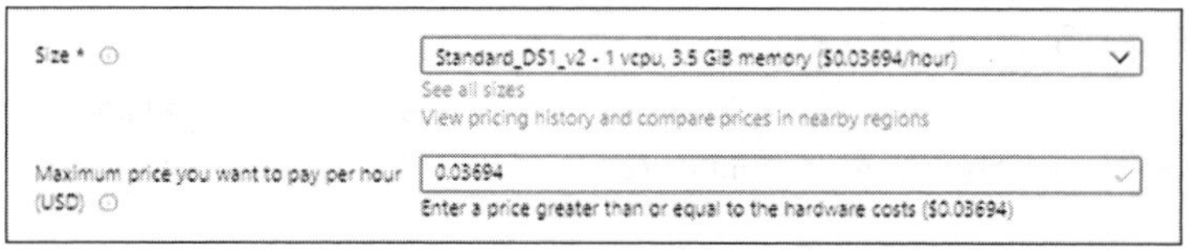

FIGURE 1-37 Setting the spot instance size and max price.

5. Click **Next** and continue creating the VM as described in the section, "Azure VM creation walkthrough."

USING AZURE POWERSHELL

You can set up a spot instance with Azure PowerShell by using the `New-AzVMConfig` command with the `-Priority` Spot and `-MaxPrice` parameters. The output of this command is passed through to the `New-AzVM` command to create a VM as a spot instance. Here's an example:

```
#Define variables
$rg = "RG01"
$vm = "VM01"
$location = "East US"
#Create Spot Instance with vmconfig
$vmConfig = New-AzVMConfig -VMName $vm -VMSize Standard_D1 -Priority "Spot" -MaxPrice -1
-EvictionPolicy Deallocate | `
New-AzVM -ResourceGroupName $rg -Location $location -VM $vmConfig
```

USING THE AZURE CLI

You can set up a spot instance with the Azure CLI by using the `az vm create` command with the `--priority` Spot and `--max-price` parameters, as follows:

```
#Define variables
rg = "RG01"
vm = "VM01"
location = "East US"
#Create Spot Instance with vmconfig
az vm create \
    --resource-group $rg \
    --name $vm \
    --location $location \
    --image WindowsServer2019Datacenter \
    --admin-username adminuser \
    --priority Spot \
    --max-price -1 \
    --eviction-policy Deallocate
```

Dedicated hosts

In a regular Azure VM setup, the underlying host can be shared across multiple clients, which can create compliance, security, and/or regulatory issues. Using a dedicated host helps address these issues.

Azure dedicated hosts provide physical servers to host Azure VMs. The physical server and its workload capacity is used exclusively by a single organization. It is not shared with other Microsoft Azure customers. Once a dedicated host is provisioned, the organization has control over its infrastructure and can define host-level maintenance policies.

> **NOTE** Dedicated hosts are ideal for environments in which hosting VM workloads on a shared environment would pose compliance or regulatory problems. By default, all dedicated hosts created for an organization are isolated from other customers in the same environment.

Benefits of dedicated hosts

Using dedicated hosts offers a few benefits. These are discussed here.

VM SKU CONSOLIDATION

You can set up VMs of different sizes on the same dedicated host. However, the VMs must be of the same series. For example, suppose you need to host VMs of different sizes within the Exds series—E2ds, E4ds, E8ds, and E16ds. In this case, you could select an Edsv4-Type 1 dedicated host to host all these VM SKUs.

Depending on the size of the dedicated host you select, you can set up different VMs, taking into account the total compute capacity available. Figure 1-38 shows how you can use 31 E2ds v4 VMs, 15 E4ds v4 VMs, or 7 E8ds v4 VMs on an Edsv4-Type1 host. Alternatively, as shown in Figure 1-39, you can use a combination of different types of VMs. (Note that this is not an exhaustive list of combinations, but rather an indicative sample set.)

VM Series

Edsv4

Dedicated Host SKUs (VM series and Host Type)	Physical cores	Available vCPUs	Available RAM	VM Size	# VMs
Edsv4-Type1	52	80	504 GiB	E2ds v4	31
				E4ds v4	15
				E8ds v4	7
				E16ds v4	3
				E20ds v4	3
				E32ds v4	1
				E48ds v4	1
				E64ds v4	1

FIGURE 1-38 Dedicated host SKUs.

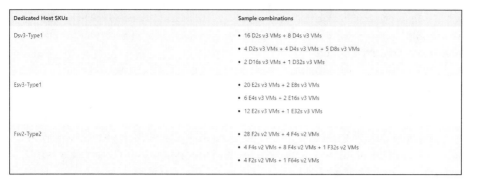

Dedicated Host SKUs	Sample combinations
Dsv3-Type1	• 16 D2s v3 VMs + 8 D4s v3 VMs • 4 D2s v3 VMs + 4 D4s v3 VMs + 5 D8s v3 VMs • 2 D16s v3 VMs + 1 D32s v3 VMs
Esv3-Type1	• 20 E2s v3 VMs + 2 E8s v3 VMs • 6 E4s v3 VMs + 2 E16s v3 VMs • 12 E2s v3 VMs + 1 E32s v3 VMs
Fsv2-Type2	• 28 F2s v2 VMs + 4 F4s v2 VMs • 4 F4s v2 VMs + 8 F4s v2 VMs + 1 F32s v2 VMs • 4 F2s v2 VMs + 1 F64s v2 VMs

FIGURE 1-39 Dedicated host types.

> **TIP** It's recommended that you identify all the different VMs you plan to use that will be of the same series and to split them between multiple similar-sized dedicated hosts to improve redundancy and reliability.

MAINTENANCE ACTIVITY MANAGEMENT

Every host in the Microsoft Azure environment must undergo regular updates to improve the reliability, availability, performance, and security of the platform's back-end infrastructure. In all shared-customer scenarios, Microsoft manages this to ensure minimal disruption and downtime in the back end. However, in some environments, applications are sensitive to such maintenance activities. Fortunately, with dedicated hosts, the organization, rather than Microsoft, can control the deployment of these updates. For example, you can control the order in which hosts are updated. You can also delay the update by as many as 35 days.

> **NOTE** If you do not perform an update within the 35-day window, Microsoft will deploy it automatically, in any random order. This ensures that the underlying host layer is always secure and is set up to provide the best possible performance across the Azure environment.

If your organization is running mission-critical or legacy applications or cannot afford any changes or updates to the underlying host layer without a planned maintenance and downtime window, dedicated hosts are a great option. Just be sure to set internal controls and processes to manage these updates on an ongoing basis to avoid unplanned outages.

BRING YOUR OWN LICENSING (BYOL)

Dedicated hosts enable you to leverage your Windows and SQL Server licensing, provided the licensing adheres to Microsoft's terms of use. Microsoft deducts the licensing costs from your ongoing VM costs, allowing for significant cost savings. In fact, cost benefits can be upwards of 30%, depending on your licensing SKUs.

SUPPORT FOR WINDOWS AND LINUX

Dedicated hosts support both Windows (with or without SQL Server) and Linux VMs on the same physical host. Be sure to take this into consideration in your planning, as it can help you maximize the use of the physical host environment by reducing the overall number of hosts required. This, in turn, can affect cost.

CO-LOCATION WITH OTHER NON-DEDICATED HOST-BASED VMS

You can use dedicated hosts alongside shared VMs. This enables you to host sensitive workloads on dedicated hosts, while running less-sensitive or non-critical workloads in a shared server environment. This combination can give you the best of both worlds, providing security, compliance, and performance for sensitive and critical workloads and cost benefits for non-critical workloads. Remember this when designing your environment; it is a key consideration.

HIGH AVAILABILITY

When you use a dedicated host, all VMs on that host may go down if the dedicated host experiences a problem. This can have a detrimental impact—especially if redundant servers for the same application are placed on the same dedicated host. It is therefore important to consider high availability when designing the environment. There are different ways to address this. Regardless of which way you choose, you will need to deploy multiple copies of each VM component across multiple hosts.

One way to address this issue is to create host groups. A *host group* is a collection of dedicated hosts in a single availability zone. To achieve high availability across zones, you can create multiple host groups (one per zone) and spread them accordingly.

You can set up VMs in different fault domains within a host group. This results in them being hosted on different physical racks in the datacenter. When you create a host group, you must specify how many fault domains the host group will be spread over. You then assign a specific fault domain to each host in the host group. The underlying managed disk services for VMs deployed to hosts with different fault domains will be set up on multiple storage stamps to increase fault-isolation protection.

> **NOTE** **Using fault domains is different from using co-location. Two hosts that have the same fault domain are not necessarily in proximity with each other.**

You can use availability zones and fault domains together to achieve a higher level of fault isolation. It is important that you specify the availability zone, fault domain count, and fault domain configuration for the host groups, hosts, and VMs at the time of creation for maximum benefits.

> **NOTE** **Every Azure subscription has vCPU quota limits on the region and VM-series level. Ensure that you have sufficient vCPUs available before creating any dedicated hosts. If you need more vCPUs, contact Microsoft support.**

Dedicated host walkthrough

The following sections step you through the process of setting up a dedicated host and adding a VM to it using the Azure Portal, Azure PowerShell, and Azure CLI.

USING THE AZURE PORTAL

To create a dedicated host and add a VM to it using the Azure Portal, follow these steps:

1. In the Azure Portal, type **dedicated hosts** in the search bar. Then, under **Marketplace**, click **Dedicated Hosts**. (See Figure 1-40.)

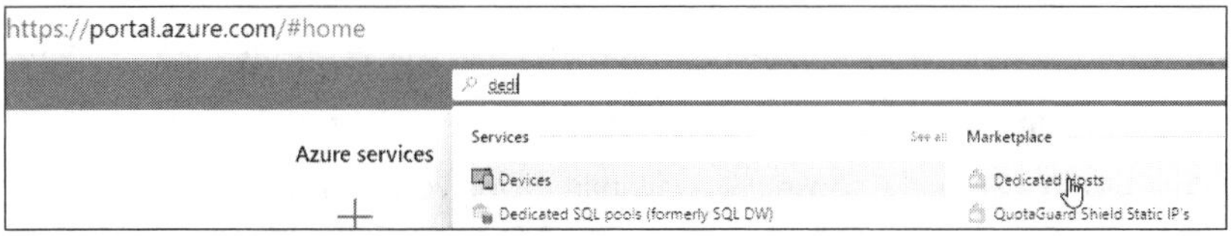

FIGURE 1-40 Searching for the dedicated hosts service.

2. In the Create Dedicated Host wizard, enter the following information (see Figure 1-41):
   - **Subscription** Select the subscription to create the dedicated host.
   - **Resource Group** Select an existing resource group or create a new one for the dedicated host.
   - **Name** Enter a unique name for the dedicated host.
   - **Location** Select the Azure region you want for the dedicated host.

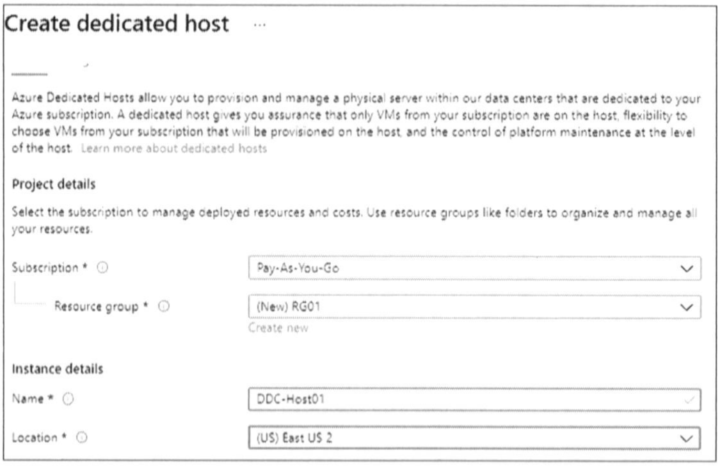

FIGURE 1-41 Creating a dedicated host.

3. Under **Hardware Profile**, you can choose an existing host group or create a new one. For this exercise, click **Create New Host Group**. (See Figure 1-42.)

FIGURE 1-42 Creating a new host group.

4. In the Create a Host Group dialog box, enter the following information (see Figure 1-43):

- **Host Group Name** Enter a unique name for the host group.
- **Availability Zone** Choose the availability zone you want to use.
- **Fault Domain Count** Specify how many fault domains the host group will support.

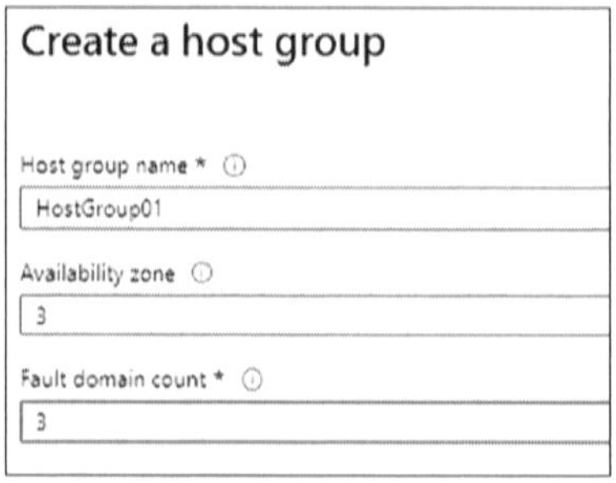

FIGURE 1-43 Setting up the host group.

5. Open the **Size Family** drop-down list and choose the family type for the VMs that will be hosted on the dedicated host. Then open the **Fault Domain** drop-down list and assign the dedicated host to a specific fault domain. (See Figure 1-44.)

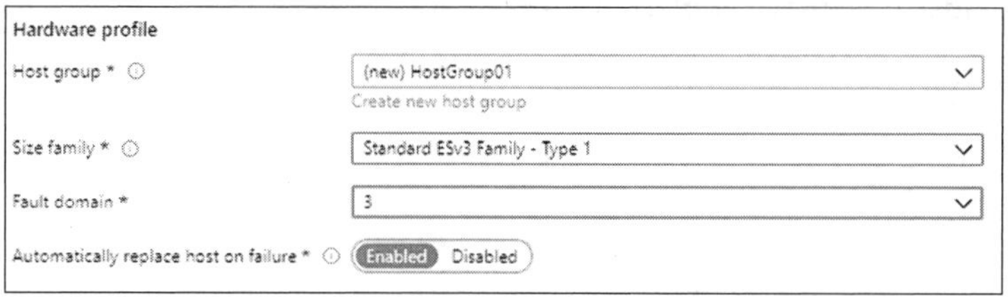

FIGURE 1-44 Setting up the hardware profile.

6. Under **Save Money**, use the option buttons to specify whether you currently have Windows Server or SQL Server licenses. (See Figure 1-45.) Then click **Next** to continue.

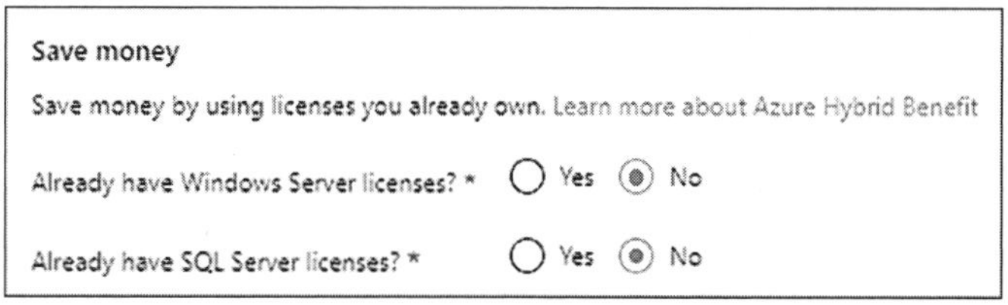

FIGURE 1-45 Configuring the Azure Hybrid Benefit.

7. In the **Tags** tab, enter any tags that you would like to apply to the dedicated host or leave the default settings as is (see Figure 1-46) and click **Next** to continue.

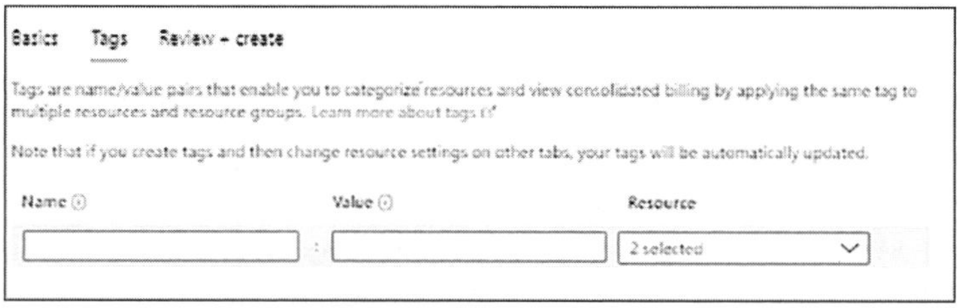

FIGURE 1-46 Setting up dedicated host tags.

8. In the **Review +Create** tab, review your settings and click **Create** to create the dedicated host.

9. After Azure creates the dedicated host, navigate to its configuration blade. Then, under **Settings**, click **Instances**. (See Figure 1-47.)

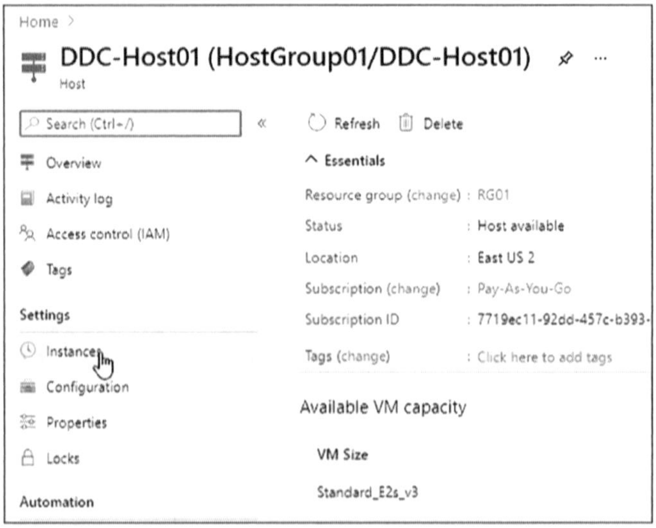

FIGURE 1-47 Setting up a VM instance.

10. Click **Add VM**. (See Figure 1-48.)

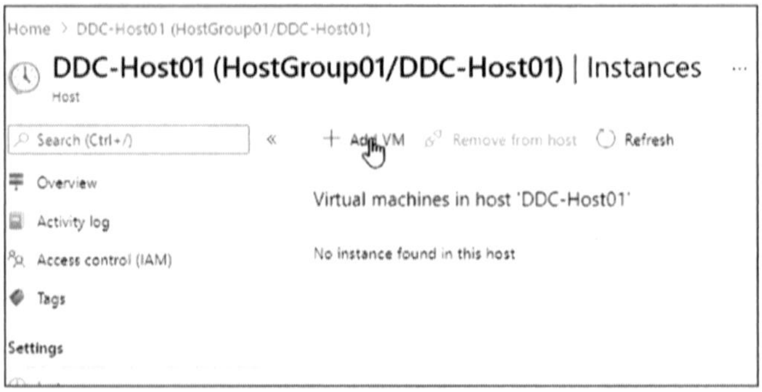

FIGURE 1-48 Adding a new VM to the dedicated host.

You'll create the VM as described in the section, "Azure VM creation walkthrough," entering the settings indicated in the following steps.

11. In the **Basic** tab, open the **Availability Options** drop-down list and choose **Select Availability Zone**. Then open the **Availability Zone** drop-down list and choose the same zone you selected for the dedicated host. (See Figure 1-49.)

12. In the **Advanced** tab, open the **Host Group** drop-down list and choose the host group you created for the dedicated host. Then open the **Host** drop-down list and choose the dedicated host you created earlier in this walkthrough. (See Figure 1-50.)

Region * ⓘ	(US) East US 2 ▾
Availability options ⓘ	Availability zone ▾
Availability zone * ⓘ	3 ▾
Security type ⓘ	Standard ▾
Image * ⓘ	▦ Windows Server 2019 Datacenter - Gen1 ▾
	See all images | Configure VM generation
Azure Spot instance ⓘ	☐
Size * ⓘ	Standard_E2s_v3 - 2 vcpus, 16 GiB memory (Price unavailable) ▾
	See all sizes

FIGURE 1-49   Set VM availability options for the dedicated host.

Host

Azure Dedicated Hosts allow you to provision and manage a physical server within our data centers that are dedicated to your Azure subscription. A dedicated host gives you assurance that only VMs from your subscription are on the host, flexibility to choose VMs from your subscription that will be provisioned on the host, and the control of platform maintenance at the level of the host. Learn more ☐

Host group ⓘ	HostGroup01 | Zone 3 | eastus2 ▾
*Host ⓘ	▲
	Select one ...
Proximity placement group	DDC-Host01 

Proximity placement groups allow you to group Azure resources physically closer together in the same region. Learn more ☐

Proximity placement group ⓘ	No proximity placement groups found ▾

FIGURE 1-50   Choosing the dedicated host.

13. Click **Next** and continue creating the VM as described in the section, "Azure VM creation walkthrough."

USING AZURE POWERSHELL

You can create a dedicated host and assign a VM to it with Azure PowerShell by using the New-AzHostGroup and New-AzHost commands, as follows:

```
#Define variables
$rg = "RG01"
$location = "East US"
$vnet = "vNet-01"
$HostGrpName = "HostGroup"
$Dhostname = "DHost-01"
$vm = "VM01"
#Create Host Group
New-AzHostGroup `
    -Location $location `
```

```
    -Name $HostGrpName `
    -PlatformFaultDomain 2 `
    -ResourceGroupName $rg `
    -Zone 1
#Create Dedicated Host
New-AzHost `
    -HostGroupName $hostGrpName `
    -Location $location `
     -Name $Dhostname `
    -ResourceGroupName $rg `
    -Sku ESv3-Type1 `
    -AutoReplaceOnFailure 1 `
    -PlatformFaultDomain 1
#Define Credentials
$cred = Get-Credential
#Create VM in Dedicated Host
New-AzVM `
    -Credential $cred `
    -ResourceGroupName $rg `
    -Location $location `
    -Name $vm `
    -HostId $dhost.Id `
    -Size Standard_E2s_v3 `
    -Image Win2019Datacenter `
    -Zone 1
```

USING THE AZURE CLI

You can create a dedicated host and assign a VM to it with the Azure CLI using the `Az vm host group create` and `az vm host create` commands, as follows:

```
#Define variables
rg="RG01"
location="EastUS2"
vnet="vNet-01"
hostgrpname="HostGroup"
dhostname="DHost-01"
vm="VM01"
#Create Host Group
az vm host group create \
    --name $hostgrpname \
    --resource-group $rg \
    --location $location \
```

```
    --zone 1 \
    --automatic-placement true \
    --platform-fault-domain-count 1
#Create Dedicated Host
az vm host create \
    --host-group $hostgrpname \
    --name $dhostname \
    --sku ESv3-Type1 \
    --location $location \
    -g $rg
#Create VM in Dedicated Host
az vm create \
    -n $vm \
    --image Win2019Datacenter \
    --host-group $hostgrpname \
    --size Standard_E2s_v3 \
    --location $location \
    -g $rg \
    --zone 1
```

Backups and disaster recovery

It is highly recommended that you put a backup and disaster-recovery solution in place for your Azure environment workloads. These can be native solutions like Azure Backup and Azure Site Recovery or third-party solutions. Having a working and tested solution in place is especially critical in scenarios in which data corruption, malicious encryption, or data loss occurs.

For most organizations, having a backup solution in place is standard practice, and has been for some time. However, because of the exorbitant costs historically associated with disaster-recovery solutions, few organizations could afford one. Azure Site Recovery drastically reduces the costs associated with building and maintaining a disaster-recovery solution, making it feasible for most organizations.

Backup

It is highly recommended that you have a backup solution in place for every production VM—either Azure Backup or a third-party solution that supports integration with Azure. Regardless of what tool you use, a detailed backup strategy is critical to recovery in the event of data corruption or a malicious attack. This strategy should include monitoring backups on a regular basis and immediately fixing any backup issues. You should also test the restoration of VM backups in isolated networks to validate that the data restores correctly and adheres to the compliance requirements of the organization.

If you are using Azure Backup, you can store VM backups redundantly across multiple geographies. This is highly recommended, as it allows you to restore data in an alternate region in case of regional failure—especially important if you have no disaster-recovery solution.

Although backing up production VMs is strongly recommended, for dev/test VMs, it might be optional, depending on the data stored on the VMs and DevOps processes in place. If cost is not a restricting factor, then consider keeping backups for the dev/test environment, but with a lower retention level than for production VMs.

Azure uses Recovery Services vaults to create, store, and manage backups. Each vault can contain backup policies and configuration for thousands of VMs and other Azure workloads that are supported for backup. You can create a vault on your own. Alternatively, enabling Azure Backup for a VM will set one up for you automatically.

> **TIP** When developing your backup strategy, discuss requirements with the security, compliance, and data protection teams to ensure that the organization's needs are met across all your VM workloads.

Managed snapshots

Managed disks support snapshots, which can be used as a backup option for dev/test VM workloads. Each snapshot is a full read-only copy of the managed disk. You can use these snapshots to rebuild a dev/test VM. You should incorporate snapshots into your backup and recovery strategy if doing so meets your organization's compliance and recovery needs. Snapshots provide a quick and easy way to manage backups for dev/test workloads.

Backup walkthrough

The following section steps you through the process of setting up Azure Backup for a VM during VM creation using the Azure Portal.

> **NOTE** You are not limited to setting up Azure Backup for a VM during VM creation. You can set it up anytime, even after the VM is up and running.

USING THE AZURE PORTAL

To set up Azure Backup during VM creation using the Azure Portal, follow these steps:

1. Follow the steps in the "Azure VM creation walkthrough" section to start the Create a Virtual Machine wizard and create a VM.

2. In the **Management** tab, locate the **Backup** section. Then select the **Enable Backup** check box.

3. Enter the following information (see Figure 1-51):

    - **Recovery Services Vault**   This will be updated automatically to show any existing Recovery Services vaults in the same region as your VM. Alternatively, a (new) tag will appear before the name of the fault; this indicates that the wizard will create one automatically. To change to a different existing vault, select it from the drop-down list. Alternatively, to create a custom vault, click the **Create New** link and follow the prompts.

    - **Backup Policy**   Click the **Create New** link. This opens the Create Policy wizard, which you can use to set up the backup policy that will define when and how often backups will take place and the retention configuration.

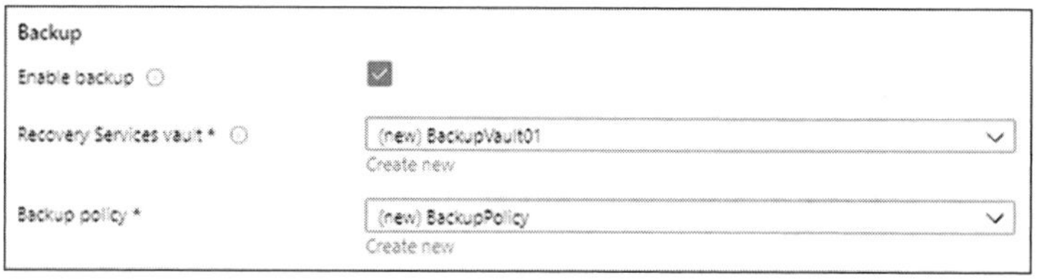

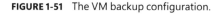

FIGURE 1-51   The VM backup configuration.

4. In the Create Policy wizard, enter the following information (see Figure 1-52) and click **Create**:

    - **Policy Name**   Enter a name for the backup policy.

    - **Backup Schedule**   Use the **Frequency**, **Time**, and **Timezone** drop-down lists to set the backup schedule.

    - **Instant Restore**   Specify the number of instant restore snapshots to take and retain. (Having more snapshots enables you to recover your VM more quickly, without having to access the backup vault.)

    - **Retention Range**   Use these settings to specify how long daily, weekly, monthly, and yearly backups should be retained.

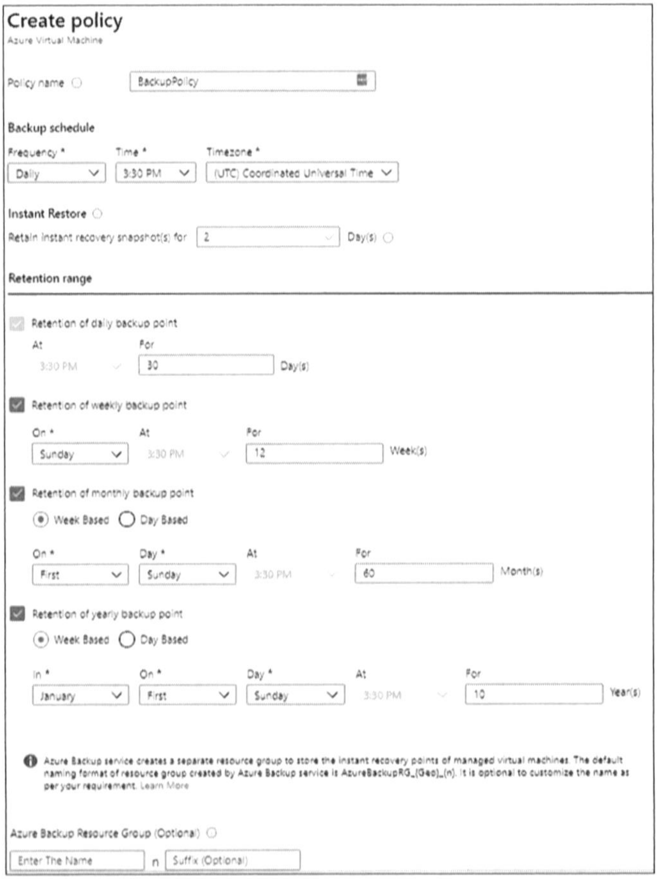

Create policy
Azure Virtual Machine

Policy name ○   BackupPolicy

Backup schedule

Frequency *   Time *   Timezone *

| Daily ∨ | 3:30 PM ∨ | (UTC) Coordinated Universal Time ∨ |

Instant Restore ○

Retain instant recovery snapshot(s) for   2   ∨   Day(s) ○

Retention range

☑ Retention of daily backup point

At   For

3:30 PM ∨   30   Day(s)

☑ Retention of weekly backup point

On *   At   For

| Sunday ∨ | 3:30 PM ∨ | 12   Week(s) |

☑ Retention of monthly backup point

⦿ Week Based   ○ Day Based

On *   Day *   At   For

| First ∨ | Sunday ∨ | 3:30 PM ∨ | 60   Month(s) |

☑ Retention of yearly backup point

⦿ Week Based   ○ Day Based

In *   On *   Day *   At   For

| January ∨ | First ∨ | Sunday ∨ | 3:30 PM ∨ | 10   Year(s) |

ⓘ Azure Backup service creates a separate resource group to store the instant recovery points of managed virtual machines. The default naming format of resource group created by Azure Backup service is AzureBackupRG_{Geo}_{n}. It is optional to customize the name as per your requirement. Learn More

Azure Backup Resource Group (Optional) ○

| Enter The Name | n | Suffix (Optional) |

FIGURE 1-52 Setting up the backup policy.

5. Continue creating the VM as described in the section, "Azure VM creation walkthrough."

Disaster recovery

A regional failure will result in all Azure VMs being unavailable until Microsoft recovers the region and brings all the workloads back online. If such an outage is not acceptable for your organization, you need to develop a disaster-recovery strategy for all production VMs (and optionally for dev/test VMs).

Azure Site Recovery natively integrates with Azure VMs to implement disaster recovery in a secondary Azure region of your choice. The service seamlessly manages replication, usually resulting in a very low recovery time objective (RTO). Azure Site Recovery also supports the creation of a recovery plan that can help automate the entire disaster-recovery process.

If Azure Site Recovery is not ideal for your environment, you can use a third-party solution that supports Azure VMs instead. Regardless of which solution you use, be sure you document the entire disaster-recovery process and test it on a regular basis to ensure your environment comes online in the secondary site per your recovery point objective (RPO) requirements.

TIP Your disaster-recovery strategy should include all interconnected components.

Site recovery walkthrough

The following section steps you through the process of setting up Azure Site Recovery during VM creation using the Azure Portal.

NOTE You are not limited to setting up Azure Site Recovery during VM creation. You can set it up anytime, even after the VM is up and running.

USING THE AZURE PORTAL

To set up Azure Site Recovery during VM creation using the Azure Portal, follow these steps:

1. Follow the steps in the "Azure VM creation walkthrough" section to start the Create a Virtual Machine wizard and create a VM.

2. In the **Management** tab, in the **Site Recovery** section, select the **Enable Disaster Recovery** check box. Then enter the following information (see Figure 1-53):

   - **Secondary Region** Choose a region to host the disaster recovery copy of the VM.
   - **Secondary Subscription** Select the subscription to set up Azure Site Recovery.
   - **Recovery Services Vault** A Recovery Service vault is automatically created. Click **Create New** if you require any customizations.
   - **Site Recovery Policy** A site recovery policy is automatically created. Click **Create New** if you require any customizations.
   - **Availability Options** Select any infrastructure redundancy options, if required.
   - **Update Settings** Specify whether Azure Site Recovery (ASR) should manage updates for the servers.
   - **Automation Account** Select an automation account or let the wizard create one to be used to automate activation.

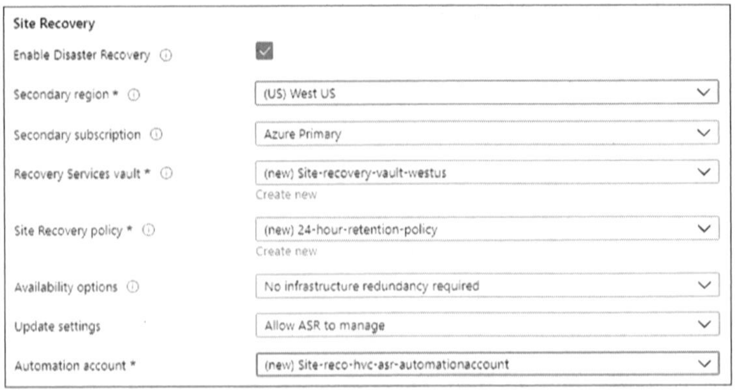

FIGURE 1-53 Set up Site Recovery options.

3. Verify that the configuration is correct and continue creating the VM as described in the section, "Azure VM creation walkthrough."

Best practices

Now that we have covered all the different aspects of setting up a VM workload in Azure, including ensuring it is highly available and cost-optimized, let's review some of the general best practices to improve the security, monitoring, and management of these workloads. These guidelines are based on real-world deployments; your use of them in your own environment should be judicious and based on your own internal reviews:

- **Limit VM-level access** Restrict administrative access to VMs to administrators who are required to carry out administrative activities. Set up access using groups so you can easily provision and de-provision access as needed. Use built-in or custom roles in Azure to restrict access on the Azure level and adopt a similar approach to limit access on the OS level. Define access permissions for different administrative roles and use RBAC to define granular permissions for those roles. This will help limit the attack surface in case of breach of credentials.

- **Limit/restrict use of generic admin accounts** Use named administrative accounts instead of generic admin accounts shared by multiple administrators. This will help identify the actors for actions that have been carried out.

- **Control network access using network security groups** Ensure only the required ports are opened on NSGs assigned on the VM or subnet level. For critical protocols such as RDP, SSH, and FTP, where the set of users accessing that protocol is limited, also define trusted network ranges to limit access.

- **Use Azure Policy to assess compliance** You can use Azure Policy to define rules to standardize the Azure environment and monitor and assess the compliance of the environment with these rules. Use Azure Policy to define VM parameters such as allowed locations, VM SKUs, backup, disk encryption, and so on, to ensure that any new VM workloads automatically adhere to best practices identified for the environment.

- **High availability and DR for critical applications** Use the high-availability options available for VMs to protect critical application workloads. For example, for a critical application or database, having multiple servers running the same application can help with load-balancing and reduce impact in case of a security breach on one of the two VMs by allowing failover to the second VM. Similarly, your disaster-recovery plan should consider security breaches that might cause access to the primary site to go offline, including scenarios such as malicious data encryption. This way, you can bring the disaster-recovery site online with data from before the malicious attack.

- **Leverage Azure Security Center** Cyberattacks are now more prevalent than ever. Constant monitoring of an environment is the only way to identify, act on, and limit the impact of a security breach. Azure Security Center provides these capabilities. If possible, you should use it to detect threats and take automated actions for remediation. If Azure Security Center does not meet your needs, you can use any number of third-party solutions instead.

- **Enforce disk encryption** Protecting data at rest in cloud environments is a key requirement for most organizations. Use Azure Disk Encryption to encrypt boot and data volumes for both Windows and Linux VMs. Organizations that require a high level of security can use customer-managed encryption keys for the encryption for complete control over the data.

- **Limit public access** Attackers constantly scan public networks for exposed IPs that can be subjected to brute-force attacks. VMs that require exposure to the public internet should be behind a WAF, Azure Firewall, or a similar service to limit exposure. If VMs require direct connectivity, it is important to limit access to only the protocols, ports, and IP ranges that need to be accessed.

- **Use just-in-time access if possible** Just-in-time access helps lock down management access to VMs. It can help control access to VMs by provisioning access when required for defined and monitored periods of time.

- **Define a patch-management strategy and monitor compliance** Unpatched environments are one of the leading causes of security breaches. It is important to have a clearly defined patch-management strategy that includes reporting and monitoring guidelines to ensure that this critical activity regularly occurs for every OEM software in the environment.

- **Deploy an antivirus and antimalware solution** Install a centralized antivirus and antimalware solution to protect against known viruses, malicious files, and zero-day attacks. Microsoft Malware is available for use with Windows VMs. Various Azure-supported third-party solutions are also available to provide this security layer.

- **Limit installed software and services**   Review the software and services installed on all VMs, especially public-facing ones, and remove any unwanted software or services to limit the attack surface due to unmonitored or unpatched code.

- **Monitor VM health and performance**   Monitoring critical processes and the overall health and performance of VMs can help you identify any breaches causing unexpected performance spikes. Identifying these in the early stages can help limit any service disruption and possibly the level of impact on the environment.

- **Back up VMs regularly**   In some malicious data-encryption scenarios, the only method of recovery is to restore data from backups. It is, therefore, important that backups are in place to assist in such recoveries.

## Chapter 2

Azure virtual machine scale sets

Overview

As the use of Azure has increased, environments have become more complex and interconnected. This has led to a growing need to easily deploy, manage, and scale virtual machines (VMs) that can be integrated with Azure load balancing and auto-scaling without too much overhead. The introduction of the Azure VM scale sets (VMSS) addressed exactly this need.

A VMSS consists of multiple VMs that are configured to be exactly the same and can be managed as a group rather than individually. This involves much less overhead while also enabling you to take advantage of the scaling and elasticity offered by the cloud. VMSS are available across all Azure regions. Moreover, Microsoft does not charge you to use them beyond the regular compute charges you pay for any other resources. This makes VMSS a very high-value proposition for many environments.

As environments transition to cloud-scale application architectures, the true power, flexibility, and benefits of VMSS become apparent. Consider a cloud-scale application architecture, in which unique and non-unique components of applications are built separately and made to run individually. Using VMSS makes it possible to keep the unique components, such as management nodes, running as individual nodes based on their specific resource requirements, while deploying the non-unique components of the workload as VMs in a scale set. As a result, capacity in terms of the number of VMs in the set becomes more important than the individual characteristics of the workload, making scale easier to achieve.

How Azure VMSS work

To build complex scalable infrastructure designs in the cloud, you must always achieve a balance between the level of control you have over the individual infrastructure resources and the complexity and placement of those resources. Platform as a service (PaaS) solutions tend to facilitate this by providing fixed architectures that you must conform to and that the application must be built around. This helps you achieve the right balance.

In many cases, using a PaaS solution is not possible, and you need to deploy a custom application architecture specific to the needs of your environment. VMSS address this by allowing a higher level of control over infrastructure than a PaaS solution, while reducing the overhead of building and scaling different resources like networking, storage, and compute, and balancing nodes across fault and update domains. In short, VMSS provide the control capabilities of infrastructure as a service (IaaS) combined with the ease of scale provided by PaaS. (See Figure 2-1.)

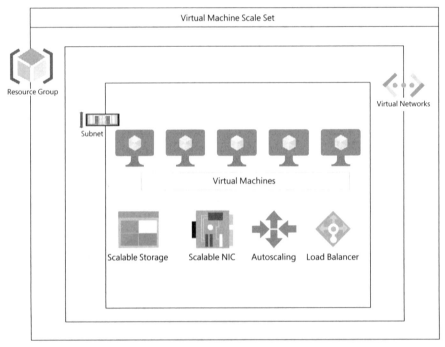

FIGURE 2-1 An Azure VM scale set built of different Azure components, including resource groups, VMs, network interface cards (NICs), storage, and extensions.

A VMSS allows for the definition of an individual compute resource, which has storage, network, and required extension properties associated with it. This saves you a lot of configuration work. Moreover, when it's time to deploy the resource, only a single call is sent to the underlying Azure fabric. This enables the Azure compute resource provider to automatically optimize both reliability and performance.

Why use a VMSS?

To provide better performance and high availability and redundancy, applications are generally distributed across multiple instances running the same application code. The application might then be accessed via a load balancer that distributes requests to one of the application instances.

To perform maintenance or update an application instance/code base, you must divert traffic to another functional application instance. Azure VMSS can help you facilitate this. On a related note, if there is an increase in demand for the application, you might a need to increase the number of application instances running the application. Azure VMSS provide the management capabilities to build and run an application across many VMs while automatically scaling resources and load-balancing traffic as needed.

VMSS features

Important features of VMSS include the following:

- **Easy creation**   You can use the Azure Portal to easily create Windows and Linux VMSS. (You will walk through this process later in the chapter.) When the scale set is created, load balancers with NAT rules to allow SSH or RDP connections are automatically implemented. These load balancers handle basic layer-4 traffic distribution as well as more advanced layer-7 traffic distribution and TLS termination.

- **Easy management**   All VM instances in a scale set are created from the same base OS image and configuration. This enables you to easily manage tens or even hundreds of VMs without having to perform additional configuration or network-management tasks. Moreover, you can change the number of VMs running in a scale set simply by issuing an API call or command (for example, through REST, the SDK, or the command line).

> **NOTE**   VMSS require you to maintain a consistent server, application, and OS configuration across your environment. In addition, applications are more reliable when the VM SKU and size, hard disk configuration, and application installs and patches match across all VMs.

- **High availability**   The number of VMs in a scale set can vary between 0 and 100. VMSS with large numbers of VMs allow for high availability. Another contributor to high availability is availability zones. These allow for the automatic distribution of VM instances in a scale set within a single datacenter or across multiple datacenter.

- **High resiliency**   Every scale set contains multiple instances of an application. So, if one instance of a VM hosting the application experiences an issue or requires maintenance, users will be able to access other instances with minimal (if any) interruption or impact.

- **Built-in autoscaling**   Demand to access an application can fluctuate during the course of the day, week, or month. VMSS can automatically increase the number of VM instances available as demand rises and reduce the number of VM instances as demand goes down. This helps minimize costs without sacrificing availability. You can easily define autoscaling rules based on your environment. For example, you can set a minimum, maximum, and default number of VMs in a scale set, as well as action triggers based on resource consumption.

> **NOTE**   When the number of VMs in a scale set increases, VMs are automatically balanced across fault and update domains to ensure high availability.

- **Large compute pools**   You can create multiple VMSS in the same VNET or subscription. You can then combine these VMSS to build large compute pools for high-volume data processing or other services.

- **Integration with Azure Resource Manager (ARM)**   With a large deployment, automating the deployment of most or all functionality, including software and VM extensions, is essential. VMSS supports this automation, including ARM template deployments that include details on the required extensions and software compatible with ARM deployments.

- **Support for Visual Studio**   When a VMSS is part of an ARM project, you can deploy standard Linux and Windows templates for Visual Studio provided in the Azure SDK. This allows for the automation of workload deployment as part of the project buildout.

- **Integration with Azure load balancers**   Azure load balancers and the Azure Application Gateway can seamlessly integrate with VMSS. As mentioned, load balancer NAT rules are automatically created when a new VM is added to a scale set. This helps ensure that the VMs always have a connection path.

- **Improved security**   Built-in control over inbound connectivity makes VMs in a scale set inherently more secure than standalone VMs with an IP address, which require the configuration of a network security group (NSG) to lock down unwanted ports and protocols.

- **Support for different tools**   You can manage VMSS using the Azure CLI, Azure PowerShell, the latest versions of the Azure-managed SDKs, and REST APIs.

- **Manual rollout of OS image updates without interruption**   You can update a scale set master or model—that is, its definition and properties—and then perform a manual rollout for all or selected VMs. This enables you to update VMSS without shutting down the entire scale set, which reduces downtime during update and maintenance activities.

Scaling considerations

Here are a few points to keep in mind with regard to scaling VMSS:

- A scale set built using an Azure Marketplace image can support as many as 1,000 VMs. If, however, a scale set is set up to support more than 100 VMs, some scenarios work differently—especially those related to load balancing. This is discussed in more detail later in this chapter in the section "Large VMSS."

- A scale set built using a custom image can support as many as 600 VMs. If, however, the scale set is set up with a user-managed storage account, it must create all OS disk VHDs in a single storage account. As a result, the maximum recommended number of VMs in a custom image scale set in user-managed storage is 20. (If overprovisioning is turned off, this limit increases to 40.) Overprovisioning is discussed later in this chapter in the section "Overprovisioning."

- Scale sets configured with user-managed storage accounts are currently limited to 5 storage accounts and 100 VMs, or 20 VMs per storage account only.

Scale sets versus VMs

As mentioned, a VMSS set consists of multiple VMs with an identical configuration built in a highly available design with interconnected components. But although a VMSS is composed of VMs, there are some features that only VMs have, and other features that are available only with VMSS. It is important to understand which technologies offer which features so you can make an informed decision about which one to use.

Here are some key advantages of VMSS:

- **Easy scaling** It is easier to scale a VMSS than it is to scale individual VMs. Scaling VMs individually involves using complex scripting and triggers, whereas you can employ the Azure autoscale service to automatically scale a VMSS.

- **Easy re-imaging** It is generally recommended to build scale sets with images. This allows for the easy addition and deletion or removal of VMs from the scale set without data loss or service interruption. It is easier to re-image scale sets than VMs.

- **Easy upgrades** You can roll out scale set upgrades very easily by using upgrade policies. There are no such scale policies for individual VMs.

- **Overprovisioning** Overprovisioning of scale sets helps increase reliability and reduce deployment times, especially during peak loads. Achieving the same outcome using individual VMs would require the use of complex code.

On the other hand, VMs have a few unique features that must be taken into consideration:

- **Image capture** You can capture an image of an individual VM but not of a VM that is part of a scale set.

- **Native to managed disk migration** Migrating from native to managed disks is possible when using individual VMs, but not when a VM is part of a scale set.

- **Use of IPv6** You can assign IPv6 to individual NIC cards on a VM, but this cannot be done for a VM in a scale set. In that case, you must assign IPv6 to the load balancer in front of the scale set.

> **NOTE** These lists cover frequently used features in both technologies. Depending on the actual environment and set of requirements, there might be other design, storage, networking, and security factors to consider.

VMSS creation walkthrough

The following sections step you through the process of creating a VMSS using the Azure Portal, Azure PowerShell, and the Azure CLI. If you are following along, be sure to select resources and resource names based on your environment, including unique VMSS, vNET, and subnet names for each of your deployments. Also, be sure to delete any unwanted resources after you have completed testing to avoid charges levied by Microsoft for these resources.

USING THE AZURE PORTAL

To create a virtual machine scale set using the Azure Portal, follow these steps:

1. Log in to the Azure Portal, type **virtual machine scale sets** in the search box to locate the service, and select it from the list that appears. (See Figure 2-2.)

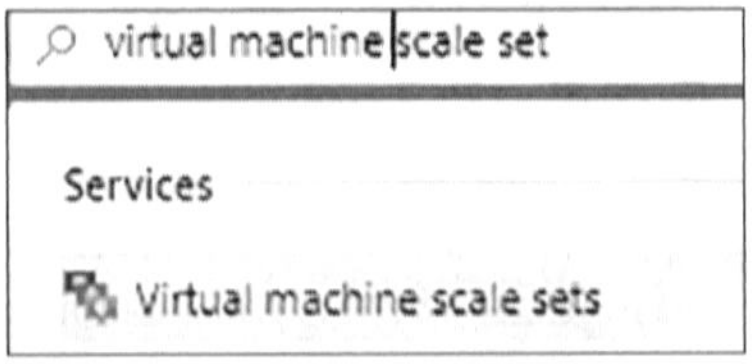

FIGURE 2-2   Search for the virtual machine scale set service.

2. Click the **Create Virtual Machine Scale Set** button to start the Create Virtual Machine Scale Set wizard. (See Figure 2-3.)

No virtual machine scale sets to display

Create a virtual machine scale set to deploy and manage a load balanced set of identical Windows or Linux virtual machines. Use autoscale to automatically scale virtual machine resources in and out. Learn more ◰

Create virtual machine scale set

FIGURE 2-3   Initiate the creation of a virtual machine scale set.

3. In the **Basics** tab of the Create Virtual Machine Scale Set wizard, enter the following information (see Figure 2-4), and click **Next**:

- **Subscription**   Select the subscription that will host the virtual machine scale set.
- **Resource Group**   Select the resource group you want to use to host the virtual machine scale set. Alternatively, to create a new resource group, click the **Create New** link and follow the prompts.
- **Name**   Type a name for the virtual machine scale set.
- **Region**   Select the region you want to use to host the virtual machine scale set.
- **Availability Zone**   Leave this set to **None** (the default).
- **Orchestration Mode**   Leave this set to **Uniform** (the default).
- **Security Type**   Leave this set to **Standard** (the default).
- **Image**   Select the OS image that should be deployed on the VMSS instance.

- **Azure Spot Instance**   Leave this unchecked (the default).
- **Size**   Select the desired size for the VMSS instance.
- **Username**   Enter the local administrator username to be set up on the instance.
- **Password and Confirm Password**   Enter the password for the local admin user.
- **Licensing**   Leave this unchecked (the default).

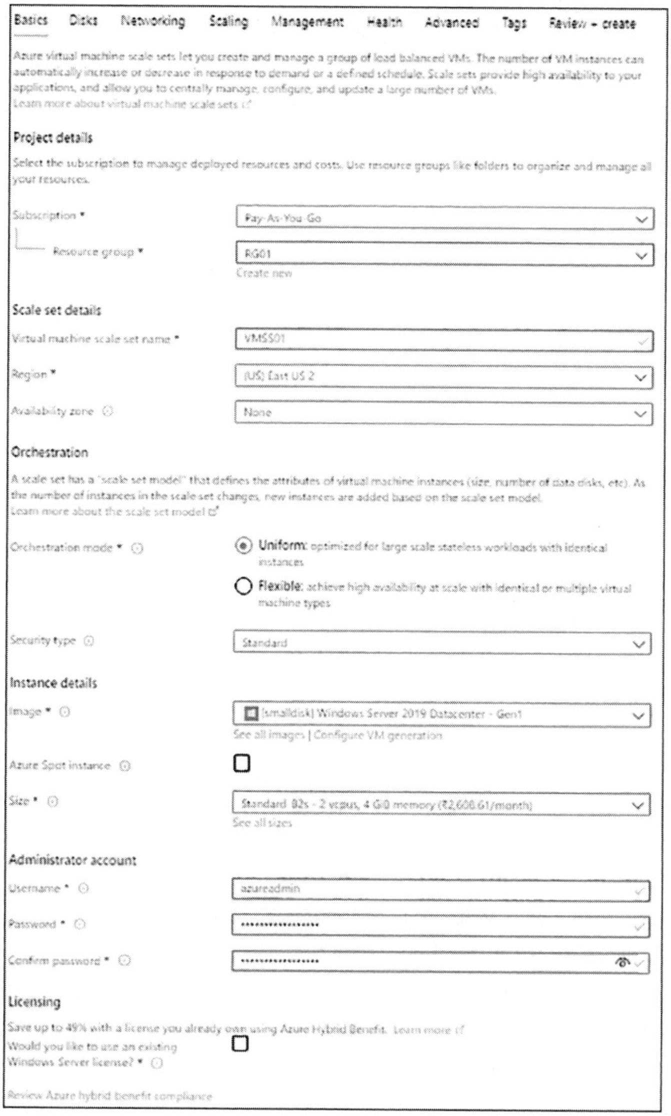

FIGURE 2-4   The Basics tab of the Create Virtual Machine Scale Set wizard.

4. In the **Disks** tab, enter the following information (see Figure 2-5) and click **Next**:

- **OS Disk Type**   Select the disk type to set up for the VM instances.
- **Encryption Type**   Leave this set to **(Default) Encryption-at-Rest with a Platform-Managed Key**.
- **Enable Ultra Disk Compatibility**   Leave this unchecked (the default).
- **Data Disks**   Leave this blank.
- **Use Managed Disks**   Leave this checked (the default).

FIGURE 2-5   The Disks tab of the Create Virtual Machine Scale Set wizard.

5. In the **Networking** tab (see Figure 2-6), enter the following information and click **Next**:

- **Virtual Network**   Select the vNET to host the VMSS. Alternatively, to create a new virtual network, click **Create Virtual Network** and follow the prompts.
- **Network Interface**   Leave this set to the default. Optionally, click **Edit** to modify the selected network interface.
- **Use a Load Balancer**   Leave this unchecked (the default).

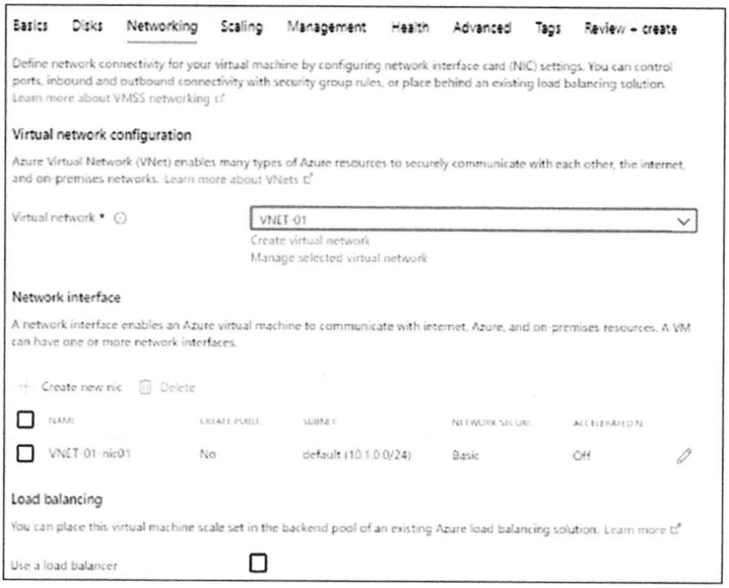

FIGURE 2-6 The Networking tab of the Create Virtual Machine Scale Set wizard.

6. In the **Scaling** tab (see Figure 2-7), enter the following information and click **Next**:

- **Initial Instance Count** Specify a value equal to or higher than **2**.
- **Scaling Policy** Leave this set to **Manual** (the default).
- **Scale-in Policy** Leave this set to **Default - Balance Across Availability Zones and Fault Domains...**.

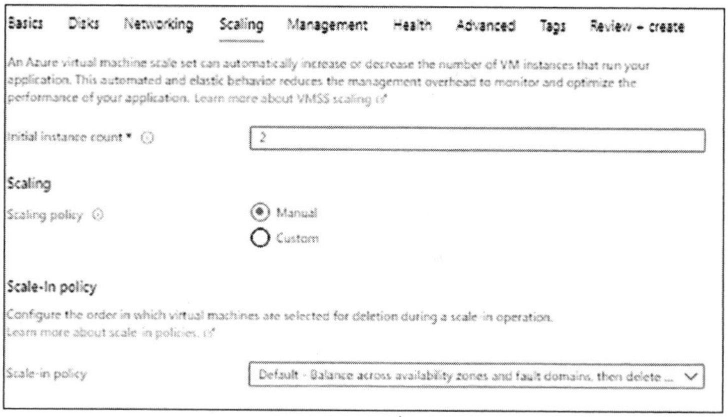

FIGURE 2-7 The Scaling tab of the Create Virtual Machine Scale Set wizard.

7. In the **Management** tab, leave the default settings as is (see Figure 2-8) and click **Next**.

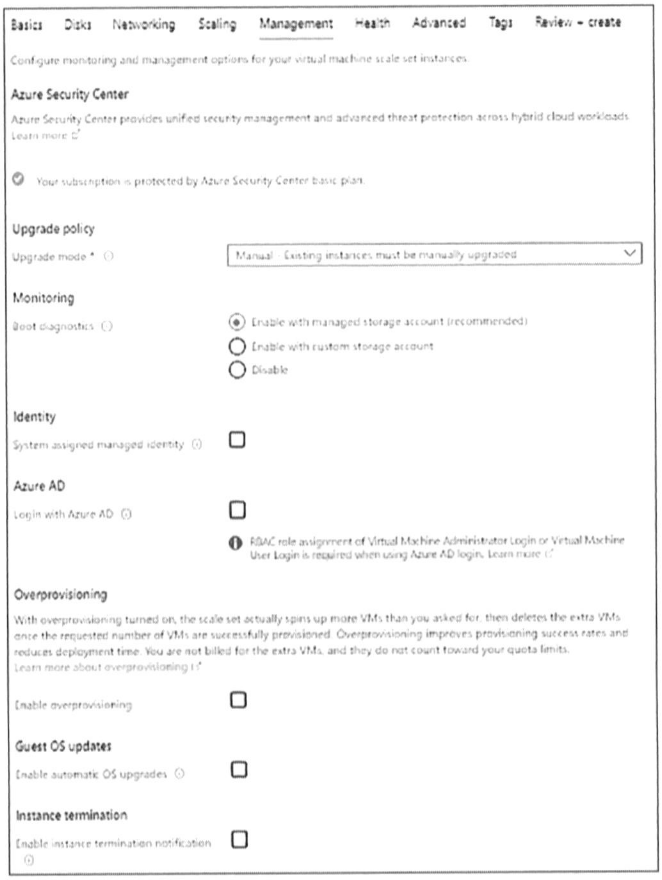

FIGURE 2-8   The Management tab of the Create Virtual Machine Scale Set wizard.

8. In the **Health** tab, leave the default settings as is (see Figure 2-9) and click **Next**.

FIGURE 2-9   The Health tab of the Create Virtual Machine Scale Set wizard.

9. In the **Advanced** tab, leave the default settings as is (see Figure 2-10) and click **Next**.

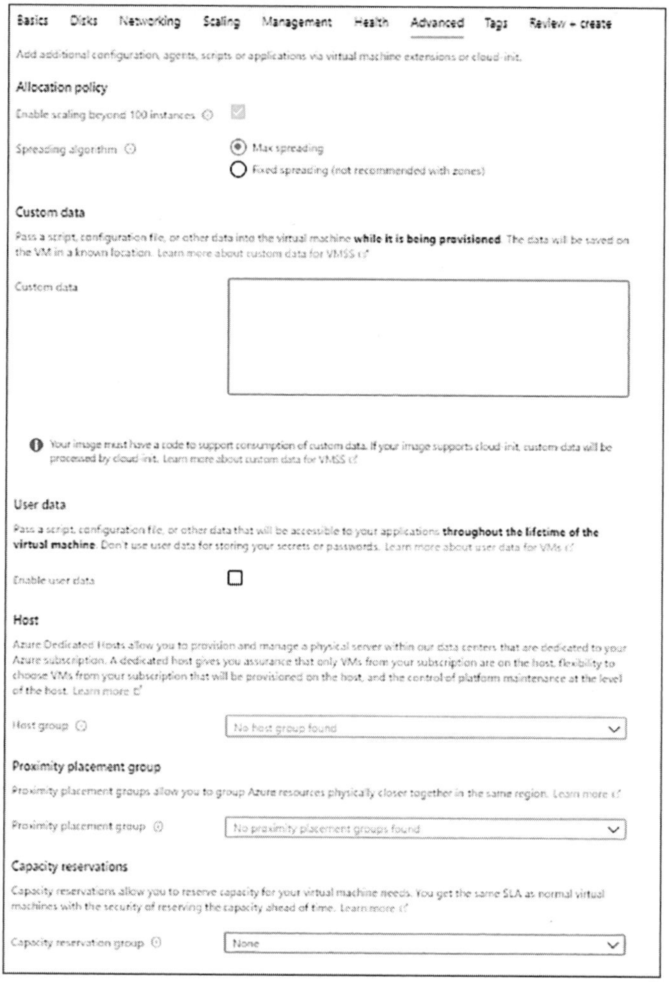

FIGURE 2-10   The Advanced tab of the Create Virtual Machine Scale Set wizard.

10. In the **Tags** tab (see Figure 2-11), enter any tags you want to associate with the VMSS and click **Next**.

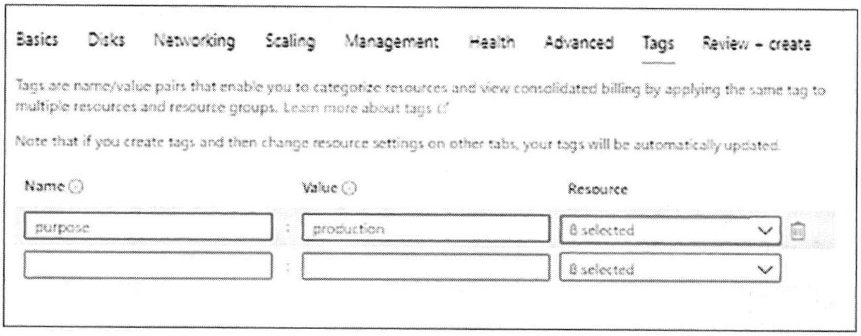

FIGURE 2-11   The Tags tab of the Create Virtual Machine Scale Set wizard.

11. In the **Review + Create** tab (see Figure 2-12), verify that your settings are correct and click **Create**.

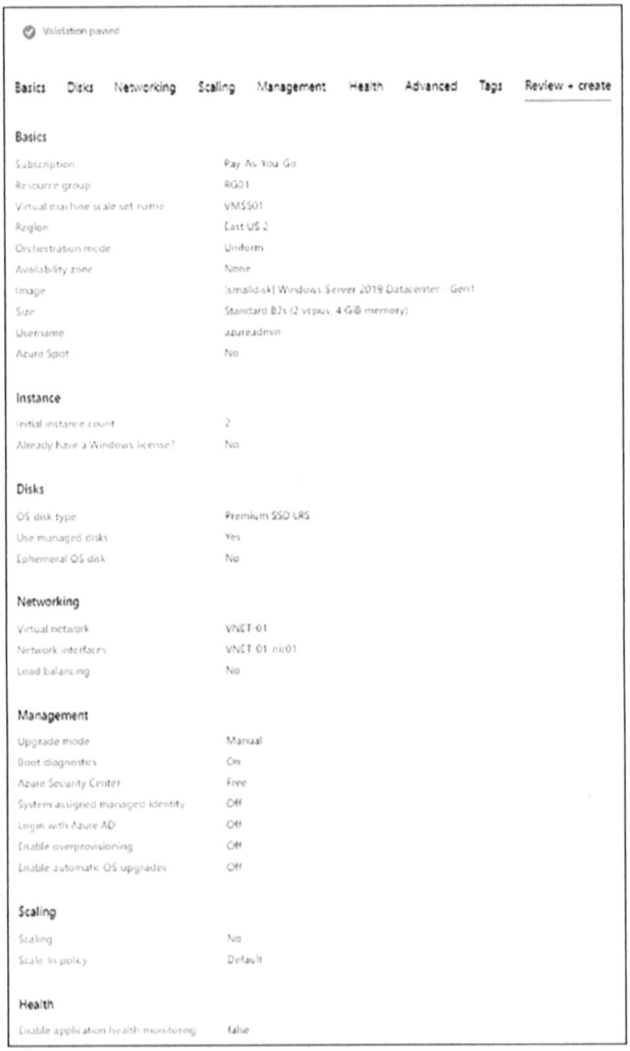

FIGURE 2-12 The Review + Create tab of the Create Virtual Machine Scale Set wizard.

USING AZURE POWERSHELL

You can create a VMSS with Azure PowerShell using the `New-AzPrivateDNSZone` command with various switches to set parameters. For example, to create the same scale set as you did in the preceding section, you use the following code snippet:

```
#Define variables
$RG = "VMSS-RG01"
```

```
$location = "EastUS2"
$vmssname = "VMSS01"
$vnet = "VMSS01-Vnet"
$subnet = "VMSS01-Subnet"
$vmsslb = "VMSS01-LB"
$vmsspip = "VMSS01-PIP"
#Create VMSS
New-AzVmss -ResourceGroupName $RG `
  -Location $location `
  -VMScaleSetName $vmssname `
  -VirtualNetworkName $vnet `
  -SubnetName $subnet `
  -PublicIpAddressName $vmsspip `
  -LoadBalancerName $vmsslb `
  -UpgradePolicyMode "Automatic"
```

USING THE AZURE CLI

You can create a VMSS with the Azure CLI using the `az network private-dns zone create` command with various switches to set parameters. The following script shows you how to set up the same scale set you created in the preceding sections with the Azure CLI:

```
#Define variables
location="eastus2"
rg="VMSS-RG01"
vmssname="VMSS01"
vmssadminuser="vmssadmin"
#Create VMSS
az vmss create \
  --resource-group $rg \
  --name $vmssname \
  --image UbuntuLTS \
  --upgrade-policy-mode automatic \
  --admin-username $vmssadminuser \
  --generate-ssh-keys
```

Large VMSS

A VMSS containing between 100 and 1,000 VMs is considered to be a large scale set. In specific scenarios, like centralized compute grids that require simplified management of worker nodes or big data deployments with large data sets, it is easier to have a single large VMSS than multiple smaller scale sets. In such scenarios, by combining the VMSS with data disks, a highly scalable environment consisting of thousands of VMs and petabytes of storage can be used to run singular operations.

A scale set can scale up to include a large number of VMs not because it allows such a large number within its scope, but because it allows for multiple placement groups to be contained within a single scale set. A placement group is similar to an availability set. It has its own upgrade and fault domains. A single placement group can contain as many as 100 VMs. By default, a scale set consists of only one placement group. However, if you set the `singlePlacementGroup` parameter to `false`, the scale set can contain multiple placement groups, with a combined limit of 1,000 VMs.

Although large scale sets might be a great option for large deployments, it might not be what's best for your environment. To determine whether large scale sets are right for you, consider the following points:

- **The VM image and number of VMs required to run the application**   If the application requires a custom OS image to be deployed, the scaling is limited to 600 VMs instead of 1,000 VMs. If, however, an Azure Marketplace image can be used, then the full limit or quota of 1,000 VMs can be used.

- **The disks that can be used by the application**   Large scale sets only use Azure managed disks. This is because user-managed disks use storage accounts, which can contain only 20 disks/VMs at a time. There is a risk of running into subscription limits for storage accounts, which can result in catastrophic outcomes if not accounted for. To limit this risk and to reduce the management overhead for the storage admin charged with managing the large number of storage accounts, large VM scale sets have been designed to work only with managed disks.

- **The application's load-balancing requirements**   Layer-4 load-balancing requirements for a large VMSS are different. It requires the use of the standard SKU, as that has the ability to load-balance traffic between multiple scale sets and multiple placement groups. If, however, the application in question requires the use of a basic load balancer, then the scale set cannot use multiple placement groups. It needs to use only a single placement group and would therefore be limited to 100 VMs. On the other hand, layer-7 load balancing, which uses the Azure Application Gateway, is supported for VMSS of all sizes.

- **The application's networking requirements**   Large VMSS do not support InfiniBand networking. If that is a requirement for an application, then a large VMSS would not be the right option for that environment. In addition, every scale set is set up inside a single subnet. Depending on the total number of VMs intended to be part of the scale set, and accounting for future growth requirements, the subnet for the scale set must have enough address space available for all the VMs that will eventually be hosted within it. Because scale sets overprovision VMs to improve deployment reliability and performance, you must also consider this when deciding on address space size. As a rule of thumb, after you calculate the final intended size of the scale set, add 20% to accommodate overprovisioning.

- **The application's availability requirements** Using a large VMSS does not change the overall availability of a scale set. VMs in different placement groups can end up on the same hardware, even though the scale of a large VMSS should minimize the impact of such a distribution logic.

Large VMSS creation walkthrough

The following sections step you through the process of creating a large VMSS using the Azure Portal, Azure PowerShell, and the Azure CLI. If you are following along, be sure to select resources and resource names based on your environment, including unique VMSS, vNET, and subnet names for each of your deployments. Also, be sure to delete any unwanted resources after you have completed testing to avoid charges levied by Microsoft for these resources.

USING THE AZURE PORTAL

To enable support of large scale sets using the Azure Portal during VMSS creation, follow these steps:

1. Follow the steps in the "VMSS creation walkthrough" section to start the Create a Virtual Machine Scale Set wizard and create a VMSS.

2. In the **Scaling** tab, in the **Instance** section, change the value in the **Initial Instance Count** box to a number higher than **100**. (See Figure 2-13.) This will automatically set the allocation policy to support more than 100 instances and create multiple placement groups in the back end to support a large VMSS.

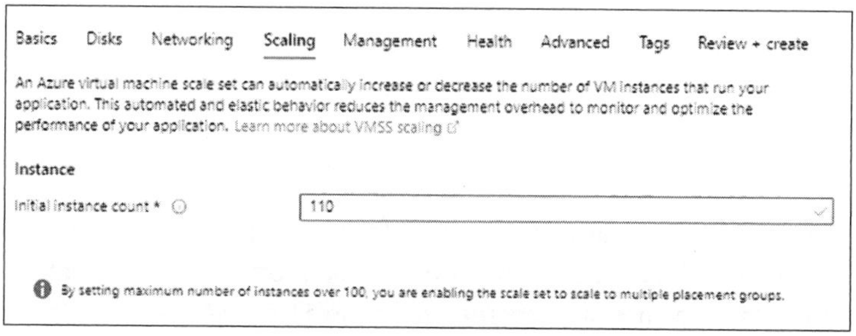

| Basics | Disks | Networking | Scaling | Management | Health | Advanced | Tags | Review + create |

An Azure virtual machine scale set can automatically increase or decrease the number of VM instances that run your application. This automated and elastic behavior reduces the management overhead to monitor and optimize the performance of your application. Learn more about VMSS scaling

Instance

Initial instance count *

    110

ℹ By setting maximum number of instances over 100, you are enabling the scale set to scale to multiple placement groups.

FIGURE 2-13 Setting the Initial Instance Count value to a number higher than 100 to enable large VM scale sets.

3. In the **Advanced** tab, under **Allocation Policy**, select the **Enable Scaling Beyond 100 Instances** check box. (See Figure 2-14.)

| Basics | Disks | Networking | Scaling | Management | Health | Advanced | Tags | Review + create |

Add additional configuration, agents, scripts or applications via virtual machine extensions or cloud-init.

Allocation policy

Enable scaling beyond 100 instances ☑

FIGURE 2-14 Setting up support for large scale sets.

4. Finish using the VM Scale Set Creation wizard to create the large VMSS, as described in the section "VMSS creation walkthrough."

USING AZURE POWERSHELL

Using Azure PowerShell to create a large VMSS involves adding the –InstanceCount parameter with a value higher than 100. This configures the scale set to support multiple placement groups. The following code shows a PowerShell script to create a large VM scale set:

```
#Define variables
$RG = "VMSS-ResourceGroup"
$Location = "EastUS2"
$VMSSName = "LargeVMScaleSet01"
$VNET = "VMSS-Vnet"
$Subnet = "VMSS-Subnet"
$vmsslb = "VMSS01-LB"
$vmsspip = "VMSS01-PIP"
#Create Large VMSS
New-AzVmss `
   -ResourceGroupName ""$RG `
   -Location ""$location `
   -VMScaleSetName $VMSSName"" `
   -VirtualNetworkName ""$vNET `
   -SubnetName ""$Subnet `
   -PublicIpAddressName $vmsspip `
   -LoadBalancerName $vmsslb `
   -UpgradePolicyMode "Automatic" `
    -InstanceCount 150
```

USING THE AZURE CLI

When using the Azure CLI to create a large VMSS, you add an --Instance-Count parameter with a value higher than 100. This configures the scale set to support multiple placement groups. The following code shows a Bash script used to create a large VMSS:

```
#Define variables
location="eastus2"
rg="VMSS-RG01"
vmssname="LargeVMScaleSet01"
vmssadminuser="azureadmin"
#Create Large VMSS
az vmss create \
   --resource-group $rg \
   --name $vmssname \
   --image UbuntuLTS \
```

```
--upgrade-policy-mode automatic \
--admin-username $vmssadmiuser \
--generate-ssh-keys --instance-count 150
```

Ensure high availability with VMSS

VMSS support several features to enable high availability. These include the following:

- Overprovisioning
- Availability zones
- Fault domains
- Autoscaling
- Vertical scaling
- Load balancing

Overprovisioning

Overprovisioning is the default behavior for a scale set. Overprovisioning results in the scale set provisioning more VMs than required or requested. The additional VMs are deleted when the required number of VMs have been successfully provisioned and are active. There is no charge for the additional VMs, and quota limits are not affected. The benefit of this feature is it improves the success rates for VM deployments and reduces wait times for new VM deployments to come online.

The application hosted within the scale set must be capable of handling this behavior. Having VMs appear and disappear can cause certain applications to behave in a confusing manner, as their code is not designed to deal with this. In such cases, you can turn off overprovisioning within the scale set templates by specifying the parameter "overprovision": "false".

> **TIP** Although scale sets that have user-managed storage with overprovisioning turned off can have more than 20 VMs per storage account, for performance reasons, it is not recommended to go beyond 40 VMs per storage account.

Overprovisioning walkthrough

The following sections step you through the process of enabling provisioning using the Azure Portal, Azure PowerShell, and the Azure CLI. If you are following along, be sure to select resources and resource names based on your environment, including unique VMSS, vNET, and subnet names for each of your deployments. Also, be sure to delete any unwanted resources after you have completed testing to avoid charges levied by Microsoft for these resources.

USING THE AZURE PORTAL

To enable overprovisioning using the Azure Portal during VMSS creation, follow these steps:

1. Follow the steps in the "VMSS creation walkthrough" section to start the Create a Virtual Machine Scale Set wizard and create a VMSS.

2. In the **Management** tab, under **Overprovisioning**, select the **Enable Overprovisioning** check box. (See Figure 2-15.)

FIGURE 2-15   Enabling overprovisioning.

3. Finish using the VM Scale Set Creation wizard to create the VMSS, as described in the section "VMSS creation walkthrough."

USING AZURE POWERSHELL

When using Azure PowerShell to create a VMSS, you add the -Overprovision parameter and set the value to $true to enable overprovisioning and $false to disable it. By default, overprovisioning is enabled, so setting this value to $true is typically not necessary. The following code shows how to use a PowerShell script to create a VMSS with overprovisioning turned off:

```
#Define variables
$location = "EastUS2"
$RG = "VMSS-RG01"
$vmssname = "VMSS01"
# Create VMSS with overprovisioning turned off (it's enabled by default)
$vmssConfig = New-AzVmssConfig -Location $location `
    -SkuCapacity 2 `
    -SkuName "Standard_DS2" `
    -OverProvision $False
New-AzVmss -ResourceGroupName $rg -Name $vmssname -VirtualMachineScaleSet $vmssConfig
```

USING THE AZURE CLI

When using the Azure CLI to create a VMSS, you add the --disable-overprovision parameter to disable overprovisioning. Overprovisioning is enabled by default. The following code shows how to use this parameter in a Bash script to create a VMSS with overprovisioning disabled:

```
#Define variables
vmssname="vmss01"
location="eastus2"
```

```
rg="vmss-rg01"
#Create VMSS with overprovisioning turned off (it's enabled by default)
az vmss create -g $rg -n $vmssname -l $location --image ubuntults --disable-overprovision
```

Availability zones

To protect a VMSS from datacenter–level failures, you can create a scale set across availability zones. Azure regions that support availability zones have a minimum of three separate zones, each with their own independent power source, network, and cooling. You can select an availability zone when you create the VMSS.

Considerations

When you deploy a regional scale set into one or more zones, you have three availability options:

- **Static fixed spreading (platformFaultDomainCount = 5)** The scale set spreads the VMs across exactly five fault domains per zone. If the scale set cannot identify five distinct fault domains per zone, the request fails.

- **Max spreading (platformFaultDomainCount = 1)** The scale set spreads the VMs across as many fault domains as possible within each zone. This might be across more than five fault domains per zone, or fewer, depending on how many are available. With max spreading, regardless of how many fault domains the VMs are spread across, only one fault domain is visible in the VMSS instance view and in the instance metadata.

- **Spreading aligned with storage disk fault domains (platformFaultDomainCount = 2 or 3)** The scale set spreads the VMs across the same fault domains as the underlying managed disks attached to the individual VMs. The number of managed disk fault domains varies between two to three per Azure region.

Unless there is a need to spread replicas across distinct hardware isolation units, max spreading would work for most deployments. It provides the best spreading and redundancy. However, if there is a need to spread replicas across distinct hardware isolation units, the recommendation would be to use spreading across availability zones and use max spreading within each zone.

Placement groups

As mentioned, a placement group is similar to an availability set, and has its own update and fault domains. A single placement group can contain a maximum of 100 VMs.

When you deploy a scale set, you can choose to deploy it within a single placement group or multiple placement groups within an availability zone. Although the scale set is regional and not zonal, you can choose to have a single placement group or multiple placement groups within the region.

By default, with new scale sets, multiple placement groups are set up for single-zone and cross-zone scale sets. However, only single placement groups are used for regional (non-zonal) scale sets.

Single-zone and zone-redundant scale sets

You can deploy scale sets within a single availability zone or across multiple availability zones. Deploying a scale set to a single availability zone would require all VMs created for that scale set to exist within that same zone—meaning that a zone outage would cause a service interruption. In contrast, with multiple zone scale sets, VMs are spread across multiple zones, thereby providing more redundancy and resiliency from zone outages. In addition, with single-zone scale sets, autoscaling works only in that zone, whereas with multi-zone or zone-redundant scale sets, autoscaling evenly balances VMs across the zones (depending on the zone-balancing policies in place).

Although using zone-redundant scale sets would seem like the ideal solution due to the added redundancy, doing so can affect the design, costs, and management overhead associated with your application design. Hence, it is important to take all the related factors into consideration, including the application redundancy and uptime requirements, before deciding which option to choose. You should also confirm that the regions most suited for your workload support availability zones to avoid issues during deployment.

Zone balancing

Zone balancing is used when scale sets are deployed across multiple zones. In such instances, it is possible to select between two types of zone-balancing algorithms:

- **Strict zone balance**   With strict zone balance, the scale set is managed such that it is considered balanced only if all zones have the same number of VMs, plus or minus one VM. For example, if a scale set is spread across three zones, and zone A has three VMs, zone B has three VMs, but zone C has two VMs, then the scale set is considered balanced because the difference is only one VM. On the other hand, if in the same scenario, zone C had only one VM, then the scale set would be considered unbalanced. On subsequent scale-out or scale-in attempts, the scale set would work toward balancing itself. Note that VM extensions are not taken into consideration when checking for this balance. This implies that VMs with failed extensions will be considered active during the balancing check.

- **Best-effort zone balance**   Best-effort zone balance has more flexibility than strict zone balance. It attempts to maintain balance, but if it is not able to do so—for example, due to an outage in a specific zone—it will temporarily operate in an unbalanced manner. It will then work toward correcting the balance in subsequent scale-in or scale-out attempts based on region availability. This distinction is important, because strict zone balance will fail scale-out or scale-in attempts if there is a possibility of an imbalance taking place, which might cause problems in the event of regional outages or if the size of the scale set must scale in specific regions due to lack of vCPU availability.

Availability zones walkthrough

The following sections step you through the process of setting up availability zones for a VMSS using the Azure Portal, Azure PowerShell, and the Azure CLI. If you are following along, be sure to select resources and resource names based on your environment, including unique VMSS, vNET, and subnet names for each of your deployments. Also, be sure to delete any unwanted resources after you have completed testing to avoid charges levied by Microsoft for these resources.

USING THE AZURE PORTAL

To set up availability zones using the Azure Portal during VMSS creation, follow these steps:

1. Follow the steps in the "VMSS creation walkthrough" section to start the Create a Virtual Machine Scale Set wizard and create a VMSS.

2. In the **Basics** tab, open the **Availability Zone** drop-down list and do one of the following:

   - Select a single availability zone (zone 1, zone 2, or zone 3) to spread the scale set across a single zone. (See Figure 2-16.)

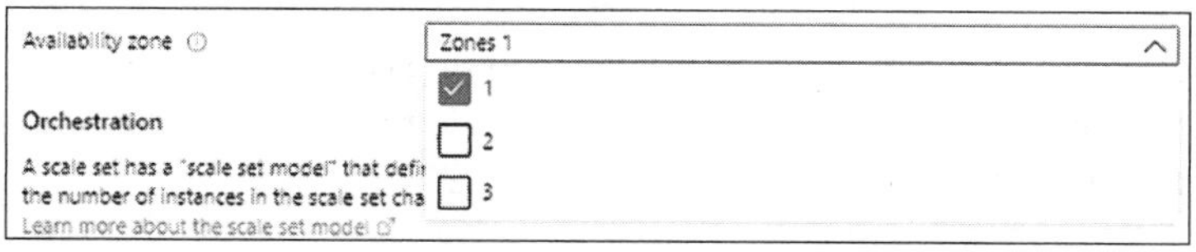

FIGURE 2-16 Single zone scale set setup.

   - Select multiple zones to create a zone-redundant scale set. (See Figure 2-17.)

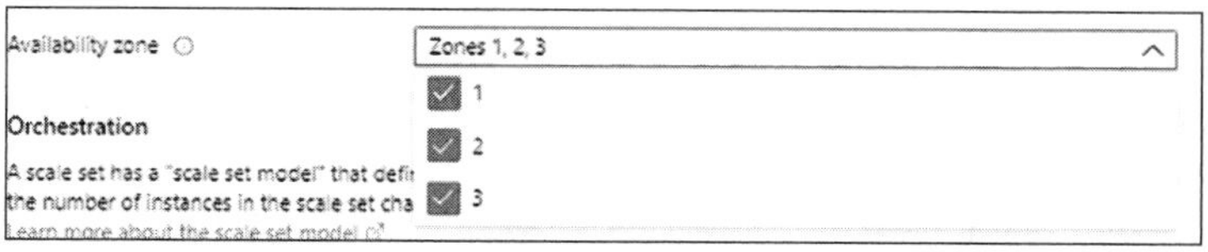

FIGURE 2-17 Different availability group options.

3. Finish using the VM Scale Set Creation wizard to create the VMSS, as described in the section "VMSS creation walkthrough."

USING AZURE POWERSHELL

When using Azure PowerShell to create a scale set, you add the –Zone parameter to enable the availability zones for that scale set. For example, the following code shows how to use this parameter in a PowerShell script for VMSS creation. Add the number of zones based on your scale-set design needs:

```
#Define variables
$RG = "VMSSResourceGroup"
$location = "EastUS2"
$VMSSname = "VMScaleSet01"
$vnet = "VMSS-Vnet"
$subnet = "VMSS-Subnet"
$publicIP = "VMSSPublicIPAddress"
# Create VMSS in availability zone
New-AzVmss `
   -ResourceGroupName $RG"" `
   -Location ""$location `
   -VMScaleSetName ""$VMSSname `
   -VirtualNetworkName ""$vnet `
   -SubnetName ""$subnet `
   -PublicIpAddressName ""$publicip `
   -LoadBalancerName "VMSSLoadBalancer" `
   -UpgradePolicy "Automatic" `
   -Zone "1", "2", "3"
```

USING THE AZURE CLI

When using the Azure CLI to create a scale set, you add the --zones parameter to enable the availability zones for that scale set. For example, the following code shows how to use this parameter in a Bash script or prompt for VMSS creation. Add the number of zones based on your scale-set design needs:

```
#Define variables
rg="VMSS-RG01"
name="VMSS-Set01"
adminusername="vmssadminuser"
# Create vmss in availability zones
az vmss create --resource-group $rg\
    --name $name \
    --image UbuntuLTS \
    --upgrade-policy-mode automatic \
    --admin-username $adminusername\
    --generate-ssh-keys \
    --zones 1 2 3
```

Fault domains

In Azure regions with no availability zones, VMSS are created with five fault domains by default. For Azure regions that do support zonal deployments, the fault domain count is one. This implies that the VM instances will be split across as many racks as possible. You must set the number of fault domains when creating a scale set, so you'll want to think about this beforehand to build for maximum resiliency.

> **TIP** It is recommended to set the number of fault domains equivalent to the number of managed disks to prevent loss of quorum if a managed disk fault domain goes down.

Fault domain walkthrough

The following sections step you through the process of setting up fault domains for a VMSS using the Azure Portal, Azure PowerShell, and the Azure CLI. If you are following along, be sure to select resources and resource names based on your environment, including unique VMSS, vNET, and subnet names for each of your deployments. Also, be sure to delete any unwanted resources after you have completed testing to avoid charges levied by Microsoft for these resources.

USING THE AZURE PORTAL

To enable fault domains using the Azure Portal during VMSS creation, follow these steps:

1. Follow the steps in the "VMSS creation walkthrough" section to start the Create a Virtual Machine Scale Set wizard and create a VMSS.

2. In the **Advanced** tab, next to **Spreading Algorithm**, select one of the following options:

   - **Max Spreading** VMs are spread across as many fault domains as possible in each zone.

   - **Fixed Spreading** VMs are always spread across exactly five fault domains. Remember, if fewer than five fault domains are available, the scale set will fail to deploy.

3. If you chose **Fixed Spreading** in step 2, enter the number of fault domains you want to use in the **Fault Domain Count** drop-down list. (See Figure 2-18.)

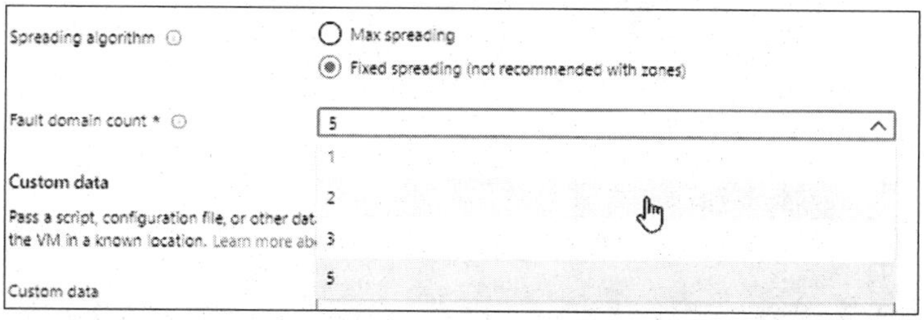

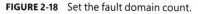

FIGURE 2-18 Set the fault domain count.

4. Finish using the VM Scale Set Creation wizard to create the VMSS, as described in the section "VMSS creation walkthrough."

USING AZURE POWERSHELL

When using Azure PowerShell to create a scale set, you add the -PlatformFaultDomainCount parameter to set the number of fault domains to be used for the scale set. For example, the following code shows how to use this in a PowerShell script for VMSS creation. Add the number of fault domains to be used based on your scale-set redundancy needs, selecting between the currently supported values of 1, 2, 3, and 5.

```
#Define variables
$RG = "VMSS-RG01"
$location = "EastUS2"
$VMSSname = "VMScaleSet01"
$vnet = "VMSS-Vnet01"
$subnet = "VMSS-Subnet01"
$publicip = "VMSSPublicIPAddress"
#Create VMSS with fault domain config
New-AzVmss `
   -ResourceGroupName ""$RG `
   -Location ""$location`
   -VMScaleSetName ""$VMSSname `
   -VirtualNetworkName ""$vnet `
   -SubnetName ""$subnet `
   -PublicIpAddressName ""$publicip `
   -LoadBalancerName "VMSSLoadBalancer" `
   -UpgradePolicy "Automatic" `
   -Zone "1", "2", "3"
   -PlatformFaultDomainCount 3
```

USING THE AZURE CLI

When using the Azure CLI to create a scale set, you add the --platform-fault-domain-count parameter to set the number of fault domains for the scale set. For example, the following code shows how to use this in a Bash script for VMSS creation. Add the number of fault domains to be used based on your scale-set redundancy needs, selecting between the currently supported values of 1, 2, 3, and 5:

```
#Define variables
rg="VMSS-RG01"
$location = "EastUS2"
$VMSSname = "VMScaleSet01"
$vnet = "VMSS-Vnet01"
#Create VMSS with fault domain config
az vmss create \
```

```
--resource-group $rg \
--name myScaleSet \
--image UbuntuLTS \
--upgrade-policy-mode automatic \
--admin-username azureuser \
--platform-fault-domain-count 3\
--generate-ssh-keys
```

Autoscaling

Now that we've covered availability and resiliency options, and highlighted a number of occasions on how autoscaling relates to scale set availability and resiliency, let's examine how autoscaling works. In this context, autoscaling describes the ability of an Azure VMSS to automatically manage VM requirements based on various rules and resource-utilization patterns. In other words, the scale set can increase or decrease the number of VM instances running the application based on the rules defined in the scale set. As VM instances are added to a scale set, they are automatically added to the load balancer, too, so traffic can be distributed to them.

Autoscaling significantly reduces the overhead associated with managing application workload capacity requirements. Indeed, it completely eliminates the need to constantly check VM utilization and decide to scale in or out. This not only reduces management overhead, but it also makes the entire process more accurate than if it were manually managed.

You define a scale set's autoscaling rules manually. First, though, you must establish what you consider to be acceptable performance, based on application requirements and customer experience testing. After you identify these thresholds, you can put in place autoscaling rules to adjust the scale set's resource capacity accordingly.

A good approach is to base rules on the percentage of VM CPU utilization within a specific period of time. For example, suppose you know from user experience testing that when CPU utilization hits 85%, performance starts to suffer. In that case, you might set an autoscaling rule to increase the number of VM instances if CPU utilization reaches 80% for a period of 15 minutes to avoid performance degradation. Conversely, you might set an autoscaling rule to decrease the number of VM instances if CPU utilization drops below 30% to avoid paying for VM instances you aren't using.

> **NOTE** You might select a higher or lower threshold of CPU usage or higher or lower time thresholds based on the environment and your knowledge of demand requirements.

You might also create autoscaling rules based on scheduled or known triggers or activities that would require a much higher or lower capacity requirement. For example:

- If business activity typically starts at 9 a.m. Monday through Friday, a burst of users will likely log in to the system at that time. In that case, it would be a good idea to create an autoscaling rule to add VM instances just before that time so they are available before users begin to log in. On the other hand, if business activity tends to drop sharply after 7 p.m. and on weekends, you can create an autoscaling rule to reduce the number of VM instances available during that time.

- If your business employs an enterprise resource planning (ERP) application, it likely sees increased usage at the end of the month or quarter. Knowing this, you could set an autoscaling rule to automatically increase the number of VM instances to accommodate this increased demand.

- If you are planning a marketing promotion, an event, or a large sale, you could schedule a one-time autoscaling rule before the activity or anticipated demand.

> **NOTE** The biggest benefits of autoscaling, apart from reduced management overhead, are cost savings and improved application performance.

Host-based metrics

The easiest metrics to use for autoscaling rules are the built-in host metrics for the various VM instances. These provide details on CPU utilization, memory demand, and disk access for each VM instance. Visibility into these metrics does not require the use of additional agents or configuration. You can configure scaling-in or scaling-out actions based on these metrics when you create a scale set or add them later using the Azure Portal, Azure PowerShell, the Azure CLI, and ARM templates.

Azure Diagnostics Extension for VMs

To obtain more detailed performance metrics, you must deploy an agent on each VM instance. One such agent is the Azure Diagnostic Extension for VMs. Once deployed, this agent provides more in-depth performance metrics, which allow for more-informed decisions regarding autoscaling rules. For example, you can consider more granular metrics like PercentageIdleTime for CPU or AverageReadTime for disks instead of the basic CPU and disk utilization metrics available using host metrics. This can help in defining more accurate scaling policies that yield higher levels of performance and cost benefits.

Azure Application Insights

You can use Azure Application Insights to monitor app-level performance metrics. To use Application Insights, you must install an instrumentation package within the application to monitor the app and send telemetry data to Azure. Once this is in place, you can access advanced application metrics such as session details, application response times, page loading performance, and so on, which you can use to define autoscaling rules. This level of granularity allows for more insightful and more efficient autoscaling actions, based on actual customer experience rather than baseline parameters.

Advanced autoscaling

In addition to setting autoscaling rules based on performance metric thresholds, a specific schedule, or a combination of the two, you can set up advanced autoscaling rules using email and webhook notifications. This approach requires the creation of multiple scaling profiles that contain a combination of triggers and scaling actions. Based on the email and webhook notifications, different profiles and their associated actions could be triggered.

Best practices and general tips for autoscaling

Following are some best practices and general tips that relate to autoscaling:

- **Set maximum and minimum values appropriately**   If the scaling logic is set such that the minimum = 4, the maximum = 4, and the current instance count is 4, no scaling action can occur. Therefore, an appropriate margin is required between the maximum and minimum instance counts, which are inclusive. Autoscale will scale between these two limits.

- **Autoscale resets any manual scaling actions**   Manual scaling is temporary unless the autoscaling rules are set or modified in line with the manual scaling actions. If you manually set an instance count value above or below the maximum, the autoscale engine will automatically bring the scale set to the minimum or maximum threshold based on the deviation on its next run. For example, if the range is set to be between 2 and 7, and there is only one instance running, autoscale would automatically scale to two instances the next time it runs. Similarly, if the instance count is manually set to scale to nine instances, on the next autoscale run, it will scale it back to seven instances.

- **Modify autoscaling rules**   You can easily modify autoscaling rules over time. So, for example, you might start with utilization rules and then gather performance metrics before deciding on scheduled rules unless you have historical data available.

- **Combine scaling-in and scaling-out rules**   While it is possible to create autoscaling rules to take only a single action (scale in or scale out), based on specific performance thresholds in a profile, it is not ideal. The more optimal approach would be to combine rules such that scaling out takes place automatically when usage is high and scaling in occurs automatically when the usage is low.

- **Diagnostics metrics for scaling rules**   There are different metrics for scaling, which include total, minimum, maximum, and average. Based on the environment in use, the most appropriate metric would differ. If you're not sure which metric is the right one, it's a good idea to start with the average metric; you can adjust it over time if needed.

- **Threshold management**   When setting metric thresholds, account for the environment in which the scale set is running and expect to perform some amount of fine-tuning and adjusting over time based on that environment. Also ensure that metrics do not overlap, clash, or conflict, as this will result in confusion and potentially inaction. Be sure to test a scaling-in and scaling-out operation by performing stress testing on the scale set if possible. This will help validate that the rules work, and that you will only need to adjust thresholds over time based on actual performance.

- **Using multiple profiles**   You can set different types of scaling rules for a scale set. This can result in a single scale set having multiple profiles with different types of policies, which are triggered based on performance, schedules, or specific date/time ranges. It is important to know the order in which autoscale processes these profiles. At present, autoscale processes them in the following order:
  - Profiles with a fixed date and time
  - Profiles with recurring schedules
  - The default profile

  Currently, only a single profile is processed at a time. This means that when a profile condition is met, autoscale applies the rules covered in that profile and ignores the rest of the profiles in the queue thereafter. Therefore, it might be best to add any rules that are required but are ignored (due to the ordering) to the profile that *is* getting processed last.

- **Scaling out versus scaling in**   For rules that manage scaling-out operations, a match with any rule will trigger the operation. However, for rules that manage scaling-in operations, all the rules must match. Be sure to test against this scenario to ensure your rules will work as expected when needed.

- **Identifying the default instance count**   The default instance count is the number of VMs running when autoscaling rules are not in effect at the start of the scale set setup. This can be due to insufficient metric information for the thresholds defined in the configuration. Make sure the minimum required number of VMs is set up correctly based on the anticipated load at that time to ensure the application performance does not suffer. Over time, this will be managed more efficiently by the system as it gathers performance metrics from the VM instances.

- **Autoscale notifications**   Autoscale records numerous actions and conditions in the activity log, such as scaling operations initiating, completing, and failing; issues with gathering metrics; and so on. You can use the Azure monitor or log monitor to set up notifications to inform administrators when such events take place. This can prompt a deeper analysis to identify whether there are incorrectly sized VM instances or other performance issues. (Incorrectly sized VM instances would require vertical scaling, which is discussed in the next section.)

Autoscaling walkthrough

The following sections step you through the process of setting up autoscaling policies using the Azure Portal, Azure PowerShell, and the Azure CLI. If you are following along, be sure to select resources and resource names based on your environment, including unique VMSS, vNET, and subnet names for each of your deployments. Also, be sure to delete any unwanted resources after you have completed testing to avoid charges levied by Microsoft for these resources.

USING THE AZURE PORTAL

To set up autoscaling using the Azure Portal during VMSS creation, follow these steps:

1. Follow the steps in the "VMSS creation walkthrough" section to start the Create a Virtual Machine Scale Set wizard and create a VMSS.

2. In the **Scaling** tab, in the **Instance** section, change the value in the **Initial Instance Count** box to reflect minimum number of VM instances for the new scale set. (See Figure 2-19.)

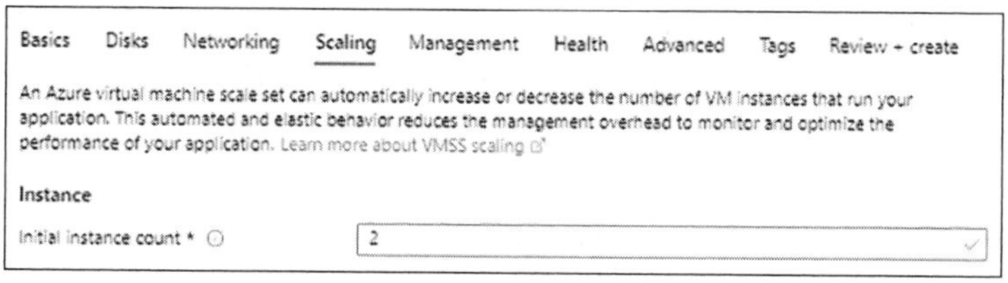

Basics	Disks	Networking	Scaling	Management	Health	Advanced	Tags	Review + create

An Azure virtual machine scale set can automatically increase or decrease the number of VM instances that run your application. This automated and elastic behavior reduces the management overhead to monitor and optimize the performance of your application. Learn more about VMSS scaling ◻

Instance

Initial instance count * ◯   [2]

FIGURE 2-19 Entering the minimum number of VM instances for the scale set.

3. In the **Scaling** section, next to **Scaling Policy**, select one of the following (see Figure 2-20):

   - **Manual**   If you select this option, all scaling-management activities will need to be performed manually.

   - **Custom**   When you select this option, you can set up the system to manage scaling activities.

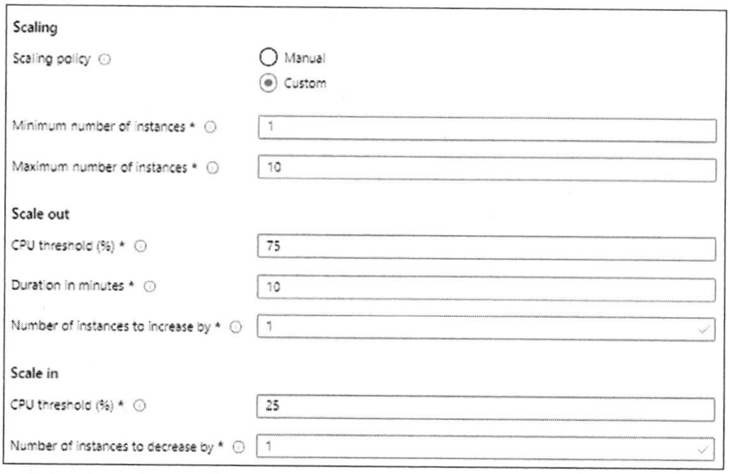

Scaling

Scaling policy ◯   ◯ Manual
                        ⦿ Custom

Minimum number of instances * ◯   [1]

Maximum number of instances * ◯   [10]

Scale out

CPU threshold (%) * ◯   [75]

Duration in minutes * ◯   [10]

Number of instances to increase by * ◯   [1]

Scale in

CPU threshold (%) * ◯   [25]

Number of instances to decrease by * ◯   [1]

FIGURE 2-20 Select the Custom scaling policy and define your autoscale thresholds.

As shown in Figure 2-20, when you select the Custom option button, you'll see several additional options:

- **Minimum number of instances**   Defines the minimum number of instances required for stable application functionality with the base application load.

- **Maximum number of instances** Defines the maximum number of instances required for stable application functionality with the maximum anticipated application load. If you aren't sure what this number should be, increase it over time while monitoring the usage of the scale set.

- **Scale Out: CPU threshold (%)** Defines the CPU threshold to monitor to trigger scale-out policies. Set this based on the threshold point at which application performance may suffer and the amount of time it takes for a new instance to be brought online to handle new sessions.

- **Scale Out: Duration in minutes** Defines the amount of time to monitor CPU utilization to trigger scale-out policies. Set this based on expected spikes in application load that stabilize quickly thereafter and the amount of time it takes for new instances to be brought online.

- **Scale Out: Number of instances to increase by** Defines the number of instances to add when threshold parameters are met. This could be a single instance or multiple instances, based on anticipated application loads derived from historical data or on scheduled or planned events.

- **Scale In: CPU threshold (%)** Defines the CPU threshold to monitor to trigger scale-in policies. Set this based on the threshold point at which application performance may continue to work efficiently and the amount of time it takes for a new instance to be brought online to handle new sessions in case there is a spike.

- **Scale In: Number of instances to decrease by** Defines the number of instances to remove each time scale-in threshold parameters are met. This could be a single instance or multiple instances, based on anticipated application loads derived from historical data or on scheduled or planned events.

4. Under **Scale-In Policy**, open the **Scale-In Policy** drop-down list and choose the policy you want to apply. (See Figure 2-21.) Your choices are as follows:

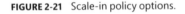

Scale-In policy

Configure the order in which virtual machines are selected for deletion during a scale-in operation.
Learn more about scale-in policies. ☞

Scale-in policy

Default - Balance across availability zones and fault domains, then delete ... ∧

Default - Balance across availability zones and fault domains, then delete VM with highest instance ID

Newest VM - Balance across availability zones, then delete the newest created VM

Review + create   ‹ Previc Oldest VM - Balance across availability zones, then delete the oldest created VM

FIGURE 2-21 Scale-in policy options.

- **Default – Balance across availability zones and fault domains, then delete VM with highest instance ID** This policy configuration results in the scale set being spread across multiple availability zones and fault domains to achieve maximum redundancy. For zonal deployments, VMs are balanced across availability zones.

On a best-effort basis, VMs are balanced across fault domains. The VM with the highest instance ID is deleted when the balancing algorithm performs its scaling in operations.

- **Newest VM – Balance across availability zones, then delete the newest created VM**   For zonal deployments, this scale-in policy configuration results in the scale set being spread across multiple availability zones. Scale-in operations will delete the newest VMs.

- **Oldest VM – Balance across availability zones, then delete the oldest created VM**   For zonal deployments, this scale-in policy configuration results in the scale set being spread across multiple availability zones. Scale-in operations will delete the oldest VMs.

5. Finish using the VM Scale Set Creation wizard to create the VMSS, as described in the section "VMSS creation walkthrough."

If autoscaling is not set up at the time of the scale set creation or if it needs to be modified at any stage, you can easily address this. You can change scaling policies as needed and even define advanced scaling configurations such as multiple scaling conditions or multiple scaling rules. Follow these steps:

1. In the Azure Portal, select the VMSS whose scaling policies you want to set or change.

2. Click the **Scaling** option in the **Settings** pane.

3. In the **Configure** tab, select one of the following options:

- **Manual Scale**   Select this to set up a manual instance count that will be a fixed count maintained for autoscaling. (See Figure 2-22.)

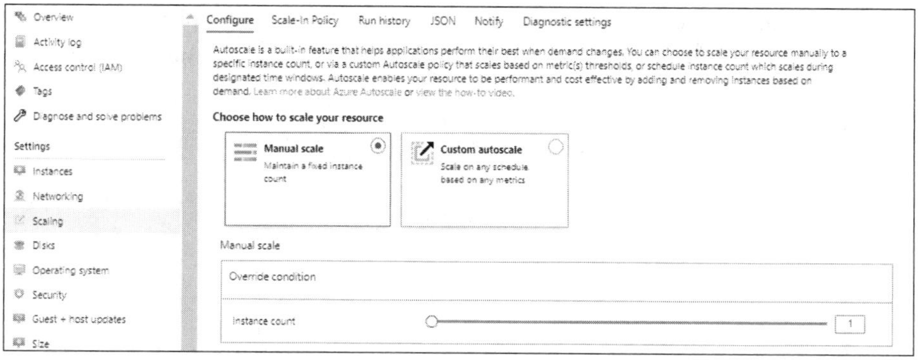

FIGURE 2-22   Set up or modify autoscaling policies for an existing VMSS.

- **Custom Autoscale**   Select this to set up more complex autoscaling rules. For example, you can set scaling logic based on CPU usage, as shown in Figure 2-23.

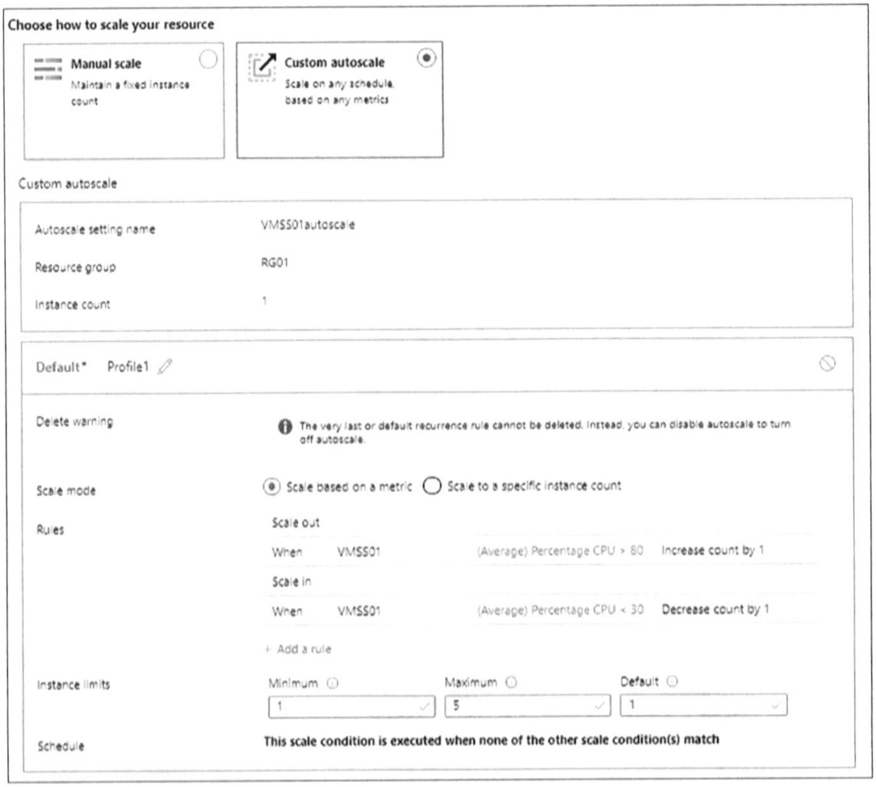

FIGURE 2-23 Custom scale set rules and thresholds to trigger scaling policy.

4. Optionally, set up an advanced scaling configuration by creating multiple scaling rules for different thresholds or parameters to achieve more fine-tuned autoscaling. (See Figure 2-24.)

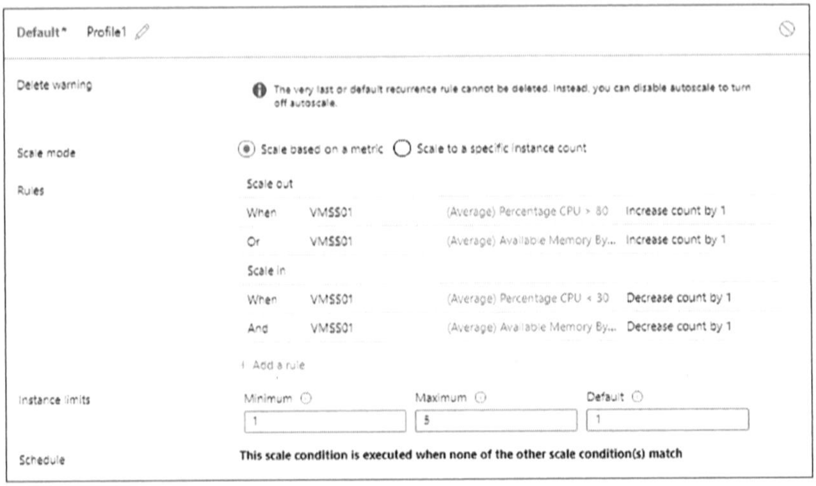

FIGURE 2-24 Create multiple custom scaling rules to monitor multiple scale set utilization conditions.

5. Optionally, define multiple profiles with different scaling rules to achieve the desired autoscaling configuration. (See Figure 2-25.) Be sure to test this to ensure that the rules do not clash or conflict.

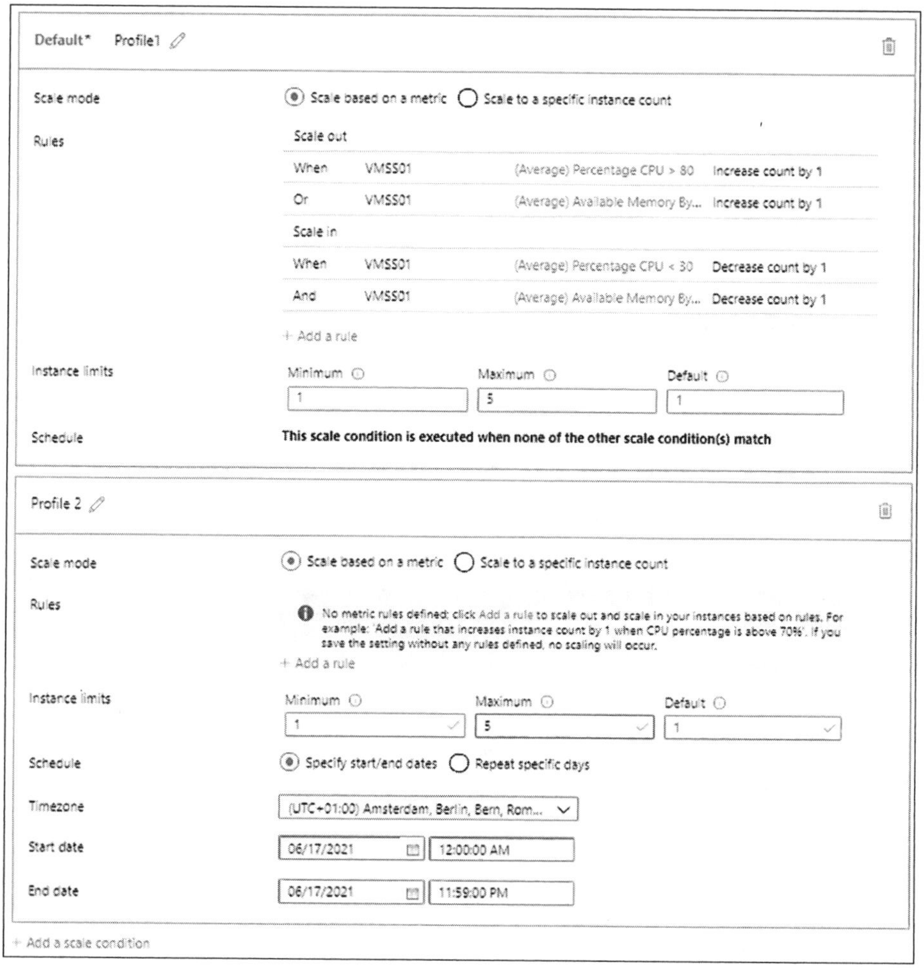

FIGURE 2-25 Configure multiple custom scaling rules.

You can set up autoscaling notifications to email administrators or specific engineers within the organization when autoscaling operations are triggered. Notifications to webhooks can also be set up using this feature. Follow these steps:

1. In the Azure Portal, select the scale set for which you want to set up autoscaling notifications.

2. Click the **Scaling** option in the **Settings** pane.

3. In the **Notify** tab, specify whether you want to email administrators or co-administrators (or both).

4. Optionally, add more administrator emails or webhooks. (See Figure 2-26.)

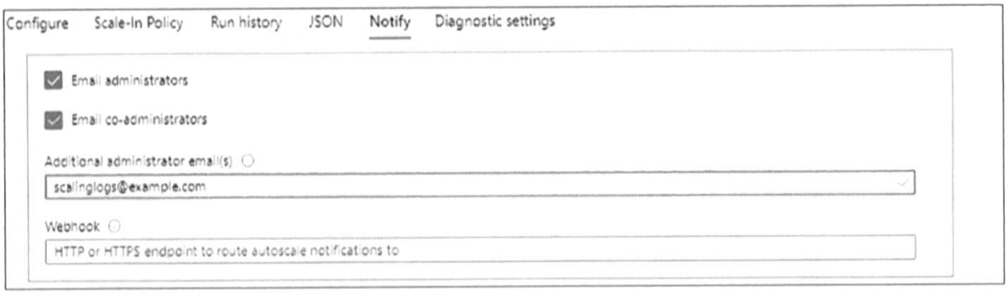

FIGURE 2-26 Setting up autoscaling notifications.

USING AZURE POWERSHELL

When using Azure PowerShell, you can use the `New-AzureRmAutoscaleRule` command to create an autoscaling rule and the `Update-AzureRMAutoscaleRule` command to modify an autoscaling rule. For example, the following code creates an autoscaling rule to check for the CPU percentage utilization for 15 minutes, and to increase the VM instance count by 2 if the average is greater than 80%.

> **NOTE** Replace the subscription ID in the following code to your own. Otherwise, the script will fail.

```
#Define variables
$subscriptionID = "12232-12148-329201-199101"
$rg = "VMSS-RG01"
$vmssname = "VMSS-01"
$location = "EastUS2"
$vnet = "VMSS01-vNET"
$subnet = "VMSS01-Subnet"
$loadbalancer = "VMSS01-LB"
#Setup autoscaling rule
New-AzureRmAutoscaleRule `
  -MetricName "Percentage CPU" `
  -MetricResourceId /subscriptions/$SubscriptionId/resourceGroups/$RG/providers/
Microsoft.Compute/virtualMachineScaleSets/$vmssname `
  -TimeGrain 00:05:00 `
  -MetricStatistic "Average" `
  -TimeWindow 00:15:00 `
  -Operator "GreaterThan" `
  -Threshold 90 `
  -ScaleActionDirection "Increase" `
```

```
-ScaleActionScaleType "ChangeCount" `
-ScaleActionValue 2 `
-ScaleActionCooldown 00:15:00
```

The following code defines the scale-in policy as NewestVM at the time of scale set creation:

```
#Define variables
$subscriptionID = "12232-12148-329201-199101"
$rg = "VMSS-RG01"
$vmssname = "VMSS-01"
$location = "EastUS2"
$vnet = "VMSS01-vNET"
$subnet = "VMSS01-Subnet"
$loadbalancer = "VMSS01-LB"
#Create VMSS with scale-in policy
New-AzVmss -ResourceGroupName $RG `
  -Location $location `
  -VMScaleSetName $vmssname `
  -ScaleInPolicy "NewestVM"
```

USING THE AZURE CLI

When using the Azure CLI to create a scale set, you can add the `az monitor autoscale create` parameter to enable autoscaling for that scale set. For example, the following code creates an autoscaling rule to set the minimum instance and maximum instance count for the scale set and to increase the instances by two each time an autoscale action is triggered:

```
#Define variables
rg="VMSS-RG01"
vmssname="VMSS01"

#Create autoscale rule
az monitor autoscale create --resource-group $rg \
  --resource $vmssname \
  --resource-type Microsoft.Compute/virtualMachineScaleSets \
  --name autoscalerule01 \
  --min-count 4 \
  --max-count 40 \
  --count 2
```

The following code sets the scale-in policy to OldestVM at the time of the scale set creation:

```
#Define variables
rg="VMSS-RG01"
vmssname="VMSS01"
adminuser="vmssadminuser"
#Create VMSS with scale-in policy
az vmss create \
```

```
--resource-group $rg \
--name $vmssname \
--image UbuntuLTS \
--admin-username $adminuser\
--generate-ssh-keys \
--scale-in-policy OldestVM
```

Vertical scaling

So far, we've covered how autoscaling can scale in and scale out—in other words, scale hori-
zontally. However, there might be instances when you need to scale up or scale down—that
is, scale vertically. With vertical scaling, the size of the VM instances, rather than the number
of instances, is increased or decreased, depending on performance needs. You might need to
scale vertically if, for example:

- Horizontal scaling takes place too often, and the autoscale service cannot keep up with
  demand.
- The application is not performing as expected because the VM instances are
  undersized.
- Autoscaling does not occur much at all because the VM instances are oversized, and
  additional instances are rarely required.

> **NOTE** There are limitations on what size a VM can be, depending on the size of the
> first VM instance in a scale set. Therefore, you must select the new size with this in mind.

You can scale vertically in one of two ways:

- By reprovisioning the VMs in the scale set—that is, removing VMs and adding new ones
  of the required size.
- By changing the size of every VM currently running to retain the data already hosted on
  these VMs.

Vertical scaling can reduce service costs by replacing oversized VM instances with smaller
ones and then reducing the number of smaller VMs that run during off-peak hours. Vertical scaling can also improve application performance because it takes less time to provision
smaller VM instances than larger ones.

You can set up vertical scaling to be triggered using webhooks based on alerts generated
by monitored metrics. Whenever an alert is generated, the webhook can trigger a set of pre-
defined automated actions, which would carry out the scale-up or scale-down operation.

Load balancing

Load balancers distribute traffic to all the VM instances in a scale set. Basic layer-4 traffic distribution to all VM instances can be handled by a load balancer. You can set up the Azure load balancer to monitor VM instances and distribute incoming traffic only to healthy VM instances. Although Microsoft does not charge you extra to set up or use scale sets, it does charge you for the use of underlying compute resources, such as the load balancer.

Load balancing walkthrough

The following sections step you through the process of setting up a load balancer for a VMSS using the Azure Portal, Azure PowerShell, and the Azure CLI. If you are following along, be sure to select resources and resource names based on your environment, including unique VMSS, vNET, and subnet names for each of your deployments. Also, be sure to delete any unwanted resources after you have completed testing to avoid charges levied by Microsoft for these resources.

USING THE AZURE PORTAL

To set up a load balancer using the Azure Portal during VMSS creation, follow these steps:

1. Follow the steps in the "VMSS creation walkthrough" section to start the Create a Virtual Machine Scale Set wizard and create a VMSS.

2. In the **Networking** tab, under **Load Balancing**, select the **Use a Load Balancer** check box. (See Figure 2-27.)

FIGURE 2-27 Set up load balancing.

3. Still in the **Load Balancing** section, enter the following information (see Figure 2-28):

   - **Load Balancing Options** Leave this set to **Azure Load Balancer** (the default).
   - **Select a Load Balancer** Choose the load balancer you want to use. Alternatively, click the **Create New** link and follow the prompts to create a new load balancer with traffic-routing rules that you define. I opted to create a new load balancer named VMSS01-lb.

> **NOTE** The Standard load balancer is the default supported option. If you need to use the Basic load balancer instead, then you must create the scale set without the load balancer. Then, after you create the scale set, you must provision the basic load balancer separately. Finally, you must add the VMSS to the back-end pool of the Basic load balancer.

- **Select a Backend Pool** Leave this set to the default. The load balancer will automatically add new VM instances to the pool for load balancing. Alternatively, click the **Create New** link to set up a new back-end pool name.

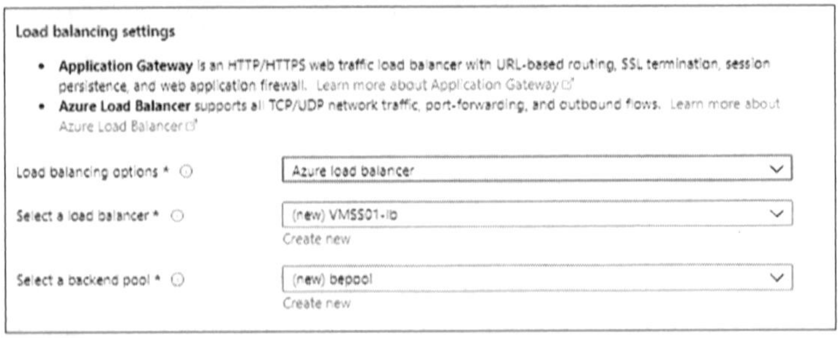

Load balancing settings

- **Application Gateway** is an HTTP/HTTPS web traffic load balancer with URL-based routing, SSL termination, session persistence, and web application firewall. Learn more about Application Gateway
- **Azure Load Balancer** supports all TCP/UDP network traffic, port-forwarding, and outbound flows. Learn more about Azure Load Balancer

Load balancing options * ○	Azure load balancer	⌄
Select a load balancer * ○	(new) VMSS01-lb	⌄
	Create new	
Select a backend pool * ○	(new) bepool	⌄
	Create new	

FIGURE 2-28 Set up load balancing configuration options.

4. Finish using the VM Scale Set Creation wizard to create the VMSS, as described in the section "VMSS creation walkthrough."

USING AZURE POWERSHELL

When using Azure PowerShell to create a scale set, you can use the –LoadBalancerName option to specify the name of the load balancer to be used or created as part of the scale set creation process. For example, the following code shows how to use this in a PowerShell script for VM scale set creation:

```
#Define variables
$rg = "VMSS-RG01"
$vmssname = "VMSS-01"
$location = "EastUS2"
$vnet = "VMSS01-vNET"
$subnet = "VMSS01-Subnet"
$loadbalancer = "VMSS01-LB"
#Create VMSS with load balancer
New-AzVmss `
  -ResourceGroupName $rg `
  -Location $location `
  -VMScaleSetName $vmssname `
  -VirtualNetworkName $vnet `
  -SubnetName $subnet `
  -PublicIpAddressName "VMSS01-PublicIPAddress" `
  -LoadBalancerName $loadbalancer `
```

USING THE AZURE CLI

When using the Azure CLI to create a scale set, you can use the --Load-Balancer option to specify the name of the load balancer to be used or created as part of the scale set creation process. For example, the following code shows how to use this in a Bash script for VM scale set creation:

```
#Define variables
rg="VMSS-RG01"
vmssname="VMSS-01"
adminusername="vmssadmin"
loadbalancer="VMSS01-LB"
vnet="VMSS01-vNet"
subnet="VMSS01-Subnet"
#Create the VM scale set with a load balancer
az vmss create \
  --resource-group $rg \
  --name $vmssname \
  --image UbuntuLTS \
  --upgrade-policy-mode automatic \
  --admin-username $adminusername \
  --generate-ssh-keys \
--public-ip-address vmss-publicipaddress-01 \
--load-balancer $loadbalancer \
--vnet-name $vnet\
--subnet $subnet
```

Maintain Azure VMSS

Maintaining an Azure VMSS involves the following tasks and tools:

- Upgrading the scale set model
- Performing automatic OS upgrades
- Updating golden OS images
- Deploying the Application Health extension and automated instance repairs
- Using Instance Protection
- Using proximity placement groups
- Checking and increasing vCPU quotas
- Enabling termination notifications

Upgrade the scale set model

A VMSS has an upgrade policy that is used to decide how VM instances within that scale set will be kept up to date with the latest scale set model. There are three upgrade modes:

- **Automatic**   Existing VM instances will upgrade as soon as new OS images/upgrades are available. The upgrade will be carried out in random order.

- **Manual** Existing VM instances will not be upgraded automatically. Instead, they will be upgraded manually by an administrator. (Note that choosing this option limits the use of the automatic OS rollback feature by using the previous OS disk.)

- **Rolling** Upgrades are rolled out automatically in batches, enabling administrators to pause the upgrades if needed—for instance, if there are reported issues post-upgrade.

Upgrade the scale set model walkthrough

The following sections step you through the process of setting model upgrade options using the Azure Portal, Azure PowerShell, and the Azure CLI.

USING THE AZURE PORTAL

To set up automatic OS upgrades using the Azure Portal during VMSS creation, follow these steps:

1. Follow the steps in the "VMSS creation walkthrough" section to start the Create a Virtual Machine Scale Set wizard and create a VMSS.

2. In the **Management** tab, under **Upgrade Policy**, open the **Upgrade Mode** drop-down list and choose **Manual…**, **Automatic…**, or **Rolling….** (See Figure 2-29.)

FIGURE 2-29 Set the upgrade policy.

If you select the Automatic option, no further configuration is needed. (See Figure 2-30.)

FIGURE 2-30 The Automatic upgrade mode requires no further configuration.

If you select the Rolling option, you'll see additional options to define the rolling upgrade batch size (as a percentage), the pause time between batches, the maximum unhealthy instances (as a percentage), and the maximum unhealthy instances upgraded (as a percentage). (See Figure 2-31.)

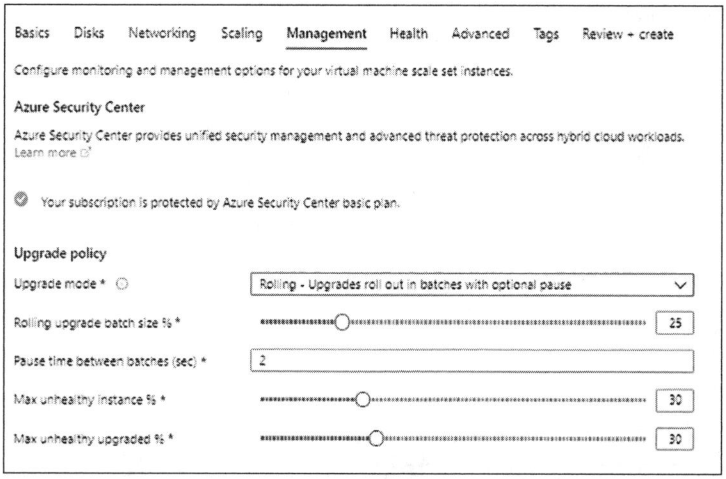

FIGURE 2-31 Set the Rolling upgrade policy.

4. Finish using the VM Scale Set Creation wizard to create the VMSS, as described in the section "VMSS creation walkthrough."

USING AZURE POWERSHELL

When using Azure PowerShell to update a VMSS, you can add the –UpgradePolicyMode parameter and set the value to Automatic, Rolling, or Manual to define this configuration. For example, the following code shows how to use this in a PowerShell script for VMSS updates:

```
#Define variables
$rg = "VMSS-RG01"
$vmssname = "VMSS-01"
$location = "EastUS2"
$vnet = "VMSS01-vNET"
```

```
$subnet = "VMSS01-Subnet"
$loadbalancer = "VMSS01-LB"
#Update scale set config
New-AzVmss `
   -ResourceGroupName $rg `
   -Location $location `
   -VMScaleSetName $vmssname `
   -VirtualNetworkName $vnet `
   -SubnetName $subnet `
   -PublicIpAddressName "VMSS01-PublicIPAddress" `
   -LoadBalancerName $loadbalancer `
    -UpgradePolicyMode "Automatic"
```

USING THE AZURE CLI

When using the Azure CLI to create a scale set, you can set the --upgrade-policy-mode parameter to Automatic, Rolling, or Manual. For example, the following code shows how to use this in a Bash script for VMSS creation:

```
#Define variables
rg="VMSS-RG01"
vmssname="VMSS-01"
adminusername="vmssadmin"
#Update scale set config
az vmss create --resource-group $rg \
   --name $vmssname \
   --image UbuntuLTS \
   --upgrade-policy-mode automatic \
   --admin-username $adminusername \
   --generate-ssh-keys \
```

Perform automatic OS upgrades

You can perform automatic OS upgrades to safely update the OS disk for all VM instances in a scale set. This process is easy to manage and highly efficient. Here are a few points to keep in mind about automatic OS upgrades:

- The latest OS images can be automatically applied after they are distributed by the image publishers, without user intervention.

- VM Instances are upgraded in rolling batches, ensuring minimal disruption and service interruption.

- Automatic OS upgrades are integrated with the Application Health extension and application health probes to allow for better monitoring and management.

- Automatic OS upgrades work for all VM sizes, and for both Windows and the latest Ubuntu and CentOS Linux images.

- Automatic OS upgrades allow for the entire process to be made manual, if needed.

- As part of the upgrade process, a new OS disk is created with the latest OS image, and the current OS disk of a VM is replaced at the time of the upgrade. All extensions and custom data scripts are thereafter run to bring the VM to the same state as the original VM. Persistent data disks are not affected and continue to be retained by the VM.

- Automatic OS upgrades can be enabled on a scale set of any size, which means they can be leveraged for scale sets ranging from a few VMs to thousands of VMs.

- To minimize application downtime, upgrades take place in batches, with no more than 20% of the scale set upgrading at any time.

> **TIP** The recommended approach is to incorporate an application heartbeat, validate upgrade success for each batch in the upgrade process, and integrate that as part of the DevOps process.

Automatic OS image upgrades walkthrough

The following sections step you through the process of enabling automatic OS image upgrades using the Azure Portal, Azure PowerShell, and the Azure CLI.

USING THE AZURE PORTAL

To enable Automatic OS upgrades using the Azure Portal during VMSS creation, follow these steps:

1. Follow the steps in the "VMSS creation walkthrough" section to start the Create a Virtual Machine Scale Set wizard and create a VMSS.

2. In the **Management** tab, under **Automatic OS Upgrades**, select the **Enable Automatic Upgrades** check box. (See Figure 2-32.)

FIGURE 2-32 Set up automatic OS upgrades.

3. Finish using the VM Scale Set Creation wizard to create the VMSS, as described in the section "VMSS creation walkthrough."

USING AZURE POWERSHELL

When using Azure PowerShell to update a VMSS, you can add the –AutomaticOSUpgrade parameter and set it to $true to enable automatic OS upgrades. For example, the following code shows how to use this parameter in a PowerShell script:

```
#Define variables
$rg = "VMSS-RG01"
```

```
$vmssname = "VMSS-01"
#Update scale set config
Update-AzVmss -ResourceGroupName $RG -VMScaleSetName $vmssname -AutomaticOSUpgrade $true
```

USING THE AZURE CLI

When using the Azure CLI to update a VMSS, you can add the `--set UpgradePolicy.AutomaticOSUpgradePolicy.EnableAutomaticOSUpgrade` parameter and set it to true to enable automatic OS upgrades. For example, the following code shows how to use this parameter in a Bash script for VMSS updates:

```
#Define variables
rg="VMSS-RG01"
vmssname="VMSS-01"
#Update scale set config
az vmss update --name $vmssname \
--resource-group $rg \
--set UpgradePolicy.AutomaticOSUpgradePolicy.EnableAutomaticOSUpgrade=true
```

Update golden OS images

To perform OS updates on VM instances in a scale set, you can update the golden image. Alternatively, you build a new golden image with the required updates and deploy it to the scale set. This would result in each VM instance being upgraded to the latest image in a rolling manner.

This is generally a non-disruptive activity, as the scale set design should help ensure minimal to no user interruption. However, if the application deployed on the scale set has compatibility issues between different OS versions and requires a subsequent update, it might be prudent to take maintenance downtime to perform these upgrade activities. This prevents you from having multiple versions of the app running at the same time.

> **TIP** If possible, you should create a continuous integration/continuous deployment (CI/CD) pipeline to integrate the deployment and upgrade of the app. This enables the scale set to automatically upgrade VM instances in a more seamless manner.

Deploy the Application Health extension and automated instance repairs

Azure VM extensions are critical to performing automated post-deployment configuration activities. In addition, extensions can be deployed for monitoring, securing, backing up, and performing other activities on the VM.

One example of an extension is the Application Health extension. You can use the Application Health extension to monitor the health of the application and automatically perform repairs when needed.

You can integrate Application Health extensions with the automated instance repairs (AIR) service to achieve high availability for the application running in a scale set. If the Application Health extension engine detects an unhealthy scale set, the AIR service can automatically delete it and deploy a new one in its place. This reduces the management overhead required to monitor and act on such failures.

AIR is currently supported for scale sets with no more than 200 VM instances. However, it is possible that this limit will change in the future to match the maximum instance limit for scale sets.

> **NOTE** Some extension deployments depend on the successful deployment of other extensions. In most production environments, this can result in multiple extensions being provisioned on each VM instance. It is important to test and validate these extensions to ensure they do not conflict or clash with resources and cause application outages. The incorrect ordering of extension deployments can result in avoidable failures.

Application Health extension walkthrough

The following section steps you through the process of enabling the Application Health extension using the Azure Portal.

USING THE AZURE PORTAL

To enable the Application Health extension using the Azure Portal during VMSS creation, follow these steps:

1. Follow the steps in the "VMSS creation walkthrough" section to start the Create a Virtual Machine Scale Set wizard and create a VMSS.

2. In the **Health** tab, under **Enable Application Health Monitoring** (see Figure 2-33), select the **Enabled** option.

FIGURE 2-33 Enable application health monitoring.

Enabling application health monitoring reveals several additional parameters (see Figure 2-34):

- **Application Health Monitor** Set the extension to use to monitor the health of the application (in this case, the Application Health extension).

- **Protocol** Select the protocol supported by the application for monitoring its health.

- **Port Number** Enter the port number that will be used to monitor application health. For highly secure environments, you may end up using a port that is not publicly exposed.

- **Path** Enter the path that corresponds with the page, application, or file that will be monitored to confirm application health status.

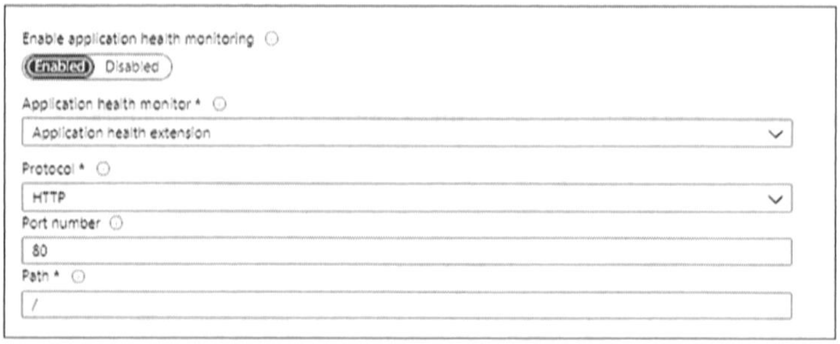

FIGURE 2-34 Application health monitoring options.

3. Choose the desired settings. Then finish using the VM Scale Set Creation wizard to create the VMSS, as described in the section "VMSS creation walkthrough."

Automatic instance repair walkthrough

The following sections step you through the process of enabling automatic instance repairs using the Azure Portal, Azure PowerShell, and the Azure CLI.

USING THE AZURE PORTAL

To enable automatic instance repairs using the Azure Portal during VMSS creation, follow these steps:

1. Follow the steps in the "VMSS creation walkthrough" section to start the Create a Virtual Machine Scale Set wizard and create a VMSS.

2. In the **Health** tab, under **Automatic Repair Policy** (see Figure 2-35), select the **Enable Automatic Repairs** check box, and enter a value in the **Grace Period** box.

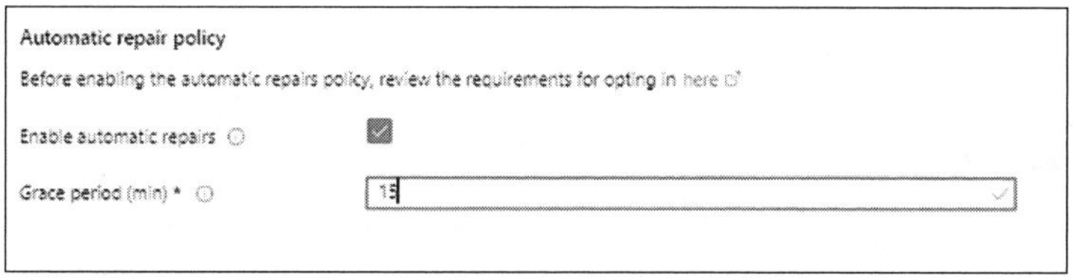

FIGURE 2-35 Enable automatic instance repair.

3. Finish using the VM Scale Set Creation wizard to create the VMSS, as described in the section "VMSS creation walkthrough."

USING AZURE POWERSHELL

When using Azure PowerShell to create a VMSS, you can enable automatic instance repairs by adding the `-EnableAutomaticRepair` and `-AutomaticRepairGracePeriod` parameters and set the values to `$true` and `PT30M`, respectively. (PT30M specifies a grace period of 30 minutes.) For example, the following code shows how to use these parameters in a PowerShell script for VMSS creation:

```
#Define variables
$location = "East US2"
$RG = "VMSS-RG01"
$VMSSName = "VMSS01"
#Update instance repair config
$vmssconfig = New-AzVmssConfig `
 -Location $location `
 -SkuCapacity 2 `
 -SkuName "Standard_DS2" `
 -UpgradePolicyMode "Automatic" `
 -EnableAutomaticRepair $true `
 -AutomaticRepairGracePeriod "PT30M"
#Create VMSS
New-AzVmss -ResourceGroupName $RG -Name $VMSSName -VirtualMachineScaleSet $VMSSconfig
```

USING THE AZURE CLI

When using the Azure CLI to create a scale set, you can use the `--automatic-repairs-grace-period` parameter with a value for the number of minutes for the grace period. This enables the configuration of automatic instance repair and sets the grace period defined in the command. For example, the following code shows how to use this parameter in a Bash script for VMSS creation:

```
#Define variables
location="EastUS2"
rg="VMSS-RG01"
```

```
adminuser="vmssadmin"
loadbalancer="VMSS01-LB"
vmssname="VMSS-01"
vmsshealthprobe="VMSS-LB01-HP01"
#Setup VMSS with automatic instance repair config
az vmss create \
  --resource-group $rg \
  --name $vmssname \
  --image UbuntuLTS \
  --admin-username $adminuser \
  --generate-ssh-keys \
  --load-balancer $loadbalancer \
  --health-probe $vmsshealthprobe \
  --automatic-repairs-grace-period 30
```

Use Instance Protection

Instance Protection enables you to set specific VM instances in a VMSS as special VMs. This results in them being treated differently from other VMs in the scale set. The difference in treatment depends on the protection properties defined for the instance. You might use this feature when you want to avoid autoscaling specific instances in a scale set or if upgrading or reimaging those instances might result in the disruption of specific activities running just on those VMs.

Azure VMSS provide two types of Instance Protection, as follows:

- **Scale-in protection**   This prevents automatic scale-in operations from taking place on the specified instance. It does not prevent user-initiated operations like deletions, nor does it prevent scale set–level operations like OS upgrades, instance deallocations, and so on.

- **Scale set–level protection**   This prevents scale set–level operations from taking place. This includes scale-in protection features in addition to preventing scale set–level operations like OS upgrades, instance deallocations, and so on. It does not protect against user-initiated actions like deletions, nor does it prevent the deletion of the entire scale set itself.

You can set up Instance Protection only after the scale set instances have been created. There are many ways of doing this, including using the Azure Portal, Azure PowerShell, the Azure CLI, or the REST API. If you need to use Instance Protection, it is important to remember to set it up after the VM instances are created.

Instance Protection walkthrough

The following sections step you through the process of enabling instance protection using the Azure Portal, Azure PowerShell, and the Azure CLI.

USING THE AZURE PORTAL

To set up Instance Protection using the Azure Portal, follow these steps:

1. In the Azure Portal, navigate to the VMSS for which you want to configure Instance Protection, and select it.

2. Click the **Protection Policy** button. (See Figure 2-36.)

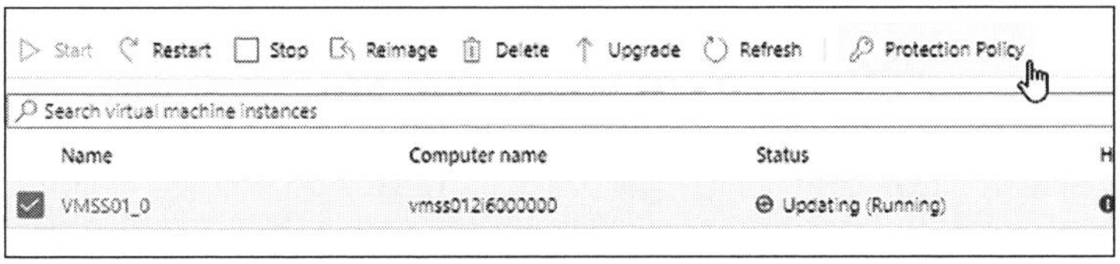

FIGURE 2-36   Set up Instance Protection.

3. In the **Protection Policy** pane, select the type of Instance Protection you want to apply and click **Save**. (See Figure 2-37.)

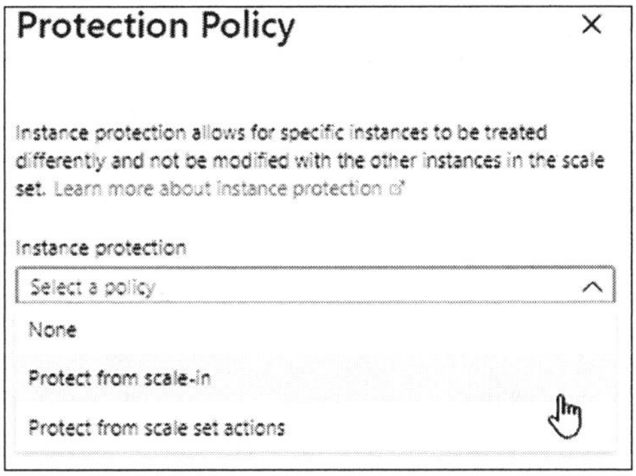

FIGURE 2-37   Change the protection policy configuration.

USING AZURE POWERSHELL

When using Azure PowerShell to update a VMSS to use Instance Protection, you add the `-ProtectFromScaleIn` parameter and set the value to $true. For example, the following code shows how to use this parameter in a PowerShell script for a VMSS:

```
#Define variables
$RG = "VMSS-RG01"
$VMSSName = "VMSS-01"
#Update Instance protection config
Update-AzVmssVM `
  -ResourceGroupName $RG `
  -VMScaleSetName $VMSSName `
  -InstanceId 0 `
  -ProtectFromScaleIn $true
```

USING THE AZURE CLI

When using the Azure CLI to create a scale set, you can use the `--protect-from-scale-in` parameter with a value of `true` or `false` to turn Instance Protection on or off. For example, the following code shows how to use this parameter in a Bash script for a VMSS:

```
#Define variables
rg="VMSS-RG01"
vmssname="VMSS-01"

#Update Instance protection config
az vmss update \
  --resource-group $rg \
  --name $vmssname \
  --instance-id 0 \
  --protect-from-scale-in true
```

Use proximity placement groups

All VMs in a single scale set are generally placed in a single Azure region. In theory, this reduces the physical distance between the instances. Using availability zones can help achieve a similar outcome. However, a single availability zone can be spread across multiple physical datacenters, which can result in much higher network latency than the application deployed on the scale set might support. To address this, you can use proximity placement groups. Proximity placement groups ensure that the VMs you use are located as close together as possible to achieve the lowest possible latency and avoid application performance issues.

Proximity placement groups can be used for VM instances in an availability set, VM instances in a single scale set or multiple scale sets, and standalone VMs. This enables multi-tiered applications to have all their interdependent workloads hosted close to each other to reduce latency across the stack.

> **TIP** It is a best practice to configure proximity placement groups at the scale set resource level rather than on individual VMs.

Proximity placement groups walkthrough

The following sections step you through the process of defining proximity placement groups using the Azure Portal, Azure PowerShell, and the Azure CLI. If you are following along, be sure to select resources and resource names based on your environment, including unique VMSS, vNET, and subnet names for each of your deployments. Also, be sure to delete any unwanted resources after you have completed testing to avoid charges levied by Microsoft for these resources.

USING THE AZURE PORTAL

To define a proximity placement group using the Azure Portal at VMSS creation, follow these steps:

1. Follow the steps in the "VMSS creation walkthrough" section to start the Create a Virtual Machine Scale Set wizard and create a VMSS.

2. In the **Advanced** tab, under **Proximity Placement Group**, open the **Proximity Placement Group** drop-down list and choose the group you want to use. (See Figure 2-38.)

> **NOTE** The proximity placement group you want to use must be created in advance so you can select it during scale set creation.

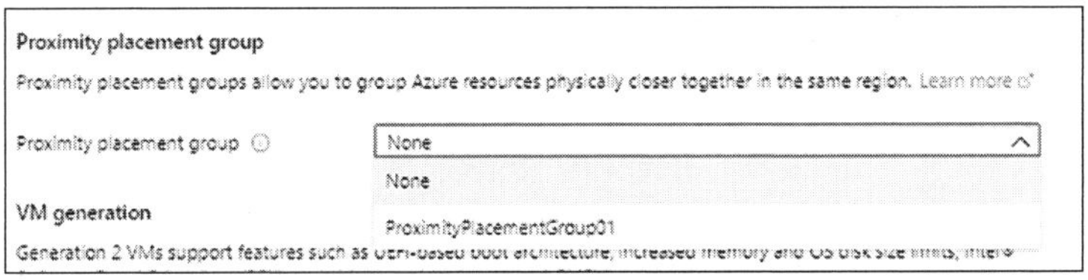

FIGURE 2-38 Set up a proximity placement group.

3. Finish using the VM Scale Set Creation wizard to create the VMSS, as described in the section "VMSS creation walkthrough."

USING AZURE POWERSHELL

When using Azure PowerShell, you can assign a VMSS to a proximity placement group during the creation process by defining the –ProximityPlacementGroupId parameter with the resource ID of the proximity placement group. To move an existing VMSS to a proximity placement group, use the following code snippet:

```
#Define variables
$RG = "RG01"
$location = "EastUS2"
$ppgroupName = "PPG-VMSS-01"
$vmscaleset = "VMSS-ScaleSet"

#Create Proximity Placement group
$ppgroup = New-AzProximityPlacementGroup -Location $location `
   -Name $ppgroupName `
   -ResourceGroupName $RG `
   -ProximityPlacementGroupType Standard
#Move an existing scale set into the proximity group
""
#Stop vm scale set
```

```
Stop-AzVmss -VMScaleSetName $vmscaleset.Name -ResourceGroupName $RG
#update scale set config
Update-AzVmss -VMScaleSetName $vmscaleset.Name -ResourceGroupName $RG -ProximityPlace-
mentGroupId $ppgroup.Id
Start-AzVmss -VMScaleSetName $vmscaleset.Name -ResourceGroupName $RG
```

USING THE AZURE CLI

When using the Azure CLI, you can set up a proximity placement group for VMSS during the creation process by defining the `--ppg` parameter with the resource ID of the proximity placement group. To do so, you must have created the proximity placement group before creating the scale set, as shown in the following sample code snippet:

```
#define variables
ppg="VMSS-PPG"
rg="RG01"
location="eastus"
vmssname="VMSS01"
#create proximity placement group
az ppg create \
    -n $ppg \
    -g $rg \
    -l $location\
    -t standard
#create scale set with the proximity placement group
az vmss create -n $vmssname -g $rg --instance-count 5 --image Win2019Datacenter --os-
disk-size-gb 40 --ppg $ppg
```

Check and increase vCPU quotas

There are two types of vCPU quotas currently available in Azure: one on the regional level and one on the VM family level. Any new VM deployment must meet the CPU limits available for both these quotas. If there are not enough vCPUs available for either of these two quotas, then the VM deployment will fail. In addition, there is a limit on the number of VMs that can be provisioned in a specific region.

It is important to be aware of these limits so scaling operations are not affected. You can check current consumption on the Subscription page in the Azure Portal in the Usage + Quotas section or by using Azure PowerShell. If consumption is too high for either the regional or VM family quota, it is recommended that you request an increase by logging a ticket with Microsoft support or by deleting unwanted or unused VMs from the subscription.

Enable termination notifications

During scale-in operations on VM instances in a scale set, the sudden loss of an instance can result in user data loss if the application is not set up to handle such activities efficiently. If termination notifications have been enabled for the scale set, the system sends a notification via the Azure Instance Metadata Service to record any termination activities. You can also set up a termination delay, which enables the transfer of load or traffic from the soon-to-be-terminated instance to other active instances in the scale set.

> **TIP**   It is helpful to test this functionality with the application deployed on the scale set to see how it affects the behavior of the scale set and the app, and if improvement in availability is achieved.

> **NOTE**   Termination notifications cannot be set on existing scale sets in Azure Portal.

Termination notification walkthrough

The following sections step you through the process of setting up termination notifications using the Azure Portal, Azure PowerShell, and the Azure CLI. If you are following along, be sure to select resources and resource names based on your environment, including unique VMSS, vNET, and subnet names for each of your deployments. Also, be sure to delete any unwanted resources after you have completed testing to avoid charges levied by Microsoft for these resources.

USING THE AZURE PORTAL

To set up termination notifications using the Azure Portal during VMSS creation, follow these steps:

1. Follow the steps in the "VMSS creation walkthrough" section to start the Create a Virtual Machine Scale Set wizard and create a VMSS.

2. In the **Management** tab, under **Instance Termination**, select the **Enable Instance Termination Notification** check box.

3. Drag the **Termination Delay (Minutes)** slider to the number of minutes you want the system to wait before sending the termination notification. (See Figure 2-39.)

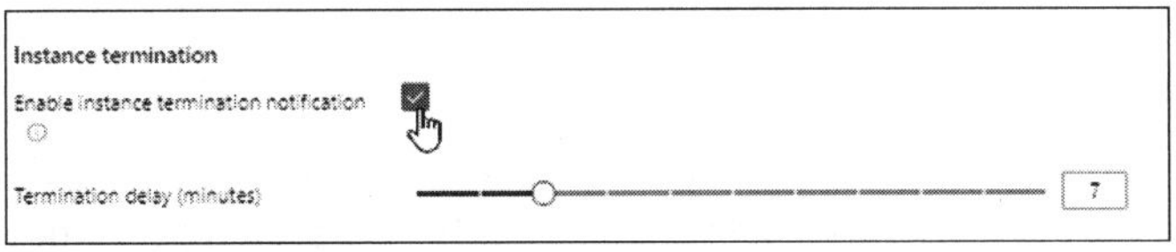

FIGURE 2-39   Set up instance termination notification.

4. Finish using the VM Scale Set Creation wizard to create the VMSS, as described in the section "VMSS creation walkthrough."

Choosing a termination delay

Consider the following factors when deciding on the termination delay:

- **Termination notifications only on delete operations** All delete operations (manual autoscale-initiated scale-in) generate termination events if your scale set has the scheduledEventsProfile parameter enabled. Other operations, such as reboot, reimage, redeploy, and stop/deallocate, do not generate termination events. Termination notifications can't be enabled for low-priority VMs.

- **No mandatory wait for timeout** You can start the termination operation at any time after the event has been received and before the event's NotBefore time expires.

- **Mandatory delete at timeout** There is no capability to extend the timeout value after an event has been generated. When the timeout expires, the pending termination event will be processed and the VM will be deleted.

- **Modifiable timeout value** You can modify the timeout value any time before an instance is deleted by modifying the notBeforeTimeout property on the scale set model and updating the VM instances to the latest model.

- **Approve all pending deletes** If there's a pending delete on VM_1 that isn't approved, and you've approved another termination event on VM_2, then VM_2 isn't deleted until the termination event for VM_1 is approved or its timeout has elapsed. After you approve the termination event for VM_1, both VM_1 and VM_2 are deleted.

- **Approve all simultaneous deletes** Extending the preceding example, if VM_1 and VM_2 have the same NotBefore time, then both termination events must be approved or neither VM will be deleted before the timeout expires.

USING AZURE POWERSHELL

You can set up termination notifications using Azure PowerShell with the –TerminateScheduledEvents and –TerminateScheduledEventNotBeforeTimeoutInMinutes parameters. The –TerminateScheduledEvents parameter can be set to either $true or $false. The –TerminateScheduledEventNotBeforeTimeoutInMinutes value needs to be defined with the minutes after which the termination timeout must take place. For example, the following code shows how to do this in a PowerShell script for a VMSS:

```
#Define variables
$location="EastUS2"
```

```
#Setup VMSS with termination notification configuration
New-AzVmssConfig `
  -Location $location `
  -SkuCapacity 2 `
  -SkuName "Standard_DS3v4" `
  -UpgradePolicyMode "Automatic" `
  -TerminateScheduledEvents $true `
  -TerminateScheduledEventNotBeforeTimeoutInMinutes 10
```

USING THE AZURE CLI

You can set up termination notifications using the Azure CLI with the `--terminate-notification-time` parameter with a timeout value in integer form based on the minutes for the timeout to be set. For example, the following code shows how to use this parameter in a Bash script for a VMSS:

```
#Define variables
rg="VMSS-RG01"
vmssname="VMSS-01"
adminusername="vmssadmin"
#Create VMSS with termination notification config
az vmss create --resource-group $rg \
  --name $vmssname \
  --image UbuntuLTS \
  --admin-username $adminusername \
  --generate-ssh-keys \
  --terminate-notification-time 20
```

Azure maintenance best practices

To enhance the stability, reliability, security, responsiveness, and performance of the underlying host infrastructure on which VMs are hosted, Microsoft Azure must perform updates on a periodic basis. These updates can be on the software or hardware level in the form of OS updates or upgrades or hardware replacement.

Microsoft performs these updates such that there are no anticipated outages on the underlying infrastructure that might affect any VM workloads running on them. However, on occasion, Microsoft may require maintenance on the underlying host, which will cause your VMs to be paused during the reboot window.

In such cases, Microsoft will convey this to the admins assigned to your Azure subscription well in advance and will await a response. If you do not respond to Microsoft, Azure's back-end service automatically performs the maintenance. If you do respond, Microsoft will expect you to carry out the required maintenance on your underlying host on your own within 35 days and provide you with the necessary steps to do so. If you fail to perform this maintenance, Azure will automatically initiate the upgrade.

For highly available infrastructure like scale sets, it is advantageous to have a pre-defined process to manage these updates on an ongoing basis. This helps ensure that when any notifications are received from Microsoft Azure regarding required maintenance, a clearly defined set of steps is carried out in an efficient manner.

Some best practices for planned maintenance are as follows:

- **Multiple admins get alerts** Set up numerous parties to receive alerts. Alerts are typically sent to the subscription owner and co-owners, but more recipients can be added by targeting activity log events.

- **Communication planning** Notify all affected parties of the upcoming maintenance requirements well in advance and after the maintenance is complete.

- **Detailed process documentation** Have a clearly documented process in place for activities to be carried out before and after the maintenance.

- **Validate the environment** Do this after the maintenance to ensure everything is working as expected.

- **Internal cross-org coordination** Ensure no other maintenance or upgrade activities are taking place around the same time.

- **Design with high availability in mind** Any unplanned downtime should not affect the overall environment.

Networking considerations and best practices

When you deploy an Azure VMSS using the Azure Portal, certain network properties are set by default—for example, a default Azure load balancer with inbound NAT rules is assigned. Depending on requirements—especially security requirements—you might need to change the default configuration. Before making such changes, be sure to discuss this with your security team to ensure you are in alignment with the appropriate policies.

Commonly used features that can be modified from the default configuration include the following:

- **Accelerated Networking** Accelerated Networking improves the network performance of a NIC by enabling single root I/O virtualization (SR-IOV) for a VM. If your environment calls for the use of this functionality, you should set the `"enableAcceleratedNetworking"` parameter to `true` in the scale set's `"networkInterfaceConfigurations"` settings or template during scale set creation.

- **DNS settings** By default, scale sets take on the specific DNS settings of the VNET and subnet in which they were created. You can, however, configure the DNS settings for a scale set directly as part of the template code. This can help ensure that the scale set is aligned with your organization's DNS-related network requirements.

- **Public IPv4 per VM** In general, individual VMs in a scale set do not require their own public IP addresses. For most scenarios, it is more secure and economical to have a single public IP associated with the load balancer or with a jumpbox in that scale set. The jumpbox helps route, control, and monitor incoming connections to the scale set. There are exceptions to this, however, such as in scenarios where workloads require direct public connectivity using unique IP addresses. In such cases, you might consider adding individual public IPs per VM.

- **Network security groups (NSGs)** NSGs allow the filtering and control of traffic to and from resources in an Azure network or an Azure VM. They also allow for the creation of security rules that detail the source, scope, protocol, and port parameters to control said traffic. You can apply an existing or pre-defined NSG to a scale set during the creation process on the Networking tab of the VM Scale Set Creation wizard, in the Network Interface section.

- **Multiple IPs per VM network interface** Every NIC attached to each individual VM in a scale set can have one or more IP configurations associated with it. Each configuration is assigned one private IP address by default based on the subnet for the scale set. In addition, each configuration can have one public IP address associated with it.

- **Multiple NICs per VM** Larger VMs can have multiple NICs. The maximum number at this time is eight NICs per VM, but it differs between VM SKUs. If multiple NICs are required per VM, you can easily achieve this if the IP address space on the virtual network and subnet(s) have been sized appropriately. It is important to note that all NICs connected to a VM in a scale set must connect to the same virtual network. The NICs can connect to different subnets, but all subnets must be part of the same virtual network.

- **Application security groups (ASGs)** ASGs help manage VM security by grouping VMs according to the applications that run on them. This allows for the use of NSGs in an application-centric manner. You can configure an existing or pre-defined ASG during the VMSS creation process in the Networking tab of the VM Scale Set Creation wizard, in the Network Interface section.

Now that we have covered all the networking features that can benefit a scale set, let's dive deeper into various high availability, redundancy, and management options.

VMSS deployment best practices

To streamline the deployment of VM Instances in a VMSS, consider the following points when formulating your deployment strategy.

Use a custom golden image

To use an application on VM instances in a scale set, there are two approaches you can take. The recommended approach is to use the application installer to create a custom VM OS image. This "golden" image should be built to auto-trigger any pre-install or post-install configuration steps using scripts so that no admin or user intervention is required during scaling operations.

The other option is to use the default OS images, called platform images in Azure, to create VM instances. In this scenario, the required application install should be automated using scripting, third-party application deployment solutions, or in the case of Windows Servers, group policy. Note that, with this approach, the time required to get the new VM instance in "usable" mode, ready to accept user connections, increases. Depending on the number of changes that need to be performed, there can be application access or performance issues. In addition, you may need to monitor or validate the functioning of the application after each scale-out operation to confirm that all required changes have taken place correctly. This can result in more complexity in your deployment and day-to-day maintenance and management. That is why it is best to adopt the golden image–based deployment option in your environment if you can, as it will help streamline the deployment and application upgrade process.

Use the Custom Script Extension for app configuration

Custom Script Extension (CSE) allows you to automate the install of applications on Azure VMs. Although you can use this approach for application installs after an instance deployment, it is recommended to instead use it only for any post-deployment configuration that must be performed on each new VM instance that you cannot incorporate in the golden image.

The CSE engine requires scripts to be provided in the Azure Portal when the extension is configured or to host them in GitHub or an Azure blob storage and reference them during configuration. The engine then uses the script directly if provided or downloads it for use at execution.

Use Windows PowerShell Desired State Configuration

Windows PowerShell Desired State Configuration (DSC) is an essential component for setup, configuration, and management of Windows Servers. In large environments that make extensive use of scale sets, it gets difficult over time to monitor and maintain the known good state of every VM instance. Windows PowerShell DSC provides a free option to help monitor and maintain this configuration state, removing the need for you to procure and deploy other complex third-party solutions.

PowerShell DSC is a configuration as code (CaC) technology that uses GitHub to enable you to configure Windows OS and deployed applications using a configuration file and Windows PowerShell.

Every VM instance has a built-in engine, which performs the required actions that you have pushed out. Using this approach, you can completely automate the ongoing monitoring and management configuration of VM instances, reducing management overhead.

Use cloud-init for Linux VMs

Similar to Windows PowerShell DSC, you can use cloud-init to perform the same set of tasks for a Linux VM. You can also use cloud-init to configure the users and security settings inside the Linux OS.

Cloud-init is compatible with most Linux distributions, and automatically uses the native tool on each distribution for command execution. This standardization makes it easy to deploy applications without customizing the install commands for each distribution type.

OS and data disks for scale sets

You can use different disk types on VM scale sets, depending on the availability, redundancy, reliability, and cost considerations for your environment. The following sections review each of these disk options in more detail to allow you to make a more informed choice for your workloads.

Disk types

VMSS currently support different disk types for use with either the OS or data disks on VM instances. These disk types are as follows:

- **Premium SSD** Currently the fastest disk types available for scale sets. These disks provide the maximum input/output operations per second (IOPS) and higher performance than other supported disk types. They are, however, the most expensive disk options, so you must consider actual application requirements and associated budgets before choosing this disk type. Premium SSD disks are supported by specific VM series like DSv2-Series, FS, and GS-series VMs. VM instances must use one of these VM series to be able to use Premium SSD disks.

- **Standard SSD** A great option for workloads that require a consistent level of performance that is higher in IOPS than Standard HDD disks but not as high as Premium SSD disks. Standard SSD disks deliver much higher redundancy, consistency, and latency than HDD disks. They are suitable for applications that need low IOPS, like web servers, small lightly used applications, and some dev/test workloads. Standard SSDs provide low–single digit millisecond latency. However, at times, actual IOPS and throughput may vary.

- **Standard HDD** Provide a significantly lower amount of IOPS than SSD disks. Standard HDD disks are, however, the cheapest disk option. They are suitable for applications where the IOPS requirements can be met using HDD disks and for dev and test workloads.

Disk types walkthrough

The following section steps you through the process of assigning a disk type to a VMSS using the Azure Portal.

To assign a disk type to a VMSS using Azure Portal during VMSS creation, follow these steps:

1. Follow the steps in the "VMSS creation walkthrough" section to start the Create a Virtual Machine Scale Set wizard and create a VMSS.

2. In the **Disks** tab, under **Disk Options**, open the **OS Disk Type** drop-down list and choose **Premium SSD**, **Standard SSD**, or **Standard HDD**. (See Figure 2-40.)

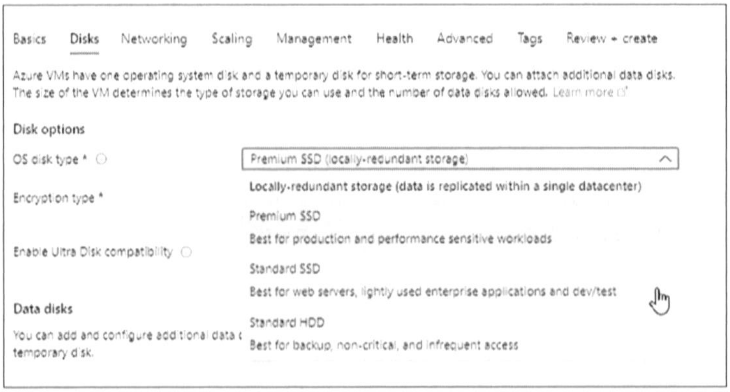

FIGURE 2-40   Set up disk options.

3. Finish using the VM Scale Set Creation wizard to create the VMSS, as described in the section "VMSS creation walkthrough."

Managed disks

Due to the high-availability requirements of scale sets, it is critical to use managed disks in conjunction with scale sets. These provide a very high level of resiliency by isolating disks for the different VM instances to reduce single points of failure in the architecture. When you integrate managed disks and scale sets, the loss of individual VM instances will not affect other VM instances or cause a major outage.

> **TIP**   You should always use managed disks with a scale set unless other technical limitations require the use of user-managed storage.

Managed disks walkthrough

Managed disks are enabled by default when you select the OS disk type. This section steps you through the process of confirming they are set up during scale set creation using the Azure Portal.

To confirm that managed disks are enabled for a scale set using the Azure Portal during VMSS creation, follow these steps:

1. Follow the steps in the "VMSS creation walkthrough" section to start the Create a Virtual Machine Scale Set wizard and create a VMSS.

2. Select the OS disk type. (See the "Disk types walkthrough" section for more information.)

3. Scroll to the **Advanced** section and ensure the **Use Managed Disks** check box is selected. (See Figure 2-41.)

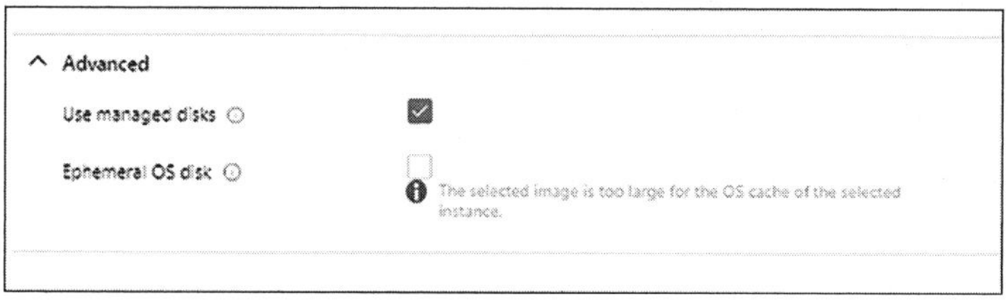

FIGURE 2-41   Confirm managed disks are set up for the scale set.

4. Finish using the VM Scale Set Creation wizard to create the VMSS, as described in the section "VMSS creation walkthrough."

User-managed storage

If managed disks are not preferable for use with a particular scale set, your other option is to employ a user-managed storage account to store the VM disks for all the VMs in the scale set. At present, you are limited to using 20 VMs per storage account. However, achieving higher IO throughput in the storage layer might result in a lower number of VMs being provisioned per account.

> **TIP**   When naming storage accounts, start each name with a different character. Also, use as many storage accounts as possible to help spread the load across the storage layer in the Azure back end.

User-managed storage walkthrough

The following section steps you through the process of setting up user-managed storage using the Azure Portal.

USING THE AZURE PORTAL

To configure the VM OS disk to be user-managed using the Azure Portal during VMSS creation, follow these steps:

1. Follow the steps in the "VMSS creation walkthrough" section to start the Create a Virtual Machine Scale Set wizard and create a VMSS.

2. Select the OS disk type. (See the "Disk types walkthrough" section for more information.)

3. Scroll to the **Advanced** section and deselect the **Use Managed Disks** check box. (See Figure 2-42.)

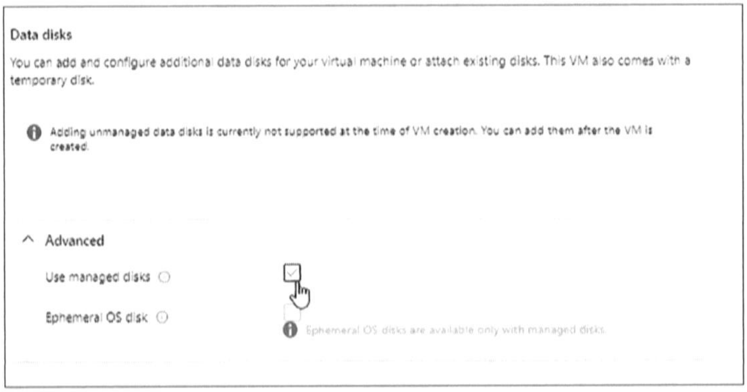

FIGURE 2-42 Set up user-managed storage.

4. Finish using the VM Scale Set Creation wizard to create the VMSS, as described in the section "VMSS creation walkthrough."

Data disks

Azure VMSS supports the use of data disks for VM instances when the scale set is created or at a later stage if the need arises. Note that simply adding the disk does not make it usable. The disk must also be mounted and formatted within the OS. Using the Custom Script Extension discussed earlier to perform these activities is advisable to reduce management overhead for subsequent operations.

Data disks can be empty (the default). Alternatively, you can duplicate an existing data disk and attach it to all VM instances in a scale set. If you are using a custom golden image, you can include the data disk containing the required data in the image. Then, when the scale set is provisioned using the custom image, it will have all the required data.

Adding unmanaged data disks is currently not supported at the time of VM creation. You can add them after the VM is created, however. Data disks are supported by and can be added and managed using the Azure Portal, Azure PowerShell, the Azure CLI, Azure templates, SDKs, and the REST API.

Data disks walkthrough

The following sections step you through the process of setting up data disks Using the Azure Portal. If you are following along, be sure to select resources and resource names based on your environment, including unique VMSS, vNET, and subnet names for each of your deployments. Also, be sure to delete any unwanted resources after you have completed testing to avoid charges levied by Microsoft for these resources.

USING THE AZURE PORTAL

To set up data disks using the Azure Portal during VMSS creation, follow these steps:

1. Follow the steps in the "VMSS creation walkthrough" section to start the Create a Virtual Machine Scale Set wizard and create a VMSS.

2. In the **Disks** tab, click the **Create and Attach a New Disk** link. (See Figure 2-43.)

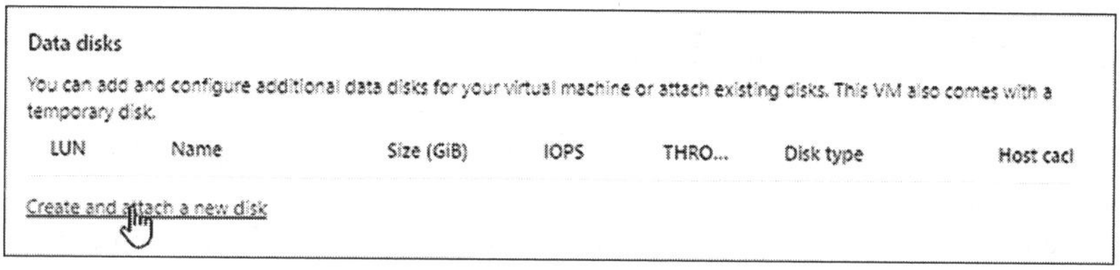

FIGURE 2-43 Set up data disks.

3. The Create a New Disk dialog box opens. (See Figure 2-44.) Type a name for the new disk in the **Name** box. Then do any of the following before clicking **OK**:

   - Set a source type by opening the **Source Type** drop-down list and choosing from the available options.

   - Change the size of the disk by clicking the **Size** link. Then, in the **Disk Size** dialog box, choose an account type, select a disk size, and click **OK**.

   - Choose an encryption type by opening the **Encryption Type** drop-down list and choosing from the available options. (The default type is encryption at rest with a platform-managed key.)

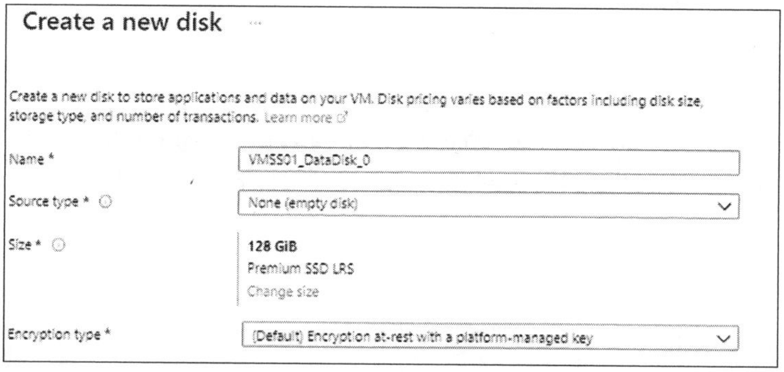

FIGURE 2-44 Create a New Disk dialog box.

The disk you created appears in the Data Disks area of the Disks tab. (See Figure 2-45.)

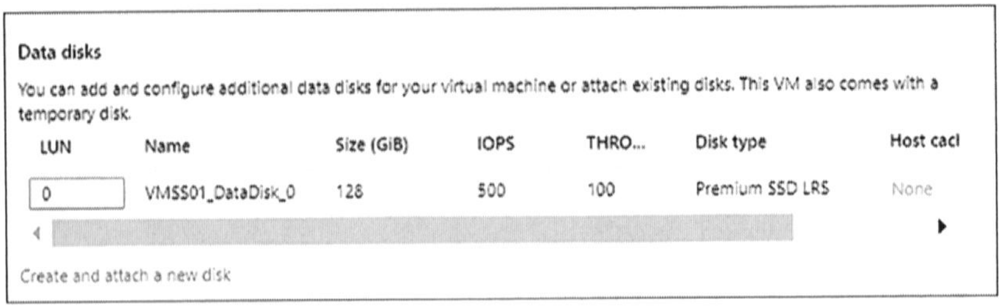

Data disks

You can add and configure additional data disks for your virtual machine or attach existing disks. This VM also comes with a temporary disk.

LUN	Name	Size (GiB)	IOPS	THRO...	Disk type	Host cacl
0	VMSS01_DataDisk_0	128	500	100	Premium SSD LRS	None

Create and attach a new disk

FIGURE 2-45   Data disks on LUN 0.

4. Finish using the VM Scale Set Creation wizard to create the VMSS, as described in the section "VMSS creation walkthrough."

Strategies for cost optimization

Microsoft provides various options to help you manage costs associated with the VM instances in a VMSS. Depending on your application design, cost-control requirements, and application capabilities, you will likely be able to benefit from some, if not most, of these options.

Spot instances

Like individual VMs, VM instances in a VMSS can be set up as Azure spot instances. This offers significant cost savings when performing scale-out operations.

Spot instances depend on the capacity available in the specific region based on the VM size, time of day, and other factors, so they do affect a scale set's availability. Therefore, specific use cases like dev/test environments, batch jobs, and similar workloads, and web applications with no user affinity requirements are great candidates for spot instances.

> **NOTE** Depending on the application or workload deployed on a scale set, spot instances can be a great option to reduce compute costs.

> **NOTE** You must set up spot instances when you create a VMSS. Once a scale set has been created, you cannot add a spot instance to it. You will need to re-create the scale set.

When you use spot instances, there is a risk of Azure evicting VMs if it needs the capacity back. However, you can establish eviction policies to dictate when and how this occurs, and what happens next.

Eviction policies are similar to the deallocation and delete options discussed in Chapter 1 of this book. If a scale set's VM instances are built from custom images and a new one can be easily brought up without manual intervention or long processing times, it might be best to set the policy to delete instead of deallocate because removing the underlying VM disk results in additional cost savings. Additionally, if you deallocate rather than delete the VMs, those VMs would count against the scale set's capacity. Moreover, being spot instances, if they can't be brought online, it would limit the number of instances that could be made available in other zonal regions to achieve capacity requirements. Setting the eviction policy to delete would alleviate this problem.

At the time of eviction, there is a 30-second window to complete any outstanding jobs before shutdown is performed. Hence, it is advisable to stress-test this in different workload scenarios to make sure there are no application errors, data loss, or locked jobs or transactions.

Spot instances walkthrough

The following sections step you through the process of setting up spot instances using the Azure Portal, Azure PowerShell, and the Azure CLI.

USING THE AZURE PORTAL

To set up spot instances using the Azure Portal during VMSS creation, follow these steps:

1. Follow the steps in the "VMSS creation walkthrough" section to start the Create a Virtual Machine Scale Set wizard and create a VMSS.

2. In the Basics tab, in the **Instance Details** section, select the **Azure Spot Instance** check box.

3. In the **Eviction Type** options that appear, select one of the following options (see Figure 2-46):

   - **Capacity Only...** Choose this eviction model if you want to evict VM spot instances if Azure needs capacity for pay-as-you-go workloads.

   - **Price or Capacity...** Choose this eviction model to specify a maximum price that you are willing to pay to run the spot instance every hour. If the cost of the instance goes beyond your maximum price, Azure will evict your VM if it needs capacity for pay-as-you-go workloads.

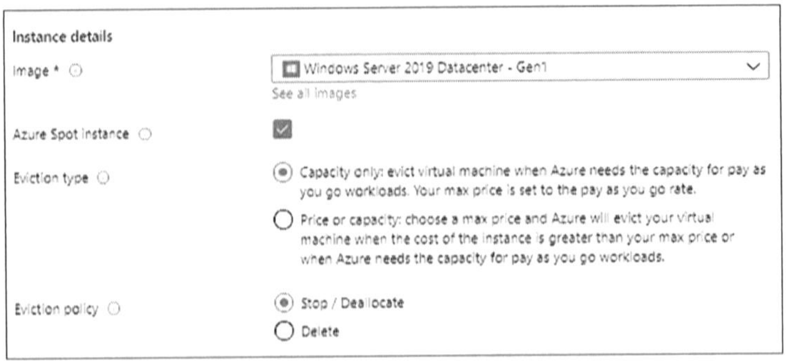

FIGURE 2-46 Eviction type options for spot instances.

4. Open the **Size** drop-down list and choose a size for the spot instance.

5. Type a maximum price in the **Maximum Price You Want to Pay Per Hour** box. (See Figure 2-47.)

> **TIP** Choose your maximum price based on historical reviews of spot prices in a particular region for a particular SKU and any budgetary considerations you might have regarding the workload.

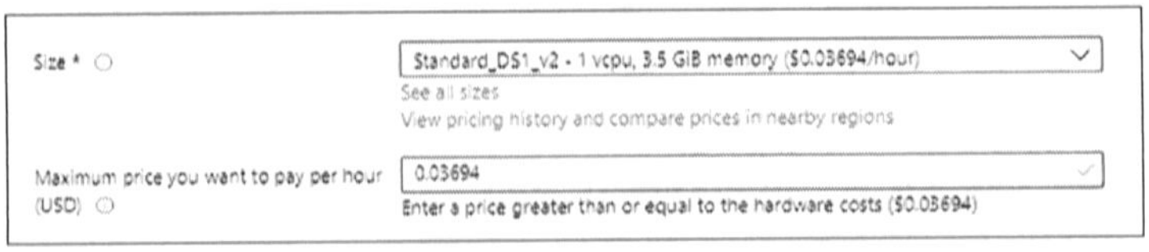

FIGURE 2-47 Choose a size for your spot instance and specify your maximum price per hour.

6. In the **Eviction Policy** section, choose one of the following options (see Figure 2-48):

- **Stop/Deallocate**   Choose this option if you want Azure to stop and deallocate an evicted spot instance so it can quickly be brought back online at a later stage. When you check this option, Azure retains the underlying disk(s), as well as any data contained within the spot instance.

- **Delete**   Choose this option if you want Azure to remove the evicted spot instance and its underlying disks. If the VMSS does not store data locally on the disks of the VMs, then this would be the best option, as it will save considerable costs.

> **TIP** Storing data locally on the VM disks in a scale set is not recommended.

FIGURE 2-48 Set up the eviction policy for spot instances.

7. Finish using the VM Scale Set Creation wizard to create the VMSS, as described in the section "VMSS creation walkthrough."

USING AZURE POWERSHELL

You can use Azure PowerShell to set up spot instances when creating a VMSS by adding the parameters '-Priority "Spot"' and '-max-price xx' (where xx is the maximum price for the spot instance) to the code or script. If you do not want spot instances to be evicted for price reasons, set -max-price to -1. (If -max-price is not specified, it will be set to -1 by default.) For example, the following code shows how to create a VMSS in the East US 2 region with spot instances that use a delete eviction policy and have a maximum price per hour of 0.01538:

```
#Define variables
$location = "East US 2"
$RG = "VMSS-RG01"
$vmssname = "VMSS01"
#Create vmss config for Spot instances
$vmssConfig = New-AzVmssConfig `
    -Location $location `
    -SkuCapacity 2 `
    -SkuName "Standard_DS2" `
    -UpgradePolicyMode Automatic `
    -SinglePlacementGroup False `
    -Priority "Spot" `
    -max-price 0.01538 `
    -EvictionPolicy Delete
#Create scale set with above config
New-AzVmss -ResourceGroupName $RG -Name $vmssname -VirtualMachineScaleSet $vmssConfig
```

USING THE AZURE CLI

You can use the Azure CLI to set up spot instances when creating a VMSS by adding the parameters '--Priority Spot' and '--max-price xx' (where xx is the maximum price for the spot instance) to the code. If you do not want spot instances to be evicted for price reasons, set the --max-price to -1. (If --max-price is not specified, it will be set to -1 by default.) For example, the following code shows how to create a VMSS (UbuntuScaleSet01) with the UbuntuLTS image and spot instances that use a delete eviction policy with a maximum price of 0.01538:

```
#Define variables
location="East US 2"
rg="VMSS-RG01"
vmssname="VMSS01"
adminusername="vmssadmin"
#Create vmss config for Spot instances
az vmss create --resource-group $rg \
```

```
--location $location \
--vm-sku Standard_DS2 \
--name $vmssname \
--image UbuntuLTS \
--single-placement-group false \
--admin-username $adminusername \
--generate-ssh-keys \
--priority Spot \
--max-price 0.01538 \
--eviction-policy Delete
```

Reserved instances

Like individual VMs, VMSS can benefit from reserved instances (RIs). To recap, RIs are VMs that are reserved on the Azure platform for a specific period of time, which can vary from one to three years. When a VM is set up as a reserved instance, the underlying hardware resources for that VM are reserved, ensuring that the VM will have access to them regardless of whether it is placed offline during the reservation period, no matter how long.

For scale sets, because the number of VMs constantly changes based on fluctuations in the utilization of resources and on your scaling policies, it might be best to start by reserving the minimum number of instances that can run at any given time in the scale set. Then, monitor the peak utilization window and VM instance requirements for the application at peak capacity. If you determine that setting up RIs for your VMSS results in cost savings, you can set them up for more of your VM instances.

Dedicated hosts

You can use dedicated hosts to host a VMSS, the same way you can individual VMs. During scale set creation, you simply specify a host group containing the dedicated hosts you want to use.

For this to work correctly, there are a few prerequisites and best practices:

- Be sure the availability settings on the VMSS and host group match. This ensures that their availability configurations are aligned. The fault domain count for the VMSS and host group should also match to ensure that VMs are spread correctly.
- You should provision dedicated hosts in advance with sufficient capacity to host the scale set VM instances. Otherwise, VM creation during VMSS creation will fail.
- The placement of VMs in the host group should be set to automatic. Manual management causes issues with new VM provisioning on scale-out operations.
- Finalize the VM SKUs required for the VM instances so that the SKU of the dedicated host can be set up to match. This will ensure that VM instances for that SKU are supported for provisioning on the dedicated host(s).
- Do not use proximity placement groups.

- Avoid provisioning VMs. Alternatively, make sure that the capacity of your dedicated host is enough to handle overprovisioned VMs. That way, there are no failures during deployment or scaling operations.

Dedicated hosts walkthrough

The following sections step you through the process of setting up a dedicated host configuration for a VMSS during VMSS creation using the Azure Portal, Azure PowerShell, and the Azure CLI. If you are following along, be sure to select resources and resource names based on your environment, including unique VMSS, vNET, and subnet names for each of your deployments. Also, be sure to delete any unwanted resources after you have completed testing to avoid charges levied by Microsoft for these resources.

USING THE AZURE PORTAL

To set up dedicated hosts configuration using the Azure Portal during VMSS creation, follow these steps:

1. Create a dedicated host by following the steps covered in Chapter 1.

2. Follow the steps in the "VMSS creation walkthrough" section to start the Create a Virtual Machine Scale Set wizard and create a VMSS.

3. In the **Advanced** tab, under **Host**, open the **Host Group** drop-down list and select the host group you want to use. (See Figure 2-49.)

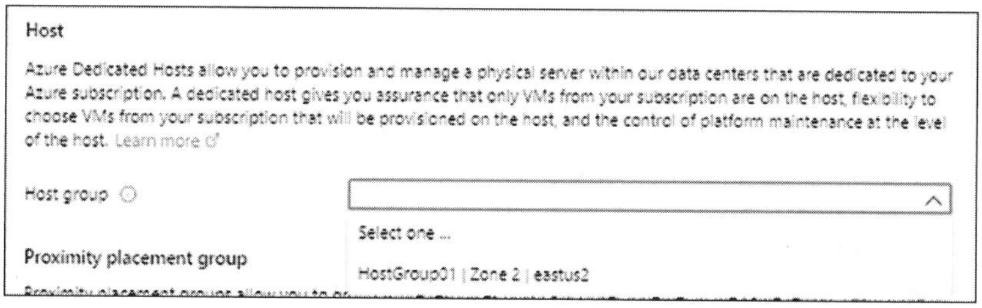

FIGURE 2-49 Set up a dedicated host.

4. Finish using the VM Scale Set Creation wizard to create the VMSS, as described in the section "VMSS creation walkthrough."

USING AZURE POWERSHELL

You can use Azure PowerShell to create a Windows Server–based VMSS with a dedicated host using the New-AzHostGroup and New-AzHost parameters. If you want to manually choose which host to deploy the scale set to, add the --host parameter with the name of the host. For example, the following code shows how to use these parameters in a PowerShell script for VMSS creation based on the setup done earlier using the Azure Portal:

```
#Define variables
$RG = "VMSS-RG01"
```

```
$location = "East US 2"
$hostgroup = "VMSS-HostGroup01"
$hostname = "VMSS-Host01"
$vmssname = "VMSS01"
$vnet = "VMSS01-vNET"
$subnet = "VMSS01-Subnet"
$vmsspip = "VMSS01-PIP"
$vmsslb = "VMSS01-Loadbalancer"
New-AzResourceGroup -Location $location -Name $rgName
$hostGroup = New-AzHostGroup `
    -Location $location `
    -Name $hostgroup `
    -PlatformFaultDomain 2 `
    -ResourceGroupName $RG `
    -Zone 1

#Create the Dedicated Host
$dHost = New-AzHost `
    -HostGroupName $hostGroup.Name `
    -Location $location -Name $hostname `
    -ResourceGroupName $RG `
    -Sku DSv3-Type1 `
    -AutoReplaceOnFailure 1 `
    -PlatformFaultDomain 1

#Create a new scale set in the host group
New-AzVmss `
    -ResourceGroupName $RG `
    -Location $location `
    -VMScaleSetName $vmssname `
    -VirtualNetworkName $vnet `
    -SubnetName $subnet `
    -PublicIpAddressName $vmsspip `
    -LoadBalancerName $vmsslb `
    -UpgradePolicyMode "Automatic"'
    -HostGroupId $hostGroup.Id
```

USING THE AZURE CLI

You can use the Azure CLI to create a Windows Server–based VMSS with a dedicated host using the az vm host group create and az vm host create commands and their related parameters. For example, the following code shows how to use this in a Bash script for VMSS creation based on the setup done earlier using the Azure Portal:

```
#Define variables
rg="VMSS-RG01"
location="EastUS2"
```

```
hostgroup="VMSS-HostGroup01"
hostname="VMSS-Host01"
adminusername="vmssadmin"
vmssname="VMSS01"
#Create a host group for the VMSS
az vm host group create \
    --name $hostgroup \
    -g $rg \
    -z 1 \
    --platform-fault-domain-count 2
    --automatic-placement true
#Create a Dedicated Host
az vm host create \
    --host-group $hostgroup\
    --name $hostname\
    --sku ESv3-Type1 \
    --platform-fault-domain 1 \
    -g $rg

#Create a VMSS
az vmss create \
  --resource-group $rg \
  --name $vmssname \
  --image UbuntuLTS \
  --upgrade-policy-mode automatic \
  --admin-username $adminusername \
  --host-group $hostgroup \
  --generate-ssh-keys \
  --size Standard_D2s_v3 \
  --zone 1
```

Azure Hybrid Benefit

You can apply the Azure Hybrid Benefit to VM instances in a scale set. Azure Hybrid Benefit is a licensing benefit that enables you to use your own on-premises Windows Server license to license servers in Azure. To do this, you must have Software Assurance or a Windows Server subscription. Using Azure Hybrid Benefit can help you significantly reduce the costs of running your workloads because you pay only for compute costs. Azure Hybrid Benefit works with both Windows and Linux VMSS.

> **NOTE** It is highly recommended that you approach your Microsoft account manager or Microsoft software licensing partner for clarity on whether your licensing qualifies for this benefit before attempting to apply it. The same is applicable for any Linux distributions that you intend to use with Azure Hybrid Benefit.

Azure Hybrid Benefit for Windows VMSS walkthrough

The following sections step you through the process of setting up Azure Hybrid Benefit for a VMSS in Windows using the Azure Portal, Azure PowerShell, the Azure CLI, and an ARM template.

USING THE AZURE PORTAL

To set up Azure Hybrid Benefit using the Azure Portal during VMSS creation, follow these steps:

1. Follow the steps in the "VMSS creation walkthrough" section to start the Create a Virtual Machine Scale Set wizard and create a VMSS.

2. In the **Basics** tab, under **Licensing**, select the **Would You Like to Use an Existing Windows Server License** check box.

3. A check box appears to prompt you to confirm that you have an eligible Windows Server license with Software Assurance or a Windows Server subscription. Select the check box to confirm. (See Figure 2-50.)

FIGURE 2-50   Set up Azure Hybrid Benefit in Windows and confirm licensing eligibility.

4. Finish using the VM Scale Set Creation wizard to create the VMSS, as described in the section "VMSS creation walkthrough."

USING AZURE POWERSHELL

You can use Azure PowerShell to enable Azure Hybrid Benefit and create a Windows Server–based VMSS by adding the –LicenseType "Windows_Server" parameter. For example, the following code shows how to use this parameter in a PowerShell script for VMSS creation:

```
#Define variables
$RG = "VMSS-RG01"
$vmssname = "VMSS01"
$location = "EastUS2"
#create VMSS with Azure Hybrid Benefit
New-AzVmss `
    -ResourceGroupName $RG `
    -Name $vmssname `
```

```
    -Location $location `
    -ImageName "Win2019Datacenter" `
    -LicenseType "Windows_Server"
```

USING THE AZURE CLI

You can use the Azure CLI to enable Azure Hybrid Benefit and create a Windows Server–based VMSS by adding the `--License-Type Windows_Server` parameter. For example, the following code shows how to use this parameter in a Bash script for VMSS creation:

```
#Define variables
rg="VMSS-RG01"
vmssname="VMSS01"
location="EastUS2"
#create VMSS with Azure Hybrid Benefit
az vm create \
    --resource-group $rg \
    --name $vmssname \
    --location $location \
    --license-type Windows_Server
    }
```

Azure Hybrid Benefit for Linux VMSS walkthrough

The following sections step you through the process of setting up Azure Hybrid Benefit for a VMSS for RHEL and SLES using the Azure Portal, Azure PowerShell, and the Azure CLI.

USING THE AZURE PORTAL

With Linux, you can apply Azure Hybrid Benefit during VMSS creation and after. To set up Azure Hybrid Benefit during VMSS creation, follow these steps:

1. Follow the steps in the "VMSS creation walkthrough" section to start the Create a Virtual Machine Scale Set wizard and create a VMSS.

2. In the **Basics** tab, under **Licensing**, select the **Would You Like to Use an Existing Red Hat Enterprise Linux Subscription** check box.

3. A check box appears to prompt you to confirm that you have an eligible Red Hat Enterprise Linux subscription. Select the check box to confirm. (See Figure 2-51.)

FIGURE 2-51 Set up Azure Hybrid Benefit in Linux during VMSS creation and confirm licensing eligibility.

4. Finish using the VM Scale Set Creation wizard to create the VMSS, as described in the section "VMSS creation walkthrough."

USING AZURE POWERSHELL

You can use Azure PowerShell to enable Azure Hybrid Benefit when creating a Red-Hat Linux Server–based or SUSE Linux Server–based VMSS by adding the `–LicenseType "RHEL_BYOS"` or `–LicenseType "SLES_BYOS"` parameter. For example, the following code shows how to use these parameters in a PowerShell script for VMSS creation:

```
#Define variables
$RG = "VMSS-RG01"
$vmssname = "VMSS01"
$location = "EastUS2"
#create VMSS with Azure Hybrid Benefit
New-AzVmSS `
    -ResourceGroupName $RG `
    -Name $vmssname `
    -Location $location `
    -ImageName "RHEL" `
    -LicenseType "RHEL_BYOS"
```

USING THE AZURE CLI

You can use the Azure CLI to enable Azure Hybrid Benefit and create a Red Hat Linux Server–based VMSS by adding the `--License-Type RHEL_BYOS` parameter. For example, the following code shows how to use this parameter in a Bash script or prompt for RHEL VMSS creation:

```
#Define variables
rg="VMSS-RG01"
vmssname="VMSS01"
location="EastUS2"
#create VMSS with Azure Hybrid Benefit
az vmss create \
--resource-group $rg \
--name $vmssname \
--location $location \
--license-type RHEL_BYOS
```

Best practices

Nowadays, every public-facing environment is under constant attack from malicious actors. For some of these malicious actors, the goal is to break into the network to steal vital or confidential information. For others, it's to spread ransomware to bring down the network and force the organization to pay a ransom.

This section covers some general and security recommendations and best practices for VMSS. Although the recommendations and best practices that follow do not comprise an exhaustive list, they are a great starting point for most environments. Keeping these recommendations and best practices in mind can help you secure your VMSS environment post-deployment.

A general recommendation is to always review which best practices will apply to your environment, test them to validate the impact, monitor them constantly, and adjust them as needed. Do this before you finalize their implementation to avoid unexpected outages.

> **NOTE** Network security best practices are covered in greater depth in *Microsoft Azure Networking: The Definitive Guide*, which is part of the same series as this book.

- **Use application gateways to manage web application traffic** With application gateways, you can use the back-end pool to host the VMSS, while front-end public-facing interfaces and HTTPS/SSL connections terminate on the application gateway. As a result, only specific resources are exposed on configurable listeners and ports, drastically limiting the attack surface for that application.

- **Use virtual networks and separate internal and public-facing workloads** It is best to host Azure resources like VMs and VMSS inside existing or new virtual networks with a subnet configuration to separate internal and public-facing workloads. This segregation can be based on public and internal-facing workloads, workload criticality, workload interdependence, or current network schema.

- **Use NSGs** It is highly advisable to use NSGs on the VM NIC or vNET level to control traffic to hosted applications or workloads on only specific trusted source IPs and application ports. Note that this applies on the individual VM or vNET level. You should validate this configuration on a regular basis to ensure that only the required source IPs and ports are still set up, as this tends to change over time with more additions than deletions or reviews taking place.

- **Use Azure Firewall for public endpoint protection** NSGs are great for protecting individual VMs or resources within a vNET. However, it is difficult to monitor traffic across the entire environment. This is where Azure Firewall comes in handy. With Azure Firewall, you can enact source IP, application port, and protocol restrictions for the entire environment. Because Azure Firewall is service-based, charges are levied based on usage, making it a very cost-effective yet secure solution.

- **Set up network traffic logging** Azure Security Center can log network traffic to identify and monitor network policies and suggestions to secure the VM instances in a VMSS. In addition, NSG flow logs can be configured to store historical data in a storage account for auditing of suspicious activity.

- **Monitor Azure activity logs** You should monitor the Azure activity log for changes to the VMSS configuration to identify unwanted or unplanned configuration modifications. For best results, set up alerts to inform admins or security experts within the organization of such changes.

- **Use Azure Policy for configuration remediation** Azure Policy is a great service to assign policy definitions for Azure resources for good governance of the Azure environment. You can use Azure Policy to monitor and remediate non-compliance due to deviations in configuration for resources, including network resources used by scale sets.

- **Standardize security configuration** You can use Azure Blueprints to combine Azure objects such as ARM templates, Azure policies, roles, and role assignments to create a single simplified security blueprint. This helps you streamline large-scale Azure VM deployments such as VMSS. Use these whenever possible, as it will help in simplifying the deployment and management of large and complex VMSS.

- **Set time synchronization for VM instances** Microsoft maintains time sources for all Azure resources. However, if your organization requires the use of custom time sources, you can set them up with group policy or local policy settings. Note that you must apply these settings to all VM instances in a scale set to ensure they are localized correctly to avoid differing log time entries.

- **Manage security logs centrally** Azure records write operations on resources to activity logs, which are stored in each resource's blade in Azure. Recording these logs in a central database like Azure Sentinel or a third-party SIEM tool can help you easily track, monitor, and audit these logs for security events. You can also use Log Analytics Workspace for long-term event log data retention from Azure VM instances in a scale set. You can automate the integration and ingestion of this data to streamline the entire security log monitoring process.

- **Audit logging** You can install diagnostic extensions on VM instances in a scale set to capture guest OS diagnostic information. This can be in the form of Windows event logs, application logs, custom logs, and Windows performance counters. In addition, you can use Application Insights to capture more advanced counters, which provide more visibility into the performance of the application hosted in the VMSS. Finally, you can use Azure Monitor to monitor performance and logs on the VM level. Working in conjunction with Application Insights, which performs the same task on the application layer, Azure Monitor makes it possible for you to better understand application performance issues and address them on the VM or application layer as indicated in the logs.

- **Centralize antimalware logging** Enable Microsoft's Antimalware for Cloud Services and Virtual Machines tool for Windows VM instances in a scale set to capture and log events in an Azure blob storage account for review. You can set up alerts for events that require follow-up. (Linux VMs require the use of a third-party tool for antimalware monitoring.)

- **Use domain authentication/Azure AD authentication to manage VM instances** This simplifies the security model and allows for easier scaling, monitoring, tracking, and reviewing of access permissions for admins and end-users.

- **Use Privileged Access Workstations (PAWs)** If feasible, use PAWs with MFA to reduce the organization's attack surface. PAWs are dedicated environments with limited access to and from Internet services, which reduces the threat vectors that the workstations are exposed to. This makes them ideal for highly sensitive activities.

- **Allow access from known IP ranges only** You can use conditional access policies and named locations to allow access only via known good IP ranges and/or countries to your Azure Portal for VMSS management. Requests from unknown IPs or countries are automatically dropped. This can prevent brute-force attack attempts.

## Chapter 3

Azure App Service

Overview

Azure App Service is a compute service within Azure that enables you to host web applications, mobile application back ends, and REST APIs. Some key features of Azure App Service include the following:

- It provides DevOps integration capabilities to allow for continuous deployment of code using Azure DevOps, Docker Hub, GitHub, and other third-party solutions.
- It allows for development in different programming languages like .NET Core, .NET, Node.js, PHP, Python, Java, and others.
- It allows for both Windows- and Linux-based applications to run at scale.

Although App Service can help address the requirements of most app deployments, there are a few key points to consider when deciding it is the best service for hosting an app. Some primary reasons to use Azure App Service are as follows:

- **Automated management** OS management activities, including patching and maintenance, are automated. This applies even to the language frameworks supported by the service. This frees development and engineering resources from the burden of managing the back-end platform so they can focus on more business-critical application-development activities.
- **Support for multiple frameworks** In addition to the different programming languages that can be used by App Service, it can also leverage PowerShell scripts and other types of executables for background services.
- **Robust scaling** Both manual and automated scaling operations are supported—including scaling up, down, in, and out. This can help organizations of all sizes embarking on their cloud journey obtain the maximum benefit from their cloud spends.
- **Global deployment** App Service deployments are supported across Microsoft's globally dispersed regions and datacenters. This allows for app hosting in regions closest to the users.
- **High availability and uptime guarantees** In addition to workloads hosted on the free and shared tiers of services, App Service workloads are guaranteed a 99.95% uptime.

- **Optimized for DevOps builds**   Continuous integration and deployment can be achieved by leveraging App Service in conjunction with Azure DevOps, Azure Container Registry, GitHub, Bitbucket, and Docker Hub. This allows for multiple staging and dev/test environments that can be used for testing, validation, and production.

- **Support for PowerShell and CLI management**   Apps can be managed using Azure PowerShell, the command-line interface (CLI), or the Azure Portal to help in DevOps and automation activities.

- **Integration with Docker and containers**   Apps can be dockerized and hosted as custom containers in App Service. Both Windows- and Linux-based containers are supported. This enables engineers with skills in managing Docker to quickly get up to speed managing Azure App Service.

- **Adherence to global compliance standards**   Compliance with ISO, SOC, and PCI standards is built in.

- **Easy to integrate with existing authentication solutions**   Various secure authentication solutions can be easily leveraged, enabling users to employ existing Azure Active Directory, Microsoft, Google, Facebook, and Twitter accounts.

- **Built-in support for mobile apps**   Mobile app features such as user authentication, notification services, offline data sync, social integration, and automated scaling are all built-in, making it easy to build and deploy apps.

- **Ability to run code and scripts in a serverless architecture**   On-demand scripts and code snippets can be executed without deploying back-end servers using serverless computing. This saves time, resources, and money, as compute costs are charged only for actual use.

- **Connectors for enterprise, SaaS, and internet-based services**   App Service has ready connectors for integration with enterprise applications, SaaS applications, and internet-based services, making it easy to integrate with the most commonly used platforms and applications.

- **Hybrid connectivity**   Support for hybrid connections is available to allow access to on-premises data sources.

- **Built-in application templates**   There are numerous application templates available in the Azure Marketplace, including templates for WordPress, Drupal, and Umbraco, to name a few. The list of templates available is quite extensive and is being updated constantly.

- **Visual Studio and Visual Studio Code integration**   Deep integration with Visual Studio and Visual Studio Code allows for streamlined app building, deployment, and troubleshooting.

- **Support for Linux languages and frameworks**   Linux containers can be run natively or using custom containers (known as Web App for Containers). This allows for the use of built-in Linux images for languages such as .NET Core, Python, Node.js, JRE, PHP, and others. Custom containers help address scenarios not covered by the built-in images.

App Service plans

App Service plans identify the hardware computing resources made available to the App Service to run the required web, API, and mobile apps. Depending on what plan you select, computing resources are dedicated solely to your organization or shared among customers. The App Service plan also defines the specifications of the back-end VM series that is allocated. This, in turn, affects the number of applications that can be hosted using those resources.

> **NOTE** One App Service plan can be used to deploy and run multiple apps.

When you create an App Service plan, you must define certain parameters for that plan. These include the following:

- The pricing tier (Free, Shared, Dedicated, Isolated, etc.)
- The region in which the apps will run (Central US, West Europe, East Asia, etc.)
- The size of the VM instances required (small, medium, large)
- The total number of VM instances required

Once the preceding parameters are defined, the resources identified in the plan are created in the selected region. Thereafter, the resources are made available for the hosting of the required apps.

Choosing the right pricing tier is key. Table 3-1 reviews the four pricing tiers.

TABLE 3-1 Pricing tiers

Pricing tier	Description	Key features
Free	Allows you to host one or more web apps without having to pay any associated compute charges.	The underlying hardware is shared between customers. You can run only 10 apps.
		You can have 10 free plans per region.
		There are time limits on CPU usage. These make this pricing tier ideal for test/dev workloads, and web APIs generally run quickly.
		There are limits on memory, storage, bandwidth, scalability, and security features.
		Uptime SLAs do not apply.
Shared	Similar to the Free tier in that the underlying hardware is shared, but offers more flexibility in terms of CPU usage and so on.	The underlying hardware is shared between customers.
		You can run 100 apps.
		You can have 10 plans within a single resource group.
		You can have unlimited shared plans per region.
		There are limits on memory, storage, bandwidth, scalability, and security features. However, CPU usage limits apply 240 minutes per day.
		A per-app charge applies.
		Uptime SLAs do not apply.

Pricing tier	Description	Key features
Dedicated	Provides compute resources that are dedicated to that customer. There are different levels available in this plan—Basic, Standard, Premium, PremiumV2, and PremiumV3—and each defines the number of VM instances that the apps in the plan get access to.	A per-instance charge applies, regardless of the number of apps running. You can scale out by increasing the number of VM instances available. You can scale up by moving from one dedicated tier to a higher one to increase the size of the VM instances. This tier supports several additional features, including features that relate to backups, security, auto-scaling, and integration with traffic management. An uptime SLA of 99.95% applies.
Isolated	Provides a dedicated set of VMs hosted in an Azure virtual network environment to support compute isolation.	Plans in this tier are deployed into an App Service Environment (ASE), described in more detail later in this chapter. Fixed charges to run the environment apply, as well as variable charges based on the number of instances. This tier provides maximum scale-out capabilities. Fine-grained control over ingress and egress application network traffic is supported. All security and scaling features are available for apps running on this tier. An uptime SLA of 99.95% applies.

NOTE As you can see, the higher the tier, the more features become available to improve security, scalability, and reliability.

Single versus multiple App Service plans

You can host multiple apps as part of the same App Service plan, potentially reducing your overall compute costs. Because multiple apps share the underlying resources allocated to the App Service plan, it is important to monitor their use.

Before you add a new app to your App Service plan, make sure its requirements align with available resources in the plan. Take these factors into consideration when deciding whether to host an app in an existing App Service plan or create a new plan for the app:

- Does the app have the same scaling needs as the rest of the apps in the current plan?

- Do the app's resource requirements (current and future) align with the available resources in the current plan?

- Does the app have any security or feature requirements that cannot be met by the existing plan?

- Does the app need to be isolated from other apps?

NOTE Adding an app to an existing App Service plan might seem cost-effective, but if doing so will affect application performance or potentially cause outages, it might not be worth it.

Azure App Service Environments

Earlier, I mentioned that the Isolated pricing tier deploys apps in an App Service Environments (ASE). An ASE is a dedicated, fully isolated environment provisioned to run apps with high levels of security and scalability. An ASE can host Windows or Linux web apps, mobile apps, function apps, and Docker containers.

Although all application workloads can be hosted in an ASE, considering the cost implications, there are certain workload types that are more appropriate for ASEs than others. When deciding if an ASE is the best choice for an app, consider these factors:

- Does the app require complete isolation and secure access to on-premises resources?
- Does the app have high memory requirements that are not met by the Dedicated tier?
- Does the app require a very high level of scalability?

If the answer to all or most of these questions is yes, then an ASE might be the appropriate choice.

Here is a list of some examples of functionality that is only possible when using an ASE:

- Hosting apps in a single-tenant environment
- Using private or internal Certificate Authority certificates
- Publishing a dedicated outbound IP address for all the apps hosted in the ASE
- Publishing and accessing apps only on a private internal IP address
- Providing the highest level of scaling possible across all App Service plans
- Securing outbound network traffic with additional network controls available with integrations that are not part of the app

An ASE is assigned exclusive access to a dedicated set of compute and network resources and is accessible only from a single subscription. Each subscription supports the deployment of 100 App Service plan instances. These can be deployed in one of three ways:

- A single App Service plan with 100 instances
- 100 App Service plans with single instances in each plan
- A combination of the two

An ASE is composed of two components:

- **Front ends** Front ends provide HTTP and HTTPS endpoints for ingress termination and load-balancing. Front ends are added automatically as scaling operations take place to handle the additional load.
- **Workers** Workers host the apps deployed by a customer. You specify the size of the workers when you select your App Service plan tier.

Both components are managed services and are deployed or removed automatically as the App Service plans are sized. Because of this design, the charges associated with an ASE are fixed every month based on the plan that is selected. Additionally, every vCPU in the plan has an associated cost, which will be levied when resources are consumed.

There are two different ways to provision network access for an ASE, depending on its public access requirements:

- **External ASE**   An internet-facing ASE is deployed with a public IP address so the apps hosted on the ASE can be accessed externally.

- **Internal ASE**   An internal ASE is deployed using an internal load balancer (ILB) IP address so it is accessible only on internal networks. This would include any networks connected over VPN or ExpressRoute.

The public virtual IP (VIP) or the ILB IP serve as the endpoints for the termination of the different protocols for client connectivity. Because there is no direct access to the VMs running in the ASE, you can create network security groups (NSGs) to manage the network traffic within the subnet where the ASE is housed. If a site-to-site VPN or ExpressRoute connection to the on-premises environment is in place, the apps hosted in the ASE can communicate with on-premises resources.

App Service walkthrough

The following sections step you through the process of creating a basic web app using the Azure Portal, Azure PowerShell, and Azure CLI. You will use sample GitHub code provided by Microsoft to create a static HTML website, which you will use later to create a Hello World web app.

> **NOTE**   You will create the same web app using all three methods. Be sure to adjust the web app's name for each deployment.

USING THE AZURE PORTAL

To create a sample static HTML website for the Hello World web app using the Azure Portal, follow these steps:

1. Log in to the Azure Portal and type **app services** in the search bar.

2. Under **Services**, click **App Services**. (See Figure 3-1.)

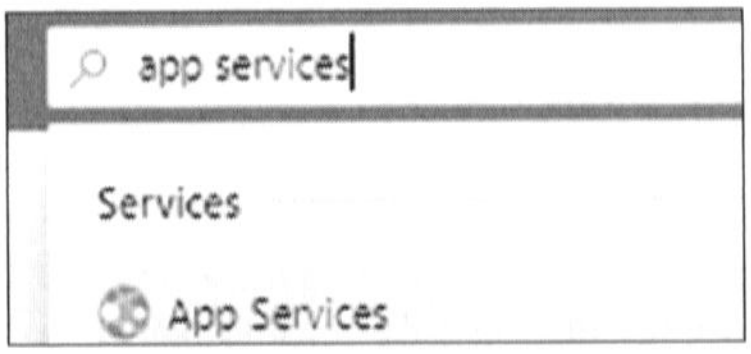

FIGURE 3-1   Selecting the App Services service in the Azure Portal.

3. Click either the **Create** button or the **Create App Service** button to launch the Create Web App wizard. (See Figure 3-2.)

Create, build, deploy, and manage powerful web, mobile, and API apps for employees or customers using a single back-end. Build standards-based web apps and APIs using .NET, Java, Node.js, PHP, and Python.

Learn more about App Service ☑

Create app service

FIGURE 3-2 Creating the first App Service.

4. In the **Basics** tab, enter the following information for the web app (see Figure 3-3):

- **Subscription**   Select the subscription that will host the web app.

- **Resource Group**   Select an existing resource group or create a new one to host the web app.

- **Name**   Enter a unique name for the web app. If the name you enter is already in use, the wizard will prompt you to select another name.

- **Publish**   Select the publishing model for the web app. Your options are Code and Docker Container. In this case, choose **Code**.

- **Runtime Stack**   Choose the runtime stack that corresponds to the app—here, **.NET 5**.

- **Operating System**   Choose an operating system for the app VM—in this case, **Windows**.

- **Region**   Select the Azure region you want to host the app.

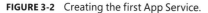

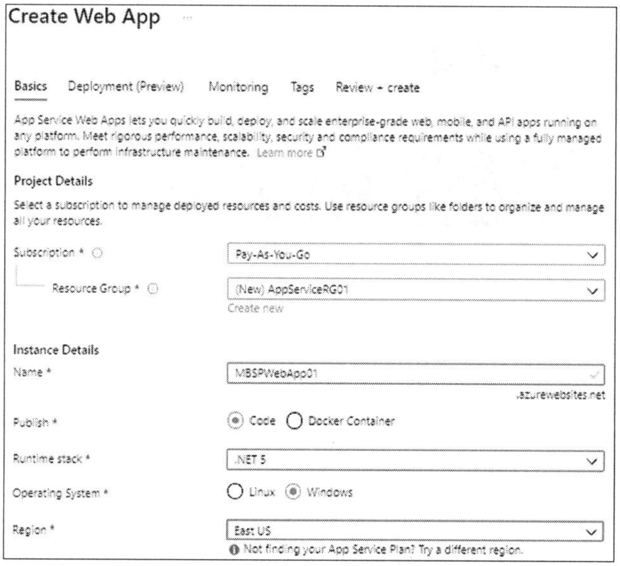

FIGURE 3-3 Setting up the basic configuration for the app.

5. Still in the **Basics** tab, under **App Service Plan**, select an existing App Service plan. Alternatively, to create a new plan, click **Create New**, type a name for the new plan, and click **OK**. (See Figure 3-4.)

FIGURE 3-4 Defining a new App Service plan.

6. In the **Sku and Size** section, click the **Change Size** link. (See Figure 3-5.)

Sku and size *	**Standard S1**
	100 total ACU, 1.75 GB memory
	Change size

FIGURE 3-5 Setting the SKU and size for the App Service plan.

7. In the Spec Picker window, choose an appropriate pricing tier based on your resource and feature requirements. In this case, click **Dev / Test**. Then choose the **F1** plan (the Free pricing tier) and click **Apply**. (See Figure 3-6.)

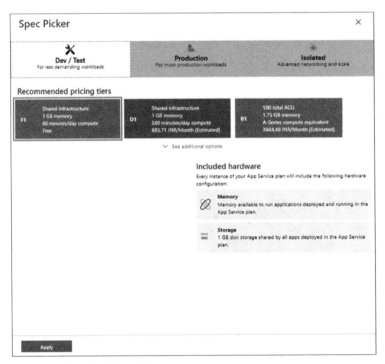

FIGURE 3-6 Set the SKU and size.

Choose a pricing tier

As you've learned, there are various pricing tiers available. Figure 3-7 shows additional Dev / Test pricing tiers, with the B1 tier selected; Figure 3-8 shows the recommended pricing tiers for production workloads; and Figure 3-9 shows recommended tiers for isolated workloads.

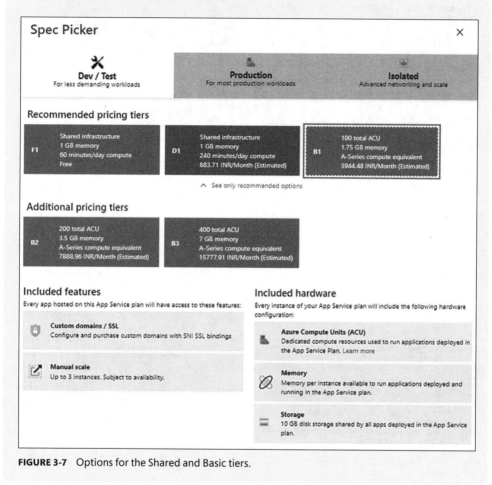

FIGURE 3-7   Options for the Shared and Basic tiers.

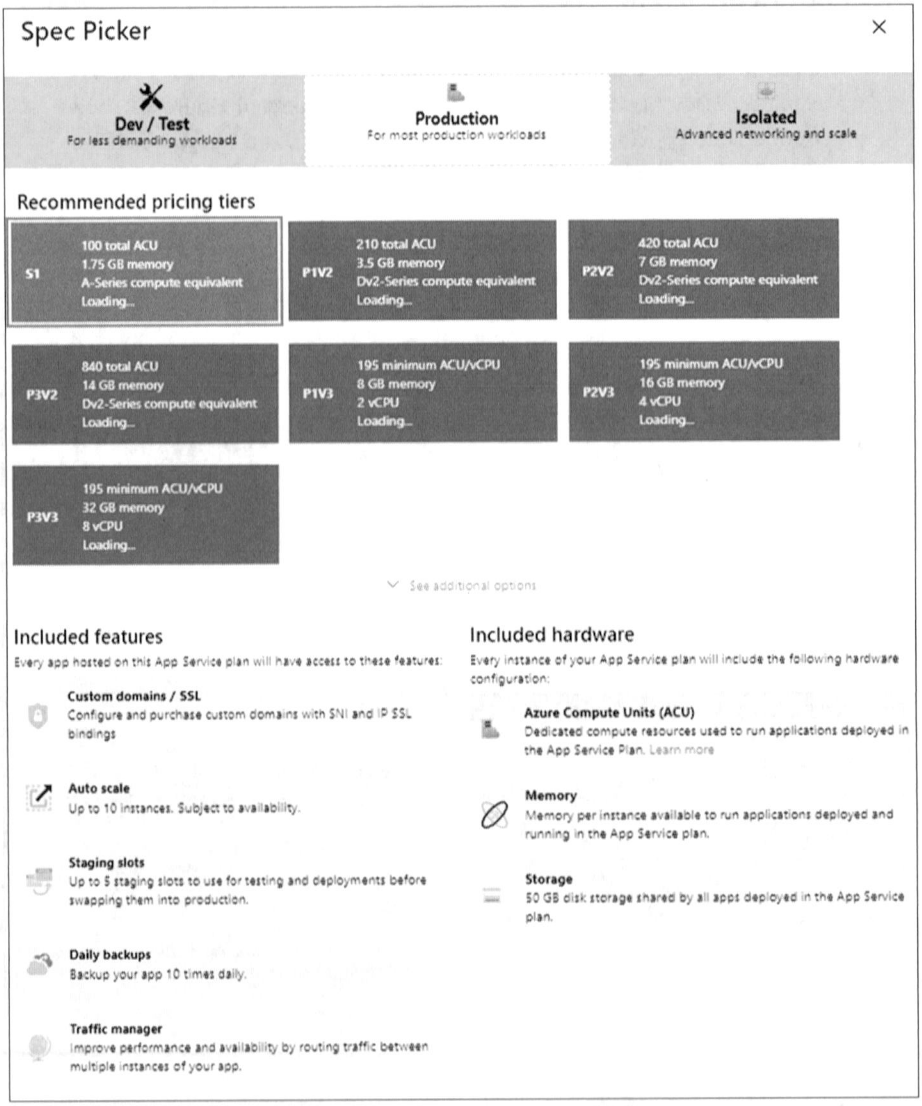

Spec Picker   ✕

✗	**▦**	**▦**
Dev / Test For less demanding workloads	**Production** For most production workloads	**Isolated** Advanced networking and scale

Recommended pricing tiers

S1	100 total ACU 1.75 GB memory A-Series compute equivalent Loading...	**P1V2**	210 total ACU 3.5 GB memory Dv2-Series compute equivalent Loading...	**P2V2**	420 total ACU 7 GB memory Dv2-Series compute equivalent Loading...
P3V2	840 total ACU 14 GB memory Dv2-Series compute equivalent Loading...	**P1V3**	195 minimum ACU/vCPU 8 GB memory 2 vCPU Loading...	**P2V3**	195 minimum ACU/vCPU 16 GB memory 4 vCPU Loading...
P3V3	195 minimum ACU/vCPU 32 GB memory 8 vCPU Loading...				

⌄ See additional options

Included features

Every app hosted on this App Service plan will have access to these features:

🛡 **Custom domains / SSL**
Configure and purchase custom domains with SNI and IP SSL bindings

↗ **Auto scale**
Up to 10 instances. Subject to availability.

Staging slots
Up to 5 staging slots to use for testing and deployments before swapping them into production.

☁ **Daily backups**
Backup your app 10 times daily.

Traffic manager
Improve performance and availability by routing traffic between multiple instances of your app.

Included hardware

Every instance of your App Service plan will include the following hardware configuration:

Azure Compute Units (ACU)
Dedicated compute resources used to run applications deployed in the App Service Plan. Learn more

∅ **Memory**
Memory per instance available to run applications deployed and running in the App Service plan.

Storage
50 GB disk storage shared by all apps deployed in the App Service plan.

FIGURE 3-8 Tiers for production workloads.

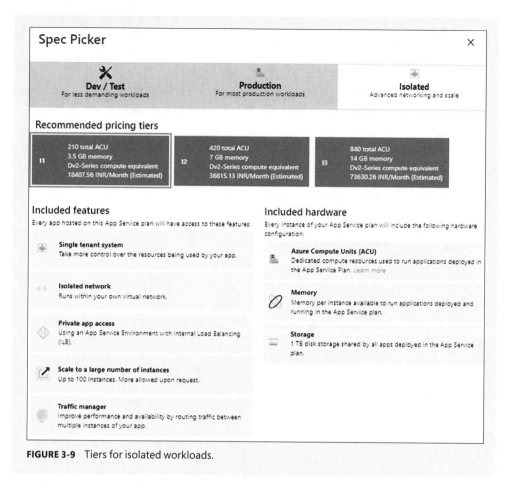

FIGURE 3-9 Tiers for isolated workloads.

8. Click **Next** twice. Then, in the **Monitoring** tab, next to **Enable Application Insights**, select the **No** option button and click **Next**. (See Figure 3-10.)

Basics   Deployment (Preview)   Monitoring   Tags   Review + create

Azure Monitor application insights is an Application Performance Management (APM) service for developers and DevOps professionals. Enable it below to automatically monitor your application. It will detect performance anomalies, and includes powerful analytics tools to help you diagnose issues and to understand what users actually do with your app. Learn more ☐

Application Insights

Enable Application Insights *   ⦿ No   ◯ Yes

FIGURE 3-10 Choosing settings in the Monitoring tab.

9. In the **Tags** tab, enter any tags that you would like to apply to identify the resources for the App Service. For example, type **ms-resource** in the **Name** column and **WebApp** in the **Value** column. (See Figure 3-11.) Then click **Next**.

FIGURE 3-11 Setting up tags for the web app.

10. In the **Review + Create** tab, review your settings and click **Create** to create the web app. (See Figure 3-12.)

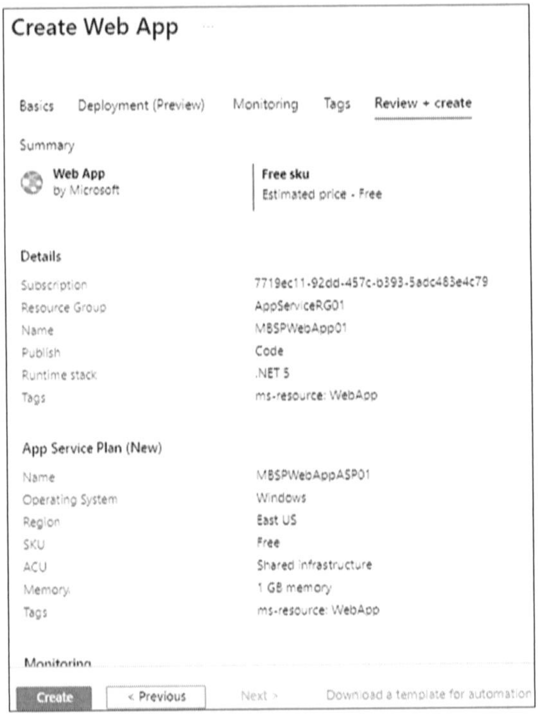

FIGURE 3-12 Reviewing the web app settings.

11. After the web app is created, click it. (In this example, it's called **MBSPWebApp01**.) Then, in the **Overview** section of the web app's page in the Azure Portal, copy the URL for the web app (located in the upper-right corner). (See Figure 3-13.)

FIGURE 3-13 Copying the web app URL.

12. Paste the URL in your web browser's address bar to see the associated website. It will look like the one shown in Figure 3-14.

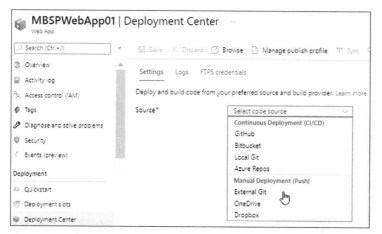

FIGURE 3-14 The default web app website.

Now you'll build the web app.

13. In the **Deployment** section of the web app's page in the Azure Portal, click **Deployment Center**.

14. In the **Settings** tab, click the **Source** drop-down list and select **External Git**. (See Figure 3-15.)

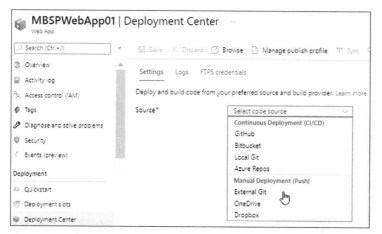

FIGURE 3-15 Setting the deployment source.

15. Under External Git, type https://github.com/Azure-Samples/html-docs-hello-world.git in the Repository box, type master in the **Branch** box, and select the Public option button next to **Repository Type**. (See Figure 3-16.)

FIGURE 3-16 Setting the External Git configuration.

16. Click **Save** to apply the changes. This will reload the code from the repository and restart the web app.

17. Verify the app details. (See Figure 3-17.)

FIGURE 3-17 The external Git configuration.

18. Click **Browse** to return to the website.

19. The website has changed, as shown in Figure 3-18, indicating that the Git repository was successfully cloned to build your web app.

FIGURE 3-18 Sample Azure App Service static HTML site.

USING AZURE POWERSHELL

You can create a sample static HTML website for the Hello World web app with Azure PowerShell using the New-AzAppServicePlan and New-AzWebApp commands. The following code shows you how. (Note that you need to connect to the Azure subscription using PowerShell first.)

Note that you need to make the following replacements in the code:

- Replace the app name with a unique name or add (Get-Random) to the end of the name to randomize it.

- Replace the Location variable with the desired Azure region.

- Replace the resource group name with an existing resource group or a different name (optional).

After the script successfully completes, browse to the web app URL to verify the application has been created successfully:

```
# Set the public GitHub repository URL, AppName and Location variables.
$githubrepo="https://github.com/Azure-Samples/html-docs-hello-world.git"
$appname="MBSPWebApp01"
$location="East US"
$resourcegroup="AppServiceRG01"
# Create a resource group to host the App Service.
New-AzResourceGroup -Name $resourcegroup -Location $location
# Create an App Service plan in Free tier.
New-AzAppServicePlan -Name $appname -Location $location -ResourceGroupName $resource-
group -Tier Free
# Create a web app using the App Service Plan.
New-AzWebApp -Name $appname -Location $location -AppServicePlan $appname -ResourceGroup-
Name $resourcegroup
# Configure GitHub deployment from your GitHub repo and deploy once.
$PropertiesObject = @{
    repoUrl = "$githubrepo";
    branch = "master";
    isManualIntegration = "true";
}
```

```
Set-AzResource -Properties $PropertiesObject -ResourceGroupName $resourcegroup
-ResourceType Microsoft.Web/sites/sourcecontrols -ResourceName $appname/web
-ApiVersion 2015-08-01 -Force
```

USING THE AZURE CLI

You can create a sample static HTML website for the Hello World web app with the Azure CLI using the `az appservice plan create` and `az webapp create` commands. The following code shows you how. (Note that you need to connect to the Azure subscription using the Azure CLI first.)

Note that you need to make the following replacements in the code:

- Replace the app name with a unique name or add ($RANDOM) to the end of the name to randomize it.
- Replace the `Location` variable with the desired Azure region.
- Replace the resource group name with an existing resource group or a different name (optional).

After the script successfully completes, browse to the web app URL to verify the application has been created successfully:

```
#!/bin/bash
# Set the public GitHub repository URL, AppName and Location variables.
githubrepo=https://github.com/Azure-Samples/html-docs-hello-world.git
appname=MBSPWebApp01
location=EastUS
resourcegroup=AppServiceRG01
# Create a resource group to host the App Service.
az group create --location $location --name $resourcegroup
# Create an App Service plan in Free tier.
az appservice plan create --name $appname --resource-group $resourcegroup --sku FREE
# Create a web app using the App Service Plan.
az webapp create --name $appname --resource-group $resourcegroup --plan $appname
# Configure GitHub deployment from your GitHub repo and deploy once.
az webapp deployment source config --name $appname --resource-group $resourcegroup
--repo-url $githubrepo --branch master --manual-integration
```

Planning deployment and operations

There are three main components to take into consideration when planning a deployment to Azure App Service:

- Deployment sources
- Build pipelines
- Deployment mechanisms

Each of these is used differently in every environment, as each environment has unique use cases and development needs. It is difficult to take a one-size-fits-all approach when planning a deployment, so it will serve you well to understand these three main components. First, though, let's discuss appropriate deployment sources.

Select an appropriate deployment source

One of the first steps in the deployment process is to identify the location where the application code will reside during the development, test, and production phases. There are two main options for this:

- **A single centralized source for all phases**   This approach involves using a centralized source such as GitHub, Azure Repos, or Bitbucket, where all the code can reside for deployments as needed.
- **A hybrid approach**   This approach involves using a combination of sources: a centralized source for testing and production and a local source on the developer's local storage for development.

The recommended approach for any enterprise environment is to identify a centralized source so that all the code repository structures can be built and maintained centrally, and code backups can be performed on a regular basis. For example, App Service has built-in integration with GitHub, which can be easily set up when the GitHub environment is online.

Deployment source walkthrough

The following sections step you through the process of setting up a different deployment source for the static web app you created earlier using the Azure Portal, Azure PowerShell, and Azure CLI. If you are following along, then make sure to adjust the web app name and variables as needed for each deployment.

> **NOTE**   Be sure to adjust the web app's name for each deployment.

USING THE AZURE PORTAL

To select a deployment source using the Azure Portal, follow these steps:

1. In the Azure Portal, select the web app you created earlier.
2. In the left pane, under **Deployment**, click **Deployment Center**.
3. In the **Settings** tab, click the **Source** drop-down list and choose **GitHub**. (See Figure 3-19.)

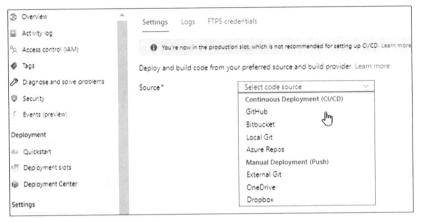

FIGURE 3-19 Selecting a new deployment source.

4. Click the **Authorize** button. (See Figure 3-20.)

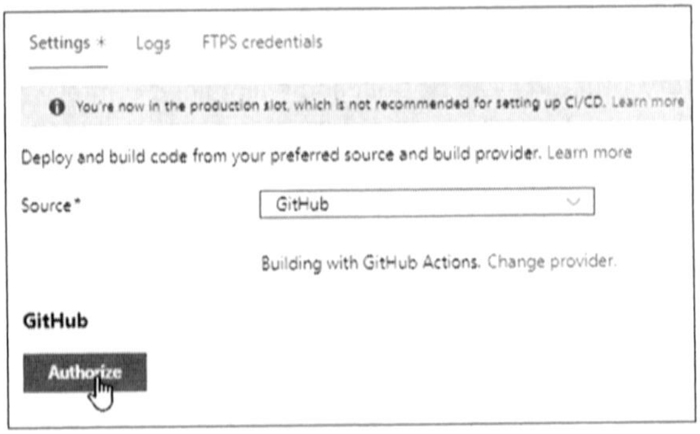

FIGURE 3-20 Authorizing the deployment source (in this case, GitHub).

5. In the Authorize Azure App Service dialog box, click the **Authorize AzureAppService** button. (See Figure 3-21.)

   In the GitHub login window that opens, enter your login credentials to begin the integration process. This may take a few minutes. When the integration process is complete, you'll see the options shown in Figure 3-22.

6. Open the **Organization** drop-down and choose the appropriate organization.

7. Open the **GitHub Repository** drop-down and choose the desired repository.

8. Open the **Branch** drop-down list and choose the branch you want to connect the app to.

9. Under **Build**, open the **Runtime Stack** drop-down list and choose the appropriate runtime stack based on your environment. Then open the Version drop-down list and select the appropriate version. (See Figure 3-23.) Finally, click **Save**.

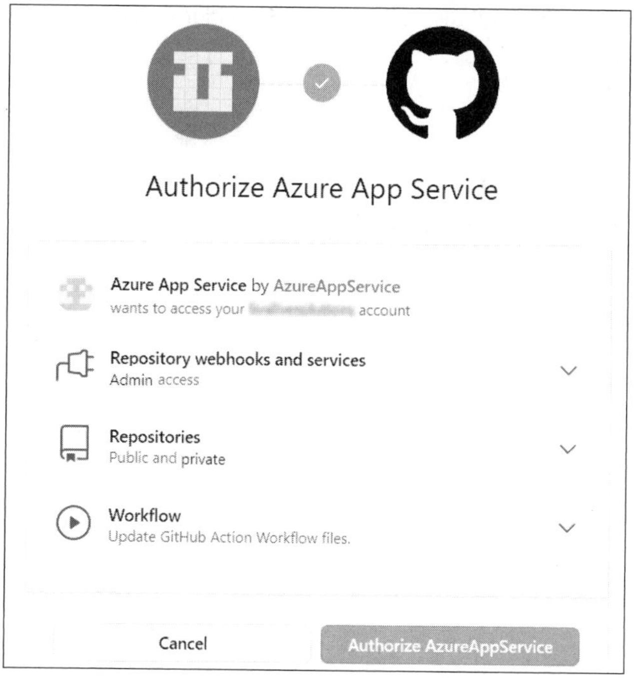

FIGURE 3-21 Authorizing the deployment source (GitHub).

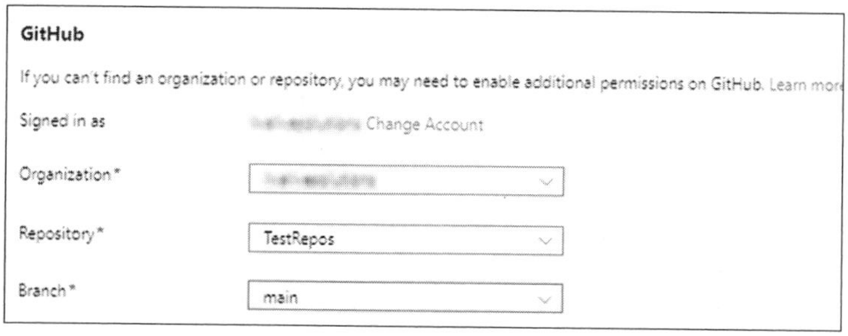

FIGURE 3-22 Setting the organization, repository, and branch under GitHub.

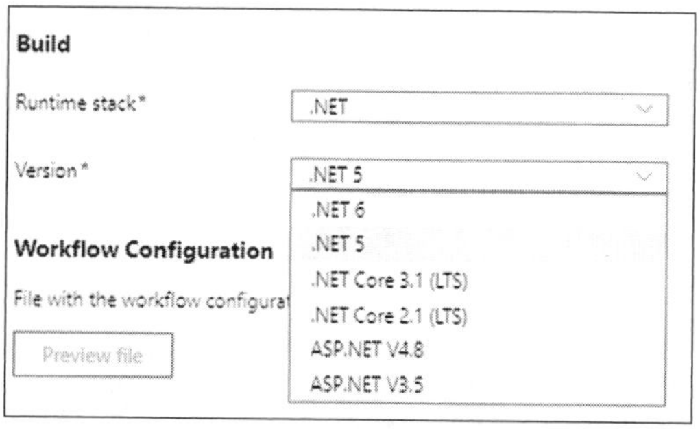

FIGURE 3-23 Selecting the runtime stack and version.

Azure shows a summary of the configuration settings. (See Figure 3-24.)

MSBPWebApp01 | Deployment Center
App Service

Search (Ctrl+/)

💾 Save   ✕ Discard   📋 Browse   📄 Manage publish profile   ↻ Sync   ♡ Leave Feedback

Deployment slots

Deployment Center

Settings | Logs | FTPS credentials

Settings

Configuration

Authentication

Authentication (classic)

Application Insights

Identity

Backups

Custom domains

TLS/SSL settings

Networking

Networking (preview)

Scale up (App Service plan)

Scale out (App Service plan)

WebJobs

Push

Deploy and build code from your preferred source and build provider. Learn more

| Source | GitHub |
| | Disconnect |

GitHub

Signed in as	liv
Organization	liv
Repository	TestRepos
Branch	main

Build

Build provider	GitHub Actions
Runtime stack	Dotnet
Version	v5.0

FIGURE 3-24   Summary of the final config is shown.

USING AZURE POWERSHELL

You can use Azure PowerShell to select a deployment source, as shown here. (Remember to adjust the value of each variable as needed for your environment.)

```
#Set the Webapp and GitHub variables
$githubrepository="{URL-of-required-GitHub-repo}"
$githubtoken="{GitHub-access-token}"
$webappname="{Name-Of-WebApp}"
$webapplocation="{WebApp-Azure-Region}"
# Setup GitHub token
$PropertyObject = @{token = $githubtoken;}
Set-AzResource -PropertyObject $PropertyObject -ResourceId /providers/Microsoft.Web/
sourcecontrols/GitHub -ApiVersion 2015-08-01 -Force
# Configure GitHub deployment from the required GitHub repo
$PropertyObject = @{
    repoUrl = "$githubrepository";
    branch = "master";
}
# Set the Webapp with the GitHub configuration
```

```
Set-AzResource -PropertyObject $PropertyObject -ResourceGroupName {resource-group-name}
-ResourceType Microsoft.Web/sites/sourcecontrols -ResourceName $webappname/web
-ApiVersion 2015-08-01 -Force
```

USING THE AZURE CLI

You can use the Azure CLI to select a deployment source, as shown here. (Remember to adjust the value of each variable as needed for your environment.)

```
#Set the Webapp and GitHub variables
githubrepos={URL-Of-GitHub-Repository}
githubtoken={GitHub-Access-Token}
WebApp={WebAppName}
ResourceGroup={ResourceGroupName}
# Configure continuous deployment from GitHub.
az webapp deployment source config --name $WebApp --resource-group $ResourceGroup
--repo-url $githubrepos --branch master --git-token $githubtoken
```

Build pipelines

A build pipeline helps automate the process of compiling, testing, and packaging source code for deployment. The pipeline reads the source code data from the deployment source and performs a series of predefined steps to prepare it for deployment.

The programming language used for the app build will determine the commands employed during the build process. This process can be executed using Azure Pipelines, a third-party solution, or locally.

Deployment mechanism

After an application package has been built, it is deployed into the web app. This action is called the *deployment mechanism*. App Service supports multiple deployment mechanisms:

- **Kudu**   This open-source engine handles continuous deployments, provides HTTP endpoints, and manages all Git deployments in Azure App Service.
- **FTP**   You can use this protocol to upload files from a source website directly to the web app.
- **WebDeploy**   This client-server tool, designed by Microsoft, syncs application content and configuration to web apps.

After the selected deployment mechanism copies the code to the web app, every VM instance running the app receives a notification regarding the availability of the new files. Each instance syncs the new files from the shared location in the web app's /wwwroot directory.

Best practices

Following are several best practices that relate to deployment.

Deployment slots

Deployment slots provide an easy way to deploy and manage code rollouts. A deployment slot creates a live App Service inside the App Service plan. You can use this to load code for testing; then, when testing is complete, you can swap the slot so the code moves to staging or production.

In the back end, the deployment slot is already live on worker instances, ready to receive connections. After the swap is performed, all settings applied to the staging or production slot will be applied to the code in the test slot (depending on which slot is selected). This makes it important to use App Service settings and connection strings to store all the required database and unique app settings required for staging or production. If this configuration is stored in the application code, the staging or production application will write to the test database instances.

It is highly recommended to use deployment slots when deploying new code to staging or production because it makes it easier to swap the previous version of the code in case of any issues. This can reduce downtime while also automating the entire DevOps pipeline workflow to build, test, and validate new code before rolling it out into production.

Deployment slots are not supported on the Free, Shared, or Basic tier plans; they are supported, however, on all plans from the Standard plan onward. For enterprise environments in which DevOps processes are in place, this would generally be the minimum plan selected. Each deployment slot has its own unique URL, which you can use to access the code in that slot for testing at no additional cost.

> **NOTE** If you scale a deployment slot up or out, all the slots on the App Service will be scaled accordingly, as they all share the same App Service plan.

Along with the codebase is a group of settings that get swapped, as follows:

- General application settings, such as the framework version, web sockets, and so on
- Connection strings (you can configure these to remain with the slot)
- App settings (you can configure these to remain with the slot)
- Public certificates
- WebJobs content
- Handler mappings

There are also settings that are not transferred during a swap. You should take these into consideration and manage the code accordingly to ensure that the right settings are applied at the time of the swap. Following is a list of some of these settings:

- Publishing endpoints
- Custom domain names
- Non-public certificates and TLS/SSL settings
- Scale settings
- WebJobs schedulers
- IP restrictions
- The Always On setting
- Diagnostic settings

Deployment slots walkthrough

The following sections step you through the process of setting up deployment slots for your web app using the Azure Portal, Azure PowerShell, and the Azure CLI.

NOTE Be sure to adjust the web app's name and variables for each deployment.

USING THE AZURE PORTAL

To set up deployment slots using the Azure Portal, follow these steps:

1. In the Azure Portal, display the page for the web app you created earlier.

2. In the left pane, under **Deployment**, click **Deployment Slots**. (See Figure 3-25.)

FIGURE 3-25 Setting up deployment slots.

3. If the web app is on the Free, Shared, or Basic tier, you will see the message shown in Figure 3-26. Click **Upgrade** to upgrade to a Standard or Premium plan. Then, in the Spec Picker window (see Figure 3-27), select a Standard or Premium plan that supports deployment slots, and click **Apply**.

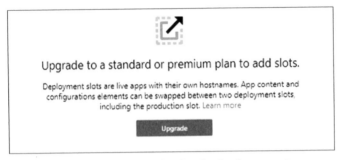

FIGURE 3-26   Upgrading the App Service plan for slot support.

Spec Picker

Dev / Test	Production	Isolated
For less demanding workloads	For most production workloads	Advanced networking and scale

Recommended pricing tiers

S1 100 total ACU 1.75 GB memory A-Series compute equivalent 5259.30 INR/Month (Estimated)	**P1V2** 210 total ACU 3.5 GB memory Dv2-Series compute equivalent 10518.61 INR/Month (Estimated)	**P2V2**	
P1V3 Premium V3 is not supported for this scale unit. Please consider redeploying or cloning your app. Click to learn more.	**P2V3** Premium V3 is not supported for this scale unit. Please consider redeploying or cloning your app. Click to learn more.	**P3V3**	

∨ See additional co

Included features   Inclu

Every app hosted on this App Service plan will have access to these features.   Every a

🛡 **Custom domains / SSL**
Configure and purchase custom domains with SNI and IP SSL bindings.

📈 **Auto scale**
Up to 10 instances. Subject to availability.

🛡 **Staging slots**
Up to 5 staging slots to use for testing and deployments before swapping them into production.

☁ **Daily backups**
Backup your app 10 times daily.

🌐 **Traffic manager**
Improve performance and availability by routing traffic between multiple instances of your app.

FIGURE 3-27   Selecting a Standard or Premium App Service Plan.

4. Click the **Add Slot** button to start the Add a Slot wizard. (See Figure 3-28.)

🔲 Save	✕ Discard	➕ Add Slot	⇄ Swap	🗒 Logs	🔄 Refresh

🚀 You haven't added any deployment slots. Click here to get started. →

FIGURE 3-28   Adding a new slot.

5. In the Add a Slot wizard (see Figure 3-29), enter a unique name for the new slot in the **Name** box. Then open the **Clone Settings From** drop-down list and specify whether the settings for the slot should be cloned from an existing web app or slot, and if so, which one. Finally, click **Add**.

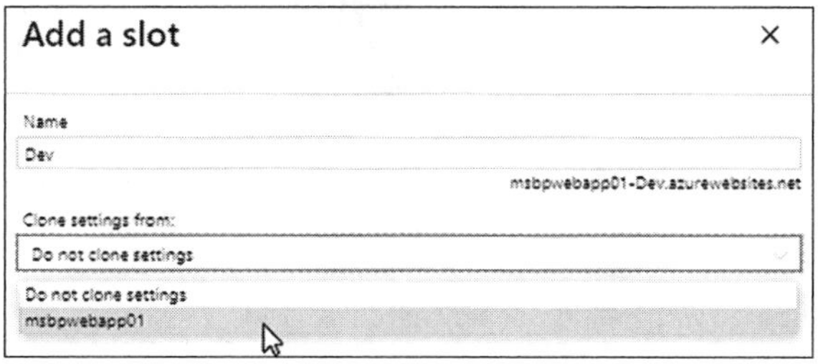

FIGURE 3-29   Selecting the new slot settings.

The new slot appears under the main production slot and any other existing slots for the web app. (See Figure 3-30.)

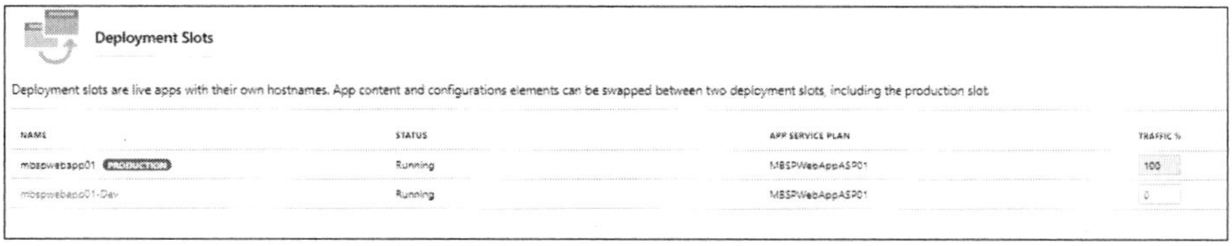

FIGURE 3-30   Multiple deployment slots.

6. Obtain the slot's URL by clicking the slot's name. The URL is displayed in the upper-right corner of the slot's Overview tab. (See Figure 3-31.)

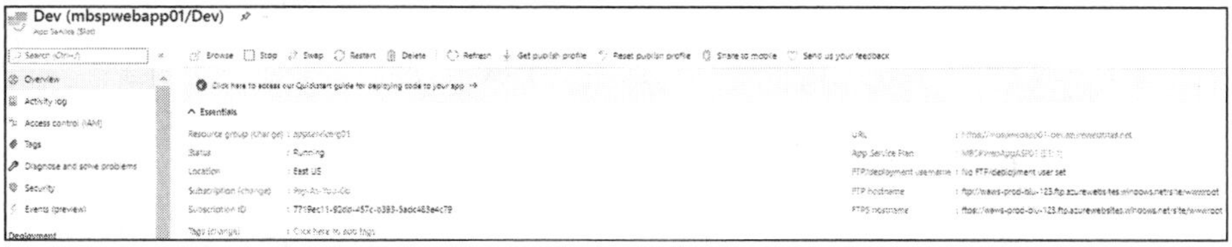

FIGURE 3-31   The new deployment slot's URL.

7. Click the URL to load the default App Service website in your web browser rather than the custom HTML site you built earlier. (See Figure 3-32.)

FIGURE 3-32 The website associated with the new deployment slot's URL.

8. Click the **Deployment Center** button on the web page to open the slot's Deployment Center page with the Settings tab displayed. Notice that the Source setting is blank. (See Figure 3-33.)

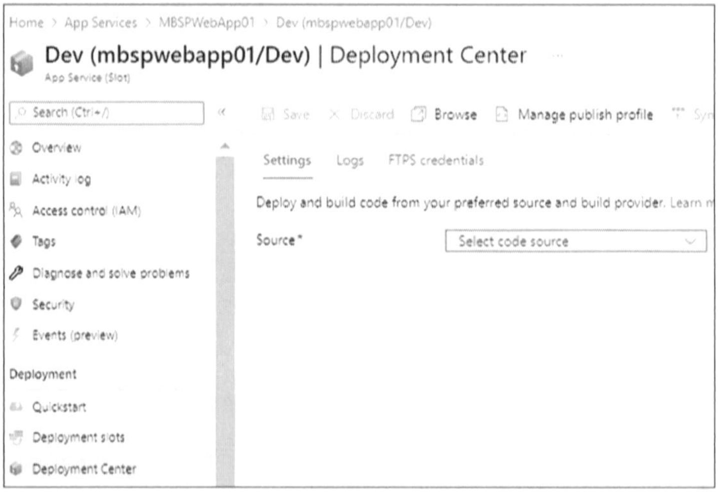

FIGURE 3-33 The slot's Deployment Center page.

9. Open the Source drop-down list and choose the same GitHub account you used earlier, but with a different branch.

USING AZURE POWERSHELL

You can create a deployment slot with Azure PowerShell by using the `New-AzWebAppSlot` command. The following code shows you how to perform this configuration for an existing web app:

```
$ResourceGroup = "AppServiceRG01"
$WebApp = "MBSPWebApp01"
New-AzWebAppSlot -ResourceGroupName $ResourceGroup -name $WebApp -slot dev
```

USING THE AZURE CLI

You can create a deployment slot with the Azure CLI using the `az webapp deployment slot create` command. The following Bash script shows you how to perform this configuration for an existing web app:

```
az webapp deployment slot create --name MBSPWebapp01 --resource-group AppServiceRG01
--slot Dev
```

Deploy code continuously only in staging or testing

You should set up the continuous deployment of code only for staging or testing slots. Setting up continuous deployment for production slots can result in code going live without proper controls.

You should also set up production branch integrations against a dummy slot in the App Service. After the code is deployed in the slot, performing a swap to make the code live is a better approach, as it provides more control over the deployment and allows easy rollback in case of issues.

Use Azure DevOps

Azure DevOps can help with the automated continuous deployment of containers to the App Service. Similarly, you can use the Deployment Center for the continuous delivery of containers to the App Service. After the integration is performed, new commits to the branch will result in the automated building, tagging, and deployment of the updated container.

GitHub Actions

GitHub Actions makes it easy to build, test, and deploy code directly from GitHub to App Service. You should employ GitHub Actions if you are using GitHub as a deployment source to help automate code deployments with proper controls and change tracking.

Multiple instances for production applications

For production applications, it is highly recommended that when you design and code the app, you keep in mind that multiple instances of the application will need to run simultaneously. This might require you to code the app to handle multiple VM instances running the app without sync issues when reading or writing data.

Running a production app with one VM instance creates a single point-of-failure. Instead, you should try to run the application with at least two or three instances, splitting your resource requirements across them, instead of one large instance. This will also help you when any upgrades are performed on the underlying VM instances, because the load will be redirected to the other available instances, preventing any downtime. Fortunately, you can easily achieve this by using the scale-out services provided by your App Service plan. (See Figure 3-34.) It is recommended that you set up automated scaling when handling increased resource or load requirements; setting up a minimum number of instances for the app up front can help mitigate a lot of basic issues.

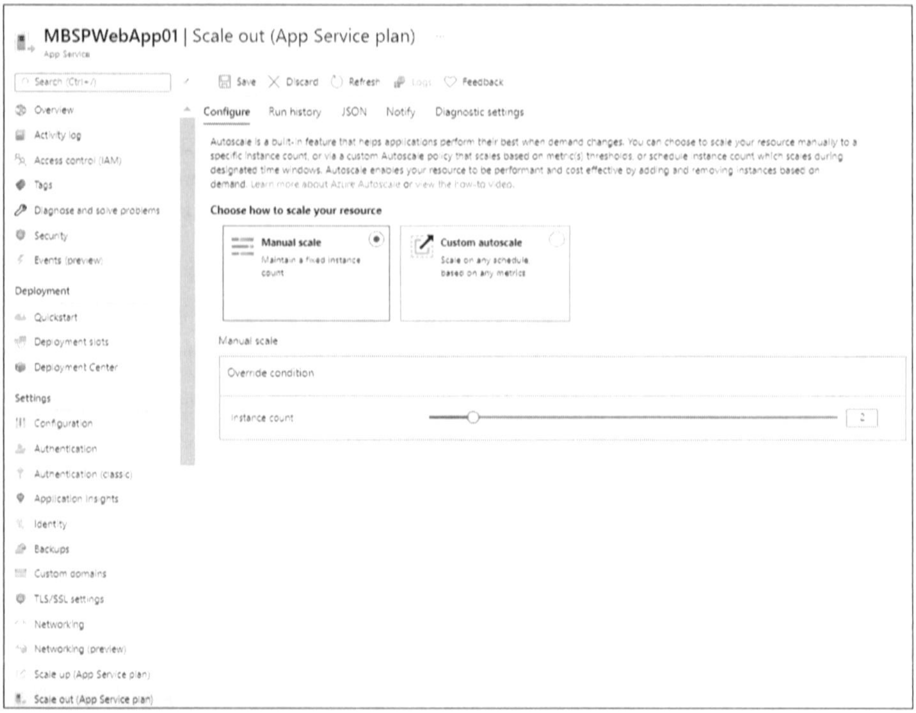

FIGURE 3-34 Scaling for multiple instances.

Collocation

It is a good practice to host all interconnected workloads in the same region—in other words, to collocate them. This helps reduce the following:

- Latency between workloads
- Costs incurred due to data transfer between regions
- Complexity in design and high-availability builds

> **NOTE** Unless there are business or security reasons for hosting workloads across regions, it is better to collocate them.

Enable Always On

Always On is an App Service feature that ensures that VM instances are kept alive, even if there are no ingress requests or traffic to the VM instances for more than 20 minutes. This can help prevent the instance from going offline due to an idle timeout, thereby creating a cold-start situation that leads to delayed response times. Always On is disabled by default, but you easily enable it using the Azure Portal (see Figure 3-35), Azure PowerShell, or Azure CLI.

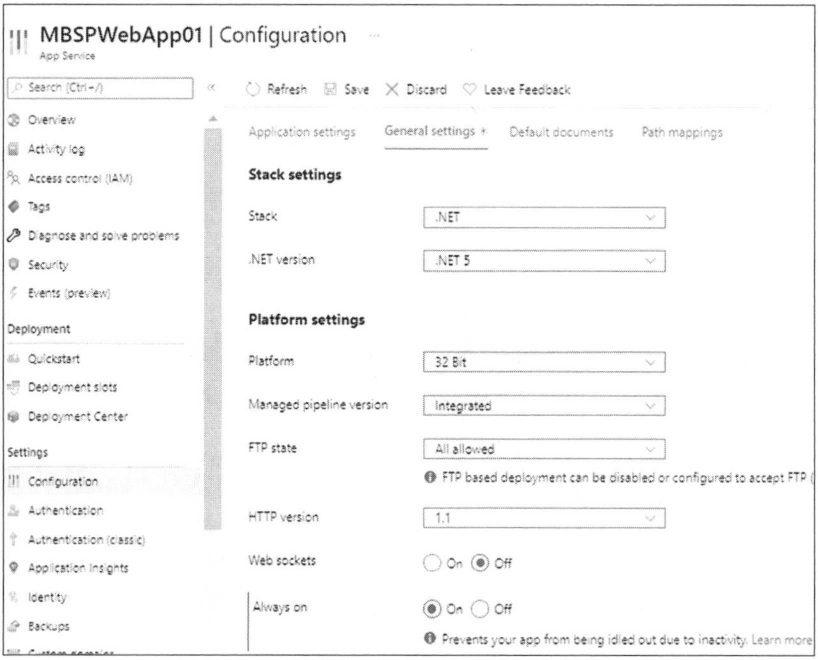

FIGURE 3-35 Enabling the Always On setting.

Disable ARR Affinity

When a client session is unexpectedly disconnected from an app, the general practice is to reconnect the user to the same app instance so the previous session can be continued. One way to do this is to enable the Application Request Routing (ARR) Affinity setting. However, when ARR Affinity is enabled, the app uses affinity cookies, which cause some VM instances to become overloaded with sessions and create load-balancing issues.

To avoid this scenario, it is recommended that you either build a stateless application or store the state information in a back-end service like a database or cache. Once that is in place, you can disable the ARR Affinity setting (see Figure 3-36), which should improve app performance.

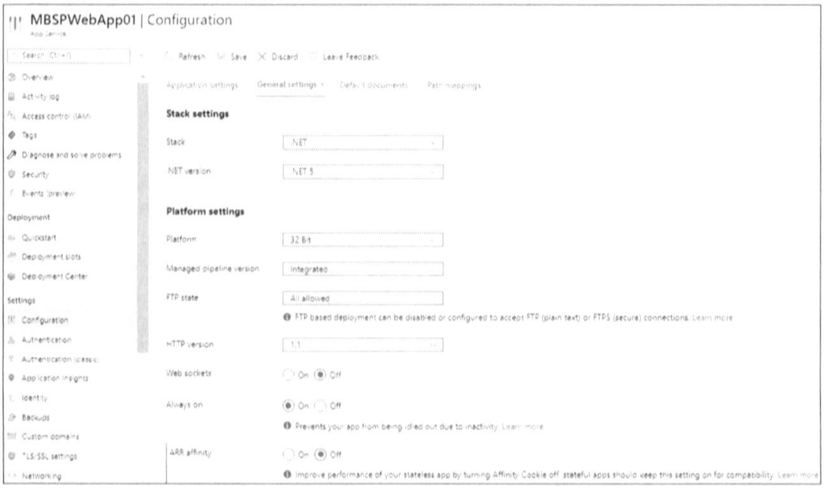

FIGURE 3-36   Disabling ARR Affinity.

Production hardware for production apps

As discussed, there are various App Service tiers available for deployment, and each tier offers specific hardware SKUs to meet different requirements. If the App Service plan is being used for a production application deployment, it is advisable to select hardware in the Production tier. (See Figure 3-37.) This ensures that the hardware resources available to the application are consistent and can be scaled automatically as required.

Define Health Check parameters

App Service has a Health Check feature that monitors the health status of running instances and automatically removes unhealthy instances from the load balancer to avoid disruption in service. This feature is disabled by default; however, it is recommended that you enable it. After you do, define the path that the service should poll on a regular basis to identify unhealthy instances. Be sure the path you select is available on all instances and is critical for the functioning of the application. This will help determine the accurate status of the application. (See Figure 3-38.)

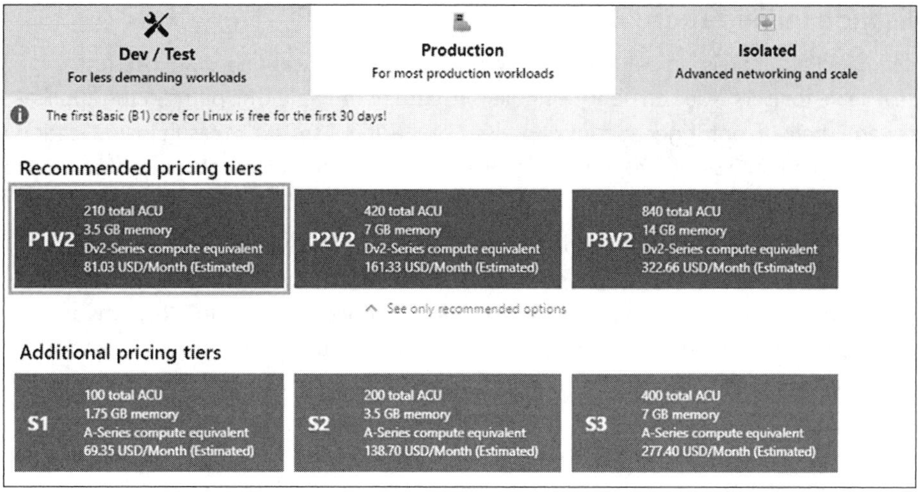

FIGURE 3-37 Selecting the production tier.

> **NOTE** The Health Check feature works only when there are two or more VM instances running in the app. If the app has only a single instance, traffic will not be blocked, even if that instance is deemed unhealthy, as there is no alternative to failover.

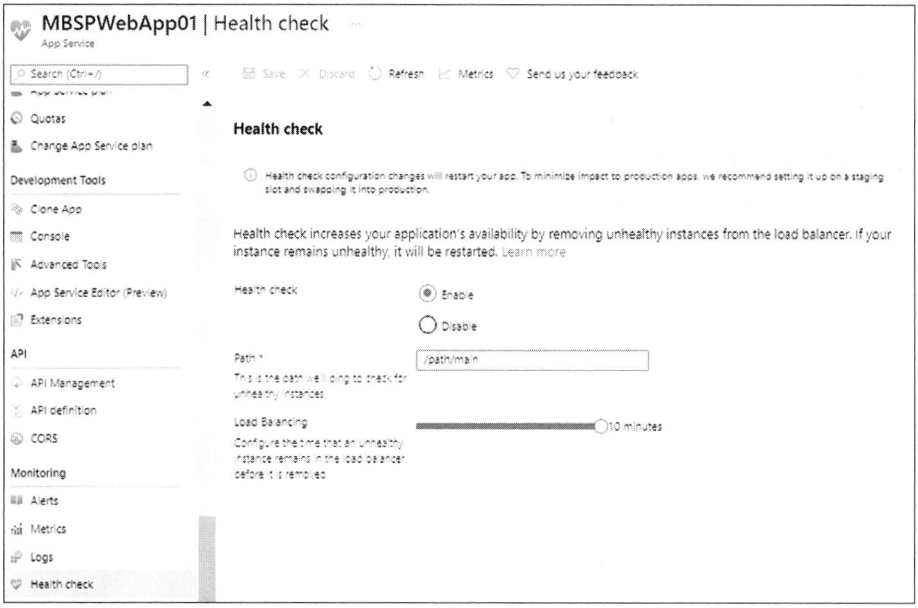

FIGURE 3-38 Configuring Health Check.

Application Initialization

Application Initialization is a great feature to warm up a new application instance before it is made available to users. You can query a single URL path or multiple URL paths in the application to warm them up or trigger a script to preload cache. If not set, it can result in application instances being put into service at the time of any restart or scale-out operation, without being ready to service clients.

In such cases, the recommended approach is to set App Initialization in the web.config file to define the different custom URL paths that need to be queried to confirm that the application is completely online before the instance is put into service. If multiple URL paths are defined, App Service will wait for all the paths to confirm their status (success or failure) before the instance is made live.

> **TIP** Set this up if you notice that new app instances are causing timeouts, access failures, or other unexpected behavior when they come online.

Auto-Heal

Auto-Heal is an App Service feature that enables you to trigger custom actions based on high memory usage, high CPU usage, and so on. The custom actions currently supported include the following:

- Email alerts to admins or stakeholders
- Automated worker process recycling
- Memory dump collection for investigation

This is a great feature, and you can configure it using the web.config tool, the Azure Portal, Azure PowerShell, or the Azure CLI.

Auto-Heal walkthrough

The following section steps you through the process of setting up Auto-Heal using the Azure Portal.

USING THE AZURE PORTAL

To set up Auto-Heal using the Azure Portal, follow these steps:

1. In the left pane of the web app's configuration page, click **Diagnose and Solve Problems**. Then, in the right pane, click **Diagnostic Tools**. (See Figure 3-39.)

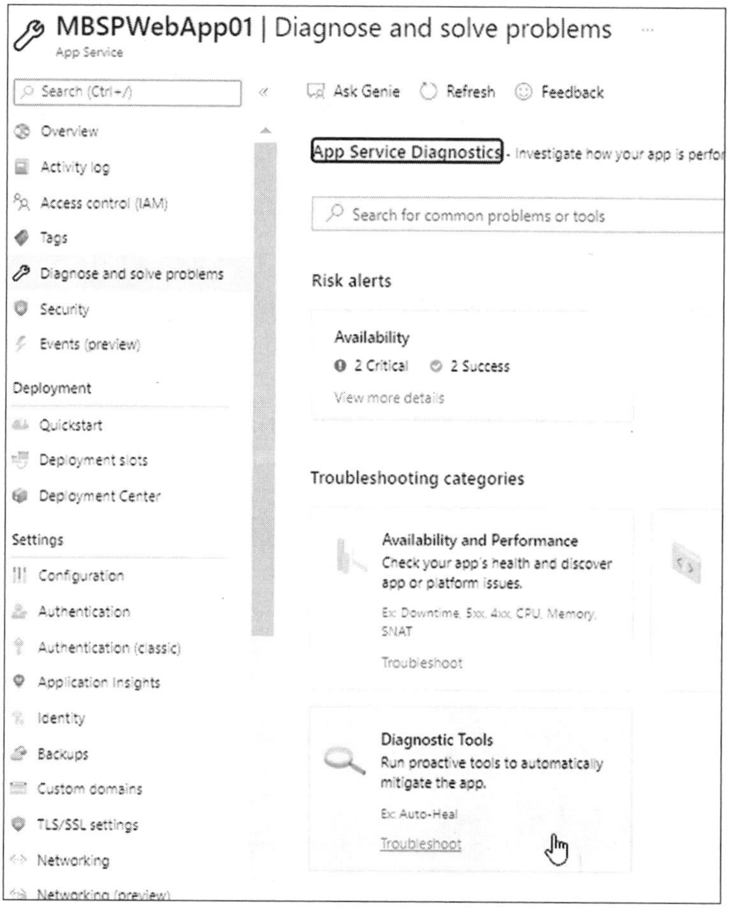

FIGURE 3-39 Selecting the Diagnostic Tools option.

2. Click **Auto-Heal**. (See Figure 3-40.)

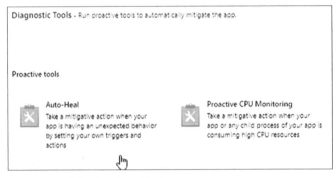

FIGURE 3-40 Selecting Auto-Heal.

3. Next to **Custom Auto-Heal Rules Enabled**, click **On**. Then define the desired conditions, actions, and override options based on your app requirements and click **Save**.
(See Figure 3-41.)

FIGURE 3-41 Enabling Auto-Heal.

Monitor disk space usage

The Azure Portal has an option to monitor App Service quotas, which you can use to monitor
an app's file system usage. For example, you might monitor this to ensure that the web folder
has a minimum of 1 GB of free disk space for faster application restarts and scale-outs. (See
Figure 3-42 and Figure 3-43.)

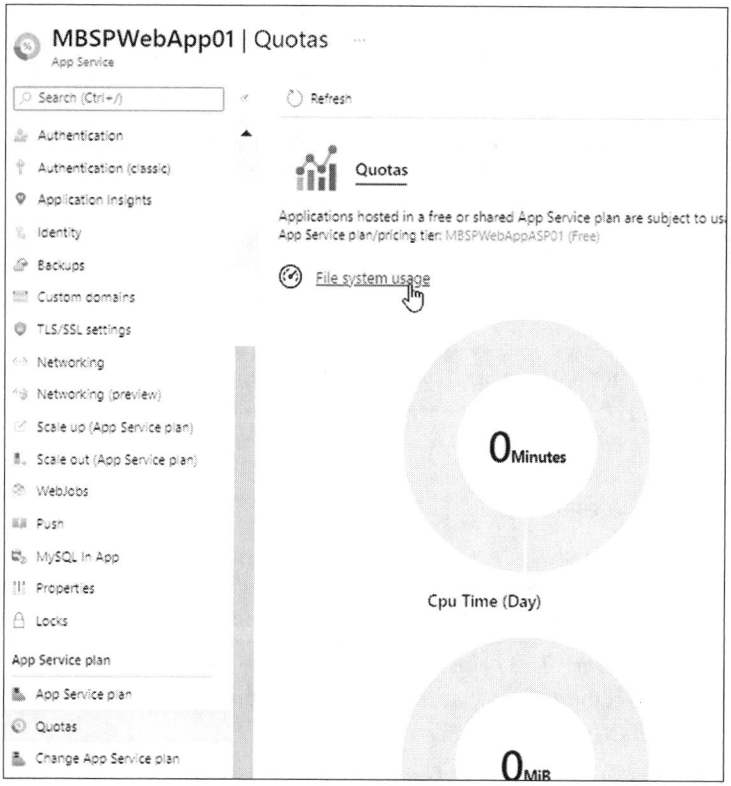

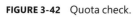

FIGURE 3-42 Quota check.

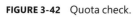

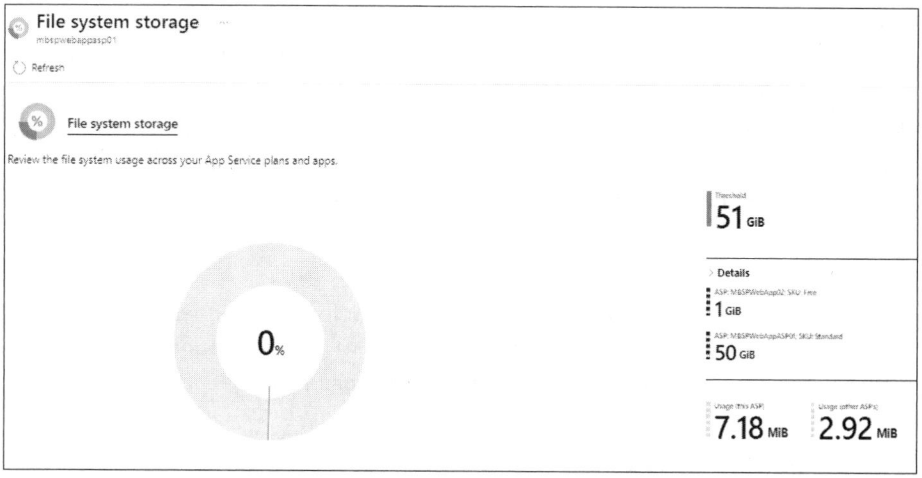

FIGURE 3-43 File system storage usage.

Enable Application Insights

Application Insights is an Azure Monitor feature to detect and analyze performance anomalies, debug code errors, and provide a better understanding of user behavior when using the app.

App Insights includes a feature called the Profiler. This feature enables you to capture the performance of the application and obtain detailed traces to identify hot code paths. (A *hot code path* is the one that take the longest to respond when handling a web request.) This can help you identify bottlenecks within an app and any dependencies. It also allows you to target development or troubleshooting efforts more appropriately.

> **TIP** Profiler works only with .NET applications. If you build an app using .NET, it is highly recommended that you set up Profiler to obtain these deep insights.

Configure monitoring and alerts

Set up monitoring for important parameters and define alerts based on appropriate thresholds. These alerts can be defined on the App Service or the App Service Plan level. There are a few recommendations for monitoring and alerting that can be configured as follows:

- **Average Working Memory Set** This helps identify the average amount of memory in MiBs used by the app. It's recommended to set this value based on the expected average memory requirements so that any breach is alerted.

- **Average CPU Percentage** This helps identify the average CPU used across all the app instances. It's recommended to set this value high enough that alerts can help either scaling or remediation actions to be taken before any service interruptions.

- **HTTP Server Errors** This helps to monitor specific HTTP status codes to identify errors or issues being encountered in web requests. It's recommended to set the value to monitor and alert for high instances of HTTP status codes greater than or equal to 400 and less than 500.

- **Average Response Time** This helps to monitor app responsiveness. If this value is too high, then it might indicate ongoing or imminent problems with the app. It's recommended to set this value for alerting based on stress testing to identify appropriate thresholds for the hosted app.

- **Average Memory Percentage** This helps to monitor the average memory used in all the instances of the app. It's recommended to set this value high enough that alerts can help either scaling or remediation actions to be taken before any service interruptions.

Deploy in multiple regions

One of the best ways to achieve high availability and ensure disaster recovery for an app is to deploy it across multiple regions. Doing so can help ensure that any regional outage does not impact app availability. This will require various other considerations as we've covered in the Disaster Recovery section later in this chapter.

However, if possible, incorporate this into the application design at the earliest stage possible.

A multi-region design can also help in routing requests to the closest datacenter based on the user's region. This can be achieved using Azure Front Door or Azure Traffic Manager to manage all the ingress traffic and route it appropriately. This can also help load-balance traffic between multiple geographies providing global load-balancing.

Plan new app deployments in existing plans

Generally, when a new workload is deployed, there is a temporary spike in resource requirements while the workload is completely online and servicing requests, at which point things stabilize and return to earlier levels until user traffic hits the new workload. If you are deploying a new workload using an existing App Service plan, you should check the CPU and memory usage to make sure there is enough spare capacity to handle this deployment spike.

If CPU or memory utilization reaches or exceeds 90%, you should bring additional VM instances online so the overall load goes down. Then you can deploy the new workload. After deployment, the App Service plan can be scaled down based on the new average resource requirements.

Scaling

Scaling is critical for applications using App Service. It can provide both performance benefits and cost savings—which can be maximized if the scaling occurs automatically.

You can achieve scaling (up or down) by changing your App Service plan tier. Be aware, however, that while a lower-tier plan will reduce your costs, it could have an impact on performance and feature availability. Therefore, it is important to identify which features you need in order to meet your application performance requirements and use this information when selecting your plan. For example:

- **Dev and test phase** Use the Free tier so no compute charges are levied.
- **General testing/pre-production release** Use the Shared tier to leverage additional features such as custom DNS and various resources.
- **Production release** Use the Basic Dedicated tier to use SSL/TLS with more resources for scaling.

> **NOTE** As your needs change or your performance metrics indicate a problem with the selected tier, you can choose a different tier—moving to a higher tier or a lower one based on your storage, compute, or memory requirements.

Scaling up or down by changing plans occurs almost immediately and requires no changes to the code or application configuration. All apps in the App Service plan are affected when scaling occurs; if you update to a higher-tier plan, each app in the plan will be able to use the new features that become available. Generally, scaling up provides access to features including (but not limited to) the following:

- More CPU, memory, and disk space
- Autoscaling
- Custom domains and SSL/TLS certificates
- Deployment slots

NOTE Of course, this will also increase the cost of the App Service plan.

In contrast, scaling down by changing plans removes or reduces the feature set, depending on which plan you choose.

In addition to scaling up or down, you can also scale out or in. Scaling out increases the number of VM instances allocated to run your app(s). For example, in the Dedicated tier, with the Premium V2 and V3 plans, you can deploy 30 VM instances, whereas in the Isolated tier, you can scale out to 100 VM instances. Scaling in is the reverse of these scenarios; you might scale in to reduce costs or unused capacity.

NOTE When you scale out, it applies to all apps running on the App Service plan on all new instances. So, each new instance runs all the apps in the plan.

All scaling operations can be performed manually or automatically—*if* your App Service plan tier supports this. Autoscaling is available only in the Standard and Premium plans on the Dedicated tier and the ASE hosted on the Isolated tier. You can perform automatic scaling based on schedules and/or metric-based rules that trigger the scaling operation.

Per-app scaling

Per-app scaling enables you to scale each app in an App Service plan independently, meaning you can configure an app to run on only a certain number of instances. For example, if your App Service plan supports 20 instances, but one of your apps requires only five instances to handle peak loads, you can use per-app scaling to set the scaling limit to five for that app. This enables you to make more appropriate use of the resources available in the App Service plan by assigning more resources only to the apps that require this.

Per-app scaling is enabled at the App Service plan level and can be configured thereafter independently for each app. Using this feature well can help you achieve the highest level of app density per App Service plan.

Scaling walkthrough

The following sections step you through the process of setting up scaling for your web app using the Azure Portal, Azure PowerShell, and Azure CLI.

USING THE AZURE PORTAL

To set up scaling using the Azure Portal, follow these steps:

1. In the left pane of the web app's configuration page, under **Settings**, click **Scale Up (App Service Plan)**. Then, in the right pane, do one of the following:

    - Click the **Manual Scale** option button. Then, in the **Manual Scale** settings, drag the **Instance Count** slider to **2**. (See Figure 3-44.)

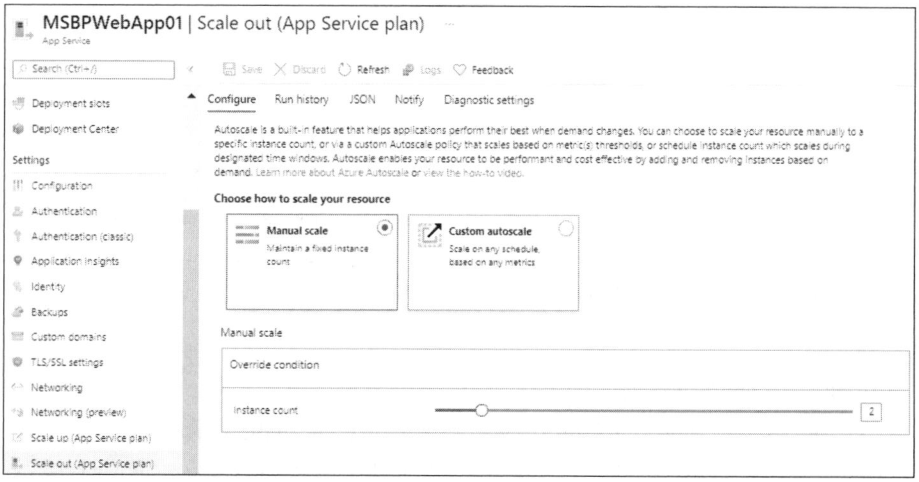

FIGURE 3-44 Manual scale configuration.

    - If you require a more advanced or custom configuration, select the **Custom Autoscale** option button and specify when you want the custom autoscaling operation to be automatically performed. (See Figure 3-45.)

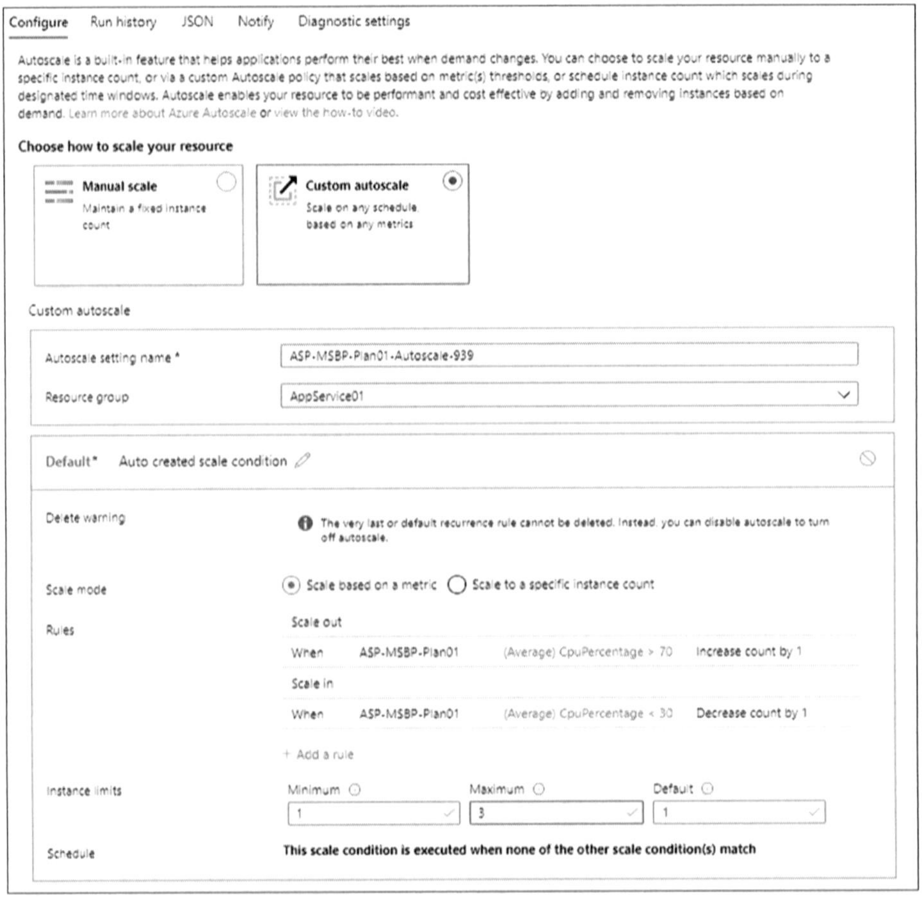

FIGURE 3-45 Custom autoscale configuration.

USING AZURE POWERSHELL

You can set up scaling with Azure PowerShell when you use the `New-AzAppServicePlan` command to create the App Service plan and employ the `-NumberofWorkers` and `-PerSiteScaling` switches. The following code shows you how:

```
#Define the variables for your environment
$ResourceGroup = "{ResourceGroupName}"
$AppServicePlan = "{Name-Of-AppServicePlan}"
$Location = "{AzureRegionName}"
#Set scaling config during plan creation
New-AzAppServicePlan -ResourceGroupName $ResourceGroup -Name $AppServicePlan
-Location $Location -Tier Standard -WorkerSize Small -NumberofWorkers 3
-PerSiteScaling $true
```

You can set up scaling with the Azure CLI when you use the `az appservice plan create` command to create the App Service plan and employ the `--per-site-scaling` and `--number-of-workers` switches. The following Bash script shows you how:

```
#Set the web app variables
WebappName="AppService$random"
Location="EastUS"
ResourceGroup = "ResourceGroup01"
# Set scaling config during plan creation
az appservice plan create --name $WebAppName --resource-group $ResourceGroup
--location $Location --sku S1 --number-of-workers 3 --per-site-scaling
```

Migrate to Azure App Service

One of the key questions in any environment is how best to migrate an existing on-premises app to App Service. To aid with this, Azure provides a free service called App Service Migration Assistant. (See Figure 3-46.) You can use this service to quickly scan and assess an existing web app to determine if it is suitable for migration. If the Migration Assistant service determines that the app is suitable for migration, you can use it to migrate the app to App Service. It is highly recommended that you use this free service to speed up and streamline app migrations.

Get a free compatibility report for your external app

Run a scan on your web app's public URL for a report of the technologies it uses and whether App Service fully supports them. If compatible, you'll be guided to download the migration assistant to simplify your migration.

Assess your web app for migration now.

Enter a public URL (https://)

FIGURE 3-46 Azure App Service Migration Assistant.

Networking considerations

As discussed, you must consider numerous deployment and operational issues when deciding on the most appropriate strategy to set up a new App Service in Azure. Similarly, you need to consider various networking solutions. The following sections cover the different networking services that are supported for integration with Azure App Service and some best practices associated with each.

By default, App Service allows all hosted apps to be accessible over the public internet. Although that might be appropriate for a large number of customer-facing apps, numerous internal or protected applications require more granular control over inbound and outbound traffic. You can set up numerous Azure services and App Service features to provide the required level of protection. Each service can help in addressing the requirements in different ways; thus, it is important to understand how each one works to design the right strategy for App Service networking.

Service endpoints and private endpoints

Azure App Service offers two types of deployment scenarios:

- **Free, Shared, Basic, Standard, Premium, PremiumV2, and PremiumV3 pricing SKUs** Apps are hosted on a multi-tenant infrastructure.
- **Isolated SKU App Service plan** A single-tenant ASE hosts all the apps directly in the client's Azure virtual network.

In a multi-tenant scenario, service endpoints enable you to define inbound traffic restrictions, allowing traffic only from a set of trusted subnets to connect to the web app. In this way, you can restrict traffic to only required resources such as VMs, other ASEs, or even other apps that use VNet Integration.

> **NOTE** You can configure service endpoints using the Azure Portal, Azure PowerShell, and the Azure CLI.

Private endpoints are available only in the PremiumV2 and PremiumV3 tier App Service plans. They allow apps hosted on the multi-tenant infrastructure to be securely connected to the customer's virtual private network. So, all inbound traffic to the web app from the customer's virtual network flows over a secure and private connection. (See Figure 3-47.)

Some key benefits of using a private endpoint include the following:

- You can restrict inbound app access to resources in a specific virtual network.
- Users and resources within the connected virtual network can access apps using an internal private IP.
- You can use a web application firewall (WAF) used along with a private endpoint for enhanced protection.
- Data leakage and data theft are difficult, as the app is accessible only on a protected network.

Some limitations when using private endpoints include the following:

- A web app can support only 100 private endpoints.
- Remote debugging is not supported.
- FTP access to the web app is not allowed.

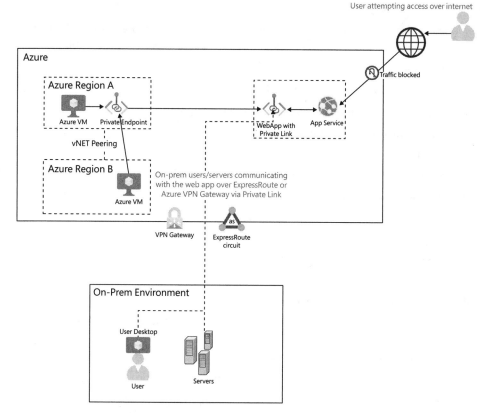

FIGURE 3-47 Private endpoint connections.

VNet integration

VNet integration helps multi-tenant apps access resources in other Azure VNet and interconnected networks. It provides outbound access from the app to the VNet and connected networks. This makes it possible for the app to access any resource located inside those networks.

This feature has two variations:

- **Regional integration** This is when the integration is with a VNet within the same Azure region as the app. Regional integration requires a dedicated subnet in the VNet for integration.

- **Gateway-required integration** This is when the integration is with a VNet in another Azure region or with a classic VNet in the same region. Here, an Azure virtual network gateway is provisioned in the destination VNet for the integration.

> **NOTE** VNet integration is an advanced feature and available only with the Standard and Premium plans.

Regional VNet integration

As mentioned, regional VNet integration is when the App Service is integrated with a VNet in the same Azure region as the app. This enables apps to access resources located within:

- The same region as the app
- Any VNet peered with the integrated VNet
- Any networks connected via ExpressRoute to the integrated VNet
- Service-endpoint secured services
- Private endpoint resources

Some restrictions with regional VNet integration include the following:

- The integration subnet must be unused and dedicated to only one App Service plan.
- The integration subnet must be /28 or larger.
- Classic VNet is not supported.
- Only one regional VNet is supported per App Service plan.

Gateway-required VNet integration

Gateway-required VNet integration is useful when an app requires access to resources located in:

- An Azure VNet in a region different from the app
- An Azure classic virtual network in the same or different region

This requires an Azure Virtual Network gateway configured with an SSTP point-to-site VPN for the integration. Once integrated, the apps can get access to resources located within:

- Any VNet peered with the integrated VNet
- Any networks connected via VPN to the integrated VNet

Some restrictions with gateway-required VNet integration include the following:

- No support for Azure ExpressRoute connections.
- Only one VNet at a time can be connected.
- An App Service Plan supports a maximum of five VNet integrations.

Traffic Manager and Azure Front Door

You can use Traffic Manager and Azure Front Door to control and distribute requests from web clients across App Service endpoints. These endpoints, which are geographically dispersed, are set to Active or Passive; based on the routing logic applied, traffic is redirected, taking into account the availability and load on the App Service endpoint.

Azure Traffic Manager is a global DNS-based load-balancing service that distributes traffic among back-end application nodes based on a load-balancing algorithm you select. It provides a public endpoint that diverts incoming client requests to the available application node hosted in Azure or in another external service.

Azure Front Door is great for application acceleration and global HTTP(S) load balancing. It provides more features than Traffic Manager and is highly recommended for use with App Service. It supports SSL offloading, Application layer processing, AnyCast routing, and content caching for faster performance and security against DDoS attacks.

Three primary routing algorithms overlap between Traffic Manager and Front Door:

- **Latency/performance** The closest app is selected based on the lowest network latency to the back ends.

- **Priority** Priority is given to the primary app defined in the configuration. Other locations hosting the same app are set up as backups so that traffic can be failed over if the primary is unavailable.

- **Weighted** Traffic is distributed across a set of apps evenly or based on a weight assigned to each app.

In addition to these three, Traffic Manager provides one additional routing algorithm:

- **Performance** Users are redirected to the closest app region based on their network latency to the app location.

Similarly, Azure Front Door provides one additional routing algorithm:

- **Geographic** Users are redirected to apps that are closest to their geographic location.

Hybrid Connections

The Hybrid Connections feature helps connect an app to on-premises resources over a secure port. It does this by setting up a relay agent, called Hybrid Connection Manager (HCM), that requires access to both the on-premises endpoint and App Service over port 443. Once the relay agent is operational, the app hosted in Azure can access resources on any TCP-enabled host endpoint on any port or application protocol. The connection is secured using TLS 1.2; in addition, shared access signature (SAS) keys authenticate and authorize resource access.

Some of the main benefits of using Hybrid Connections are as follows:

- Secure access to on-premises resources over private or public networks.

- Service-based provisioning, making it fast to set up and configure.

- Works on port 443, making it easier to handle across most firewalls.

- Multiple networks can be accessed using the same relay agent.

- No dependency on application protocol, language, or port requirements, as long as TCP support is available.

However, Hybrid Connections has a few limitations:

- It only supports TCP. It does not support the UDP protocol.

- It cannot be used to mount network-enabled drives remotely to the app.

- It uses dynamic port mapping for app access.

Network security groups

You can use network security groups (NSGs) to block both ingress and egress traffic to all resources in a VNet. For apps that use the regional VNet integration feature:

- Egress traffic can be managed using NSGs.
- Ingress traffic management requires the use of the Access Restrictions feature.

Route tables

Route tables help to set up custom routes required to enforce a specific routing configuration. You can use route tables to route outbound traffic as needed.

Azure DNS private zones

Once an app is integrated into a VNet, the DNS server configured for the VNet is applied to the app as well. If the VNet is set to use Azure DNS private zones, this would cause issues for the app, because by default, it does not support private DNS zones. However, you can enable this support configuring application settings to force all outbound traffic from the app via the VNet and require the use of the Azure DNS private zone.

Backup and restore

Azure App Service has a built-in backup and restore feature available for the Standard, Premium, and Isolated tiers. This feature allows you to create backups manually or on an automated schedule. Backups can be retained indefinitely, which is useful for organizations with long-term data-retention requirements.

The Azure App Service backup feature can currently back up the following:

- File contents
- The application configuration
- Databases interconnected for use with the app, including Azure SQL Database, Azure Database for MySQL, and Azure Database for PostgreSQL

Some key features of this built-in backup service are as follows:

- Each backup is triggered as a full backup rather than an incremental backup. This makes restore operations fast and reliable, as dependencies on earlier backups are reduced.
- Restore operations can restore to the existing app or to a new app. This is useful in scenarios in which you need to create a new test or dev environment from a recent backup.
- You can schedule backups using the Azure Portal, Azure PowerShell, or the Azure CLI.

It's important to be aware of a few limitations when setting up the backup feature:

- Backups are supported for a maximum of 10 GB of app and database content. In addition, backups of individual databases can have a maximum size of 4 GB. Backups exceeding this size will fail.

- This feature is supported only for the Standard and Premium Dedicated tiers and the Isolated tier.
- If VNet integration is in place, the backup and restore features cannot be used at the same time.
- The Azure storage required to store the backups should be in the same subscription, and preferably the same region, as the App Service.
- The firewall service for the storage account should not be configured or online.
- Backups for in-app MySQL databases are automatic, without the need for any configuration steps. However, if manual configuration settings, such as connection strings, are put in place, automated backups will not work correctly.
- TLS encryption for MySQL or PostgreSQL will cause backups to fail. If that is a requirement for the environment, consider a third-party backup solution.

Backup walkthrough

The following sections step you through the process of setting up backups for your web app using the Azure Portal, Azure PowerShell, and the Azure CLI.

> **NOTE** Adjust the storage names per your requirements.

USING THE AZURE PORTAL

To set up backups using the Azure Portal, follow these steps:

1. In the left pane of the web app's configuration page, under **Settings**, click **Backup**. (See Figure 3-48.) By default, no backups are configured.

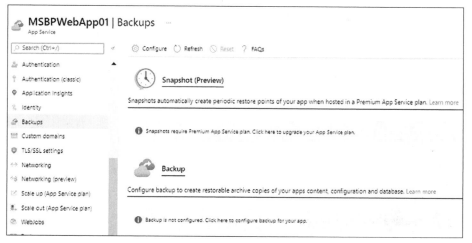

FIGURE 3-48 Backup configuration for web apps.

2. Under **Backup**, click the **Backup Is Not Configured. Click Here to Configure Backup for Your App** link. (See Figure 3-49.)

FIGURE 3-49 Backup is not configured.

3. In the Backup Configuration page, enter the following information (see Figure 3-50):

   ■ **Backup Storage**   Click the container in which you want to store the backup.

   ■ **Scheduled Backup**   Click **On**.

   ■ **Backup Every**   Specify how frequently backups should occur, in days or hours.

   ■ **Start Backup Schedule From**   Specify the date, time, and time zone when the backup schedule should start.

   ■ **Retention (Days)**   Specify how long (in days) the backup should be retained.

   ■ **Keep At Least One Backup**   Click **Yes** to ensure that at least one backup is always retained.

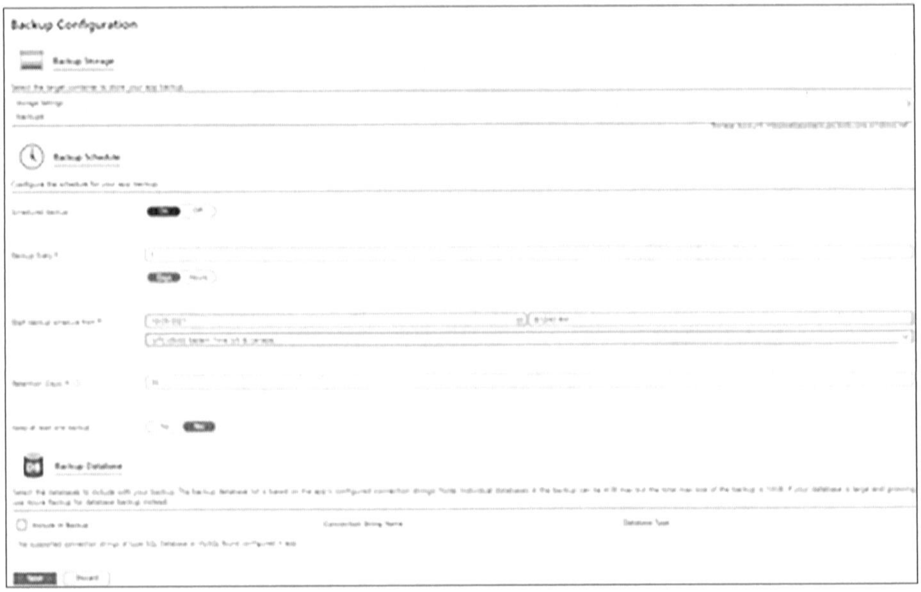

FIGURE 3-50   Configuring backup settings.

USING AZURE POWERSHELL

You can set up backups for a web app with Azure PowerShell using the `New-AzWebAppBackup` command. This command triggers a one-time backup. To schedule a backup, you must use the `Edit-AzWebAppBackupConfiguration` command.

To trigger a one-time backup, use the following code:

```
#Set variables
$resourcegroup="AppServiceRG01"
$appname="mywebapp$(Get-Random -Minimum 100000 -Maximum 999999)"
$storageaccountname="backupsstorage"
$storagecontainer="backups"
$location="East US 2"
$backupname="BackupOnce"
# Generate an SAS token for the storage container, valid for one month.
$sastokenUrl = New-AzStorageContainerSASToken -Name $storagecontainer -Permission rwdl
-Context $storageaccountname.Context -ExpiryTime (Get-Date).AddMonths(1) -FullUri
# Create a one-time backup
New-AzWebAppBackup -ResourceGroupName $resourcegroup -Name $appname -StorageAccountUrl
$sastokenUrl -BackupName $backupname
```

To schedule a backup, use the following code:

```
#Set variables
$resourcegroup="AppServiceRG01"
$appname="MSBPAPP01"
$storageaccountname="backupsstorage"
$storagecontainer="backups"
$location="East US 2"
# Generate an SAS token for the storage container, valid for 1 year.
$sastokenUrl = New-AzStorageContainerSASToken -Name $storagecontainer -Permission rwdl
-Context $storageaccountname.Context -ExpiryTime (Get-Date).AddYears(1) -FullUri
# Schedule a backup every day, beginning in two hours, and retain for 30 days
Edit-AzWebAppBackupConfiguration -ResourceGroupName $resourcegroup -Name $appname
-StorageAccountUrl $sastokenUrl -FrequencyInterval 1 -FrequencyUnit Day
-KeepAtLeastOneBackup -StartTime (Get-Date).AddHours(2) -RetentionPeriodInDays 30
```

USING THE AZURE CLI

You can set up backups for a web app with the Azure CLI using the `az webapp config backup create` command. This command triggers a one-time backup. To schedule a backup, you must use the `az webapp config backup update` command.

To trigger a one-time backup, use the following code:

```
#!/bin/bash
#Set variables
resourcegroupname="AppServiceRG01"
```

```
appname=MSBP-APP01
storagename=backupsstorage
location="EastUS2"
backupcontainer="backups"
backupname="backuponce"
expirydate=$(date -I -d "$(date) + 2 months")
# Generates an SAS token for the storage container, valid for one month.
sastoken=$(az storage container generate-sas --account-name $storagename
--name $backupcontainer --expiry $expirydate --permissions rwdl --output tsv)
# Construct the SAS URL for the container
sastokenurl=https://$storagename.blob.core.windows.net/$backupcontainer?$sastoken
# Create a one-time backup
az webapp config backup create --resource-group $resourcegroupname --webapp-name
$appname --backup-name $backupname --container-url $sastokenurl
```

To schedule a backup, use the following code:

```
#!/bin/bash
#Set variables
resourcegroupname="AppServiceRG01"
appname=MSBP-APP01
storagename=backupsstorage
location="EastUS2"
backupcontainer="appbackup"
expirydate=$(date -I -d "$(date) + 1 month")
# Generate an SAS token for the storage container, valid for one month.
sastoken=$(az storage container generate-sas --account-name $storagename
--name $backupcontainer --expiry $expirydate --permissions rwdl --output tsv)
# Construct the SAS URL for the container
sastokenurl=https://$storagename.blob.core.windows.net/$backupcontainer?$sastoken
# Schedule a backup every day and retain for 10 days
az webapp config backup update --resource-group $resourcegroupname --webapp-name
$appname --container-url $sastokenurl --frequency 1d --retain-one true --retention 10
```

Disaster recovery

In the event of a region-wide failure of the Azure infrastructure, causing App Service and all hosted apps to go offline, you would need to bring App Service back online in another available region and restore your data within that new region. You can achieve this in multiple ways, including the following:

- **Multi-site architecture**   You can set up App Service in such a way that the same apps are published across multiple Azure regions and the database is replicated geographically. Moreover, you can set up any interdependent components in a multi-site design or set them up to work with high availability (HA). This type of design is also called an active-active datacenter design.

- **Standby site** You can preconfigure the standby region with all required apps and interconnected services and replicate required data to that site. The standby site can then be brought online in the event of a disaster. This type of design is also called an active-passive with hot standby design.

- **Cold recovery** A cold recovery is where a failover site is identified, and all required services and data are restored and brought online on that site after a disaster, either manually or automatically. This type of design is also called an active-passive with cold standby design.

There are numerous factors to consider when developing a disaster-recovery strategy, especially for cold-recovery scenarios. Be sure to consider the following points in your planning:

- Identify all interconnected components within the App Service and decide on the best strategy to make them either region-independent or restorable in another region when required. These should include (but are not limited to) the following:
    - Deployment slot configurations
    - TLS/SSL certificates
    - Azure Key Vault configuration, including secrets, certificates, and managed identities
    - Integrations with load balancers, Azure Traffic Manager, WAFs, or Azure Firewall
    - Integrations using Hybrid Connections, site-to-site VPNs, or ExpressRoute
    - Integrations with third-party services that must be rebuilt

- Refer to the product documentation or configuration of each service to validate data replication or availability in the desired failover region in the event of a disaster.

- Identify and document the steps to restore each service (and the configuration required to reintegrate it, if needed), and the order in which each service should be restored.

- Test the restoration procedure, if possible, on a regular basis.

- Identify the testing parameters after restoration to validate a successful restore.

- Regularly review procedures and processes in place to ensure any changes in the environment, in product features, or in Microsoft's terms of service are taken into account in the event a restoration operation becomes necessary.

> **NOTE** Only the Premium tier supports moving an app from one region to another. However, in a disaster scenario, Microsoft enables this functionality for all App Service plans. So, apps can be migrated, restored, or downloaded, regardless of plan.

Cost considerations

It's relatively easy to set up and scale up Azure App, but you can incur unwanted costs if you don't plan and monitor it. To better gauge and manage your monthly spend, it is therefore important to understand the different elements in the App Service environment that are subject to charge.

The main resource charges are associated with compute resources for VM instances. These charges depend on the App Service plan tier and the number of VM instances deployed. The charges levied are based on the number of times the instances are online. It is highly recommended to monitor the usage of instances and identify areas where you can better manage it. This can help you significantly decrease your spending.

In addition to compute resources, Microsoft charges for some additional resources, including the following:

- App Service domains
- App Service certificates
- IP-based certificate bindings
- Storage for backup and diagnostic logging
- A virtual network for the Isolated tier ASE

NOTE Your monthly bill will provide a detailed breakdown of the charges associated with each of these different resources.

There are various ways to optimize costs associated with App Service and related workloads. Here are just a few:

- **Host multiple apps in a single plan** One of the best ways to optimize costs is to collocate multiple apps within the same App Service plan. This will require you to analyze application and API loads to determine which apps to host together. On a related note, you can move apps to different App Service plans within the same region and resource group to optimize usage over time based on load analysis. You'll want to consider this when deciding which plan to use to host your app.

NOTE Hosting multiple apps on a plan results in higher app density. This can help you reduce the number of plans you need, thereby optimizing costs.

- **Use the Free or Shared tier to host test and dev workloads** Using the Free or Shared tier for dev and test workloads can help keep costs low during those stages. These tiers are also an excellent choice for most environments for hosting functions, scripts, and code snippets, depending on their runtime and SLA requirements.

- **Use the Standard tier or above to host production workloads**   Using the Standard tier or above to host production workloads ensures those workloads are covered by the App Service SLA. This is because the hardware available on these tiers provides much better performance than the hardware resources allocated to the Free and Shared tiers. The Standard and above tiers also offer better memory, storage, security, and scaling features.

- **Use autoscaling**   Be aware that the cost of running workloads on the Standard or higher tiers is much higher. Therefore, to optimize costs, you should use autoscaling to remove VM instances when they are inactive. Autoscaling is supported in the Standard Dedicated tiers and can be used both to scale out and to scale in, ensuring that only the compute resources required are online.

- **Reserve instances**   The Dedicated PremiumV3 and Isolated tiers enable you to reserve and pre-pay for instances at a discount for use later on. You can reserve between one and three years in advance; the longer the reservation period, the cheaper it is. If you know the minimum number of compute resources you will require for the next one to three years, it would be advisable to reserve them to obtain the significant cost benefit.

> **NOTE**   If you use more compute resources than you reserved, the additional compute resources will be charged at the normal rate rather than the discounted rate. Therefore, you should monitor the usage of the apps hosted in the App Service plan over time to determine if additional reservations are required.

- **Set up budgets**   Setting up a budget can help stakeholders keep better track of their costs and (hopefully) eliminate overspending. You can set up alerts to notify application admins if spending does exceed your budget, enabling them to take immediate action to reduce the spend.

- **Monitor your spending**   Once your budget is in place, it is important to monitor your costs on a regular basis to identify unwanted spends and areas that might be ripe for optimization. Trend analysis of this data can also help in forecasting for future planning.

- **Analyze in PowerBI or Excel**   You can export the data you collect over time when monitoring costs to Microsoft PowerBI or Microsoft Excel to analyze historical trends across datasets. You can do this on a scheduled basis—daily, weekly, or monthly— making it possible to perform a long-term analysis.

- **Avoid post-deletion charges**   Even if you delete all the apps in an App Service plan, charges for that plan, and the number of VM instances deployed, will continue to apply. To avoid incurring these charges, you should delete the plan or scale it down to the Free tier. You can also remove other associated resources manually, such as the following:

    - Virtual networks created for the Isolated tier
    - The Key Vault used to store TLS/SSL certificates

- Log Analytics workspaces for log ingestion and analysis
- Backup and diagnostic logging storage accounts

Security recommendations

There are numerous security recommendations to consider when hosting apps on App Service. These are some of the most common ones:

- **Use the latest version if possible**   Make sure the platforms, frameworks, programming languages, and protocols used by your apps are up to date. This can significantly reduce the attack surface.

- **Turn off anonymous access**   Anonymous access is one of the leading causes of data theft. Unless there is a need to allow anonymous requests, it is recommended that you disable it completely. If you absolutely must allow anonymous requests, expose only the app elements that require anonymous access while securing all other APIs or access points.

- **Use the built-in authentication module**   Rather than using custom code, employ the built-in authentication module to handle all authentication and authorization requests. This helps reduce coding errors that might pose a security threat—not to mention saving you time and effort.

- **Protect access to back-end resources**   Make sure back-end resources are protected by using authentication. This authentication could call for either the user's identity or their managed identity. Managed identity is an identity managed by the Azure platform itself. This makes it easy to maintain because it eliminates the need to rotate secrets manually.

- **Map custom domains and use certificates**   It is a good practice to map custom domains for apps. This makes it easier for end-users to access the app. App Service supports several types of certificates, based on security needs:

  - **Free App Service Managed certificate**   This is a free certificate issued by DigiCert, which is automatically renewed every six months. Be aware that this certificate has some limitations. For example, it does not allow exports, it is not supported with ASE, and it does not support wildcard certifications. In addition, it does not support client authentication and does not integrate with Traffic Manager. However, if these are acceptable, then it is a great option.

  - **App Service certificate**   This is a certificate issued by GoDaddy. There are two types currently available: Standard and Wildcard. The certificate is stored in Azure Key vault and automatically renewed.

  - **Third-party certificate**   This is a certificate procured from a trusted third-party certificate provider. These certificates can either be imported into Azure Key Vault and then imported into App Service or imported directly into App Service.

- **Private certificate** This is a certificate created by the customer using an internal PKI infrastructure. This certificate is best for apps used for internal testing or for apps used by internal employees on managed devices. This certificate requires the certificate chain to be deployed on the device. The certificate can be imported into Azure Key Vault and then imported into App Service or imported directly into App Service.

> **IMPORTANT** Be sure to provision a well-known SSL/TLS certificate so client browsers connect over HTTPS without errors.

- **Use certificates to limit access** If you need to limit access to the application to specific clients, using a certificate for client authentication is highly recommended, as it blocks connections from clients missing the required certificate.
- **Use HTTPS instead of HTTP** Although App Service allows both HTTP and HTTPS connections, it is highly recommended that all HTTP requests be redirected to HTTPS. This ensures that all connections are secured by default using the SSL/TLS certificate deployed for HTTPS. All authentication and client communication would take place on a secure channel, reducing traffic snooping.
- **Disable TLS 1.0** Industry standards such as PCI DSS have deemed TLS 1.0 as an unsecure protocol. It is highly recommended that you disable TLS 1.0, forcing all apps to use TLS 1.1 or, preferably, TLS 1.2. Figure 3-51 shows the settings to use HTTPS only and to disable TLS 1.0.

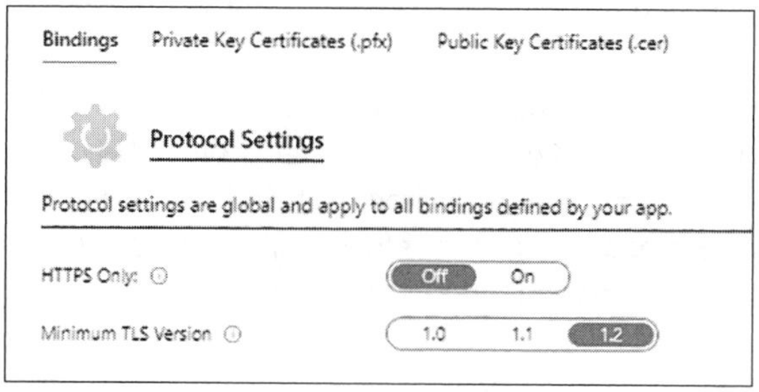

FIGURE 3-51 Setting HTTPS only and specifying the minimum TLS version.

- **Encrypt communication** When integrating apps with other Azure services such as Azure Storage, Azure SQL Database, or other database services, all communication between the workloads remains within the Azure back end. However, that traffic is on shared network infrastructure within Azure. Therefore, it is highly recommended that you encrypt this traffic to ensure that all communication is secure at all times.

- **Secure FTP traffic**   Use the FTP protocol judiciously, only when required. In addition, use it only over SSL/TLS so that all communication is secure. In short, avoid using FTP unless absolutely necessary.

- **Use Key Vault or environment variables**   Use Azure Key Vault and managed identity for secure storage, access, and management of application secrets. This includes API tokens, database credentials, and private keys that are otherwise included in the application code. If you cannot use managed identities, then it is recommended that you use environment variables in app settings and connection strings to store these values. These are stored securely with encryption and are decrypted just before being passed on to the application's process memory. The Azure platform manages the encryption keys and rotates them on a regular basis, making the system very difficult to breach.

- **Define IP restrictions (if necessary)**   Depending on your application access requirements, access to the app can be restricted for certain IP addresses or IP ranges only. This can help secure access especially for highly sensitive apps where the users accessing the application are known and access has to be limited to known networks only.

- **Define dynamic access restrictions**   For apps hosted on a Windows-based App Service, you can prevent external distributed denial of service (DDoS) attacks defining the following parameters to dynamically restrict access:
  - Deny IP address based on the number of concurrent requests.
  - Deny IP address based on the number of requests over a period of time.

- **Use the Isolated pricing tier for network isolation**   The Isolated tier is best used for apps that require all network infrastructure to be isolated and dedicated for use by a single organization only. If your organization has compliance or security needs that require such enforcement, use the Isolated tier.

- **Protect communications when accessing on-premises resources**   On-premises resources can be accessed using Hybrid Connections, via site-to-site VPNs, or by connecting the ASE directly to an on-premises environment. Each of these methods provides secure access to resources. Based on the network topology in place, select the best method for your environment, making sure all communication is directed over the selected channel only.

- **Use NSGs for ingress traffic**   Use NSGs to protect and manage ingress traffic and network access. Expose only the required endpoints and prevent access to others. Periodically review the NSG configuration to make sure no unwanted endpoints are exposed.

- **Leverage Azure Security Center**   You should use the Azure Security Center service to periodically carry out security assessments. You should also implement recommendations issued by Azure Security Center to plug security holes and employ its Integrated Threat Intelligence functionality to prevent traffic from known-malicious IP addresses.

- **Use Azure Policy**   Use Azure Policy to define and implement built-in policies for App Service, such as HTTPS enforcement, minimum allowed TLS version, and enforcement of a virtual network service endpoint.

- **Use Azure Activity Log to monitor changes**   After policy definitions are in place, you can use Azure Activity Log to monitor configuration changes to network resources, network settings, and any resources related to App Service.

- **Use Azure Monitor for centralized logging**   You can store Azure Activity and App Service Diagnostic Logs in Azure storage, Log Analytics, or event hubs. Azure Monitor then uses these to centrally monitor events and changes.

- **Encrypt source data at rest**   It is a recommended practice to encrypt application source data at rest. This means encrypting the data stored in Azure storage with platform- or customer-managed encryption keys and using Azure Key Vault to inject application secrets at runtime as part of the application settings.

- **Use WAF for inbound traffic**   Secure access to an internet-facing application using the WAF deployed in front of the app. Then use service endpoints and access restrictions on the WAF to secure ingress traffic. A WAF protects internet-facing applications from DDoS attacks, URI filtering, and SQL injection attacks.

- **Use Azure Firewall for outbound traffic**   Use the Azure Firewall service to centrally divert all outbound traffic. This allows the enforcement of traffic-management policies and captures and monitors logs for centralized analysis.

## Chapter 4

Azure Virtual Desktop

Overview

Azure Virtual Desktop (AVD) is a desktop-as-a-service that is built to run at scale in Microsoft Azure. It is a virtualization service for both desktops and applications that combines and leverages different Azure services for compute, storage, networking, security, and monitoring, to deliver a complete solution.

> **NOTE** Azure Virtual Desktop (AVD) used to be called Windows Virtual Desktop (WVD). Occasionally you might see references to WVD instead AVD in this chapter and in Microsoft's own products.

Key features

Features of AVD include the following:

- You can publish virtual desktops and apps on the Windows Server OS and the Windows 10 Desktop OS, giving users a familiar experience to their on-premises environment.
- AVD allows integration across Azure services for load balancing, high availability, security, identity and access controls, monitoring, and diagnostics.
- You can use existing on-premises custom OS images to deploy session hosts if the ones provided in the Azure Gallery and Marketplace do not meet your compliance and regulatory needs.
- You can deploy multiple pools for user or app segregation to address a variety of workload requirements.
- You can assign users to multiple app groups, thereby reducing the complexity of permissions and of the access control model.
- Support for a simplified deployment and management experience using the Azure Portal, Azure Virtual Desktop PowerShell, the Azure CLI, and REST APIs enables administrators to quickly get up to speed with AVD.
- You can give users access to full desktops, to individual apps, or to a combination of the two.

- A new Reverse Connect protocol allows secure access using reverse connections to the AVD service. No inbound ports need be exposed on the back-end VMs hosting virtual desktops or apps.

Benefits of AVD are as follows:

- AVD makes it possible to quickly deploy secure multi-user/multi-session Windows 10 virtual desktops and scale them depending on changing organizational requirements. This makes it a compelling service for organizations looking to provide secure remote work capabilities for their employees across various devices using the familiar Windows 10 interface.

- AVD enables users to employ company-provided or personal devices like laptops, tablets, and smartphones, whether they are Android or iOS, and experience a secure Windows 10 experience.

- You can virtualize Microsoft 365 apps for enterprise and optimize them to work with AVD and the Windows 10 multi-session OS.

- Along with Windows 10, you can use Windows 7 as the client OS for single-user virtual desktops. Microsoft will provide free extended security updates for the OS. (Expect this to change in the future, however, as Windows 7 is officially at end-of-life except for in certain use cases.)

- You can easily migrate existing on-premises Remote Desktop Services (RDS) desktops and apps to AVD, making it easier for organizations to get rid of legacy hardware and to benefit from the scalability, availability, and security of the cloud.

- AVD reduces security and management overhead, as Microsoft manages the back-end infrastructure and provides gateway, broker, and web access functionalities. You manage only the image and session host VMs.

- Using the Windows 10 multi-session desktop OS supported only in AVD can help reduce costs by pooling compute, storage, and networking resources while maintaining the resources provisioned for users.

- You can use Azure Automation for cost-management purposes, while still delivering the required capacity and availability in the environment.

Although Microsoft has had desktop and app virtualization solutions that leverage RDS and Hyper-V for many years, there was no full-fledged service in the Azure cloud that could provide all the different security and scalability features that AVD does. This has resulted in AVD quickly becoming one of the most widely used cloud-based desktop solutions.

Now that you have an overview of AVD, let's dive deeper into how AVD uses different Azure services to deliver a complete enterprise-ready solution.

Core concepts

This section covers some core AVD concepts so you can better understand how to use this service in small and large environments to address various requirements.

Use cases

It is easy to set up a test environment to validate how AVD performs for any given organization based on the user and app requirements of that environment. It is, nonetheless, important to understand the best use cases for AVDs to obtain the maximum benefit from the service:

- Remote work scenarios in which organizations want to enable employees to work from home in a secure manner.
- Mergers and acquisitions scenarios that require the quick integration of new employees into existing work processes.
- Scenarios in which elastic demand is needed to address the needs of short-term employees or contractors.
- Scenarios in which regulatory compliance requirements mean the organization must secure desktops but reduce administrative overhead and minimize user impact in the process.
- Scenarios in which security and data-privacy requirements mean the organization must secure end-user desktops gracefully yet swiftly.
- Scenarios in which a test and development environment is needed for app and policy compatibility testing.
- To host legacy or custom apps for engineering or design, which require specialized environments for use in a managed environment.
- To migrate to supported Windows OS releases with minimal end-user disruption.
- To provide employees with BYOD options and with the flexibility to work from different locations and using different devices in a unified and secure manner.

Although this is an extensive list, there might be other use cases specific to your environment based on cost, IT administrative needs, or other requirements. You must take these into account and validate that the ADE environment will provide a solid basis for long-term success.

Architecture

ADE consists of numerous components that must come together to provide a fully scalable and secure desktop in the cloud. Although many of these components are deployed and managed by Microsoft, many of them are deployed, managed, and secured by the customer. Figure 4-1 shows a standard AVD architecture that includes all the available components.

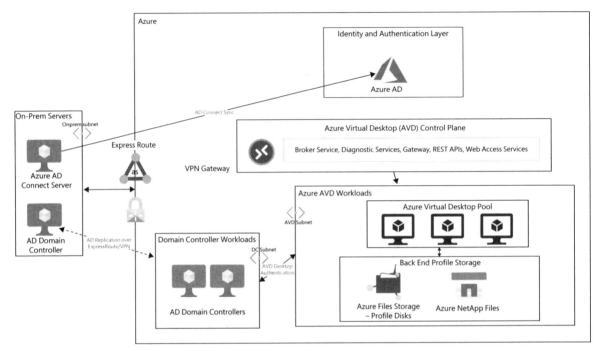

FIGURE 4-1 Azure Virtual Desktop components overview.

> **NOTE** The architecture shown in Figure 4-1 includes components that can be used for integration with existing on-premises networks and apps.

The design shown in Figure 4-1 includes the following components:

- **The AVD control plane** This consists of Web Access, Gateway, Connection Broker, Diagnostics, and Extensibility Components services. The AVD control plane is built and managed by Microsoft as a shared service.

- **Virtual networks, subnets, AVD VMs/host pools, and back-end storage (using either Azure files or Azure NetApp files)** The end-customer builds and manages these.

- **The ExpressRoute or VPN connection** This helps connect the on-premises environment with the AVD infrastructure in the cloud.

- **Customer-managed on-premises AD Domain Services server(s) and the Azure AD Connect server** These integrate with Azure Active Directory, web, application, and database server(s), which you can use as is for app publishing.

- **Azure Active Directory** This manages the identity and authentication layer.

> **NOTE** You can use multiple subscriptions, to increase capacity and availability based on customer needs. You can also build and scale customer-managed elements independently based on high-availability and performance requirements.

AVD control plane

The AVD control plane is a set of Microsoft-managed back-end service components that are completely managed and scaled per load across the entire AVD infrastructure. As mentioned, components of the AVD control plane include the following services:

- **Web Access**   The Web Access service enables users to access the AVD environment using an HTML5-compatible web browser from a variety of operating systems. It provides a user-friendly experience in BYOD and remote work scenarios.

- **Gateway**   The Gateway service allows any AVD client to securely connect to a virtual desktop and to apps hosted on the virtual desktop over the internet. It serves as an intermediary layer that coordinates connections between the client and the AVD VMs.

- **Connection Broker**   The Connection Broker service manages the load-balancing and session distribution of connections to virtual desktops and apps. It also manages the reconnection of existing sessions to the original virtual desktop (if possible) to ensure session continuity.

- **Diagnostics**   The Diagnostics service is an event aggregator that marks actions carried out by administrators or users in the AVD environment as successful or failed. These events can then be queried to identify components that are failing or have failed to initiate corrective action.

- **Extensibility Components**   You can manage AVD using the Azure Portal, the Azure PowerShell, or REST APIs. This extensibility also allows you to integrate third-party tools to extend and enhance the capabilities of the AVD environment.

Session connectivity

AVD uses the Remote Desktop Protocol (RDP) for session display and user input over network connections. Although RDP was released several years ago, with Windows NT 4.0 Terminal Server Edition, it has been constantly updated and improved with every subsequent Windows release. It is an extremely reliable protocol used extensively across most environments for remote session management. It requires ports to be opened on the firewall to access the underlying desktops or apps.

> **NOTE**   From the beginning, RDP developed to be independent of its underlying transport stack. Today, it supports multiple types of transport.

Reverse Connect

Reverse Connect is a new transport protocol built for AVD to establish remote sessions. It uses outbound HTTPS connections to the AVD infrastructure for a secure client connection. This is unlike the traditional on-premises RDS environment where a TCP listener is used for incoming RDP connections.

The most important aspect of this protocol is that it does not require any session host VMs to be directly exposed to the internet or any incoming ports to be opened. All communication between the host pool(s) and the back-end AVD control plane components occurs using HTTPS (port 443) only. This allows you to further secure connections using conditional access policies, such as source IP addresses, time of day, client OS, and so on.

Design considerations

Azure Virtual Desktop is made up of a number of different components and Azure services that work in concert. It is important to understand these components before designing the AVD solution to ensure that you incorporate them in the right manner.

Service locations

In an AVD environment, multiple resources are created, including the host pool, session hosts, app groups, and workspaces. There are some general best practices to keep in mind when deciding where to host these resources, such as the following:

- Service metadata is geographically hosted based on the location of the host pool.
- It is best to locate session hosts and app groups in the same location to avoid data transfer between locations.
- Workspaces are app groups that should be set up in the same location so that updates to each go hand in hand.
- If possible, it is best to host an app group and the related host pool in the same location.

> **NOTE** Most Azure service resources are created in a specific location.

Data storage location

Different components in the AVD environment store user data, VM data, and metadata. It is important to understand where and how this data can be stored to plan and select the hosting location.

You can use any available Azure region to host VM disks and user data using Azure Files, file servers, or other storage services. Companies are not currently required to host this data in specific regions; they can host this data in different regions based on user proximity, cost, security, data compliance, and administration needs.

Metadata contains information like AVD workspace names, host pool names, app group names, and user principal names in a datacenter. Whenever a service object is created, you must specify a location for it; this determines where metadata for the object will be stored. You are currently limited to storing metadata only in certain regions. So, it is best to select the Azure region that is closest to the primary access location, depending on what regions are available.

Because Microsoft manages storage, you should be aware that metadata is encrypted at rest and is synchronized to another region within a specific geography for redundancy and failover.

This is not the case for VM and user data, such as system OS, app settings, and user files. These reside in the region selected by the admin, and redundancy must be built and managed by the customer. In other words, Microsoft's scope of services does not include the setup, maintenance, and recovery of these services or data sources.

Service limitations

Correctly designing your solution in the design phase helps alleviate issues during the growth/scaling phase. Although AVD is highly scalable, you should consider some Azure platform and AVD control plane limitations during the design phase to avoid issues later on:

- Microsoft has a recommended limit of 5,000 VMs per Azure subscription per region. This applies to all supported Windows 10 Enterprise releases (single or multi-user sessions). To accommodate more user sessions, it is best to scale the hosts up with higher resources rather than scale out beyond the 5,000 VMs.

- Automated scaling is limited to around 1,200 VMs per Azure subscription per region. As shown earlier in the "Architecture" section, you can use a hub-and-spoke model to deploy VMs across multiple subscriptions to bypass scaling limits.

- There are API throttling limits of 600 VM reboots per hour for Resource Manager subscriptions. Although this will rarely cause issues for most enterprises, it is important to be aware of requirements for frequent VM reboots to remove app locks or perform frequent patching or updates. In such instances, performing the reboots on the OS level using either Microsoft or third-party management tools can help bypass this limitation.

- The session host VM name prefixes, which are provided when the VM is deployed, cannot exceed 11 characters because instance names are auto-assigned using the remaining four characters. (NetBIOS has a limitation of 15 characters for every Windows computer account, and all session hosts in Azure must adhere to this.)

- Although not impactful in most environments, a single resource group can contain no more than 800 instances of resources. To bypass this limitation, create more resource groups.

- When deploying using ARM templates, there is a limit of 200 VMs per availability set. Without availability sets, this limit changes to 399 VMs. So, you can always increase the limit by switching off availability sets either in Azure Portal host pool enrollment or in the ARM template code.

Host pools

A host pool is a grouping of multiple session host VMs for user consumption. Ideally, all VMs are set up using the same image or template and would be grouped together as part of a host pool. This ensures consistency in experience for all users associated with that host pool. All apps, configurations, and updates should be the same across the entire set of session host VMs in a host pool. Users assigned to an app group are associated with each host pool for the publishing of specific apps or remote desktops.

Types of host pools

Two types of host pools can be deployed in an AVD environment: personal host pools and pooled host pools.

A *personal host* pool is one in which each session host VM is assigned to individual users. The assignment can be managed automatically or manually (directly). Automatic assignment takes place when a user connects to a host pool for the first time. Any available session host is automatically assigned to that user; the user then is connected to that host each time they sign in. This is also referred to as a *persistent desktop experience* because when a VM is assigned to a user, it allows the user to store data locally and retrieve it at any time. So, users can customize their desktop experience—including the apps that are installed—based on their own needs, without affecting the experience of other users.

> **NOTE** The session host VMs can have different resource (compute, disk, network) sizing if the assignment will be managed manually. In case of automatic assignment, it is best to have the same VM sizing for all the session hosts.

A *pooled host* pool is one in which multiple session host VMs are pooled together for use by multiple users. In this scenario, all the VMs in the pool should have the same sizing, apps, and configurations to allow for efficient load-balancing. The operating system of the underlying VMs can be either a supported Windows Server OS or Windows 10 Enterprise multi-session OS. This is also called a *non-persistent desktop experience* because users are load-balanced across numerous session hosts, depending on host availability and on the load-balancing algorithm assigned to that host pool. Because it's not guaranteed that users will sign back into the same host each time, their ability to customize their desktop experience is limited, because they do not have administrative rights on the host. Users should not store data locally to avoid data loss due to session host switchover. Instead, they should use file shares, sync desktop documents using OneDrive, and employ other similar technologies to access their data.

Load-balancing methods for pooled host pools

AVD provides two types of load-balancing algorithms for pooled host pools. Each algorithm has a different way of determining which session host will be assigned to a user when they connect to the host pool:

- **Breadth-first load balancing** This type of load-balancing algorithm distributes all user sessions evenly across all session hosts in the host pool. The host-selection process is randomized. Rather than automatically selecting the host with the lowest number of sessions, the system identifies the five hosts with the fewest session and randomly assigns one of those hosts to a new user session. This type of load balancing provides an optimal user experience because the session load is shared evenly across hosts.

- **Depth-first load balancing** This type of load-balancing algorithm first saturates an entire session host with the maximum user sessions allowed for a host in the host pool. When a session host reaches its limit, the load balancer diverts all new user connections to the next available session host in the host pool, until *that* session host reaches its limit. When selecting a host for a new session, the system chooses the session host with the most sessions that hasn't reached its limit. If multiple hosts match these criteria, then the first host to respond to the query is selected. This type of load-balancing is ideal for enterprises that want more control over the number of VMs allocated to a host pool for cost-control purposes.

There are a few caveats to note:

- Each host pool can use only one load-balancing method at any given time. However, you can change this method any time you want to.

- In case a user has disconnected and is trying to reconnect to the host pool before the earlier session has been logged off, they will be reconnected to the same session as before. This happens with both load-balancing methods.

- If any session host is set to prevent new connections, that host will be ignored by the load-balancing algorithm during host selection. This happens regardless of the host's current utilization and active status.

Host pools walkthrough

The following sections step you through the process of creating host pools for your deployment using the Azure Portal, Azure PowerShell, and the Azure CLI.

> **IMPORTANT** If you are following along, you'll want to select resources and unique resource names based on your environment for each of your deployments.

> **IMPORTANT** If you are following along, delete any unwanted resources after you have completed testing to reduce charges being levied by Microsoft for these resources.

USING THE AZURE PORTAL

You can use the Azure Portal to set up personal host pools and pooled host pools. To set up a personal host pool, follow these steps:

1. Log in to the Azure Portal and type **Azure Virtual Desktop** in the search bar.
2. Under **Services**, click **Azure Virtual Desktop**. (See Figure 4-2.)

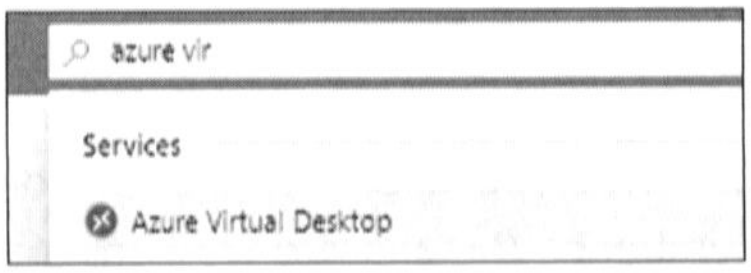

FIGURE 4-2 Searching for the Azure Virtual Desktop service.

3. In the left pane, under **Manage**, click **Host Pools**.
4. Click the **Create** button to start the Host Pool Creation wizard. (See Figure 4-3.)

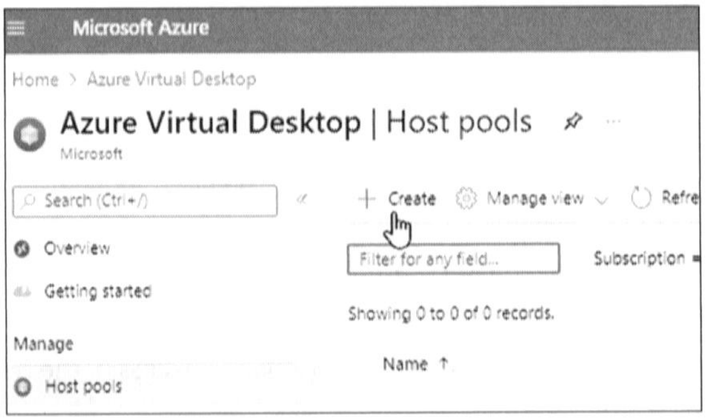

FIGURE 4-3 Host Pool creation.

5. In the **Basics** tab, enter the following information (see Figure 4-4):

   ■ **Subscription** Select the subscription that will host the AVD infrastructure.

   ■ **Resource Group** Select an existing resource group or create a new one to host the AVD environment.

   ■ **Host Pool Name** Enter a name for the host pool.

   ■ **Location** Select the Azure region you want to host the host pool metadata.

   ■ **Validation Environment** Specify whether this host pool will work as a validation environment. Set this to **No** for now.

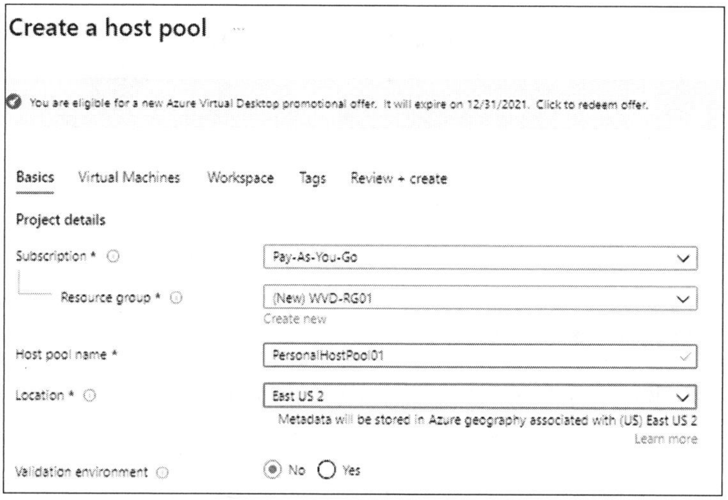

FIGURE 4-4 Setting the host pool basic config.

6. Open the **Host Pool Type** drop-down list and choose **Personal**.

7. The **Assignment Type** drop-down appears. Open this drop-down list and choose **Automatic**. (See Figure 4-5.) Then click **Next**.

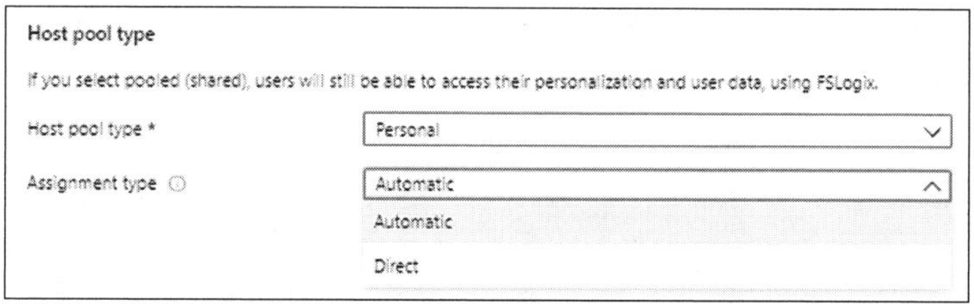

FIGURE 4-5 Choosing personal pool type and the pool's assignment type.

8. In the **Virtual Machines** tab, next to **Add Virtual Machines**, click the **No** option button, as shown in Figure 4-6. (You will add VMs later.) Then click **Next**.

FIGURE 4-6 Adding VMs (or not).

9. In the **Workspace** tab, next to **Register Desktop App Group**, click the **No** option button, as shown in Figure 4-7. (You will do this later, too.) Then click **Next**.

FIGURE 4-7 Registering the desktop app group (or not).

10. In the **Tags** tab, enter the following tags to assign them to this host pool and its associated resources (see Figure 4-8). Then click **Next**.

   ■ **Name**   WVD-Environment-Type.

   ■ **Value**   Personal.

   ■ **Resource**   Leave this set to the default.

Basics   Virtual Machines   Workspace   Tags   Review + create

Tags are name/value pairs that enable you to categorize resources and view consolidated billing by applying the same tag to multiple resources and resource groups Learn more ☑
Note that if you create tags and then change resource settings on other tabs, your tags will be automatically updated

Name ○	Value ○	Resource
WVD-Environment-Type	: Personal	7 selected ⌄ 🗑
	:	7 selected ⌄

FIGURE 4-8 Setting up tags.

11. In the **Review + Create** tab, review your settings and click **Create**. (See Figure 4-9.) The new host pool will appear in the list of personal host pools in the Azure Portal. (See Figure 4-10.)

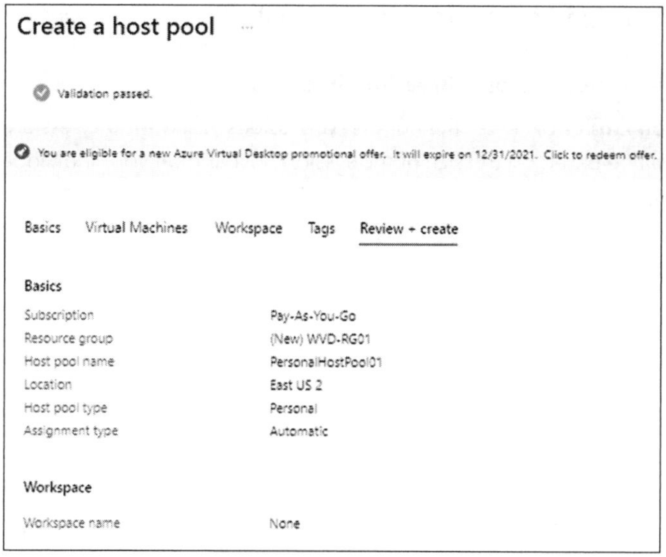

FIGURE 4-9 Reviewing and creating a personal host pool.

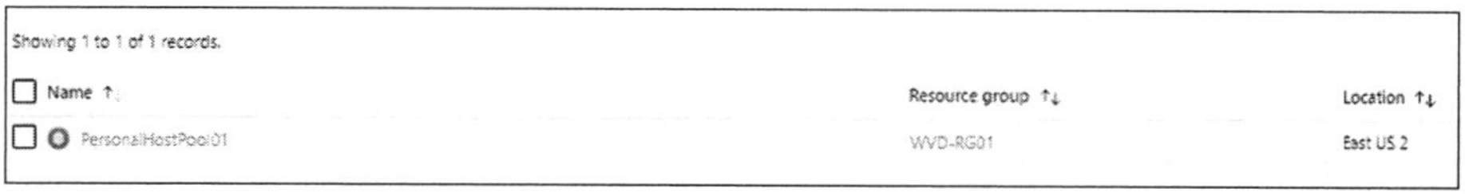

FIGURE 4-10 Confirming the creation of the personal host pool.

Setting up a pooled host pool is similar to setting up a personal host pool. Follow these steps:

12. Repeat steps 1 through 5. Be sure you choose a unique host pool name.

13. Open the **Host Pool Type** drop-down list and choose **Pooled**. (See Figure 4-11.)

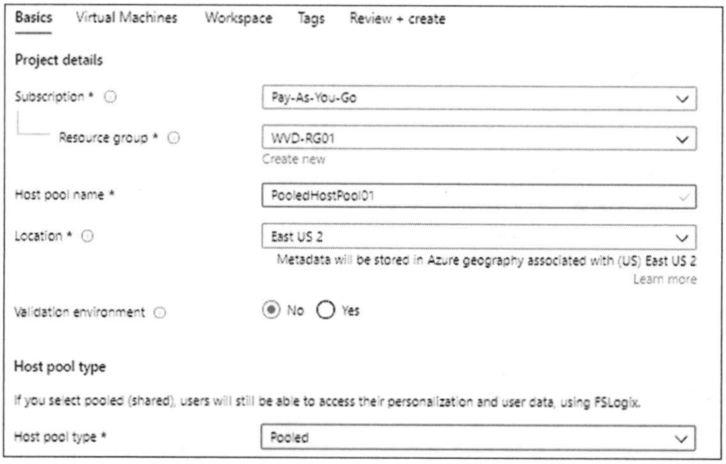

FIGURE 4-11 Creating a pooled host pool.

14. The **Load Balancing Algorithm** and **Max Session Limit** settings appear. Open the **Load Balancing Algorithm** drop-down list and choose the correct algorithm for your environment. In this case, I've chosen **Breadth-First**.

15. In the **Max Session Limit** box, enter the number of sessions you want the session host to support. This will be based on the size of the session host and on your individual session requirements. In this case, I've entered **20**. (See Figure 4-12.)

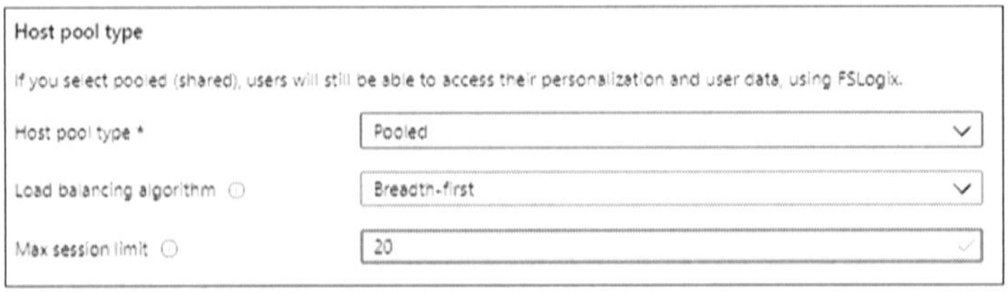

FIGURE 4-12   Setting the maximum session limit.

16. Repeat steps 8 through 11. The new host pool will appear in the list of pooled host pools in the Azure Portal. (See Figure 4-13.)

FIGURE 4-13   Confirming the creation of the pooled host pool.

USING AZURE POWERSHELL

You can create a host pool with Azure PowerShell using the New-AzWvdHostPool command with various switches to set its parameters.

For example, to create a personal host pool as shown in the steps earlier, you could use the following code. Be sure to either delete the previous host pool setup or give this a different name. Replace all the variables as per your environment:

```
New-AzWvdHostPool -ResourceGroupName WVD-RG01 `
            -Name PersonalHostPool `
            -Location 'eastus2' `
            -HostPoolType 'Personal' `
            -PersonalDesktopAssignmentType Automatic `
            -LoadBalancerType Persistent `
            -RegistrationTokenOperation 'Update' `
            -ExpirationTime $((get-date).ToUniversalTime().AddDays(1).ToString('yyyy-MM-
             ddTHH:mm:ss.fffffffZ')) `
            -Description 'Description' `
            -FriendlyName 'Friendly Name' `
```

```
            -VMTemplate $null `
            -ValidationEnvironment:$false `
            -PreferredAppGroup Desktop
```

Here's the code to create a pooled host pool:

```
New-AzWvdHostPool -ResourceGroupName WVD-RG01 `
            -Name PooledHostPool01 `
            -Location 'eastus2' `
            -HostPoolType 'Pooled' `
            -LoadBalancerType 'BreadthFirst' `
            -RegistrationTokenOperation 'Update' `
            -ExpirationTime $((get-date).ToUniversalTime().AddDays(1).ToString('yyyy-MM-
              ddTHH:mm:ss.fffffffZ')) `
            -Description 'Description' `
            -FriendlyName 'Friendly Name' `
            -MaxSessionLimit 20 `
            -VMTemplate $null `
            -ValidationEnvironment:$false `
            -PreferredAppGroup Desktop
```

USING THE AZURE CLI

You can create a host pool with the Azure CLI by using the az desktopvirtualization hostpool create command with various switches to set its parameters. The following Bash script shows you how. Be sure to either delete the previous host pool setup or give this a different name. Replace all the variables as per your environment.

To create a personal host pool, you could use the following code:

```
az desktopvirtualization hostpool create --host-pool-type Personal --load-balancer-type
Persistent --location eastus2 --name personalhosts2 --resource-group WVD-RG01
--description 'Test Pool' --friendly-name 'Personal Host Pool'
--personal-desktop-assignment-type Automatic"
```

Here's the code to create a pooled host pool:

```
az desktopvirtualization hostpool create --host-pool-type Pooled --load-balancer-type
BreadthFirst --location eastus2 --name pooledhostpool01 --resource-group WVD-RG01
--description 'Test Pool' --friendly-name 'Pooled Host Pool' --max-session-limit 20
--personal-desktop-assignment-type Automatic
```

Validation pool

A validation pool is a special type of host pool for which Azure will apply back-end service updates before rolling them out to your other host pools. Having a validation pool enables you to ensure that service updates will not negatively affect the functionality of your apps, resulting in downtime.

TIP It is highly recommended that you have a validation pool in every environment, regardless of size or complexity.

You can set a host pool as a validation pool when you create the host pool or at some later point in time. You should build the validation pool using the same image or template as the production pool. This enables you to test your apps after service updates with complete confidence in the outcomes.

NOTE Azure Service updates take place on a monthly basis. Critical updates have a different cadence, however; depending on their criticality, these updates can be issued at any time.

It is important to have a documented process in place for using validation pools after service updates. After a service update is applied to the validation pool, have a set of users sign in to the validation environment and perform all manner of checks to ensure the environment is working as expected.

Validation pool walkthrough

The following sections step you through the process of setting up a validation pool.

USING THE AZURE PORTAL

To set up a validation pool using the Azure Portal during host-pool creation, follow these steps:

1. Follow the steps outlined in the preceding walkthrough to launch the Create a Host Pool wizard.
2. Next to **Validation Environment**, select the Yes option button, as shown in Figure 4-14. Then complete the wizard as described previously to create the validation pool.

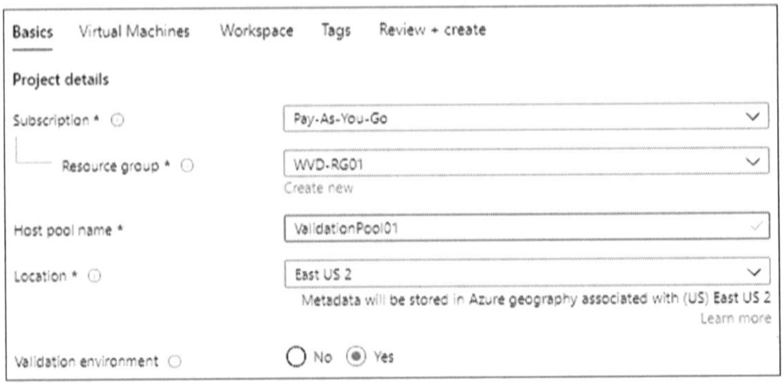

FIGURE 4-14 Creating a validation pool during host-pool creation.

To set up a validation pool using the Azure Portal for an existing host pool, follow these steps:

1. Open the existing host pool's page in the Azure Portal.
2. In the left pane, click **Properties**.
3. Under **Configuration**, next to **Validation Environment**, click the **Yes** option button. (See Figure 4-15.)

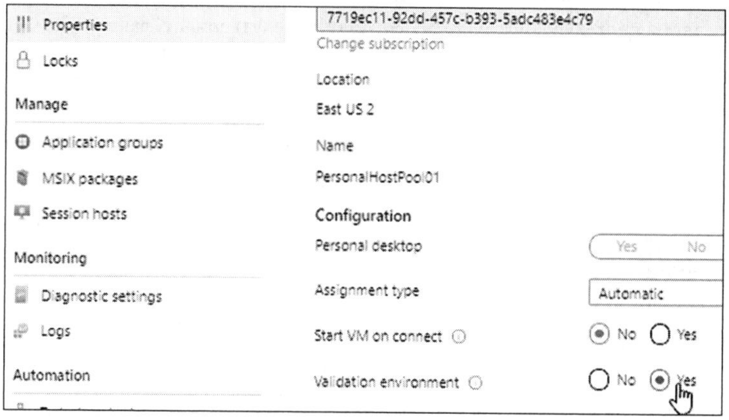

FIGURE 4-15   Creating a validation pool after host-pool creation.

USING AZURE POWERSHELL

You can create a validation pool with the same PowerShell script you used to create a host pool, but with the addition of the –ValidationEnvironment switch set to $true. The following code shows you how:

```
New-AzWvdHostPool  -ResourceGroupName WVD-RG01 `
            -Name PooledHostPool01 `
            -Location 'eastus2' `
            -HostPoolType 'Pooled' `
            -LoadBalancerType 'BreadthFirst' `
            -RegistrationTokenOperation 'Update' `
            -ExpirationTime $((get-date).ToUniversalTime().AddDays(1).ToString('yyyy-MM-
              ddTHH:mm:ss.fffffffZ')) `
            -Description 'Description' `
            -FriendlyName 'Friendly Name' `
            -MaxSessionLimit 20 `
            -VMTemplate $null `
            -ValidationEnvironment:$false `
            -PreferredAppGroup Desktop `
            -ValidationEnvironment:$true
```

You can create a validation host with the same Azure CLI Bash script you used to create a host pool, but with the addition of the `--validationenvironment` switch set to `true`. The following code shows you how:

```
az desktopvirtualization hostpool create --host-pool-type Pooled --load-balancer-type
BreadthFirst --location eastus2 --name pooledhostpool01 --resource-group WVD-RG01
--description 'Test Pool' --friendly-name 'Pooled Host Pool' --max-session-limit 20
--personal-desktop-assignment-type Automatic --validation-environment true
```

App groups

An app group is a collection of applications, installed on a session host in a host pool, which can be made available to users. There are two types of app groups in the AVD environment:

- **Desktop app groups**   These give users access to the full desktop experience.
- **RemoteApp app groups**   These give users access to only the RemoteApps that are individually published.

Whenever a host pool is created, by default, a desktop app group (named Desktop Application Group) is automatically created to provide access to the full desktop experience. (You can delete this group if it is not required.) A RemoteApp app group is not created by default. If you want to publish RemoteApps, however, you must create one.

In environments in which different apps must be published for different groups of workers, you can create multiple RemoteApp app groups to facilitate this. A RemoteApp app can be part of both multiple RemoteApp app groups and the worker profiles that use that app group. For example, a specialized engineering app might only be part of a RemoteApp app group used by the engineering team, whereas an Office app might be part of multiple RemoteApp app groups, including the one used by the engineering team.

Users access AVD resources like RemoteApps or the full virtual desktop only after they have been assigned to the appropriate app groups. When deciding on an assignment strategy, keep these caveats in mind:

- Although users can be part of both a desktop and a RemoteApp app group, they can launch only one type of app group in a given session.
- When a user is assigned to multiple app groups in the same host pool, they will see all the resources in all those app groups.
- Each Azure Active Directory tenant can support only 200 app groups.
- App groups must be in the same location as the workspaces. (You'll learn more about workspaces shortly.)
- All app groups related to a host pool must be registered to the same workspace.

App groups walkthrough

The following sections step you through the process of creating an app group using the Azure Portal, Azure PowerShell, and the Azure CLI.

USING THE AZURE PORTAL

To create an app group using the Azure Portal, follow these steps:

1. In the **Azure Virtual Desktop** page, under **Manage**, click **Application Groups**.

   A list of app groups appears. As shown in Figure 4-16, two app groups are created already—one for each of the host pools you created earlier.

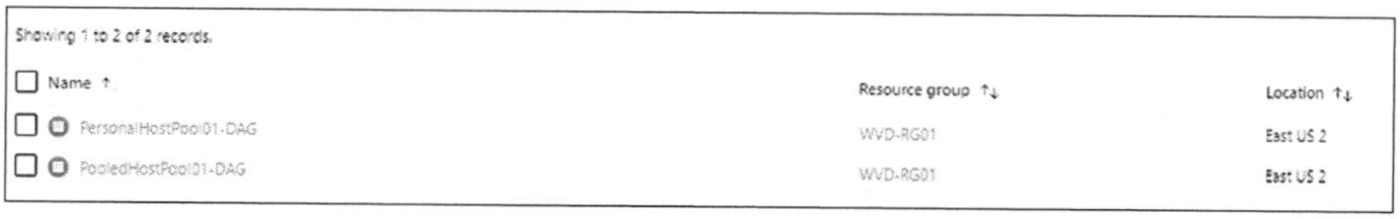

Showing 1 to 2 of 2 records.		
Name ↑	Resource group ↑↓	Location ↑↓
PersonalHostPool01-DAG	WVD-RG01	East US 2
PooledHostPool01-DAG	WVD-RG01	East US 2

FIGURE 4-16   List of app groups.

2. Click the **Create** button to start the **Create an Application Group** wizard.

3. In the **Basics** tab, enter the following information (see Figure 4-17) and click **Next** twice to skip the Applications tab and progress to the Assignments tab. (You'll add applications later.)

   - **Subscription**   Select the same subscription as the host pools.

   - **Resource Group**   Select the same resource group as the one used by the host pool you want to associate with the app group.

   - **Host Pool**   Select the host pool to associate with the app group. Be sure to select a pooled host pool. If you select a personal host pool, you will get an error asking you to select another host pool, as shown in Figure 4-17.

   - **Location**   This is set automatically and is grayed out.

   - **Application Group Type**   **RemoteApp** is automatically selected, and **Desktop** is grayed out because a desktop group has already been created by default.

   - **Application Group Name**   Type a name for the app group.

4. In the **Assignments** tab, click **Add Azure AD Users or User Groups** (see Figure 4-18).

5. Select an AD user group that contains all the users to whom you want to give access to the apps in the app group and click **Add**.

6. Click **Next** twice to advance to the **Tags** tab. (You'll register the app group to a workspace in the next section.)

7. In the **Tags** tab, enter any tags that you would like to apply (see Figure 4-19) and click **Next**.

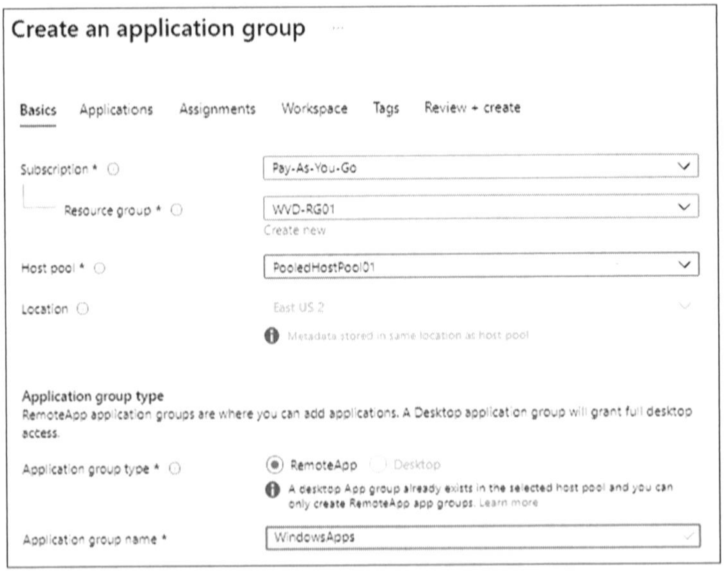

Create an application group ...

Basics   Applications   Assignments   Workspace   Tags   Review + create

Subscription * ○   Pay-As-You-Go   ▽

    └─ Resource group * ○   WVD-RG01   ▽
                                     Create new

Host pool * ○   PooledHostPool01   ▽

Location ○   East US 2   ▽
                                     ⓘ Metadata stored in same location as host pool

Application group type
RemoteApp application groups are where you can add applications. A Desktop application group will grant full desktop access.

Application group type * ○   ⦿ RemoteApp   ○ Desktop
                                     ⓘ A desktop App group already exists in the selected host pool and you can only create RemoteApp app groups. Learn more

Application group name *   WindowsApps

FIGURE 4-17   The Basics tab of the App Groups Creation wizard.

Basics   Applications   **Assignments**   Workspace   Tags   Review + create

Add users who you want to have access to this application group. You can always add or manage assignments any time later.

Name ↑↓

+ Add Azure AD users or user groups

FIGURE 4-18   Adding assignments.

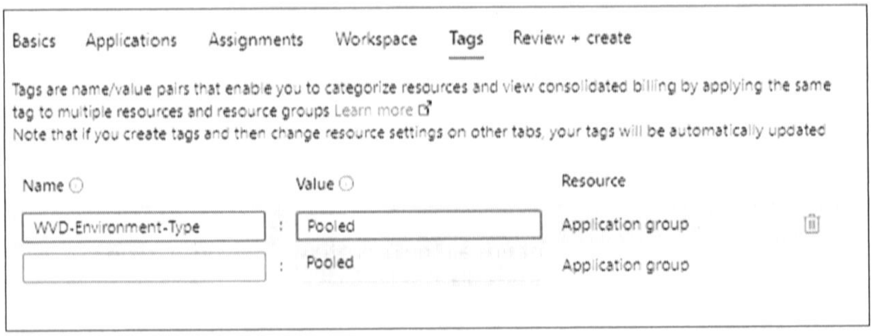

Basics   Applications   Assignments   Workspace   **Tags**   Review + create

Tags are name/value pairs that enable you to categorize resources and view consolidated billing by applying the same tag to multiple resources and resource groups Learn more ⬈
Note that if you create tags and then change resource settings on other tabs, your tags will be automatically updated

Name ○	Value ○	Resource
WVD-Environment-Type	: Pooled	Application group 🗑
	: Pooled	Application group

FIGURE 4-19   Adding tags.

8. In the **Review + Create** tab, review your settings and click **Create** to create the app group. (See Figure 4-20.)

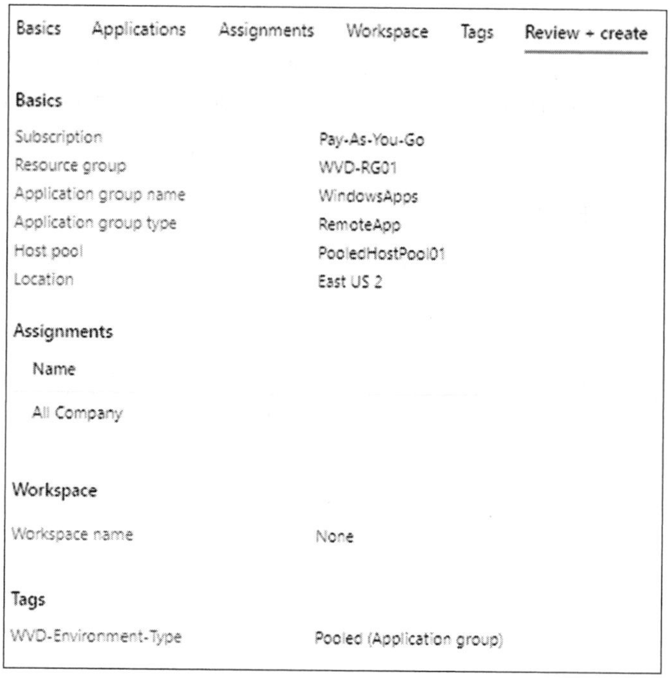

FIGURE 4-20 Reviewing the app group settings.

USING AZURE POWERSHELL

You can create an app group with Azure PowerShell using the `New-AzWvdApplicationGroup` command with various switches to set the app group's parameters. The following code shows you how:

```
New-AzWvdApplicationGroup -Name WindowsApps -ResourceGroupName WVD-RG01
-ApplicationGroupType "RemoteApp" -HostPoolArmPath '/subscriptions/7719ec11-92dd-457c-b393-
5adc481214c79/resourceGroups/WVD-RG01/providers/Microsoft.DesktopVirtualization/hostPools/
PooledHostPool01'-Location "East US 2"
```

USING THE AZURE CLI

You can create an app group with the Azure CLI `az desktopvirtualization applicationgroup create` command with various switches to set the app group's parameters. The following Bash script shows you how:

```
az desktopvirtualization applicationgroup create --location "eastus2" --description
"WVD Application Group for Pooled Desktops" --application-group-type "RemoteApp"
--friendly-name "WindowsApps" --host-pool-arm-path "/subscriptions/7719ec11-92dd-457c-
b393-5adc12a3e4c79/resourceGroups/WVD-RG01/providers/Microsoft.DesktopVirtualization/
hostPools/PooledHostPool01" --name "WindowsApps" --resource-group "WVD-RG01"
```

Workspaces

A *workspace* is a collection of app groups. In each AVD tenant, each app group must be associated with a workspace. This enables users to see and use the desktops and remote apps assigned to each app group.

Workspaces walkthrough

The following sections step you through the process of creating a workspace using the Azure Portal, Azure PowerShell, and the Azure CLI.

USING THE AZURE PORTAL

To create a workspace using the Azure Portal, follow these steps:

1. In the **Azure Virtual Desktop** page, under **Manage**, click **Workspaces**.

2. Click the **Create** button to start the Create a Workspace wizard. (See Figure 4-21.)

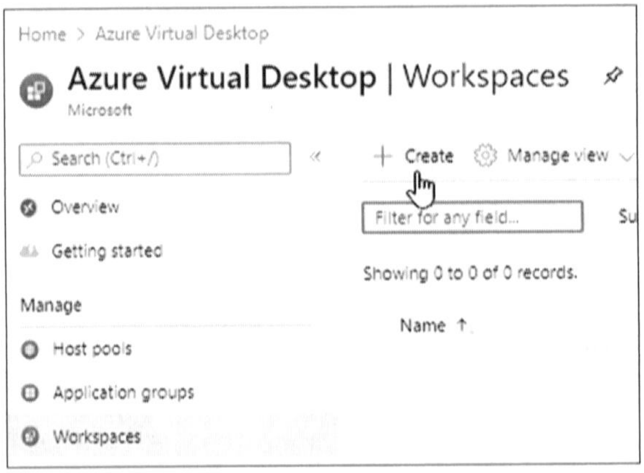

FIGURE 4-21   Creating a workspace.

3. In the **Basics** tab, enter the following information (see Figure 4-22) and click **Next**:

   - **Subscription**   Select the same subscription as the host pools.
   - **Resource Group**   Select the same resource group as the one used by the app group you want to associate with the workspace.
   - **Workspace Name**   Enter a unique name for the workspace.
   - **Friendly Name**   Enter a friendly name for the workspace.
   - **Description**   Optionally, enter a description for the workspace.
   - **Location**   Select the location where you want to create—ideally, the same region as the Azure host pools and app groups.

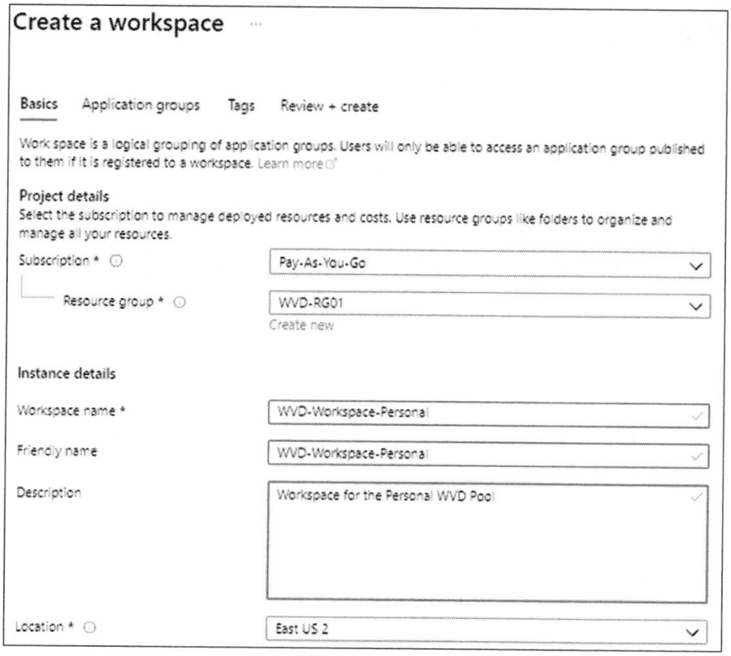

FIGURE 4-22 The Basics tab of the Create a Workspace wizard.

4. In the **Application Groups** tab, next to **Register Application Groups**, select the **Yes** option button.

5. Click the **Register Application Groups** link. (See Figure 4-23.)

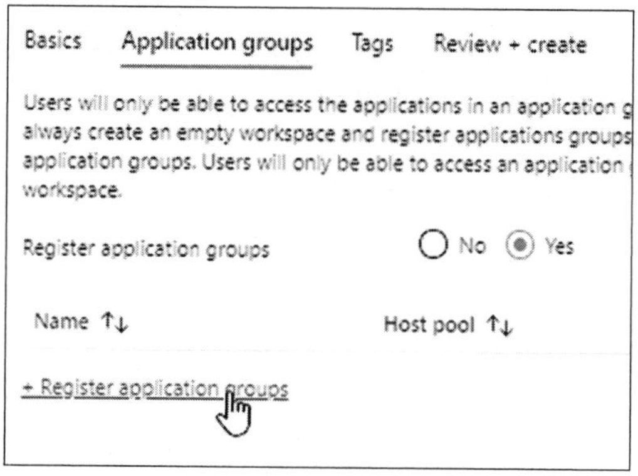

FIGURE 4-23 Registering app groups.

6. Click the **WindowsApps** app group you created earlier and click **OK**. (See Figure 4-24.)

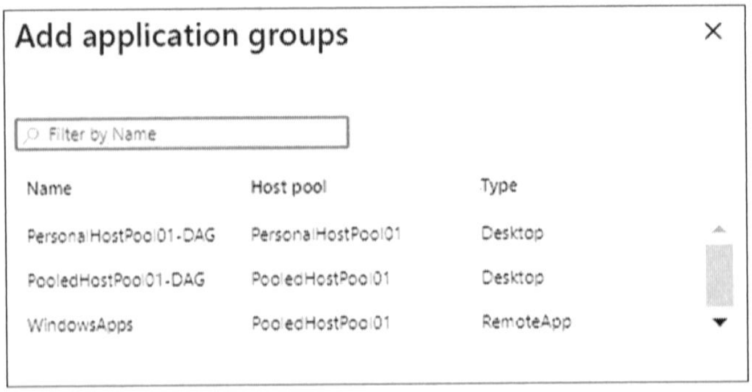

Add application groups ✕

Filter by Name

Name	Host pool	Type	
PersonalHostPool01-DAG	PersonalHostPool01	Desktop	
PooledHostPool01-DAG	PooledHostPool01	Desktop	
WindowsApps	PooledHostPool01	RemoteApp	

FIGURE 4-24   App group selection.

7. Verify the app group appears in the Application Groups tab (see Figure 4-25) and click **Next**.

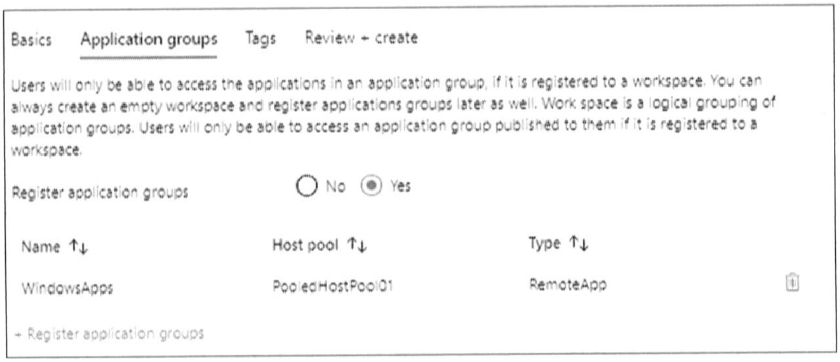

Basics   Application groups   Tags   Review + create

Users will only be able to access the applications in an application group, if it is registered to a workspace. You can always create an empty workspace and register applications groups later as well. Work space is a logical grouping of application groups. Users will only be able to access an application group published to them if it is registered to a workspace.

Register application groups   ○ No ⦿ Yes

Name ↑↓	Host pool ↑↓	Type ↑↓	
WindowsApps	PooledHostPool01	RemoteApp	🗑

+ Register application groups

FIGURE 4-25   App group setup.

8. In the Tags tab, enter any tags you want to apply to identify this workspace, and click **Next**. In this case, I've entered these tags (see Figure 4-26):

- **Name**   WVD-Environment-Type
- **Value**   Personal

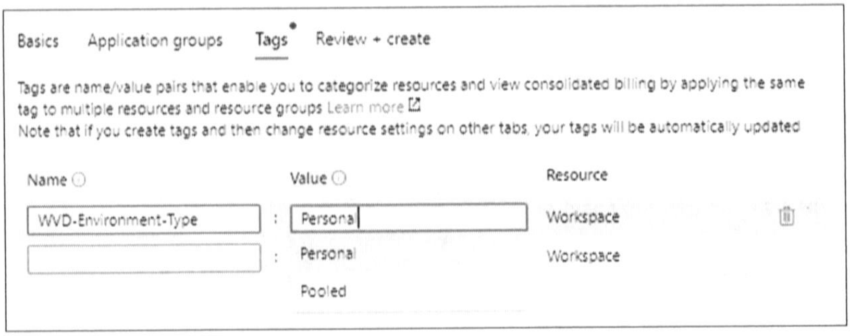

Basics   Application groups   Tags •   Review + create

Tags are name/value pairs that enable you to categorize resources and view consolidated billing by applying the same tag to multiple resources and resource groups Learn more ☑
Note that if you create tags and then change resource settings on other tabs, your tags will be automatically updated

Name ⓘ		Value ⓘ	Resource	
WVD-Environment-Type	:	Personal	Workspace	🗑
	:	Personal	Workspace	
		Pooled		

FIGURE 4-26   Adding tags to the workspace.

9. In the **Review + Create** tab, review your settings and click **Create** to create the workspace. (See Figure 4-27.)

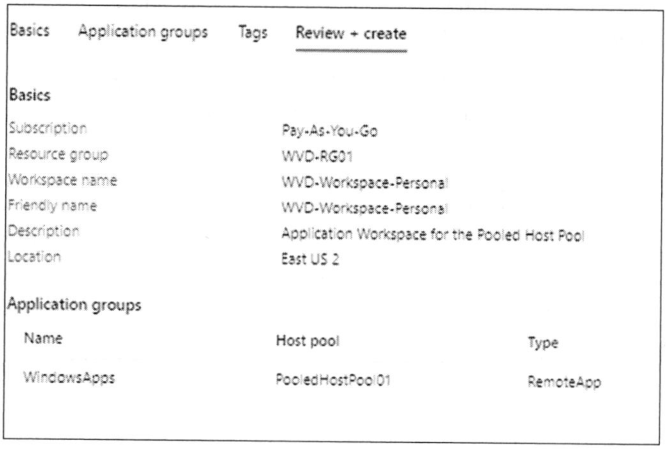

Basics   Application groups   Tags   Review + create

Basics

Subscription   Pay-As-You-Go
Resource group   WVD-RG01
Workspace name   WVD-Workspace-Personal
Friendly name   WVD-Workspace-Personal
Description   Application Workspace for the Pooled Host Pool
Location   East US 2

Application groups

Name   Host pool   Type

WindowsApps   PooledHostPool01   RemoteApp

FIGURE 4-27   Reviewing the workspace settings.

USING AZURE POWERSHELL

You can create a workspace using the Azure PowerShell `New-AzWvdWorkspace` command with
various switches to set the workspace's parameters. The following code shows you how:

```
New-AzWvdWorkspace -ResourceGroupName WVD-RG01 -Name WVD-Workspace-Pooled -Location
'eastus2' -FriendlyName 'WVD-Workspace-Pooled'-ApplicationGroupReference $null
-Description 'Workspace for Pooled Desktops'
```

USING THE AZURE CLI

You can create a workspace using the Azure CLI `az desktopvirtualization workspace create`
command with various switches to set the workspace's parameters. The following Bash script
shows you how:

```
az desktopvirtualization workspace create --resource-group "WVD-RG01" --location
"eastus2" --description "Workspace for Pooled Desktops" --friendly-name "WVD-Workspace-
Pooled" --tags WVD-Environment-Type="Pooled" --name "WVD-Workspace-Pooled2"
```

Session hosts

Session hosts are the underlying VM instances that host session-based desktops and apps
accessed by AVD end-users. When a user connects to the AVD environment, the connection
traverses through the Web Access, Gateway, and Broker services to land on a session host,
which loads the user's profile data along with the apps provisioned for the user.

In smaller deployments, you can provision session hosts individually as part of the AVD tenant and host pool. In larger deployments, it's best to use golden images that contain all the required apps and configuration. This facilitates the automated provisioning of large numbers of session hosts on an ongoing basis.

There are numerous factors to consider when deciding on the operating system, VM size, and licensing model for session hosts. These are covered in the following sections.

Operating systems supported

AVDs session hosts support different Windows operating systems in line with Microsoft's OS lifecycle policies. Only 64-bit operating systems are supported. Currently, this support extends to the following OS images. However, this might change based on the time of your deployment. Check the latest guidance to choose the best OS image for your needs:

- Windows Server 2019
- Windows Server 2016
- Windows Server 2012 R2
- Windows 10 Enterprise multi-session
- Windows 10 Enterprise
- Windows 7 Enterprise

> **NOTE** Windows 10 Enterprise N, Windows 10 LTSB, Windows 10 LTSC, Windows 10 Pro, and Windows 10 Enterprise KN OS images are not supported. Similarly, Windows 7–based desktops cannot use VHD or VHDX-profile solutions.

Table 4-1 shows the OS deployment and automation options.

TABLE 4-1 OS deployment and automation options

Windows OS	Azure Gallery Images	Manual host deployment	ARM templates	Azure Marketplace provisioning
Windows Server 2019	Yes	Yes	No	No
Windows Server 2016	Yes	Yes	Yes	Yes
Windows Server 2012 R2	Yes	Yes	No	No
Windows 10 Enterprise multi-session, version 1909 and later	Yes	Yes	Yes	Yes
Windows 10 Enterprise, version 1909 and later	Yes	Yes	Yes	Yes
Windows 7 Enterprise	Yes	Yes	No	No

As you can see, Windows Server 2016 and Windows 10 single-user and multi-session currently provide maximum flexibility and support. Regardless, you want to select the OS that is most suitable to meet your environment's automation requirements. If you have OS support restrictions based on app compatibility limitations, consider these when designing the auto-mation for the environment.

Windows 10 Enterprise multi-session

Windows 10 Enterprise multi-session is a new Remote Desktop Session Host (RDSH) that allows multiple concurrent interactive sessions. (Previously, this was possible only using Windows Server OS.) This gives users the Windows 10 experience they are used to on their PCs but allows IT to take advantage of the cost benefits of per-user Windows licensing (rather than the Remote Desktop Services (RDS) client access license required by the RDS on Windows Server OS).

Windows 10 Enterprise multi-session is a virtual edition of Windows 10 Enterprise. Its ProductType property has a value of 3, the same as Windows Server OS. This keeps the Windows 10 Enterprise multi-session OS compatible with existing RDSH multi-session–aware apps, existing RDSH management tools, and low-level system performance optimizations built and tested for RDSH environments.

Application installers that are designed to work only when the ProductType property is set to Client will prevent app installation on Windows 10 multi-session OS. To avoid this, either confirm with the app vendor or test on a standalone Windows 10 Enterprise multi-session VM to be sure app installation works as expected.

Windows 10 Enterprise multi-session is optimized for AVD. It can't be run in an on-premises production environment or activated using Key Management Service (KMS) on-premises. Microsoft's licensing agreement deems it a violation if Windows 10 Enterprise multi-session is set up to run outside of Azure for production purposes.

VM sizing

It is important to size session host VMs correctly to ensure an optimal experience for users of the AVD environment. Although you can change the VM sizing and scaling to address performance bottlenecks, you should plan and test the initial size with the following considerations in mind:

- **App performance requirements**   Consult with the app developer(s) to obtain their sizing recommendations. If dealing with multiple custom apps, combine the recommen-dations for each app to calculate the overall resource requirements.

- **Number of users (average) anticipated**   Estimate how many users, on average, are expected to use the AVD environment to calculate minimum resource requirements for the VM hosts.

- **Number of users (peak load) anticipated**   Estimate how many users during peak loads are expected or what their overall resource requirements will be to calculate the maximum resource requirements for the VM hosts.

- **Windows OS core recommendations**   For Windows 10 multi-session OS, the recom-mended minimum number of vCPU cores is four. This takes into account the fact that UI components use two parallel threads for heavy rendering activities. The recommended maximum number of vCPU cores is 24. This is because the system's synchronization overhead increases as the number of cores increases. If the number of vCPU cores exceeds 16, the overhead reduces the benefits of the additional cores. It is therefore better to use two 16-core VMs rather than a single 32-core VM.

Take these factors into consideration when calculating the minimum and maximum anticipated loads to determine how many VM session host instances you need to provision.

> **NOTE** These calculations will help you identify a good starting point for your AVD infrastructure. You continue to monitor the usage of the session hosts over time, however, so you can resize the environment based on actual observed performance if needed.

Licensing

The OS licensing for session host VMs is part of the Microsoft 365 or Windows E3 licensing or of the traditional Remote Desktop Client Access License (CAL). Table 4-2 shows the different licenses supported for the different operating systems.

TABLE 4-2 Licensing requirements

OS	Required license
Windows 10 Enterprise multi-session or Windows 10 Enterprise	Microsoft 365 E3, E5, A3, A5, F3, Business Premium Windows E3, E5, A3, A5
Windows 7 Enterprise	Microsoft 365 E3, E5, A3, A5, F3, Business Premium Windows E3, E5, A3, A5
Windows Server 2012 R2, 2016, 2019	RDS Client Access License (CAL) with Software Assurance

When you have the correct licensing to run Azure AVD workloads in place, you can run the session host VMs using Azure Hybrid Benefit, negating the need to pay for another Windows license. Since this is limited to the session host VMs, this licensing benefit does not apply to other VMs running as domain controllers, file shares, and other related services.

> **NOTE** The preceding Microsoft 365 licensing SKUs also provide the required licensing to access the AVD environment.

Scaling

Because session host VMs are VMs in the Azure back end, you can automate scaling to shut down and deallocate unused session hosts during off-peak hours, the same way you can regular VMs. You can then turn them back on during peak hours, ensuring user sessions are handled efficiently and that end-users don't experience any performance impact. Microsoft provides a low-cost scaling-automation tool that you can set up quite easily to achieve this. Refer to the complete, up-to-date guidance provided by Microsoft online to put this in place.

High availability

While designing your AVD solution, you should consider the high-availability requirements for various components to meet your organization's redundancy needs. Although the components managed by Microsoft are designed and built with high availability in mind, and are not managed by the customer, the redundancy of components like session host VMs, associated VM disks, and user profile storage are managed by the customer. The following sections discuss how to achieve high availability for these components.

Use availability sets

One of the easiest ways to achieve high availability for session hosts is to deploy them in an availability set. As discussed in Chapter 2, "Azure virtual machine scale sets," putting a VM (including a session host VM) in an availability set spreads them over multiple physical computer racks, servers, storage devices, and network devices within the same Azure datacenter, and puts them in different fault and update domains to protect them from failures or outages related to service updates. So, in the event of any hardware or software outage, only a subset of the session host VMs would go offline, and user sessions would fail over to the remaining VMs that are online and accessible. This is a great way to ensure redundancy on the local datacenter level within an Azure region.

> **NOTE** You can set this up at the time deployment using the Azure Portal, Azure PowerShell, the Azure CLI, or an ARM template.

Use availability zones

To achieve high availability in the event of a local datacenter failure within an Azure region, you can use availability zones. An availability zone is a physical datacenter location within an Azure region. Each availability zone is composed of one or more datacenters, equipped with its own independent power, cooling, and networking. Most Azure regions have three availability zones to provide utmost resiliency within the region.

> **NOTE** Currently, not all Azure regions support availability zones. So, be sure to select an Azure region that provides this capability if you require it.

Like availability sets, availability zones use fault and update domains. If three or more VMs are created across three availability zones in a particular Azure region, those VMs are spread across three fault and update domains—one in each availability zone. This ensures resiliency even if one of the zones or datacenters is completely offline.

> **NOTE** Although the datacenters within an availability zone are in the same region, they are typically located between 20 and 50 miles apart. However, they are connected via high-speed network connections to achieve low latency between workloads.

You should use availability zones in only scenarios in which uptime requirements are high, because hosting resources in availability zones has cost implications. Considering that you can easily deploy session host VMs using the golden image, it might be more cost-effective to use automation to quickly deploy new hosts in case of a zone outage. What you choose to do will depend on your availability requirements, the impact of an outage on business revenues, and app-latency requirements. You should discuss this with all stakeholders before deciding whether to use availability zones for the AVD environment.

Reserved instances

You can use reserved instances (RIs) to reduce the cost of session host VMs. With RIs, you reserve and pre-pay for the compute resources required to run your session host VMs in advance.

You can set up all session host VMs as RIs. However, if there is a set of VMs that will be brought online only for brief scheduled periods of time to handle peak loads, it is best to calculate the cost savings achieved by the scaling automation versus those achieved by using RIs before choosing which approach to take.

It might be possible to use the two options in combination to achieve maximum cost benefits—setting up RIs for one subset of session host VMs and setting up shutdown-startup automation for another.

WVD agent

Every session host VM requires the installation of a WVD agent and agent bootloader. The WVD agent allows for connectivity between the AVD service and the VMs. Because the agent is the intermediary between the service and the VM, if there are any with this agent, the session host VMs won't connect to the service and will be unavailable to accept client connections—even if the VM is online and available.

In the event of failed agent installations or upgrades, the agent will stop communicating with the AVD service. This would require an uninstall and re-install of the agent installer. If the agent is installed correctly but not loading on boot, the issue might be related to the agent bootloader and would require more analysis or reinstallation.

Agent registration

Once a VM is registered to a host pool, the VM agent regularly updates the VM's token whenever the VM is active. The certificate is thereafter valid for a period of 90 days. It is therefore recommended that all the session host VMs are brought online for 20 minutes every 90 days so that these tokens can be updated along with any other stack component and agent updates that must be applied. If any session host VM is not turned on during a 90-day period, it will result in the token expiring and the VM being unavailable for use in the host pool. It will require manual intervention to refresh this token by reinstalling the VM agent on the affected host.

Agent updates

Updates of WVD agents are performed automatically by the existing WVD agent in coordination with the AVD service as new updates are released. These updates might contain new functionality or security or bug fixes. It is important that the WVD agent be kept up to date to ensure that security and bug fixes are applied consistently across the environment.

The WVD agent queries the AVD service on a regular basis for any component updates that might be available. If updates are found, the agent is automatically updated within two to three minutes, with no impact on the VM. The older version of the agent is retained as a backup, so if there are any issues after update, it can be rolled back to the earlier version.

Microsoft performs agent updates at different intervals over a period of five days across all Azure subscriptions. However, updates are performed over a period of 24 hours for a single broker region. All VMs in a host pool are updated at different intervals during that period.

Deploying apps to session hosts

You can deploy apps to AVD session host VMs using one of the following methods:

- Installing apps in the golden image.
- Leveraging centralized management tools like SCCM or Intune.
- Dynamic app provisioning using AppV, VMWare AppVolumes, or Citrix AppLayering.
- Building custom scripts using Microsoft tools or third-party tools.
- Using MSIX App Attach to containerize and attach the required apps (apps are not installed on the OS but are instead mounted on virtual disks dynamically as needed).

MSIX App Attach is the latest app-packaging format built by Microsoft. It provides the following benefits:

- The OS, user, and app data are separated through the containerization of the app data.
- Apps need not be repacked when delivered dynamically.
- It reduces session host resource requirements, which helps reduce costs.
- It speeds up user logins.
- Because it uses a 64k block, MSIX App Attach reduces the network impact.
- It is specifically designed to support cloud solutions.
- Duplicate files across Windows and apps are removed, and app files are shared, which reduces disk utilization by session hosts.
- All apps run independently of each other and do not affect any other app during app updates—even if there are shared files involved.
- MSIX App Attach APIs support Windows 10 Enterprise and Windows 10 Enterprise multi-session, version 2004 or later, making it ideal for all supported versions of the Windows client OS.
- There are no limits on how many apps you can deploy using MSIX App Attach.

There are, however, a few limitations to using MSIX App Attach of which you should be aware:

- MSIX images are deployed on a per-machine basis, not on a per-user basis. As a result, the number of users who can use an MSIX image handle depends on the size of the VM's file system disk and network throughput. Azure Files has a limit of 2,000 open handles per file.

- Support for Azure AD Domain Services is currently not available.

- Application layering is not supported by all apps. This limits the apps from being repackaged into an MSIX file. Some types of apps that face this limitation include antivirus and anti-Malware software, Active-X and Silverlight, VPN client software, and software drivers.

Windows OS servicing

It is important to keep your AVD instances up to date on a monthly basis to ensure compliance and security. There are several options for updating session host VM instances. These include the following:

- **Microsoft Endpoint Configuration Manager (MECM)**　You can use MECM to update server and desktop operating systems on a regular basis with automation to schedule and validate successful deployments.

- **Windows Updates for Business (WUB)**　You can use WUB to update desktop operating systems like Windows 10 Enterprise multi-session in an automated manner with the latest patches released by Microsoft.

- **Azure Update Management Service (AUMS)**　You can use AUMS to update server operating systems like Windows Server 2019, 2016, and 2012 R2. You can then use Azure Log Analytics service to check for compliance to ensure the updates have deployed successfully.

- **Deploy a new image**　You can use a new (custom) image to deploy session hosts every month with the latest Windows and app updates pre-installed and tested. This enables you to test the host image in a validation pool before deployment in production.

Session host walkthrough

The following section steps you through the process of creating a session host using the Azure Portal.

USING THE AZURE PORTAL

To create a session host using the Azure Portal, follow these steps:

1. In the **Azure Virtual Desktop** page, under **Manage**, click **Host Pools**.

2. In the **Host Pools** page, click on the personal or pooled host pool that you want to use as a session host. For this example, I have selected **PersonalHostPool01**.

3. In the left pane of the host pool's page, under **Manage**, click **Session Hosts**.

4. Click **Add** to start the Create a Session Host wizard. (See Figure 4-28.)

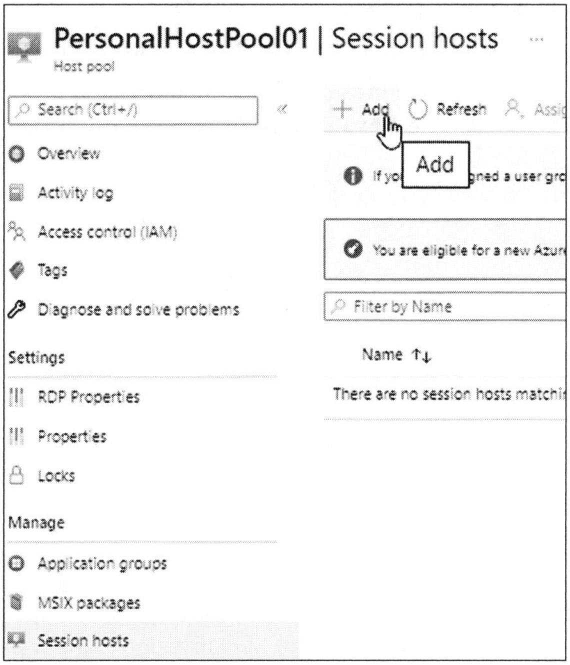

FIGURE 4-28   Adding a session host.

5. The values in the **Basics** tab should already be populated and grayed out. (See Figure 4-29.) Click **Next** to continue.

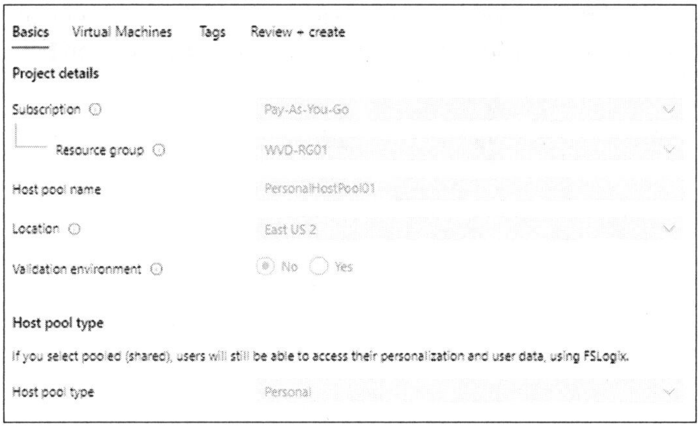

FIGURE 4-29   The Basic tab of the Create a Session Host wizard.

6. On the **Virtual Machines** tab, enter the following information (see Figure 4-30):

- **Resource Group** This should be the same resource group as the host pool.
- **Name Prefix** Enter a unique name prefix for the session host.
- **Virtual Machine Location** Indicate where you want to create the session host.
- **Availability Options** Specify whether the session host should be part of an availability zone. For this example, select **Availability Zone**.

| Basics | Virtual Machines | Tags | Review + create |

Host pools are a collection of one or more identical virtual machines within Azure Virtual Desktop environments. Here you give details to create a resource group with virtual machines in an Azure subscription. Learn more

Add virtual machines	No ● Yes
Resource group	WVD-RG01
Name prefix *	WVD-PPool
	ⓘ Session host name must be unique within the Resource Group.
Virtual machine location ○	East US 2
Availability options ○	Availability zone

FIGURE 4-30 The Virtual Machines tab of the Create a Session Host wizard.

7. Still in **Virtual Machines** tab, enter the following information (see Figure 4-31):

- **Availability Zone** Select the availability zone you want to assign to the session host, based on your AVD environment design. In this example, select **1**.
- **Security Type** Leave as Standard.
- **Image Type** Choose **Gallery**. (The other option, **Storage Blob**, is not available because you do not have a disk blob available for VM creation.)
- **Image** Select the required Windows 10 Enterprise image from the group of marketplace images made available by Microsoft—in this case, **Windows 10 Enterprise, Version 20H2**.

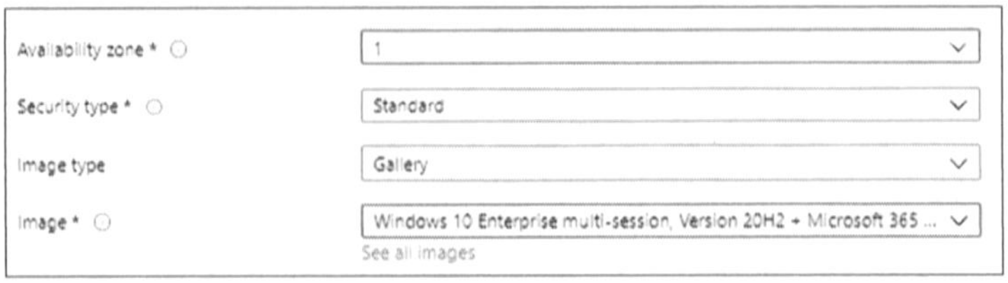

Availability zone * ○	1
Security type * ○	Standard
Image type	Gallery
Image * ○	Windows 10 Enterprise multi-session, Version 20H2 + Microsoft 365 ...
	See all images

FIGURE 4-31 Session host image selection.

8. Still in **Virtual Machines** tab, enter the following information (see Figure 4-32):

- **Virtual Machine Size** You can leave this set to the default (as I've done here) or customize it based on the requirements of your environment.

- **Number of VMs** A session host pool can have more than one VM. Set this value based on your design requirements. In this example, set it to **2**.

- **OS Disk Type** Choose the disk type based on your app requirements. In this case, choose **Standard SSD**.

- **Boot Diagnostics** Leave this set to the default value (**Enable with Managed Storage Account**) or select a custom storage account if required.

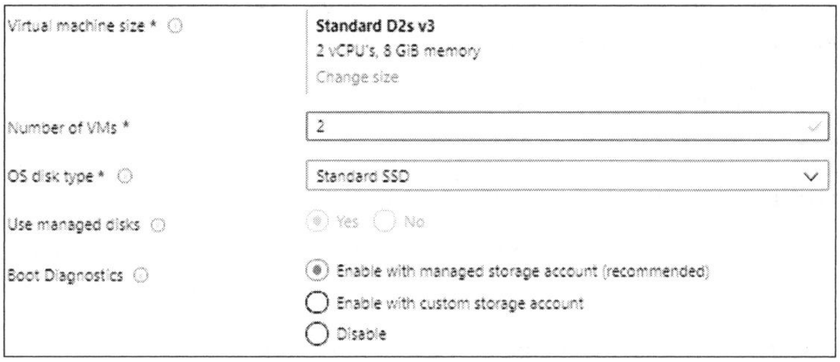

FIGURE 4-32 Setting VM values.

9. Still in **Virtual Machines** tab, under **Network and Security**, enter the following information (see Figure 4-33):

- **Virtual Network** Select the virtual network to create the session hosts.

- **Subnet** Select the subnet you want to use.

- **Network Security Group** Choose **Basic**.

- **Public Inbound Ports** Select **No**.

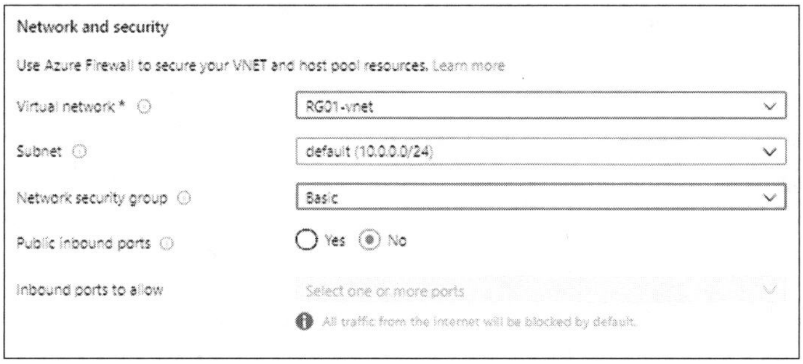

FIGURE 4-33 Setting the VM network configuration.

10. Still in **Virtual Machines** tab, under **Domain**, open the **Select Which Directory You Would Like to Join** drop-down list and choose **Azure Active Directory**.

Active Directory options

You choose Azure Active Directory if you have integrated your Azure Active Directory DS or on-premises Active Directory domain with Azure Active Directory using Azure AD Connect. If, however, you have an Active Directory DC online in Azure or on-premises Active Directory that is reachable by the session host VMs, you would choose Active Directory. If you choose Active Directory, a set of options related to Active Directory appears (see Figure 4-34):

- **AD Domain Join UPN**   Enter the user account of an admin from the domain. You'll use this to join the session host VM to the domain.
- **Password**   Enter the password for the preceding user account.
- **Specify Domain or Unit**   Select the **Yes** option button if you want to place the session host VM in a specific organizational unit (OU) in Active Directory.
- **Domain to Join**   Enter the name of the domain to join.
- **Organizational Unit Path**   Enter the OU path where the session host VM should be placed in Active Directory.

FIGURE 4-34   Active Directory settings.

11. Next to **Enroll VM with Intune**, click the **No** option button. (See Figure 4-35.) Then click **Next**.

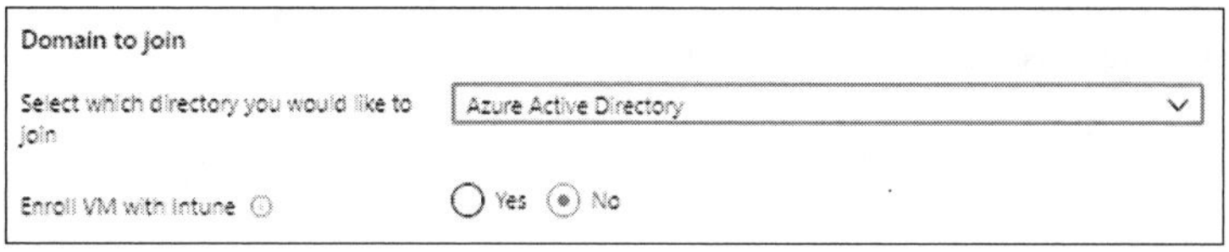

FIGURE 4-35 Domain settings.

12. In the **Tags** tab, enter any tags that you would like to apply (see Figure 4-36) and click **Next**.

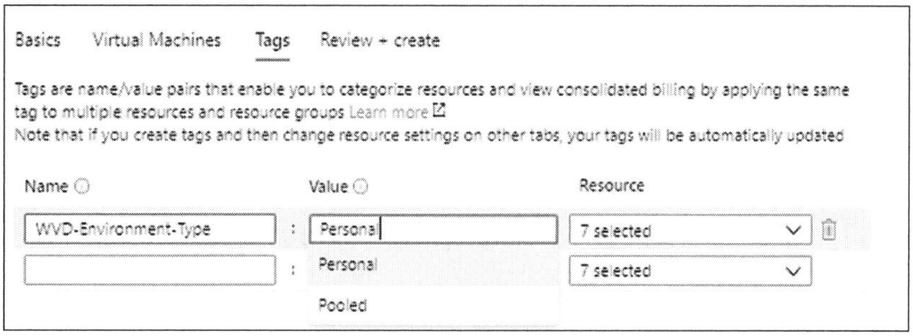

FIGURE 4-36 Setting tags for the session host.

13. On the **Review + Create** tab, review your settings and click **Create** to create the session host VMs.

The creation process takes some time to complete. The Deployment Is in Progress will indicate what phase of the process is currently underway. (See Figure 4-37.) For more information about a particular phase, you can click the Operation Details link. You can also click the Operation Details link if the creation process fails to understand why. (Click the link next to the failed step.)

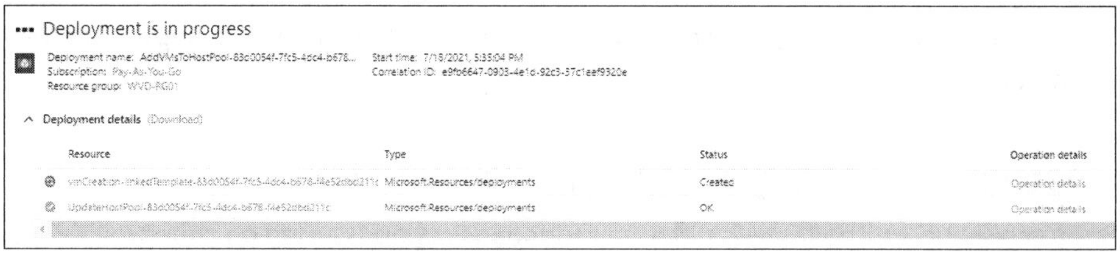

FIGURE 4-37 Monitoring deployment progress.

14. When the session host VMs have been created successfully, they will be visible in the host pool page in the Session Hosts pane. (See Figure 4-38.)

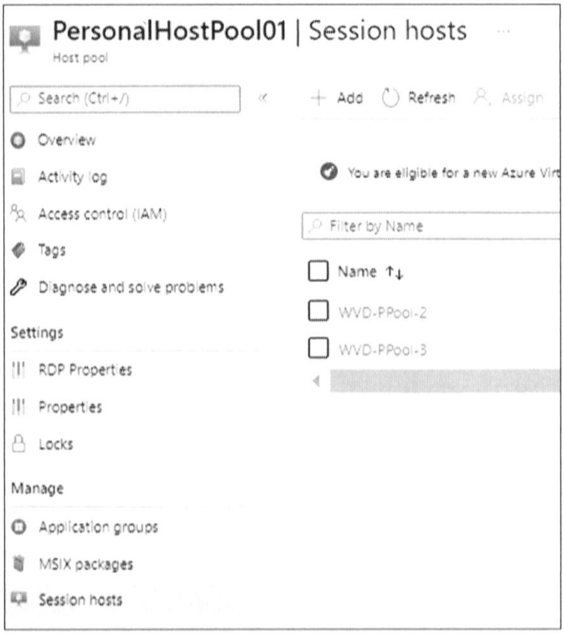

FIGURE 4-38   Confirming the session host VMs were created.

Store user profile data

You can store user profile data in Azure Storage using Azure Files. Azure Files secures this stored data by using encryption at rest and in transit and by integrating various identity options like on-premises Active Directory and Azure Active Directory. This makes it easy to manage user access permissions. Azure Files also supports numerous redundancy options, like Azure backups, snapshots, and so on, which enables you to maintain backup copies for easy restoration.

Data redundancy and high availability

You can set up Azure Files with different redundancy options based on your organization's resiliency requirements. These options are as follows:

- **Locally redundant storage (LRS)**   Using LRS ensures that each file is replicated and stored three times within the Azure storage cluster spread across a single Azure data-center. Any hardware failure on the storage layer due to power-supply issues, hard-disk issues, or other issues contained within the storage unit would not result in data loss or hamper data access. LRS is the most cost-effective redundancy option. However, other redundancy options offer better protection against datacenter-wide outages—for example, due to a fire or some other disaster.

- **Zone redundant storage (ZRS)** Using ZRS ensures that each file is replicated and stored three times within three distinct and physically isolated storage clusters. Because a zone is spread across three Azure datacenters, this provides multi-datacenter redundancy. All write operations are replicated across the three availability zones and accepted only after they have been committed to all three zones. ZRS is more expensive than LRS, but it provides a significantly higher level of protection. However, a zone-wide outage would still result in data loss.

- **Geo-redundant storage (GRS)** Using GRS ensures that files are replicated and stored six times between two Azure storage clusters—three times in an Azure storage cluster in the primary region, and three more times in an Azure storage cluster in a secondary region. In the event of a disaster, Microsoft manages the failover to the secondary site (although you can perform this failover manually if required). GRS provides the highest level of redundancy, but at a higher cost.

> **NOTE** GRS is currently available only for Azure Files Standard storage.

Backups

Although the preceding redundancy options do provide a certain level of resiliency and recoverability in case of outages, there are scenarios in which data corruption can take place. For such scenarios, you must make regular backups with Azure Backup for easy restoration when needed. Although AVD supports third-party backup solutions, Azure Backup provides a built-in, easy, and cost-effective solution that is suitable for most organizations.

AVD can leverage Azure Backup to back up the various components in AVD. These include the following:

- **Session hosts** You can back up all AVD session hosts using Azure Backup's VM backup capabilities. This is a stable, proven technology in the Azure IaaS stack that can easily scale up to provide backups for as many hosts as needed and retain those backups for as long as is required based on your organization's compliance policies.

- **Storage** Regardless of what technology is in use for user data or profile storage— Azure blob storage or Azure Files—you can leverage Azure Backup to create regular backups. This technology has been available for numerous years and is extremely stable for regular and long-term retention of user or profile data.

- **Service metadata** Azure manages the backing up of service metadata. Backup and redundancy for this type of data fall outside the customer's scope.

- **Web Access, Gateway, and Broker services** Azure manages the backing up of these components, which are part of the AVD control plane. Backup and redundancy for these services fall outside the customer's scope.

There are numerous benefits to using Azure Backup for AVD backups, including the following:

- **No infrastructure required**   Azure Backup does not require the deployment of any infrastructure to support the backing up of AVD session hosts or storage.
- **Customized retention**   You can set backup-retention policies according to your organization's policies to meet daily, weekly, monthly, and yearly retention requirements.
- **Built-in management**   All configuration for scheduling and managing backups and restores is built into the service and does not require the use of additional services or components.
- **Fast restores**   Snapshots are used for file share backups, which allow for fast restoration of required data. VM restores are also performed very quickly compared to other third-party solutions that might not use Azure as their data store.
- **Alerting and reporting**   You can use the management interface to set up alerts for backup and restore failures for timely intervention. The reporting module provides deeper insights on the backups performed.

Disaster recovery

Most mid- to large-scale enterprises see virtual desktops as critical to their environment. The impact of extended downtimes can be exorbitant, so organizations look to disaster-recovery solutions to address such scenarios.

For AVD, one of the best ways to ensure recovery in the event of a disaster is to implement disaster-recovery solutions for each of the various components that are managed by the end-customer. Components managed by Microsoft are designed with disaster recovery in mind, and failover of these components is managed by Microsoft as part of their service contracts and guarantees.

When a disaster occurs in an Azure region, back-end service infrastructure components automatically fail over to the designated secondary location and continue servicing clients normally. So, users will be able to sign into the AVD service. However, unless the other customer-managed components are available, they won't be able to perform any work functions.

The various components in the end-customer scope include the following:

- Session host VMs, including storage used for VM disks
- User profile data
- Dependent network shares
- Virtual networks connecting all these components
- Network components connecting the on-premises environment to the AVD environment

For users to access these components during a region-wide outage, each of them must be replicated to a different location. You can automate the failover between these sites or manage it manually. The following sections cover some of the recommended ways in which you can replicate each of these components or make them available in the secondary region.

VM redundancy

The first components to target are the session host VMs. There are two suggested methods to build redundancy for these VMs:

- **Replicating them using Azure Site Recovery**   You can replicate all pooled and personal desktop VMs to a secondary region using Azure Site Recovery. Azure Site Recovery is a service that is built into Azure to provide disaster-recovery services for VMs, storage, and other Azure services using replication solutions and automation tools and scripts. You can configure all your VMs in both pooled and personal host pools to use Azure Site Recovery. You can then bring the VMs back online using recovery plans. This approach works for both pooled and personal desktops.

- **Setting up multiple regions with the required VMs in advance**   You can set up multiple host pools across multiple Azure regions with the required session host capacity but keep the VMs in the secondary site offline. You can set up all the required AVD configurations, including app groups and workspaces, in the hosts in the secondary site. You can use Azure Site Recovery to power on the VMs using recovery plans in the event of a disaster. This approach is viable for pooled desktop VMs, as these VMs should not have any user data stored locally.

> **TIP**   Personal desktops allow users to store data locally and customize their desktop experience. If your AVD environment includes personal desktops, then you should consider the first approach—replicating VMs using Azure Site Recovery (or a third-party replication and recovery tool).

If you use Azure Site Recovery, the AVD agent in the secondary site VMs will automatically connect to the AVD service instance nearest to them using the latest service tokens. This eliminates the need to register these VMs in the secondary site manually. This also automatically adds them to the host pool in the secondary site and makes them available for end-users once they are re-logged.

vNETs

The next critical component to consider is the virtual network infrastructure used by the AVD environment to connect end-users to on-premises resources and business apps. If all components will be failed over to a secondary site, you should set up virtual networks in that secondary site to match the setup in the primary. This makes it easier to duplicate and maintain changes in the primary site to the secondary one. If users need to access any on-premises resources using the VPN, ExpressRoute, or other virtual WAN solutions, then those must be re-established after failover in the secondary site.

> **TIP** You can use Azure Site Recovery to build and maintain the VNet configuration in the secondary region. This eliminates the need for peering in advance and maintains all the required settings in line with the primary site network.

User identities

The domain controller, hosted on-premises or (preferably) in the Azure environment, manages user identities. You must make these available from the secondary site, too. You can achieve this in one of the following ways:

- If using an on-premises domain controller, make sure the secondary site is connected to it.
- Set up a domain controller in the secondary site.
- Use Azure Site Recovery to replicate the AD domain controller.

The recommended approach is to set up a domain controller in the secondary site to provide extremely low latency between the session hosts and the DCs in Azure. However, if that is not possible or acceptable for security or compliance reasons, then ensure there is good connectivity between the on-premises domain controller and the secondary region environment.

User profile data

You can replicate user profile data stored in FSLogix profiles to the secondary site, depending on the solution used to store the profiles:

- **Azure Files**   Use native replication for replication to the secondary site.
- **Azure NetApp Files**   Use native replication for replication to the secondary site.
- **Shared network drives stored on file shares**   Use Azure Site Recovery for the VM(s) or third-party solutions for replication.
- **Cloud Cache for profile storage**   Cloud Cache inherently allows for the replication of profile data to the secondary site.

Network shares (optional)

If users need access to company or departmental data in the AVD environment, you can create network shares to make this data available in the secondary site, depending on how the shares are set up in the primary site. Some of these options are similar to the ones available for FSLogix profile storage:

- **Azure Files**   Use native replication for replication to the secondary site.
- **Azure NetApp Files**   Use native replication for replication to the secondary site.

- **Shared network drives stored on file shares** Use Azure Site Recovery for the VM(s) or third-party solutions for replication.

Applications

Be sure to consider all the business apps employed by users in the AVD environment. To identify the ideal replication solutions, consider the apps and their data-storage options, and discuss this with the app vendor or refer to its documentation. Replication might involve the use of a single replication solution like Azure Site Recovery, a similar third-party replication solution, or a combination of solutions, depending on the app and database in use.

Best practices

After you set up all the various components for recovery to the secondary site, there are a few recommended practices to follow:

- Carry out testing of the disaster-recovery site.
- Document all recovery procedures (automated and manual).
- Allocate the responsibility of the various disaster-recovery activation and testing procedures to clearly defined roles or identified personnel.
- Regularly test the disaster-recovery plans and process to validate that all the required components come up as needed and that data is available.
- Document any changes to the primary site and incorporate them into the secondary-site configuration and recovery plan (in advance, if possible).

There are also a few suggestions on how to test the recovery plan:

- Perform recovery tests during a maintenance window to avoid user disruption.
- Communicate the recovery test plan to end-users well in advance, with frequent reminders as the test dates approach to ensure users can flag possible obstacles or planned business events to avoid business disruption.
- If necessary, turn off access to the primary site session host VMs so users do not accidentally access and make changes to those VMs during the test window.
- Test and validate all business-critical apps with relevant stakeholders and document the outcomes.
- Identify and carry out any corrective actions, if needed, before the next testing window, and document the changes for future validation.

> **NOTE** Microsoft recommends conducting tests with up to 100 VMs at a time. If more session host VMs exist, Microsoft recommends that the failover be performed in batches with a gap of at least 10 minutes between each batch.

Authentication

Some AVD components require you to set up authentication for users to be able to access and use the AVD service. These include authentication to the AVD service itself, the session hosts, and the AVD control plane for management access. Each of these is explained here in more detail.

AVD service

The following support authentication to the AVD service:

- On-premises users synced to Azure AD (also known as *hybrid identities*)
- On-premises users synced to Azure AD and federated using Active Directory Federation Services (ADFS)
- Cloud-only Azure AD users in session hosts using only Azure AD-joined VMs

> **NOTE** Standalone AD deployments federated with ADFS are not supported. This is because the AVD service requires users to be discoverable through Azure AD.

Session-host access

AVD supports NTLM and Kerberos authentication for access to session host VMs. The following three approaches are the most commonly used:

- Deploy a domain controller in the same VNet as the session hosts.
- Set up a VPN to access an on-premises domain controller.
- Set up Azure AD DS integrated with Azure AD.

Consider this when planning the design of the underlying network architecture.

Use built-in roles to provision access

Azure uses Role-Based Access Controls (RBAC) for rights assignment to users and admins for resources across the environment. AVD leverages the same RBAC model with a set of custom built-in roles specific to the AVD infrastructure management.

Let's briefly review the different built-in roles and their purpose to get a better understanding of how they can be used for simplified access management in the AVD environment:

- **Desktop Virtualization Contributor**   Allows the assigned administrator to manage all aspects of the AVD deployment except compute resources.
- **Desktop Virtualization Reader**   A view-only administrator role that allows the assigned administrator to review all aspects of the deployment but not to make changes. You might assign this role to auditors or external consultants who are tasked with reviewing your environment design and configuration for reporting purposes.

- **Host Pool Contributor** Allows the assigned administrator to manage all aspects of the host pools deployed in the environment and gives access to all resources. It does not allow the administrator to create session host VMs or create host pools, but rather gives them the ability to manage them.

- **Host Pool Reader** A view-only administrator role that allows the assigned administrator to review everything related to host pools in the AVD environment but not to make changes.

- **Application Group Contributor** Allows the assigned administrator to manage all aspects of app groups except publishing app groups to users or user groups.

- **Application Group Reader** A view-only administrator role that allows the assigned administrator to review everything related to app groups in the AVD environment but not to make changes.

- **Workspace Contributor** Allows the assigned administrator to manage all aspects of the workspaces set up in the AVD environment. It is best to use this role in conjunction with the Application Group Reader role so the assigned admin gets read access to all the app information for the app groups associated with the workspaces.

- **Workspace Reader** A view-only administrator role that allows the assigned administrator to review everything related to workspaces in the AVD environment but not to make changes.

- **User Session Operator** Allows the assigned administrator to manage user session activities like sending messages, disconnecting, and logging out sessions. This role does not grant access to session host management activities like adding or removing session hosts, setting host maintenance or drain mode configuration, or other similar activities.

- **Session Host Operator** Allows the assigned administrator to view and manage session hosts, including performing activities like removing session hosts and maintaining the host using drain mode. Admins assigned this role do not have the ability to add session hosts using the Azure Portal because write permissions for host pool objects are not assigned as part of this role. However, if a valid registration token and compute permissions are provisioned through another role, the admin can add session hosts to the host pool.

Network considerations

Following are two network-related recommendations for ensuring that the AVD environment performs optimally:

- The round-trip latency for traffic from the user network to the session hosts in the chosen Azure region should be less than 150 ms. Be sure to check this from the various known networks from which the virtual desktops would be accessed before selecting the region to host the session hosts and host pools.

- Although the regions that support the storage of virtual desktop metadata are currently limited, if possible (based on latency testing and other factors), it is best to host the session hosts in the same Azure region as the metadata service, as this improves network performance.

On the subject of networking, it is increasingly common for organizations to track and control user traffic on their workstations within the office networks and, in some cases, even on their home networks when using company devices. In the AVD environment, you can achieve this by using a proxy server to manage all communication, including DNS and internet traffic. Be aware, however, that if the proxy server's connection to the Azure environment has high latency, there will be a related impact on the AVD cluster, which can hamper the user experience. It is therefore important to choose proxy servers that exhibit low latency. It's best to test the proxy server to validate its performance when connected to the various regions where session hosts are located. Perform this validation on a regular basis to confirm that the latency has not gone up dramatically over time and identify backup proxy options to switch to before affecting the user experience.

Security

Security in the AVD environment is applicable on different levels. Some security recommendations apply to the overall AVD environment and are useful to protect the access and management layers within the environment. Other recommendations apply on the session-host level to protect and secure VM instances accessed by the users.

Security for the overall WVD environment

Let's start by covering security recommendations that apply to the overall AVD environment. These focus on protecting the identity, access, and management layers, and provide guidance on areas to monitor to identify possible surface areas of attack:

- **Use Conditional Access**   Conditional Access enables you to control which users can access resources in Azure, from which locations, at what times of day, and using which devices. This enables organizations to control access on various levels based on their compliance and security needs. You can customize Conditional Access to use some or all of these capabilities. It is a good practice to use Conditional Access to control access to the AVD environment, as its granular controls can prevent malicious actors from accessing the environment, even if they breach the password for one of the users.

- **Delegate access**   Delegating access restricts users in the AVD environment to accessing only those resources that are necessary to perform their official work activities. This access level might be different for different user groups or the same across the organization. Identify the various user groups in your organization, their role requirements, their associated permission requirements on the virtual desktop, and plan permission assignments accordingly. AVD uses the Azure RBAC model for access delegation. This makes it easy to assign access to different users or user groups by either using existing built-in roles or creating custom roles that contain the specific permission sets required by the users. You can apply the permissions thereafter on the host pool, app groups, or workspace level, providing granular control on every level.

- **Use Azure Security Center** Azure Security Center helps manage vulnerabilities; maintain access compliance in accordance with standard frameworks like PCI, HIPAA, and so on; and strengthen the overall security posture of the AVD environment. For these reasons, it is a good practice to enable Azure Security Center for all subscriptions, session hosts, and other VMs and storage accounts associated with the AVD environment.

- **Use Secure Score** Secure Score is a free service provided by Microsoft that scans the environment to identify configuration settings that deviate from Microsoft's recommendations and best practice guidelines. Secure Score provides a list of recommendations, ranked by priority or criticality, as well as guidance to help you quickly address the recommendation. Microsoft regularly updates Secure Score as new best practices, services, and field recommendations are compiled. It is best to review them monthly or quarterly and implement any new recommendations that are relevant for your environment.

- **Use multi-factor authentication** This service is provided in Azure as part of most Azure AVD licensing SKUs. Multi-factor authentication is an easy way to protect every environment—even if user passwords are breached using brute-force attacks. It is highly recommended that you enable multi-factor authentication for all administrators and users in the environment.

- **Collect audit logs** The AVD environment generates numerous audit logs, and viewing and managing these logs on an individual basis can be quite cumbersome. Fortunately, Microsoft provides the audit log collection service to consolidate and analyze these logs. Some key audit logs to collect are as follows:

  - AVD diagnostic log
  - Session hosts log
  - Azure Active Directory log
  - Azure activity log
  - Azure Active Directory Activity log

- **Use RemoteApps** You can enable AVD access by providing access either to the entire virtual desktop environment or to individual required apps only by using RemoteApps. Using RemoteApps exposes only a small subset of the session host VM to users when they access an app. This reduces the attack surface and limits users' access to the session host VM. The app experience is still seamless, as users can work with the app without needing to log in to the entire desktop.

- **Use Azure Monitor** Azure Monitor can help you monitor AVD service usage and session host health and availability. Use Azure Monitor to build and consume dashboards to monitor the health of various AVD components and set up service health alerts to be notified promptly of critical user-impacting events.

Security for session hosts

Session host VMs are the main component employed by users when they log into the AVD environment. Securing these VMs is critical to ensuring the security of the overall AVD environment. Following are some best practices to keep session host VMs secure:

- **Delegate permissions to shadow users** In environments in which user support is delegated, helpdesk admins need not have full admin rights on session host VMs. Instead, you can delegate specific permissions to shadow users in the AVD environment. This enables helpdesk admins to provide support to the users without assigning extended permissions, thereby reducing the attack surface in the event their credentials are breached. You must assign these permissions on the session host VM level by targeting the Windows management namespace. To ensure they are applied consistently across the environment, you should assign them either on the golden image used to build the session host VMs or as a computer startup script applied to the session host VMs.

- **Apply endpoint protection for hosts** Securing session host VMs starts with deploying an endpoint protection solution to detect known malicious code. Depending on your organization's preferences, you can use Windows Defender Antivirus or deploy a third-party antivirus solution. Be sure to set any exclusions for storage, app executables, or database files on a global level so they are applied across all session hosts.

- **Use an endpoint detection and response (EDR) solution** For advanced detection and response to known and unknown malicious software on session host VMs, use an EDR solution such as Defender ATP, which is provided within Azure, or a third-party solution. It is a good practice to have an EDR solution in place to protect the environment from advanced attack vectors.

- **Manage threats and vulnerabilities** Azure Security Center is a great service built into Azure to analyze and identify vulnerabilities in server operating systems deployed across the AVD environment. Azure Security Center can integrate with Defender ATP to manage threats and vulnerabilities on the operating systems. Or you can integrate and leverage various third-party threat and vulnerability management solutions found in the Azure Marketplace.

- **Patch software vulnerabilities**   Patching software vulnerabilities on the operating system and application layers is critical to ensuring that the environment is as secure as possible. Malicious actors regularly attack known vulnerabilities; simply patching these vulnerabilities on a monthly or bi-weekly patching cycle can mitigate numerous security risks. It is also a good practice to update golden images with the latest deployed patches to keep them up to date so that new VMs deployed using these images are up to date as soon as they are online.

- **Enact idle time and disconnection policies**   Identify a suitable threshold for idle time and disconnection policies to obtain the right mix of resource savings and prevent data loss and user interruption. If there are apps in the environment that have long-running processes, such as rendering and simulation software, consider larger timeout windows to avoid data loss.

- **Lock out the screen for idle sessions**   Set the Windows screen to lock and require reauthentication during idle times so that malicious actors do not exploit unattended workstations to gain access to the AVD environment.

- **Establish tiered admin access**   Users should always be given access only to the resources they need to perform their work functions efficiently. If certain users require extended access for app deployment or configuration, it is best to identify the use times for such access and provide the additional rights only for that period. If this is not possible, then use app-deployment tools such as Microsoft SCCM or Intune to publish apps or configurations to limit the need for extended access.

- **Control user access to internal and external resources**   Control user access to internal and external network resources like file shares, internal and external websites, and web services using services like Azure Firewall, network appliances, proxy servers, and so on. Restrict access to only those services or websites the user needs to carry out their work activities. Be sure to test this from different network segments to ensure that access to the AVD environment and the required internal and external resources is working correctly.

- **Deploy security for Office apps**   In most environments, Office apps are deployed on session hosts in default mode, with little to no security applied. It is important to keep these apps up to date and to identify policies specific to your environment that can help restrict access to functionality that is not needed—for example, using group policies or applying restrictions on the golden image for new session host deployments. Make sure the policies you deploy do not hamper user productivity by testing with users across company segments with different work profiles.

- **Redirect devices**   Use device-redirection policies to prevent the redirection of drives, USB devices, and printers from the user's local device to the remote desktop sessions to which they are connected. This can prevent data leaks that occur inadvertently or maliciously if a user's account is hacked. It is a good practice to set these restrictions unless redirection is required for operational reasons.

- **Set up permission controls on file systems** Use NTFS and share permissions on local and remote file shares to allow user access to only required levels. This can help prevent the spread of malicious code or unauthorized data access.

- **Prevent access to Windows Explorer** Without proper permission controls, users can employ Windows Explorer to gain entry to local and network drives to which they do not need access. It is a good practice to prevent access to Windows Explorer completely or hide all sensitive drives using group policy to prevent misuse.

- **Use just-in-time access controls** Use just-in-time access controls to provide direct RDP access to session hosts and other critical VMs in the environment. This can help you keep track of access sessions and limit the attack surface in case of a breach.

- **Prevent unwanted software deployment** Use technologies like App Locker to allow access only to required apps on session host VMs. This can help limit the attack surface and prevent malicious apps from running without being allow-listed.

Integration with Azure DevTest Labs

Azure DevTest Labs enables developers to efficiently self-manage VMs and PaaS resources without waiting for approvals. Essentially, DevTest Labs creates tools consisting of preconfigured solutions or Azure Resource Manager (ARM) templates. These have all the necessary tools and software needed to create environments in minutes rather than hours or days.

Azure DevTest Labs provides a mini Azure control plane that empowers teams to create and manage environments in a self-service manner. The biggest benefits are the cost, security, and compliance controls it provides for building a compliant desktop solution, and the agility it gives end-users by being a self-service solution. This, of course, comes at a cost, as organizations still must engineer their desktop solution. The good news is that DevTest Labs and Azure provide all the pieces needed for this solution.

Benefits of Azure DevTest Labs include the following:

- Fast VM creation
- The ability to customize and approve a set of VM images for use
- Custom VMs containing all the required software and tools for quick consumption
- Custom package builds that are a combination of custom images and the latest software builds that are installed automatically on VM creation
- Extension installs on VMs after provisioning
- Auto-startup and auto-shutdown schedules for VMs
- The ability to limit the number of VMs users can create
- Cost monitoring and alerting for optimization

There are two main reasons to combine these services:

- AVDs can front-end the connectivity for DevTest Labs workloads, providing a secure model for connectivity when used by developers to manage individual developer desktops.

- Azure DevTest Labs provides the ability to build single session hosts and give self-service capabilities to end-users while maintaining central control.

Other best practices

Following is a list of some other commonly used practices across large AVD deployments to help you better manage and monitor the environment:

- **Set up email discovery**   One way end-users connect to their published virtual desktops is to use feed URLs. However, it is always a challenge for IT to provide these complex feed URLs, and for users to retrieve it each time they require it without making mistakes. To make it easier for end-users to connect to their published virtual desktops, you can use DNS configuration to set up email discovery. This enables users to discover their feed using their email address. Be sure to set this up in all environments unless there is a special security need to hide feed URLs.

- **Use language packs**   In situations in which users will employ the AVD environment in different geographical areas or using different languages, it's important for users to be able to customize their Windows 10 language. You can achieve this building dedicated host pools with the various languages and publishing them to the required users. Alternatively, you can make all users part of the same host pool but give them access to hosts with different language images, allowing them to select the one they prefer. This method is a lot more efficient to manage and maintain.

- **Integrate with Azure Advisor**   Azure Advisor is a service that analyzes the configuration and telemetry of associated Azure resources to identify recommendations that can help address general problems. It is a good practice to integrate the AVD environment with Azure Advisor to benefit from this functionality. This can help you reduce user complaints about common issues, thereby saving time, effort, and money.

- **Use Microsoft Endpoint Manager or Microsoft Intune**   It is a good practice to use either Microsoft Endpoint Manager, a unified platform that includes Microsoft Endpoint Configuration Manager and Microsoft Intune, or Microsoft Intune alone. This can help ease management overhead by:

  - Managing automated app deployments and upgrades on session hosts

  - Keeping Windows 10 session hosts up to date

  - Monitoring compliance on session hosts for antivirus and firewall configurations

  - Managing group policy related settings deployed on session hosts

Publish apps

Once all the session hosts are deployed, the next step is to publish the required apps for users to access. You do this if users will not be given access to the entire virtual desktop, but only to the remote apps.

There are three types of apps that are generally published, as follows:

- **Built-in apps** These are the default apps installed on the base Windows image. Examples include Calculator, Notepad, File Explorer, and so on.

- **Third-party installed apps** These are the third-party apps installed on the session host images and VMs. Examples include Microsoft Office Suite, Adobe Reader, Microsoft Teams, and so on.

- **Custom apps** These are customer-specific apps installed on the session host images and VMs. These are installed in custom paths and require guidance from the app developer for ideal installation and use.

> **NOTE** After an app is published, its default icon should be updated to reflect its actual icon, if available. (Look ahead to Figure 4-42.) This will make it easier for users to identify the app. Icons with image formats of PNG, BMP, GIF, JPG, JPEG, and ICO are supported.

App publishing walkthrough

The following section steps you through the process of publishing a built-in app and a third-party app using the Azure Portal.

USING THE AZURE PORTAL

To publish a built-in app and a third-party app using the Azure Portal, follow these steps:

1. In the **Azure Virtual Desktop** page, under **Manage**, click **Application Groups**.
2. In the **Application Groups** page, click the app group that you would like to use to publish apps—in this case, **WindowsApps**. (See Figure 4-39.)
3. In the left pane of the **WindowsApps** group page, under **Manage**, click **Applications**. (See Figure 4-40.)
4. Click **Add**.
5. In the **Add Application** dialog box, open the **Application Source** drop-down list and choose **Start Menu**. (See Figure 4-41.)

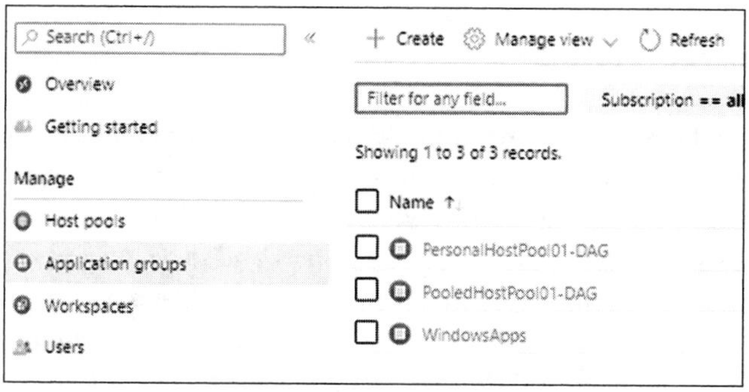

FIGURE 4-39 Selecting an app group.

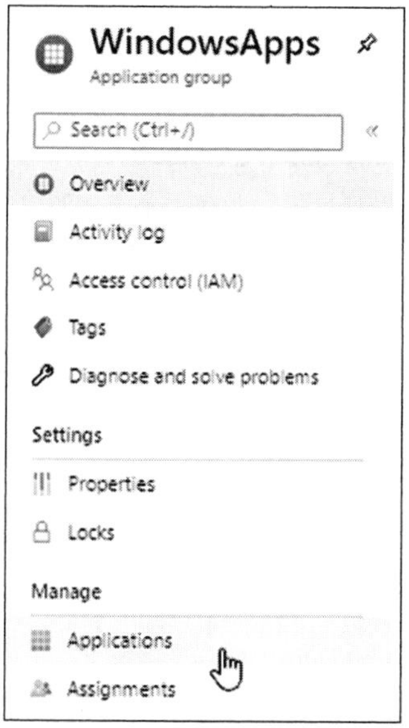

FIGURE 4-40 Adding applications to an app group.

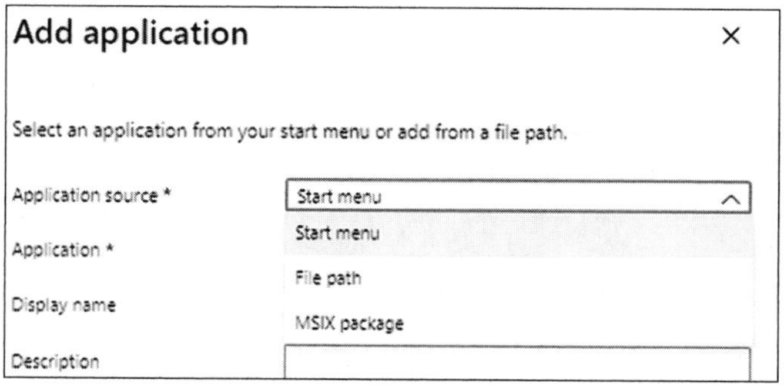

FIGURE 4-41 Selecting the application source.

Other application sources

In addition to the Start Menu option—which you choose to load apps that already have shortcuts published in the Start menu—you can choose the File Path option or the MSIX Package option. Choose File Path if you want to enter all the details for your app manually, such as the app path, name, icon, details, and so on. Alternatively, choose MSIX Package if you want to enter details for an MSIX app package that has been provisioned within the AVD configuration. Note that some settings available in the Add Application drop-down list change, depending on which of these options you choose.

6. Open the **Application** drop-down list and choose **Notepad**.

   As shown in Figure 4-42, the remaining settings are populated automatically.

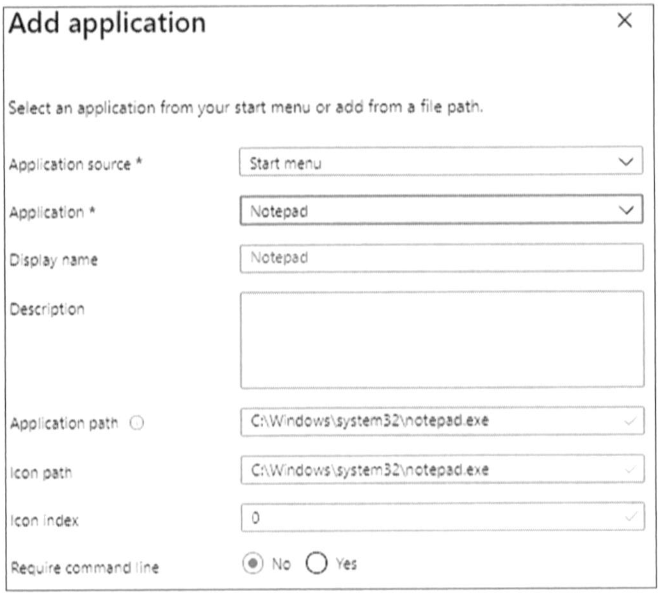

Add application   ✕

Select an application from your start menu or add from a file path.

Application source *	Start menu ⌄
Application *	Notepad ⌄
Display name	Notepad
Description	
Application path ○	C:\Windows\system32\notepad.exe
Icon path	C:\Windows\system32\notepad.exe
Icon index	0
Require command line	⦿ No ○ Yes

FIGURE 4-42   Adding the Notepad app.

7. Click **Add**.

8. Repeat these steps to add a third-party app—in this case, Acrobat Reader DC. (See Figure 4-43.)

> **NOTE**   If the third-party app does not appear in your app list, you will need to install it on all the session host VMs. Then you can publish it.

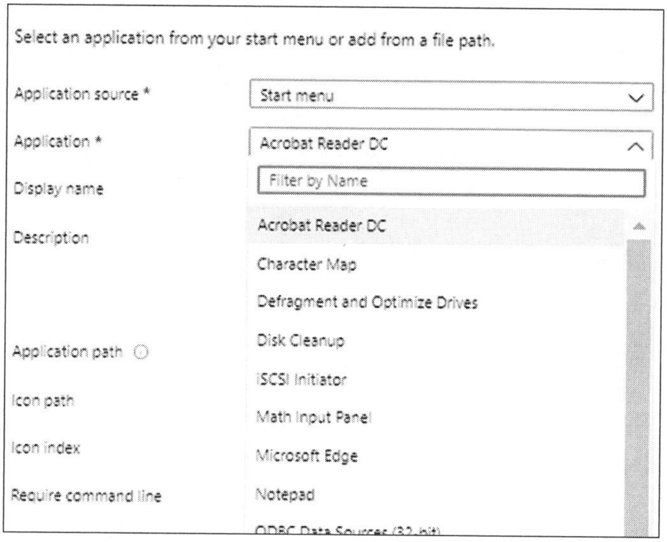

FIGURE 4-43 Adding a third-party application.

After you publish the apps, users who connect to the AVD service will be able to view them and launch them for use. (See Figure 4-44.)

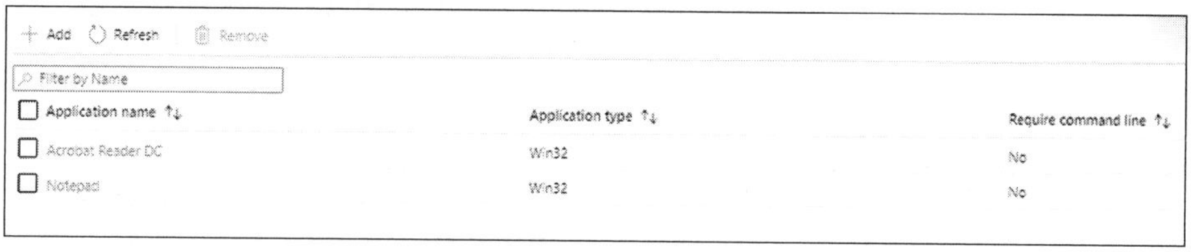

FIGURE 4-44 List of published apps.

## Chapter 5

Azure Container Instances

Overview

Azure Container Instances (ACIs) enable organizations to deploy containers in the cloud on-demand, without having to build and manage the back-end VM infrastructure. A serverless Azure environment completely managed by Microsoft, ACIs allow organizations to use containers without requiring the implementation of a container-orchestration solution such as Kubernetes. This makes it easy for organizations to get up and running with container instances extremely quickly. ACI supports both Windows and Linux container deployments using the Azure Portal, Azure PowerShell, the Azure CLI, and ARM templates.

Some common use cases for ACI include the following:

- Event-driven applications and task automation
- Batch processing jobs
- Applications that require occasional and unpredictable bursts of high capacity

> **IMPORTANT**   ACI provides the fastest and easiest method to run containers in Azure without any VM infrastructure management or orchestration-service integrations.

Key features

Some key features of ACIs are as follows:

- **Support for Docker images**   ACI supports the use of Docker images from a container registry, such as Docker Hub or Azure Container Registry. Docker Hub and Azure Container Registry are cloud-based container repositories to build, test, store, and share containers.
- **Public internet access**   ACIs enable developers to expose a container group directly to the internet with a fully qualified domain name (FQDN) and a public IP address. It also enables developers to set up a custom DNS name label for their application to make it accessible using the azureregion.azurecontainer.io DNS suffix.

- **Secure communication**   ACI requires all secure communications between servers and applications to use TLS 1.2 only. Older protocols such as TLS 1.0 and TLS 1.1 are no longer available for use.

- **Interactive shell support**   ACI provides an interactive shell that enables developers to run commands while a container is actively running. This helps when troubleshooting issues on running containers.

- **Security on the hypervisor level**   ACI ensures that applications running in containers hosted in a multi-tenant environment like Azure using shared infrastructure remain completely isolated and function as they would in a dedicated virtual machine (VM).

- **Support for resource customization**   Containers are generally used to run a single application, API service, or batch job. Different applications, API services, and batch jobs require different resource levels. Assigning the same level of resources to all containers would be an extremely expensive option. Fortunately, ACI enables users to specify the memory and the number of vCPU based on the actual needs of the container. This helps reduce the resources allocated and thereby better control and manage expenses incurred.

- **Azure Files for persistent data storage**   Users can mount Azure Files shares on ACI instances to provide persistent storage that allows containers to retrieve state data post reset.

Benefits of container services

There are a few key benefits to using ACIs. First, ACIs support both Windows- and Linux-based container groups. However, at present, there are a few features that are available only for Linux container groups, including the following:

> **IMPORTANT**   Features might change in time; hence, you should check the latest guidance on this before deployment.

- **Support for mounting Azure Files shares**   Users can mount a server message block (SMB) file share stored on Azure Storage to the container for file sharing.

- **Support for mounting a Git repo volume**   Users can mount a directory to the container and place a copy of the Git repository into it when the container starts.

- **Support for mounting a secret volume**   Users can mount a secret volume that provides sensitive information to a container that is required during runtime.

- **Support for mounting an emptyDir volume**   Users can mount an empty directory for all containers in a container group to facilitate data sharing between them.

- **Support for deployment on an Azure virtual network** This allows for secure communications with other resources located in the virtual network and on interconnected on-premises networks.

- **Support for multiple containers in a container group** ACIs support multiple containers in a single container group, thereby allowing other interconnected containers that are useful for monitoring, logging, and configuration activities to load alongside the application container.

- **Support for Azure Monitor resource usage metrics** You can use Azure Monitor to monitor ACI instance resource usage metrics to reveal detailed patterns around resource consumption to enable planning and optimization.

Additionally, both Windows and Linux containers generally start much faster than containers hosted on VMs. Because Azure manages the underlying VM infrastructure, ACI can bring containers online within seconds. Note, however, that Linux containers load much faster than Windows containers due to the size of the OS.

Finally, containers can be grouped together to share the same resources, local network, storage volumes, and lifecycle policies. For example, you might have a container that contains an application, back-end services, logging operations, and so on. You can then schedule the container group to run, so all the containers inside the group run together. (This is currently supported only for Linux containers.)

Deployment considerations

There are a number of features to consider when planning the deployment of ACIs. Let's dive deeper into each of these.

Container groups

As mentioned in the preceding section, a container group is a group of containers that share the same resources, local network, storage volumes, and lifecycle policies. A container group is scheduled on the same underlying host machine.

For example, a container group could consist of the following:

- An application container and a logging container, so the application container can store all the logging information in the logging container.

- An application container and a monitoring container, so the monitoring container can continuously monitor the health status of the application container. This can help in raising alerts and carrying out automated remediation actions.

- An application front-end container and an application back-end container, where the front-end services client requests and the back-end retrieves client data.

- A single functional task divided into a number of container images for independent management by different teams.

> **IMPORTANT** Most deployments include container groups so that interconnected containers run together.

Deployment

A container group can be deployed using one of the following:

- **Azure Resource Manager (ARM) template** ARM templates allow the implementation of infrastructure as code. An ARM template can deploy containers along with other Azure services, such as an Azure Files share. This makes it the ideal method of deployment when multiple Azure services are to be deployed along with the container instances.
- **YAML file** A YAML file is a structured configuration file that provides the ACI service with details of the container instances to deploy. It is the recommended method of deployment when only container instances are being deployed.

Resource grouping

ACI combines all the resources required by the different container instances in a container group before allocating the underlying infrastructure. It is important to define the resource requirements of each container instance based on the workload running therein to allow for optimal allocation.

Service limits

ACI has a few service limits that you must account for as part of the deployment-planning exercise. Some key limits include the following:

- **100 standard SKU container groups per region per subscription** A standard SKU provides the shared underlying infrastructure to run the container instances.
- **Zero dedicated SKU container groups per region per subscription** A dedicated SKU provides dedicated hardware on which to run the container instances.

> **IMPORTANT** By default, container groups on a dedicated SKU are blocked. If you need to be able to use container groups on a dedicated SKU, you must issue a support request to Azure support. You can also raise the group limit for standard SKUs by contacting Azure support.

- **60 containers per container group** A container group can support a maximum of 60 containers. You should avoid setting up containers that are not interdependent or interconnected in the same container group if there is a possibility of hitting this limit.

- **20 volumes per container group**   A maximum of 20 volumes are supported per container group. In case you are reaching the limit, see if any volumes overlap based on their purpose or contents.

Container instance resources

You can set up every container instance to request the minimum and maximum resources required. This enables each instance to initially request a certain amount of resources, and to scale up if required based on the maximum resource allocation on the instance level and the available resources on the container group level. To identify the ideal resource allocations and limits on the container group level, you must understand the minimum, average, and peak resource requirements across all containers.

> **NOTE**   The underlying service infrastructure for ACIs requires a small amount of resources to run. This is taken from the overall resource allocation done on the container group level. Although this amount is minimal, you must account for it by maintaining a small buffer in your resource calculations.

Networking

One of the key features of ACIs is the ability to publish container instances publicly using a FQDN and a public IP address. This makes it possible to access container instances on particular ports externally using the FQDN/IP address. Individual container instances can be exposed on different ports to make the required services available externally. At the same time, all container instances can communicate with each other internally, without requiring additional port configuration between the container instances.

> **NOTE**   The public IP address and FQDN are associated with the container group created for the container instances. If the container group is deleted, the public IP and DNS FQDN are both released back to the Azure service and made available for reuse across the Azure platform.

Container instances with private network access can communicate with other internal resources hosted on an Azure virtual network or another private network connected to the Azure virtual network via VPN/ExpressRoute. You can achieve this by deploying the container groups in an Azure virtual network. This gives all the container instances in that group the ability to communicate with other private resources/services in a secure manner.

Storage

Storage in container instances is non-persistent. However, you can make persistent storage available to container instances using different storage services available in Azure and hosted outside of Azure. These include the following:

- **Azure Files share** You can create a volume on an Azure Files share using the Azure Storage service and make it available to container instances using the SMB protocol to store, read, and write persistent data. This can also help instances share data among each other.

- **Secret volume** A secret volume provides read-only storage to store sensitive information required by a container instance during startup or runtime. Sensitive information could include SSH keys, database credentials, and so on, which should be accessible only by the container instances. These can be stored as files on the secret volume, and the volume mapped to all container instances in a container group.

- **Empty directory** An empty directory can be mapped to provide writeable storage to container instances in a container group. This can be a shared directory for data sharing or used for other purposes, such as storing checkpoint files, logs, or other data required by the other container instances, or as a scratch volume. The maximum size for an empty directory is currently 50 GB.

- **Git repo volume** A Git repo volume is a clone of an existing Git repository copied and mounted to a container instance at startup.

Each of these can be mapped to specific paths within the individual containers in a group.

Walkthrough

Let's walk through the process of creating a basic container instance using the Quickstart images provided by Microsoft in Azure. You will build these using the Azure Portal, Azure PowerShell, and the Azure CLI.

> **IMPORTANT** If you are following along, be sure to select resources and resource names based on your environment, including a unique container instance name for each of your deployments.

USING AZURE PORTAL

To create a container instance using the Quickstart image with the Azure Portal, follow these steps:

1. In the Azure Portal, type **container instances** in the search box to locate the service and select it from the list that appears.

2. Click **Create** or **Create Container Instances** to start the **Create Container Instance** wizard. (See Figure 5-1.)

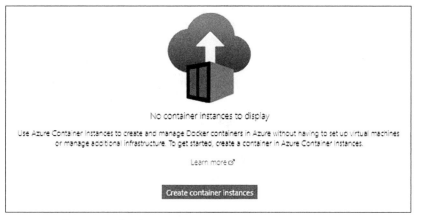

No container instances to display

Use Azure Container Instances to create and manage Docker containers in Azure without having to set up virtual machines or manage additional infrastructure. To get started, create a container in Azure Container Instances.

Learn more ⧉

Create container instances

FIGURE 5-1   Create container instance.

3. In the **Basics** tab of the **Create Container Instance** wizard, enter the following information (see Figure 5-2), and click **Next**:

- **Subscription**   Select the subscription that will host the container instance.

- **Resource Group**   Select the resource group you want to use to host the container group. Alternatively, to create a new resource group, click the **Create New** link, and follow the prompts.

- **Container Name**   Type a name for the container. If the name you type is already in use, the wizard will prompt you to select another name.

- **Region**   Select the Azure region in which you want to host the container instance.

- **Image Source**   Select the **Quickstart Images** option button. This enables you to select from pre-built images provided by Microsoft to quickly obtain the container instance with a test or temporary image.

> **NOTE**   In addition to the Quickstart Images option button, there are two other Image Source options. Azure Container Registry enables you to connect to an Azure Container Registry to select an existing image for deployment, and Docker Hub or Other Registry allows you to connect to a third-party registry service such as Docker Hub to select an existing image for deployment.

- **Image**   Click the drop-down list and select the **mcr.microsoft.com/azuredocs/aci-helloworld:latest (Linux)** image.

- **Size**   Choose to keep the instance size at the default setting. Alternatively, click the **Change Size** link and follow the prompts to customize the resources required. (See Figure 5-3.)

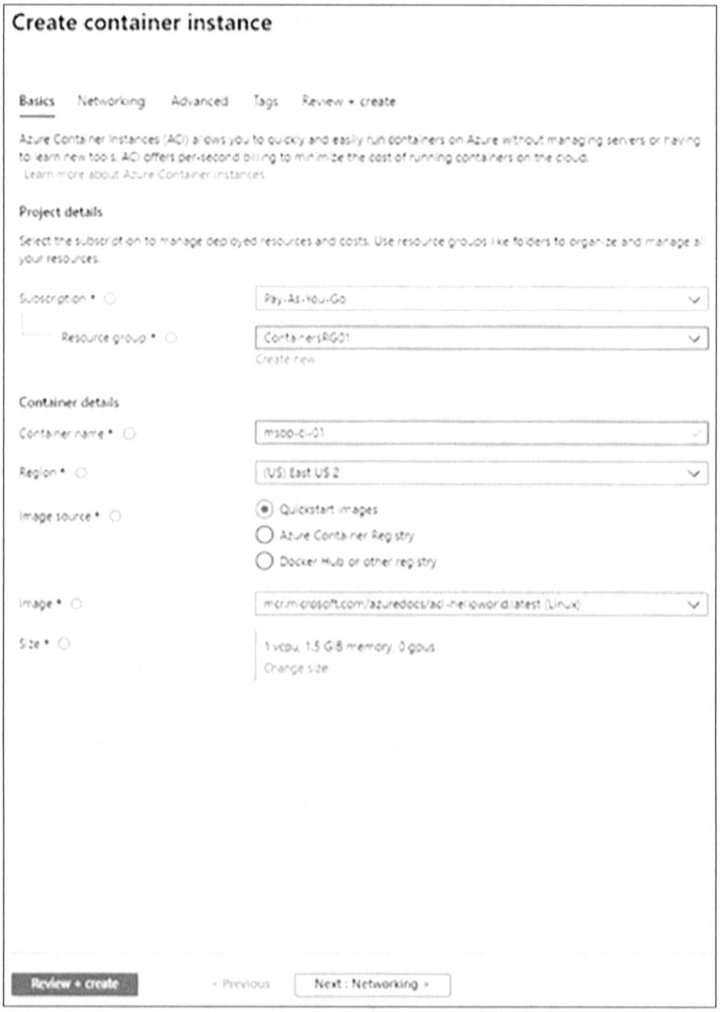

FIGURE 5-2 The Basics tab of the Create Container Instance wizard.

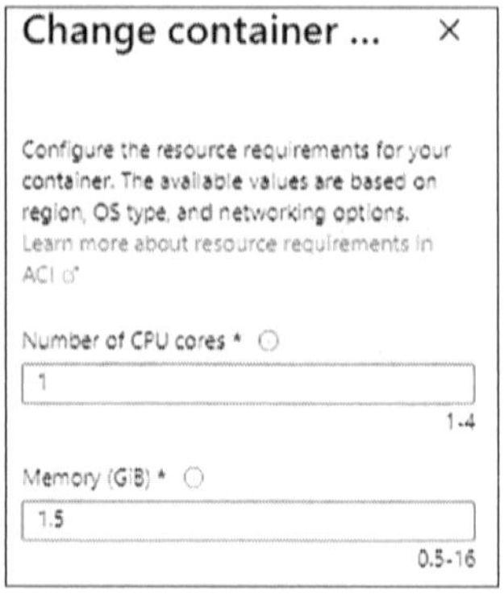

FIGURE 5-3 Customize the container instance size.

4. Enter the following information on the **Networking** tab (see Figure 5-4) and click **Next**:

- **Networking Type**   Select the **Public** option button to make the container instance available publicly.

> **NOTE**   The other options in the Networking Type section are Private and None. Select Private to make the container instance available internally via other Azure virtual networks and inter-connected networks. Select None to limit access to the container instance publicly and internally. This will allow access to container logs using only the command line.

- **DNS Name Label**   Type a DNS name label. This label must be unique across all publicly accessible container instances. If the name you type is already in use, the portal will display an error and prompt you to enter a different label.
- **Ports**   Leave the default setting as is. This port will be opened on the container instance for access.
- **Ports Protocol**   Leave the default setting as is.

FIGURE 5-4   The Networking tab of the Create Container Instance wizard.

5. On the **Advanced** tab (see Figure 5-5), enter the following information and click **Next**:

- **Restart Policy**   Select the policy you want to apply for instance restarts on exit. In this case, leave the default setting, **On Failure**, as is.
- **Environment Variables**   Enter the desired settings here—in this case, the default settings.
- **Command Override**   Enter the desired setting here—in this case, the default setting.

FIGURE 5-5 The Advanced tab of the Create Container Instance wizard.

6. In the **Tags** tab, enter any tags required for the container instance, and click **Next**.

7. On the **Review + Create** tab, review your settings and click **Create**. (See Figure 5-6.)

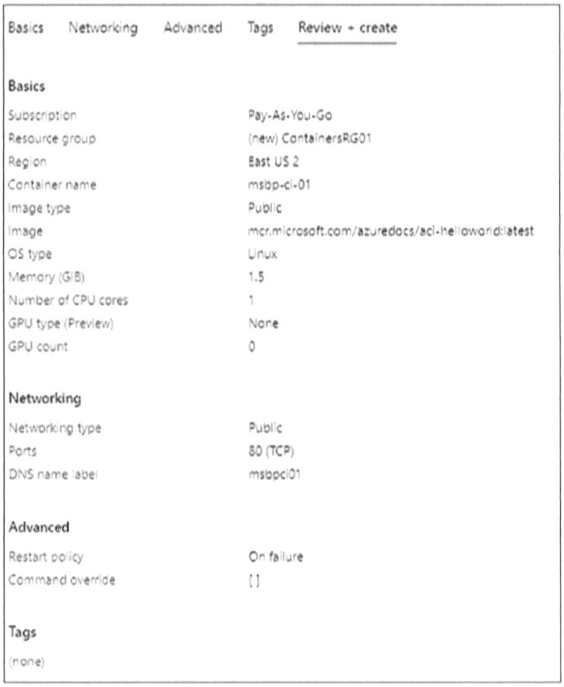

FIGURE 5-6 Review and create your container instance.

8. Select the instance in the Azure Portal. You'll see the FQDN for the instance in the **Overview** section. (See Figure 5-7; the FQDN entry is on the far right.)

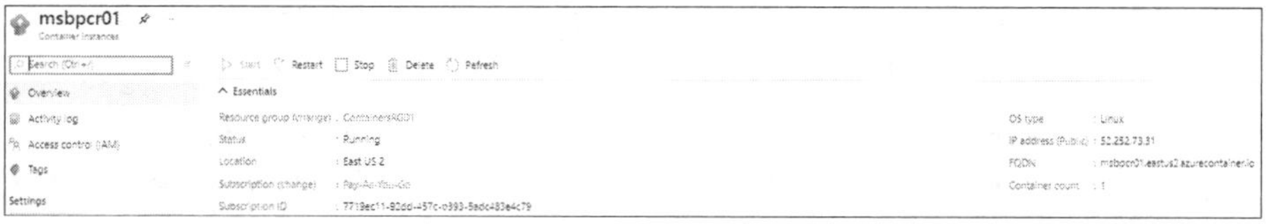

FIGURE 5-7 Container instance overview.

9. Browse to the FQDN location in a web browser to verify that the container instance is online. (See Figure 5-8.)

```
msbpcr01.eastus2.azurecontainer.io
```

Welcome to Azure Container Instances!

FIGURE 5-8 The container instance FQDN in a web browser.

USING AZURE POWERSHELL

You can use the New-AzContainerGroup Azure PowerShell command to create a container group with a container instance, as shown in the following code snippet. Use this snippet to create the same container as you did in the Azure Portal. Be sure to either delete the previous instance or give this new instance a different name:

```
# Create a resource group to host the container instance. In case of using an existing
resource group skip this command and enter the required existing resource group in the
next section.
New-AzResourceGroup -Name ContainersRG01 -Location EastUS2
#Create Container group using the Hello World Quickstart Linux image
New-AzContainerGroup -ResourceGroupName ContainerRG01
-Name msbpcr01 -Image mcr.microsoft.com/azuredocs/aci-helloworld:latest
-OsType Linux -DnsNameLabel msbpcr01 -Ports 80
```

USING AZURE CLI

You can use the az container create Azure CLI command to create a container group with a container instance, as shown in the following code snippet. Use this snippet to create the same container as you did in the Azure PowerShell. Be sure to either delete the previous instance or give this new instance a different name:

```
# Create a resource group to host the container instance. In case of using an existing
resource group skip this command and enter the required existing resource group in the
next section.
az group create --name ContainerRG01 --location eastus2
#Create Container group using the Hello World Quickstart Linux image
az container create --resource-group ContainerRG01 --name msbpcr01
--image mcr.microsoft.com/azuredocs/aci-helloworld --dns-name-label msbpcr01 --ports 80
```

Container orchestration

Container orchestration comes into the picture when environments have a number of containers that need to be deployed and managed in an automated fashion. Although you can combine container instances in container groups, as the number of container instances goes up, managing each individual instance adds significant overhead.

Using container-orchestration tools such as Azure Kubernetes Service (AKS), you can automate container scaling and upgrade coordination and management, while ACI handles basic container-scheduling activities. This helps large environments with hundreds or even thousands of containers efficiently scale and manage them.

Container registry

A container registry provides a single storage to build, store, scan, and manage container images and associated artifacts. There are three types of container registries that can be used with ACI:

- **Azure Container Registry**   Azure Container Registry is a fully managed and geo-replicated container registry service provided in Azure. There are a few benefits to using this service compared to other container registry services, as detailed here:
  - Faster deployment to ACI compared to private registry services.
  - Faster deployment of new containers using existing container images.
  - Geo-replication of the registry, providing a redundant environment that is available across Azure regions.
- **Private container registry**   A private container registry is an independently managed and hosted registry service maintained outside of Azure. This allows organizations to use their existing private container registry to deploy containers in ACI. An organization might do this for any of the following reasons:
  - Security requirements for self/managed hosting outside of Azure.
  - Existing investments in a container registry service.
  - Faster deployment using an existing service versus migrating to Azure Container Registry.

- **Other public container registry services** These include services such as those provided by Docker, AWS, Google, and OpenShift. Not all of these are supported for use with ACIs; therefore, it is important to verify the available support during deployment planning. Use these only if you need to continue to use an existing container registry service instead of moving to Azure Container Registry.

Best practices

There are a few best practices for deployment to consider, depending on your specific environment needs. Following is a small list of these best practices, along with guidance to assist you during deployment planning:

- **Keep container image sizes small** Although ACIs currently support a maximum container image size of 15 GB, you should try to minimize container sizes to avoid slow startup times.

- **Use Azure Container Registry for production deployment** Although you can use other container registries for development and testing phases, to reduce the load times of production workloads, it is highly advisable to host your container images in Azure Container Registry. To simplify architecture and management, it is best to migrate completely to Azure Container Registry, but if that is not possible for all environments, you should at least manage production deployments there.

- **Use approved container images and registries** Use only approved container images for production deployments, and have tools and processes in place to detect and prevent the use of unapproved container images. You can achieve this by using Azure Container Registry to allow only images that have been signed by their trusted publishers. Or go one step beyond and permit the use of approved image registries only. This will limit the ability to introduce unknown images into the environment.

- **Use version tags** It is a recommended practice to have a defined and structured mechanism to tag container images. Use image version tags to identify the required image rather than specifying the latest tag, which can result in the accidental deployment of untested code.

- **Use GitHub actions for automation** You can use GitHub actions to automate the deployment of containers directly to ACIs. If GitHub is the deployment source being used for an environment, use this feature to automate deployment actions.

- **Allocate minimum and maximum resources** Have a minimum allocation of 1 vCPU and 1 GB of memory for any container group. (Individual container instances hosted in the group can be set up with less than 1 vCPU and 1 GB of memory.) Set the maximum resource allocation based on the combined resource requirements of the container instances and their minimum, average, and maximum requirements, with an additional buffer for the ACI service.

- **Encrypt deployment data using customer-managed keys** The ACI service stores certain data related to the containers it runs, such as deployment metadata, environment variables, sensitive keys required during runtime, and persistent logs. This data is automatically encrypted by the Azure service using Microsoft-managed keys with 256-bit AES encryption. This should suffice for most organizations. However, to accommodate compliance or security needs, customer-managed keys can be used in place of Microsoft-managed keys for this encryption. Make sure key management and rotation processes and guidelines are in place.

- **Use Azure Logic Apps for automation** ACIs support a connector to Azure Logic Apps, which you can use to set up workflows and automated tasks for container group deployment and management—for example, monitoring for Azure Logic Apps triggers to initiate the creation or deletion of container groups.

- **Export container group configuration** After you configure a container group, you can export the configuration to a YAML file using the Azure CLI or Azure PowerShell. This makes it possible to restore or perform new builds of container groups in the event of any disaster or recovery scenario. It's a good practice to version-control the exports to make it easy to identify them and to set up automation to regularly perform this task in environments where the configuration changes on a regular basis.

Security best practices

Along with the deployment best practices covered in the preceding section, there are several security-related best practices to consider. A number of these relate to compliance and security guidelines and needs of an organization. Several common ones are listed here:

- **Enforce the principle of least privilege** You can reduce the attack surface in the event of a security breach by running containers only with the level of access needed to manage their specific jobs rather than with root or extended access—a concept called the principle of least privilege. This limits the access an attacker has to the overall environment.

- **Scan container images** Use Azure Security Center to scan container images stored inside Azure Container Registry for potential vulnerabilities. Alternatively, you can use third-party scanning tools from Twistlock, Trend Micro, and others to scan images stored in Azure Container Registry or any private registry.

- **Secure access to the container registry** It's best to use a private registry service like Azure Container Registry or Docker Trusted Registry, as these enable you to granularly define access and to prevent the introduction of unwanted images. Azure Container Registry uses Azure role-based access control (RBAC), making it easier to define access based on specific admin role activities.

- **Protect access to production containers** Limit access to production containers to privileged users who require access. Use Azure RBAC to restrict access to such users.

- **Use Azure Key Vault to secure credentials**   Azure Key Vault is a managed service provided in Azure to store sensitive information, such as certificates, passwords, and connection strings. This information is encrypted by Microsoft, and the keys are under Microsoft's management. You can use this service to store sensitive information rather than storing it within the application code or files on the container instances. Azure Key Vault encrypts data at rest and in transit when the data is shared with other Azure services.

- **Use dedicated hosts for maximum isolation**   ACI provides a dedicated SKU, which you can use to access dedicated physical server hardware in the selected Azure region to run the containers. This provides the maximum level of isolation possible for the container images. This can be a great option for organizations requiring adherence to certain compliance and regulatory guidelines for their container workloads.

- **Use Azure Firewall for better traffic management and control**   Instead of making a container instance accessible directly over the public internet, use Azure Firewall to route ingress traffic to the container instances. This adds a layer of security for the workloads and makes it easier to define complex access rules. It also allows you to route all outbound traffic from the container instances via Azure Firewall, making it easier to monitor and manage this traffic, too.

- **Use a vulnerability-management solution**   Use a vulnerability-management solution to detect, identify, and manage threats on container images and on running containers. Having a solution in place that is integrated into the DevOps lifecycle can help mitigate known issues during the development phase itself.

- **Enable logging for administrative access**   Logging all administrative access to containers can help in audits and in retracing actions performed before any incident or breach. Integrated solutions like Azure Monitor can be used for this purpose.

- **Use Azure Monitor**   Azure Monitor can be integrated with ACI to monitor resource usage, network usage, and file access by container instances. This provides insights into resource consumption and access, and helps when troubleshooting issues, planning capacity, and managing access.

- **Use network segmentation**   In environments that require a high level of security and network controls, you can perform network segmentation between container instances to protect instances from a breach in another instance's subnet. You can either do this manually during the deployment planning phase or automatically using third-party tools that monitor and manage the nano-segmentation required during runtime.

- **Approve required files and executables for use during runtime**   Providing a safe list of files and executables to be allowed access for use during runtime can significantly reduce the attack surface on a container instance. Incorporating this from the development cycle stage provides a baseline for the container and makes it easier to troubleshoot in the event of anomalies and unexpected behaviors during runtime.

- **Remove unnecessary services and processes**   This reduces the attack surface and the number of potential vulnerabilities that need to be monitored and managed for.

## Chapter 6

Azure Functions

Overview

Azure Functions is a serverless compute service that provides on-demand access to infrastructures to run and scale applications dynamically. It eliminates the need to deploy, maintain, and manage servers in Azure, enabling organizations to focus on deploying and managing their application code.

You can use Azure Functions for trigger-based apps to:

- Build web APIs for trigger-based actions.
- Process bulk data streams.
- Manage message queues.
- Process IoT streams.

The back-end infrastructure resources are updated and managed completely by Microsoft. This frees up your organization to focus on your application code and the associated triggers. Developers can build and deploy code and allow Azure Functions to handle the rest.

The compute-on-demand provided by Azure Functions helps in two ways:

- You can use Azure Functions to deploy the required business or system logic in available blocks of code or to build custom code for deployment. You can then define event triggers to initiate the function app.
- Azure Functions provides additional resources as needed to the function app for the duration of demand. As soon as demand falls, the extra resources are removed automatically.

Azure Functions hosting options

A hosting plan defines the set of resources available to host function apps. There are features available for the function app for scaling, resource limits, networking integrations, and security changes based on the hosting plan. There are three types of hosting plans available for both Windows and Linux virtual machines:

- Consumption plan
- Premium plan
- Dedicated (App Service) plan

Consumption plan

The Consumption plan is a pay-as-you-go plan that supports automatic scaling based on event-driven triggers. Each host in the Consumption plan has 1 CPU and 1.5 GB of memory. Based on the number of events triggering the function, more hosts will be made available for consumption. Then, when the number of events diminishes, the hosts will be automatically scaled back down to reduce associated charges.

Currently, the Consumption plan grants 1 million requests for free use, after which billing begins. However, this could change, so it is important to refer to the up-to-date documentation on the Microsoft site during planning.

The Consumption plan has numerous limitations, which relate to the maximum runtime, resource availability, and storage size supported by apps hosted in the plan. Take these into consideration when identifying the right plan to host your app.

Premium plan

The Premium plan provides automatic scaling capabilities, which can help function apps scale, and supports a much higher processing volume than the Consumption plan. In addition, some worker instances are constantly kept online, ensuring they are always warm and available when needed. And when required, even buffer worker instances are brought online and warmed up to ensure quick scaling.

> **NOTE**   With the Premium plan, Azure Functions automatically scales based on demand, using pre-warmed workers, which run applications without delay after being idle, run on more powerful instances, and connect to virtual networks.

The key benefits of the Premium plan are as follows:

- Pre-warmed worker instances, ensuring continuous availability
- More powerful hosts that support up to four CPUs and 14 GB of memory
- More predictable pricing compared to the Consumption plan
- Much longer runtimes than the Consumption plan
- Connectivity to virtual networks in Azure and interconnected on-premises resources
- The ability to define inbound network traffic IP restrictions

Dedicated plan

The Dedicated plan runs functions within an App Service plan. It is ideal for long-running functions that cannot be executed with the timeouts that apply on the Premium plan.

The key benefits of the Dedicated plan are as follows:

- You can employ existing underutilized App Service Environment (ASE) instances for maximum efficiency.
- Custom OS images are required to run function app code.
- You can use both manual and automatic scaling.

> **NOTE** Automatic scaling in the Dedicated plan is not as fast compared to the elastic scaling capabilities available in the Premium plan.

Durable Functions

Azure Functions was primarily designed to process large, rapid bursts of events in a stateless manner. However, over time, as the role of Azure Functions has expanded, there was a need to support stateful functions for scenarios such as execution retries based on checkpoints rather than completely re-executing all tasks. Durable Functions extends the capabilities of Azure Functions to support such scenarios. It enables you to define stateful workflows by keeping track of the state, checkpoints, and restarts, so you can easily implement the required business logic. At present, Durable Functions supports code written in C#, JavaScript, Python, F#, and PowerShell, but support for more languages could be added over time.

Triggers

Every function requires a trigger, which causes the function to initiate. Each function is invoked based on how that trigger is defined. Each function must have only one trigger. There are different types of triggers. A few of these are detailed here:

- **HTTP trigger**   Initiates a function with an HTTP request. This type of trigger helps build serverless APIs and respond to webhooks.
- **Timer trigger**   Invokes a function based on a set schedule.
- **Queue trigger**   Invokes a function when a message is added to an Azure storage queue.
- **Service bus trigger**   Invokes a function to respond to messages from a Service Bus queue.
- **Blob storage trigger**   Invokes a function when a change takes place in a blob storage, such as the addition or modification of a blob.
- **Event Hub trigger**   Invokes a function based on specific events in an Event Hub stream.

Consider a scenario in which an online retail store receives orders on a web page. These orders must be processed and entered into the back-end database—in this example, Cosmos DB. A function app set up with a service bus trigger can pick up the order information from a service bus queue, process it, and send the output to the Cosmos DB database back end. (See Figure 6-1.)

Service bus trigger–based function app

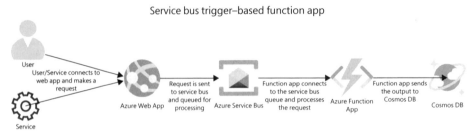

FIGURE 6-1   Service bus trigger–based function app.

Now consider another scenario that requires data from a PDF file to be read and stored in a back-end SQL database. In this scenario, a function app set up with an Azure storage queue trigger can read the PDF file from the blob storage and push the file to Cognitive Services, which can then write the output to the SQL DB. (See Figure 6-2.)

Queue trigger–based function app

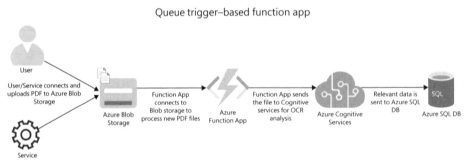

FIGURE 6-2   Queue trigger–based function app.

Bindings

A binding is a method of connecting a resource to a function for data input or data output, to be captured in parameters. For example, you can use the content of an Event Hub queue message as an input parameter to a function, and you can use the output return value of a function to create a queue message. Note that bindings are optional, and that every function can have one or more bindings (input and/or output).

> **NOTE**   Triggers and bindings make it possible to set up function parameters to receive or send data and avoid hardcoding access to other services directly.

Azure Functions walkthrough

The following section steps you through the process of creating a function app using the Azure Portal. Specifically, you will create an HTTP trigger–based app using the default code available in Azure.

USING THE AZURE PORTAL

To create a function app using the Azure Portal, follows these steps:

1. Log in to the Azure Portal and type **function** in the search bar.

2. Under **Services**, click **Function App**. (See Figure 6-3.)

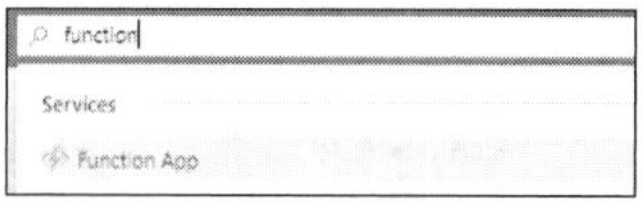

FIGURE 6-3 Search for the Function App service.

3. In the function app service page, click the **Create Function App** button to start the **Create Function App** wizard. (See Figure 6-4.)

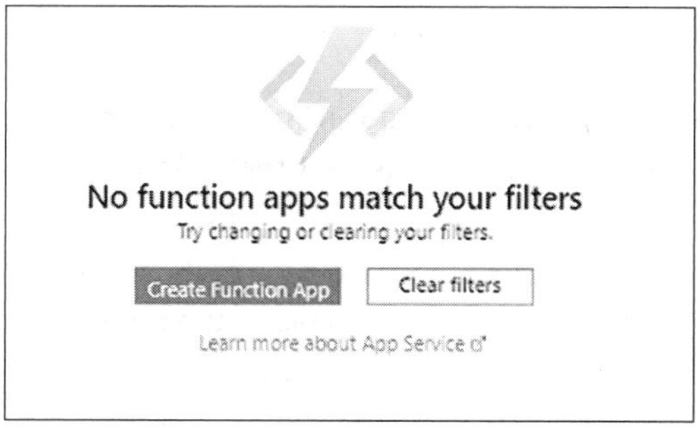

FIGURE 6-4 Creating a function app.

4. In the **Basics** tab of the Create Function App wizard, enter the following information (see Figure 6-5) and click **Next**:

- **Subscription** Select the subscription that will host the function app.

- **Resource Group** Select an existing resource group or create a new one for the function app.

- **Function App Name** Enter the name for the function app.

- **Publish** You can publish the function app using code or a Docker container. In this case, choose **Code**.

- **Runtime Stack** Select the application runtime stack—in this case, **.NET**.

- **Version** Select version **3.1**.

- **Region** Select the Azure region where you want to host the function app.

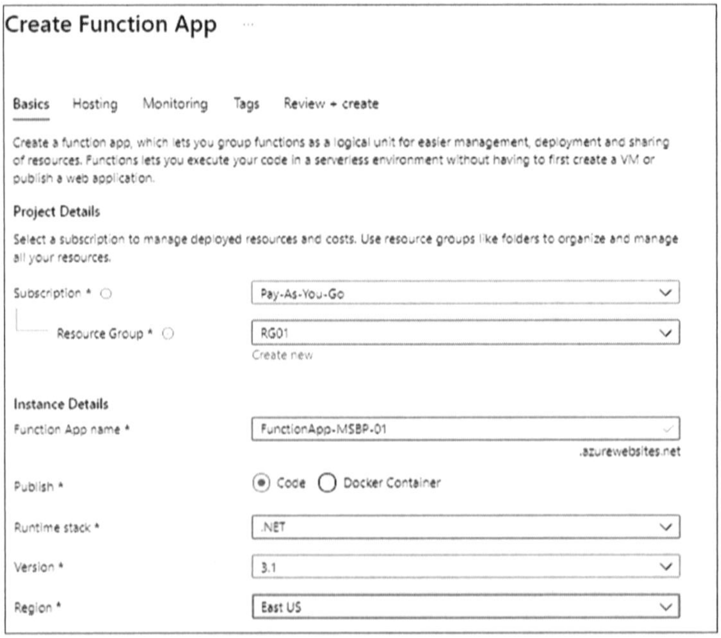

FIGURE 6-5 The Basic tab for the Create Function App wizard.

5. In the **Hosting** tab, open the **Storage Account** drop-down list and choose an existing storage account for the function app. Alternatively, click the **Create New** link to create a new storage account specifically for this function app (recommended).

6. Next to **Operating System**, click either the **Linux** option button or the **Windows** option button—in this case, the **Windows** option button. (See Figure 6-6.)

FIGURE 6-6 Setting up the storage account and OS.

7. Still in the **Hosting** tab, under **Plan**, open the **Plan Type** drop-down list and choose **Consumption (Serverless)** (see Figure 6-7). Then click **Next**.

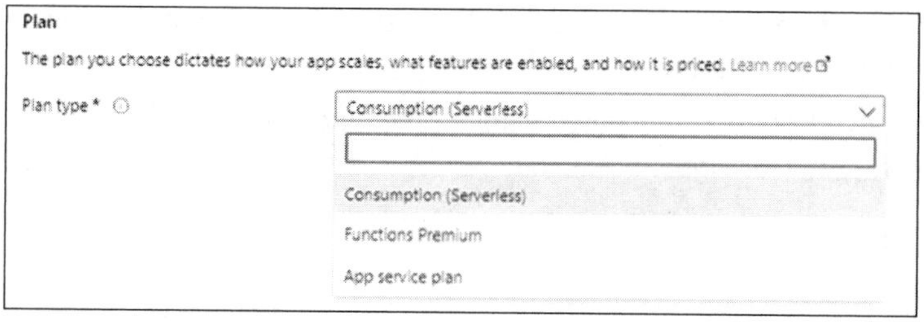
Plan
The plan you choose dictates how your app scales, what features are enabled, and how it is priced. Learn more
Plan type *
Consumption (Serverless)
Consumption (Serverless)
Functions Premium
App service plan

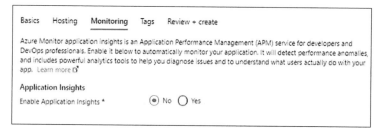

FIGURE 6-7 Selecting the hosting plan type for the function app.

8. In the **Monitoring** tab, you have the option to enable Application Insights. For now, click the **No** option button next to **Application Insights** (see Figure 6-8) and click **Next**.

Basics
Hosting
Monitoring
Tags
Review + create
Azure Monitor application insights is an Application Performance Management (APM) service for developers and DevOps professionals. Enable it below to automatically monitor your application. It will detect performance anomalies, and includes powerful analytics tools to help you diagnose issues and to understand what users actually do with your app. Learn more
Application Insights
Enable Application Insights *
No
Yes

FIGURE 6-8 Leaving Application Insights disabled for now.

9. In the **Tags** tab, enter any tags you want to apply to the function app, and click **Next**.
10. On the **Review + Create** tab, review your settings and click **Create** to create the function app.
11. After the function app is created, click the **Go to Resource** button.
12. On the function app's page (see Figure 6-9), click **Functions** in the left pane. Then click the **Create** button to start the Create Function wizard.

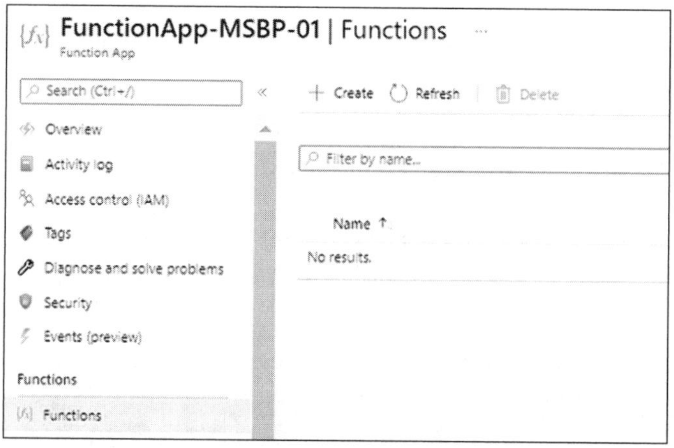
FunctionApp-MSBP-01 | Functions
Function App
Search (Ctrl+/)
Create
Refresh
Delete
Overview
Activity log
Access control (IAM)
Tags
Diagnose and solve problems
Security
Events (preview)
Functions
Functions
Filter by name...
Name
No results.

FIGURE 6-9 Creating the function.

13. In the Create Function wizard, open the **Development Environment** drop-down list and choose **Develop in Portal**.

14. Under **Select a Template**, choose a template for the function app's trigger—in this case, **HTTP Trigger**. (See Figure 6-10.)

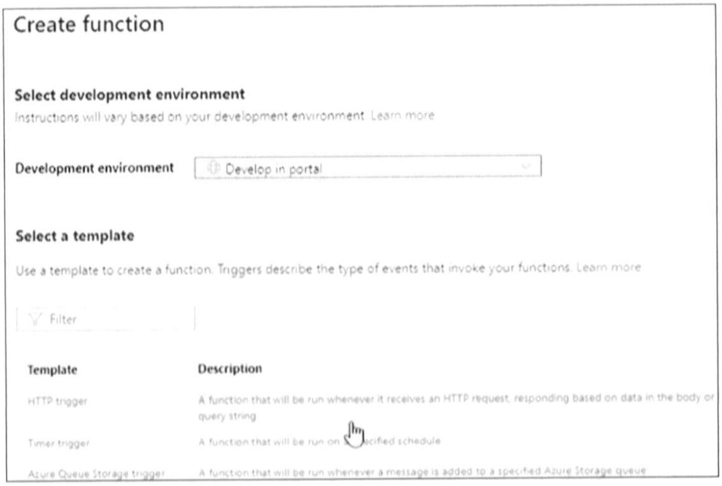

FIGURE 6-10 Selecting the trigger.

15. Under **Template Details**, in the New Function box, type a name for the new function.

16. Open the **Authorization Level** drop-down list and choose **Anonymous**. (See Figure 6-11.) Then click **Create**.

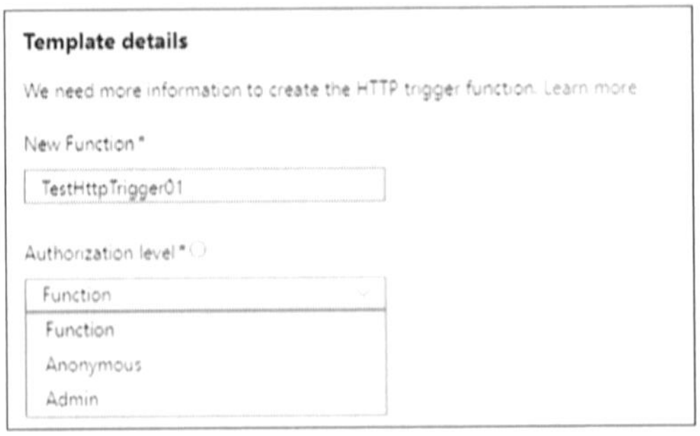

FIGURE 6-11 Setting the function name and authorization level.

17. After the function is created, click **Code + Test** in the left pane of the trigger's page.

The function code appears. As you can see, it is a simple HTTP function that will show an output based on the variable passed to it.

18. Optionally, customize the message shown, if required. (See Figure 6-12.) Then click the **Test/Run** button to test the function.

FIGURE 6-12 Customizing the default function code.

19. In the **Input** tab, in the **Body** section, enter the value for the name parameter. (See Figure 6-13.) Then click **Run**.

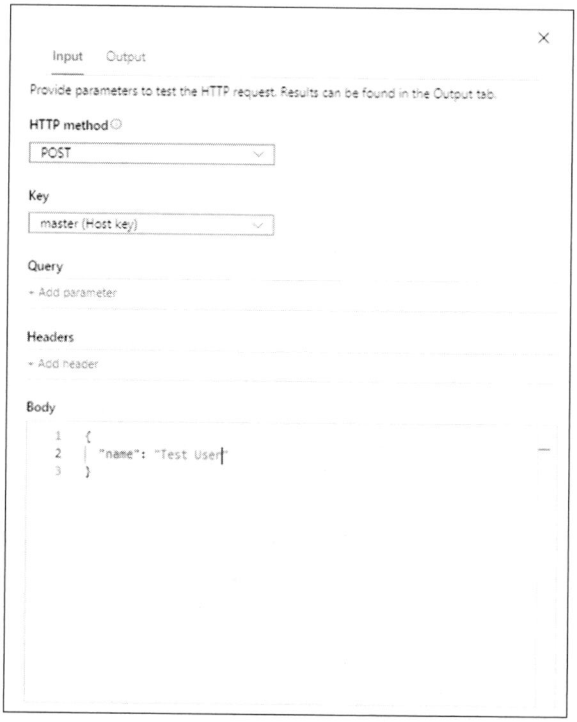

FIGURE 6-13 Setting up the name parameter in input.

The Output tab shows the expected output of the function. (See Figure 6-14.) Assuming the output is as you expected, you can test it using a web browser.

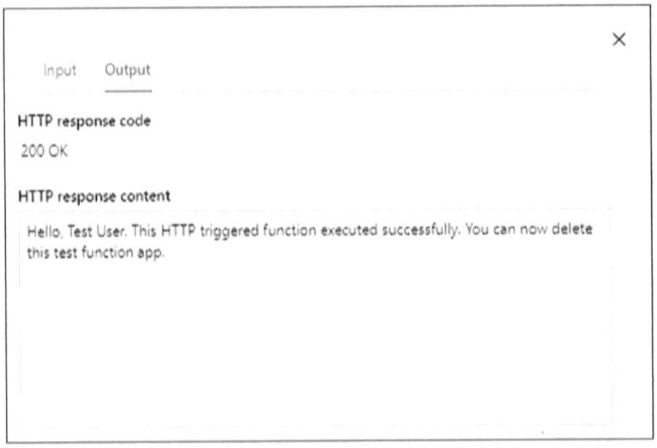

FIGURE 6-14 Output of the function.

20. Click the **Get Function URL** button. (See Figure 6-15.)

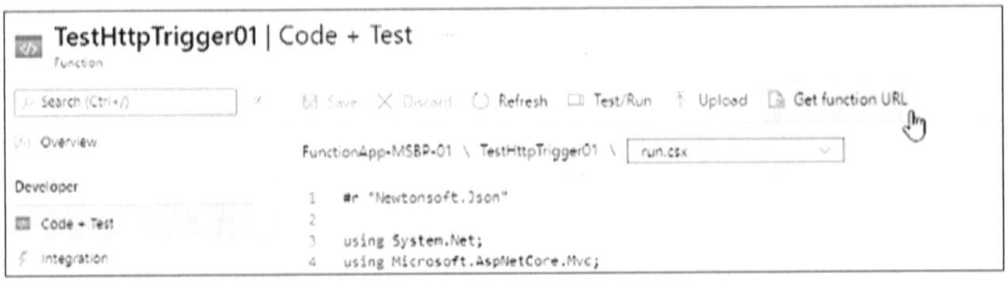

TestHttpTrigger01 | Code + Test
Function

Search (Ctrl+/)   Save   Discard   Refresh   Test/Run   Upload   Get function URL

Overview

FunctionApp-MSBP-01 \ TestHttpTrigger01 \ run.csx

Developer   1   #r "Newtonsoft.Json"
Code + Test   2
Integration   3   using System.Net;
                                   4   using Microsoft.AspNetCore.Mvc;

FIGURE 6-15 Getting the function URL.

21. Click the **Copy to Clipboard** button to copy the URL, as shown in Figure 6-16.

Get function URL

                                                              Copy to clipboard
Key   URL
default   https://functionapp-msbp-01.azurewe...

FIGURE 6-16 Copying the URL.

22. Open your web browser and paste the URL into the address bar. Then, at the end of the URL, type **?name=**, set the expected parameter, and press **Enter**. (See Figure 6-17.)

https://functionapp-msbp-01.az   ×   +

←   C   https://functionapp-msbp-01.azurewebsites.net/api/TestHttpTrigger01?name=TestUser

FIGURE 6-17 Pasting the URL into your web browser.

23. Confirm that the output is correct output in the web browser. (See Figure 6-18.)

FIGURE 6-18 Confirming the output.

Deploy function apps

You can use various technologies to deploy function apps in different ways. The following sections explain this in more detail. Once you have a better understanding of the available options, you can decide on the right tool and deployment strategy.

Deployment methods

There are multiple methods available in Azure Functions for code deployment. These are as follows:

- **External package URL**   If the function app is hosted in a remote package—for example, a ZIP file—you can set up an external package URL to point to the location of the file. At the time of execution, the file will be downloaded and the app will run in Run from Package mode.

- **ZIP deploy**   ZIP deploy is another way to push a ZIP file containing the function app. All files for the function app must be part of the ZIP file.

- **Linux Docker container**   You can deploy a function app in Linux Docker container using the Azure Function App on Container Deploy task.

- **Web Deploy (MSDeploy)**   The Web Deploy method packages and deploys Windows-based function applications. Although this is supported for use with Windows apps, the recommended method is ZIP Deploy.

- **Source control**   You can set up continuous deployment using cloud-based repositories such as GitHub, Azure Repos, or Bitbucket for function app deployments. This is the preferred method of deployment for projects that require integration of multiple sources and frequent contributions for the team to be merged for deployments.

- **Local Git**   You can set up a local Git repository hosted on a client PC as a source to push code to Azure for the deployment of a function app.

- **Cloud sync**   You can use the cloud sync deployment method if the application content is stored in cloud repositories such as Dropbox and OneDrive.

- **FTP**   With one-time or irregular deployment requirements, you can use FTP to directly upload files to Azure Functions for app deployment.

- **Portal editing**   Azure provides a portal-based editor that you can use to build and edit code for the function app.

To deploy the code, follow these steps:

1. Open the function app's page.

2. Click **Deployment Center** in the left pane.

3. In the right pane, open the **Source** drop-down list and choose the deployment source method. (See Figure 6-19.)

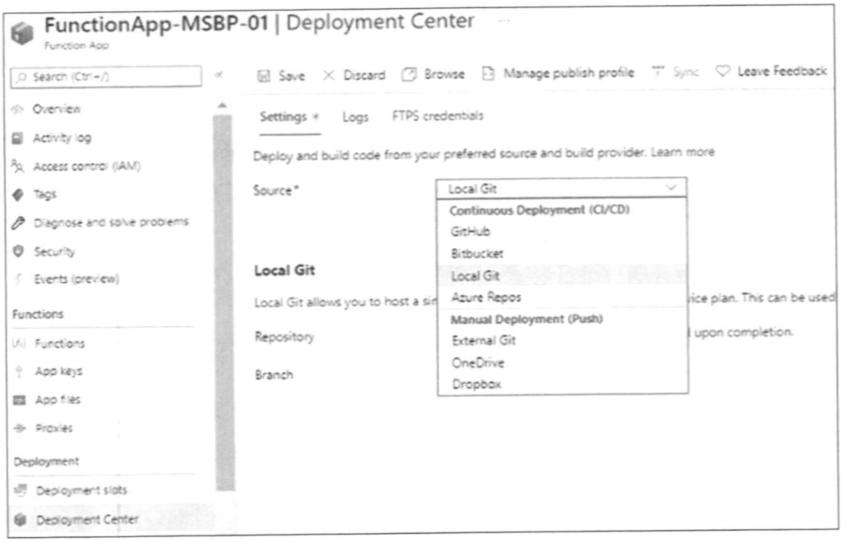

FIGURE 6-19 Selecting the deployment source method.

Deployment technologies

There are different technologies and tools available to deploy code to Azure Functions.

The following table provides a list of these along with ideal use cases for each. The deployment technology used is generally correlated to the deployment method to be used for the function app. The deployment method in turn is connected to two factors:

1. The requirements of the application or the development team.

2. The development cycle stage being deployed for.

This means that the deployment method and deployment tools used during development might differ from the ones used for production. The product code lifecycle management processes employed during development and production would primarily influence this.

The deployment tools and methods currently available, along with some suggestions on use cases, are as follows:

- **Tools-based deployment**   There are three tools that you can use to publish function apps:
    - Visual Studio
    - Visual Studio Code
    - Azure Functions Core Tools

It is best to use these during the initial development stages of a project or for ad-hoc deployments instead of as a deployment and management strategy for production builds.

- **Source control–based deployment** App Services allows you to integrate function app deployment using Deployment Center or Kudu to different sources that support continuous deployment of code. These are the primary tools that you can leverage to establish DevOps in your environment when using functions with App Services.

- **External pipelines** Azure supports Azure Pipelines and GitHub actions to establish DevOps pipelines that you can use for code validation, testing, and deployment. This is the recommended approach for production deployments at a minimum, if not for all development deployments, too.

Deployment slots

When a deployment is committed, any existing ongoing executions are permitted to complete or time out before new code is loaded to begin processing new requests. To avoid such scenarios, or to gain better control on the deployment of any code, it is advisable to use deployment slots. Deployment slots help provision different versions of code for different purposes—for example, production, staging, dev, and test.

Using deployment slots provides multiple benefits:

- **Separation of environments** You can separate production code from staging, dev, and test code to make sure no accidental commits are performed in production.

- **Warm start** Deploying code to a slot enables the app to come online and warm up before the slot is swapped to make the code live.

- **Easy rollbacks** You can easily revert any unanticipated issues after deployment of new code by swapping the slots back to their earlier configuration.

> **NOTE** Any scaling on the production slot will result in the scaling of all other slots, and vice-versa.

To create a deployment slot, follow these steps:

1. Open the function app's page.
2. Click **Deployment Slots** in the left pane.
3. In the right pane, click the **Add Slot** button and follow the prompts in the Add Slot wizard. (See Figure 6-20.)

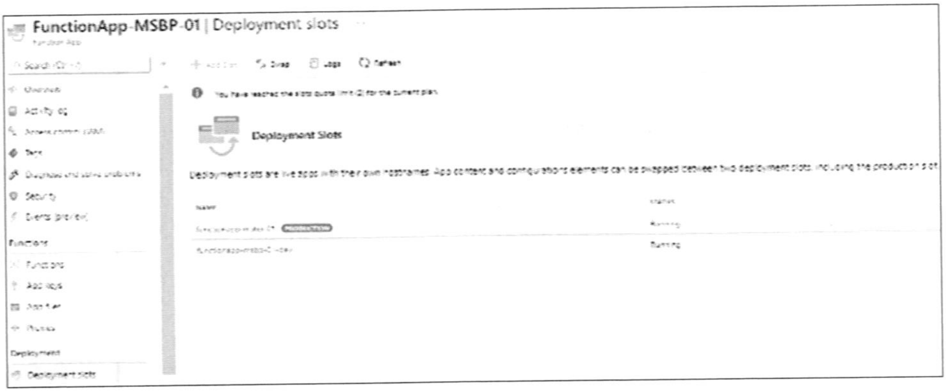

FIGURE 6-20 Setting up deployment slots.

Event-driven scaling

Azure Functions supports event-driven scaling in the Consumption and Premium plans. When a scaling event takes place, additional host instances are made available to run the function app, thereby increasing the available CPU and memory resources.

There are some differences in the way scaling occurs under each plan. For example, in the Consumption plan, each function app within a plan scales independently, whereas in the Premium plan, all apps share the underlying host resources; therefore, any app being scaled will result in all apps being scaled to the same level. Also, when scaling in, with the Consumption plan, the number of hosts could eventually be scaled down to zero if no functions were running for an extended period. In contrast, with the Premium plan, the user can specify a minimum number of hosts.

Numerous factors can impact scaling behavior. For example:

- **Scale controller** The scale controller monitors and manages scaling in a function app. The scale controller checks the rate of event generation and determines the scaling action to take—scaling in to reduce the number of available resources or scaling out to increase it. Based on the trigger used for the function app, the scale controller adjusts its unit of measurement. For example, for an Azure queue storage trigger, scaling is based on the queue length and the age of the oldest message.

- **Cold start** This refers to scenarios in which the number of active instances is scaled down to zero. This occurs if the function app has been idle for a period of time. When the next request comes in, the required instances are brought online and scaled up if necessary. This results in some latency when the request is processed. Depending on the number of dependencies required by the function app, the cold start time can be extended. Cold starts apply when using the Consumption plan. If you need to maintain a minimum number of hosts online and provide faster scaling, you should use the Premium or Dedicated plan.

- **Scaling factors**   Scaling behavior depends on numerous factors, including the following:
  - **Allocation of new instances**   HTTP and non-HTTP triggers have a different rate for allocation of new instances. For HTTP triggers, this can be as low as once per second, whereas for non-HTTP triggers, it can be much slower—one every 30 seconds. This can affect app performance.
  - **Max instance support**   With the Consumption plan, every function app can scale to a maximum of 200 instances. With the Premium plan, this limit is lowered to 100 instances, but with a higher number of resources available per instance.

Scaling management

Function apps can depend on other services or components for data input and data output. In such cases, the scaling of a function app can be affected by throughput limits on these services or components—for example, throughput limits on a connected database or storage service. In such scenarios, you need to do one of the following (see Figure 6-21):

- Scale the limits on those services in parallel.
- Cap function app instances to scale to limits that are compatible with available capacities on the associated services or components.

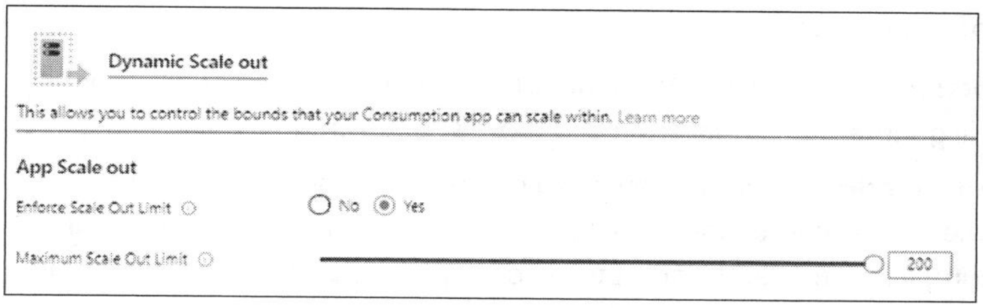

FIGURE 6-21   Setting scale-out limits.

Best practices

You can optimize function apps in to improve the reliability, security, and performance of the app. The following sections contain the most widely used best practices that you can incorporate into your environment based on your application design and requirements.

Reliability best practices

Nowadays, function apps are used to run critical functionality for organizations. So, it's critical to ensure that your apps are running with a high level of reliability to avoid a breakdown in business processes. Following are some recommended practices to incorporate in your function app to improve its reliability:

- **Avoid long-running functions** Each hosting plan (Consumption, Premium, and Dedicated) supports different app-timeout durations. Long-running functions can reach these limits quite easily and cause timeout issues. You should monitor such functions to identify areas that can be broken down into smaller function sets to speed up execution and response times. This will improve the function app's reliability.

- **Use cross-function communication** Cross-function communication is important in scenarios in which the state information of one function is used as an input or trigger for another function. You can address this in a few different ways:
    - **Durable Functions** Durable Functions provide capabilities to build and manage stateful apps and communication between multiple functions.
    - **Storage queues** Storage queues provide a cheap alternative to Durable Functions and can be used in scenarios in which building Durable Functions is not possible. There is a limit of 64 KB on messages stored in a storage queue.
    - **Service bus queues** Service bus queues provide an alternative to storage queues in cases in which a higher limit than 64 KB is required. Service bus queues support messages up to 1 MB in size.
    - **Service bus topics** Service bus topics are useful in scenarios in which message filtering is required before queue processing.
    - **Event Hubs** You can use Event Hubs in scenarios in which you need to support high volumes of communications.

- **Use stateless functions** Any state data should be associated with the application or event data. This will generally help make the app more scalable and reliable.

- **Write idempotent functions** Idempotence is a property that allows any function to be run multiple times without affecting the final result beyond the first iteration. This can help in triggering a function at different times of day based on resource availability or in retriggering a function due to timeouts or failure.

- **Use defensive programming principles** Defensive programming implies that functions are designed to take exception and failure scenarios into account such that retriggering the function will continue the operation from the point of failure. Even downstream services associated with the function will require consideration in the design phase to ensure that every aspect of the function can easily recover in the event of a failure or timeout.

Organizing functions

You can set up multiple functions as part of a single- or multiple-function app. Depending on the pricing plan, the apps will scale together or independently and share underlying resources. This will in turn influence performance and security.

Here are some organizational factors that can affect the performance and scaling of a function app:

- In the Premium and Dedicated plans, every function shares the same underlying resources. The more functions in a function app, the more this resource sharing can affect performance due to excessive usage or a fault in a single function in the app.

- Having multiple functions within a function app can cause the app to start up slowly. This is especially impactful in cold-start scenarios you might encounter when using the Consumption plan. If this poses a problem for your organization, you might need to upgrade to the Premium or Dedicated plan, both of which offer always-on functionality.

- A function that stores large amounts of data in memory can have a detrimental impact on all functions within the app. In such scenarios, consider hosting such functions in their own app.

- Functions that have much higher memory requirements can create a memory crunch for other functions in the same app when running on the Premium or Dedicated plan. In such scenarios, it may be better to host these functions in their own hosting plan. This makes it easier to scale them independently without affecting other functions.

- In the Consumption plan, all apps are scaled independently. If your environment will be using the Consumption plan, it is recommended to host each app within its own plan, as this will reduce the dependency between the apps without affecting scaling, performance, or cost.

Organizational factors that relate to configuration and deployment include the following:

- All functions in a function app share the same host.json file, which manages the advanced behavior of the function triggers and Azure Function runtime. If any function requires its own independent host.json file due to conflicting configuration or custom configuration requirements, it might be best to host it in an independent function app.

- In scenarios in which different functions use different deployment methods or different deployment slots, it might be better to host them in different function apps.

Organizing functions based on permission requirements requires you to take into account the functions' authorization and authentication requirements for when choosing a hosting plan. For example, suppose every function in a function app shares the same application settings. These settings would include connection strings and stored credentials. In scenarios where security is of paramount importance and access is to be limited to the maximum possible extent, it would be best to host only those functions that require the same level of access permissions in the same function app to avoid giving unwanted access to other functions.

Performance and scalability

Many factors influence how instances of a function app perform and scale. Following are a few factors to consider to optimize the performance and scalability of a function app:

- **Create connections to external resources** You can reuse connections to external resources to avoid creating duplicate connections and consuming additional resources. There are connection limits on each function app instance; reusing client connections can help you avoid hitting this limit and prevent a scale-out event.

- **Enable Application Insights** Enabling Application Insights can help you monitor a function app's performance metrics, such as runtime executions, resource usage, and so on. This helps you better understand app behavior and plan for changes either in your hosting strategy or your code. Figure 6-22 and Figure 6-23 show the settings to enable Application Insights.

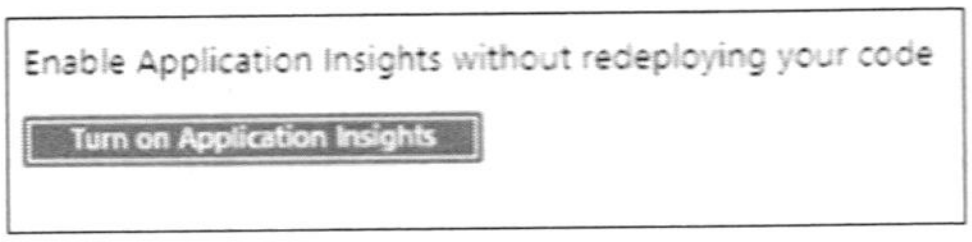

FIGURE 6-22 Enabling Application Insights.

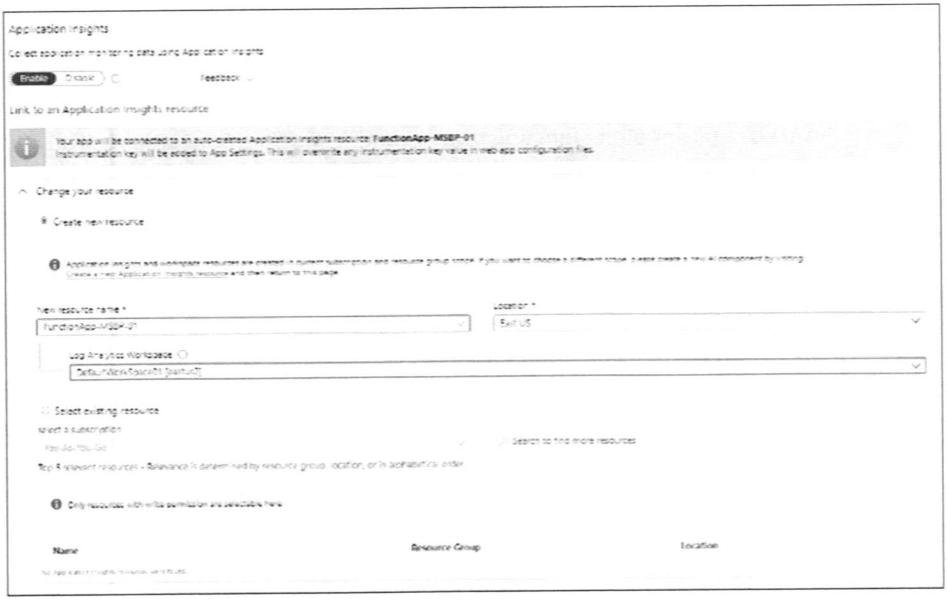

FIGURE 6-23 Setting up Application Insights.

- **Separate function apps for production and dev/test**   In the Premium and Dedicated plans, underlying resources are shared by all functions in the function app. In such scenarios, it might be best to host production functions separately from dev/test functions in different function apps. This can help you prevent a code bug in dev/test causing performance degradation or an outage in production.

- **Host shared components in common storage**   If functions share any components, such as class files, it may be advisable to host the shared assembly in a shared storage location. This helps ensure that any assembly changes are deployed consistently across all functions in the app.

- **Don't use verbose logging in production code**   Ensure that verbose logging is turned off in production code, as it can have a negative impact on application performance. You should enable verbose logging only in scenarios in which debugging is required, and only for the period during which you need to collect logs.

- **Use multiple worker processes**   One of the best ways to improve function performance is to configure them to invoke multiple worker processes per host to increase parallel processing. By default, this is set to a single worker process, and can be scaled up to 10 worker processes per host. As additional hosts are added to the app during scaling, more worker processes are used to distribute the load and improve performance.

- **Batch messages if possible**   Batching messages can help improve app performance, as multiple messages can be received in a single batch for processing. This can result in better execution performance as the host is in a warm state for multiple messages. Certain triggers such as Event Hub triggers support this capability, and if possible, should be used. You can define the maximum batch size to control the maximum number of messages received in each batch if you observe performance issues over time.

- **Set up concurrency if required**   You can set up concurrency to define the maximum concurrent requests that a function app can handle. You can define this using the host.json file. All functions in a function app will then share the concurrency limit. This can help ensure that apps accept only a certain threshold of requests to maximize app performance. In scenarios in which you know the acceptable load limits for functions in a function app, you can use this to optimize performance.

Storage best practices

Storage is a critical element in function app design. Here are a few best practices related to storage accounts used in function apps that can help improve their performance and security:

- **Set up shared storage accounts**   Every function app must be associated with a storage account when it is created. If a function generates lots of storage transactions, it can result in performance degradation for other functions sharing the same storage account. If there are functions in an app that can generate high storage transactions, it is best to use a dedicated storage account for that function app. In addition, if there is a function that writes lots of data to storage, it may be advisable to separate those write operations to another storage account instead of sharing the storage account used by the function app. This will maximize the performance of the function app.

- **Choose a storage location in the same region**   It is best to locate the storage account and function app in the same Azure region. This reduces latency and improves app performance. This is the default behavior when you use the Azure Portal; indeed, you cannot select another storage account. In certain scenarios, though, it might be necessary to use a storage account in another region due to compliance or security reasons. In such cases, you can use PowerShell or CLI to deploy the function app and specify the storage in another region during the creation process.

- **Encrypt storage data**   All data in the storage account used by the function app is encrypted at rest by default using platform-managed keys. This meets most security requirements. However, if your organization requires the use of its own encryption keys, you configure the storage account accordingly.

- **Use file shares for Linux apps**   Linux function apps support the use of Azure file shares for existing machine learning models or application data. You should use this functionality when possible instead of duplicating data for use by Linux function apps. Windows function apps currently do not support this functionality; however, this could change in the future.

Security best practices

Following are recommended best practices to improve the security posture of your function app. Make use of these based on your application design and setup:

- **Integrate Azure Security Center**   Azure Security Center performs free assessments of potential security vulnerabilities in the function app configuration. It is recommended that you use this feature to address potential loopholes in the function app security configuration.

- **Log and monitor functions**   You can monitor functions for security and performance in multiple ways, including the following:

  - **Application Insights**   Integrate functions with Application Insights to collect application logs, monitor performance and errors to detect anomalies, better understand app usage metrics, and diagnose problems.

  - **Azure Monitor**   Integrate functions with Azure Monitor to centrally log all events taking place on the functions in the app. This can help correlate performance or system issues with ongoing issues with other integrated services or system components.

  - **Azure Log Analytics**   Integrate functions with Azure Log Analytics by streaming all platform logs and metrics to a Log Analytics workspace. This enables you to conduct historical performance analysis and plan for future growth.

- **Azure Sentinel** You can use Azure Sentinel to monitor security events to prevent or plug security vulnerabilities in the function app. Azure Sentinel can read logs streamed to a Log Analytics workspace and provide a detailed analysis.

- **Allow only HTTPS connections** By default, function endpoints support both HTTP and HTTPS connections. However, it is best to allow HTTPS connections only to ensure that all communication is encrypted by default. Redirecting all HTTP connections to HTTPS can help mitigate the risk of unencrypted communications. (See Figure 6-24.)

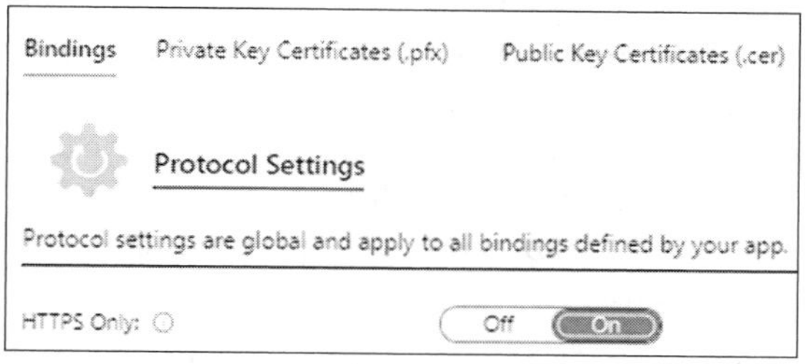

FIGURE 6-24 Allowing only HTTPS connections.

- **Use TLS 1.2 or above** Microsoft is deprecating TLS 1.0 and 1.1 across all its platforms. It is therefore recommended that you set any new deployments to use TLS 1.2 by default and to migrate any existing deployments using TLS 1.0 or 1.1 to TLS 1.2 or newer as soon as possible. (See Figure 6-25.)

FIGURE 6-25 Setting the Minimum TLS version.

- **Limit the use of access keys** You can use access keys to prevent anonymous users from accessing HTTP endpoints. Although allowing anonymous users might be acceptable during development or testing, it is not recommended in production deployments. It is better to use identity and access solutions such as Azure AD or other third-party solutions to ensure that application access is not defined in API keys shared publicly via the app access URLs.

- **Implement app-level authentication and authorization** You can integrate various identity-management solutions, such as Azure Active Directory (AAD) with function apps for client authentication. This makes it easier to identify each individual user accessing the app and customize access policies based on the profile information.

- **Implement API-level authentication and authorization for management purposes** Azure provides the Azure API Management (APIM) service to integrate and securely manage all function app APIs. This helps ensure that API access is controlled, monitored, and managed per your organization's security requirements.

- **Limit user-management permissions to function apps** You can set up users with management permissions for function apps using built-in Azure roles, such as Contributor, Owner, and Reader. You should limit management permissions based on user roles and limit the users who have more access than required for their daily activities. If a user requires Owner-level control for a specific set of activities, provide the access for the period of the activity and limit it thereafter.

- **Use Azure Key Vault** Avoid storing secrets in function app code and application settings. Instead, use Azure Key Vault to store secrets, and integrate the function app with Azure Key Vault to access the required secrets at runtime and when required. This makes it easy for multiple function apps using the same connection strings and secrets to access them from the shared Key Vault without having to manage the application settings across each function app individually.

- **Use managed identities** You can set up managed identities in Azure Active Directory (AAD) to create platform-managed IDs, which can be used to provision service level access. For example, a managed identity used in a function app can be given access to Azure Key Vault or to Azure queue or Azure storage. Because managed identities are managed by Azure, there is no requirement for key rotation on a regular basis, as the platform takes care of this. Use managed identities whenever possible instead of secrets to improve the function app's security posture.

- **Restrict CORS access to specific domains** Cross-origin resource sharing (CORS) allows web apps from different domains to make requests to the HTTP trigger endpoints in a function app. Azure provides built-in support for managing CORS headers in HTTP requests. You can allow required domains access to the endpoint to prevent cross-site scripting attacks. It is recommended that you avoid the use of wildcards to prevent exposure of access to all sites and opening the function app to such attacks.

- **Perform data validation** Perform data validation for any data input to or output from a function app. This helps ensure that no injection attack can be used to provide unvalidated data to the function app or modify data from a function app before it is passed to a downstream service.

- **Disable FTP or enforce FTPS** FTP is an unencrypted protocol and not recommended for use in most scenarios. By default, an FTP endpoint is enabled for deployment for every function app and is accessible using deployment credentials. It is recommended to avoid using FTP for deployments and to disable the protocol completely. If FTP must be used, you can enable FTPS to secure the communication channel (see Figure 6-26).

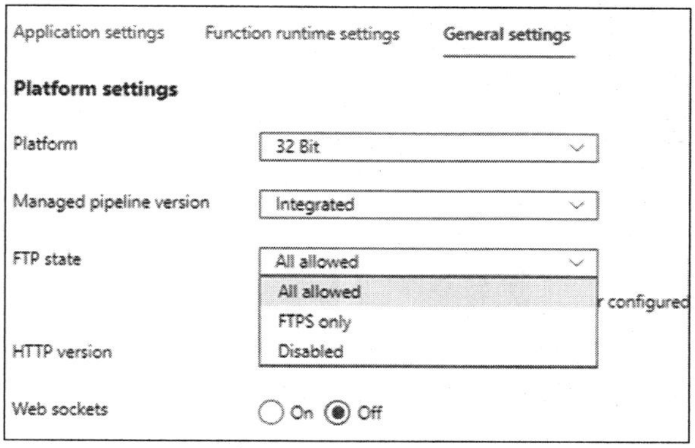

FIGURE 6-26 Setting up FTPS only.

- **Use access restrictions**   Azure provides an access restrictions feature to define allow/deny access lists to control network access to function apps. You can prioritize rules to address different types of access scenarios. By default, no rules are defined, which permits traffic from any address. If traffic to the function app is to be restricted from known sources, use this feature to secure network access.

- **Use a Private Endpoint for secure internal access**   You can integrate function apps with a private virtual network in Azure and any other interconnected networks using an Azure Private Endpoint. This opens secure private access to the functions from resources running in the Azure virtual network and on-premises networks connected over ExpressRoute or Site-to-Site VPN.

- **Deploy your function app in isolation**   For environments in which security is of utmost concern, you can deploy function apps using the Dedicated plan in an Azure ASE. This provides the function apps with a dedicated hosting environment that you can set up to control all incoming requests.

- **Use a gateway service**   You can use Azure Application Gateway or Azure Front Door with a web application firewall (WAF) to monitor and prevent attacks on a function app. Currently, function apps running in an Azure ASE on a Dedicated plan or function apps using Private Endpoints support such an integration. For environments in either scenario, consider the use of these services to secure the function app.

Index

Plug into learning at

MicrosoftPressStore.com

The Microsoft Press Store by Pearson offers:

- Free U.S. shipping

- Buy an eBook, get three formats – Includes PDF, EPUB, and MOBI to use with your computer, tablet, and mobile devices

- Print & eBook Best Value Packs

- eBook Deal of the Week – Save up to 50% on featured title

- Newsletter – Be the first to hear about new releases, announcements, special offers, and more

- Register your book – Find companion files, errata, and product updates, plus receive a special coupon* to save on your next purchase

Microsoft Press

**Find more Definitive Guides to Azure success
at MicrosoftPressStore.com**